TENNYSON

Walker & Boutall Ph.Sc.

Alfred Tennyson,
from the portrait painted by Samuel Laurence.

ALFRED LORD TENNYSON

A MEMOIR

By HIS SON

I have lived my life, and that which I have done
May He within Himself make pure!

VOLUME I

GREENWOOD PRESS, PUBLISHERS
NEW YORK

First Greenwood Reprinting, 1969

Library of Congress Catalogue Card Number: 69-14111

THESE VOLUMES ARE DEDICATED

BY PERMISSION

TO THE QUEEN

———————

An Unpublished Version of "To the Queen," 1851.

THE NOBLEST MEN METHINKS ARE BRED
OF OURS THE SAXO-NORMAN RACE;
AND IN THE WORLD THE NOBLEST PLACE,
MADAM, IS YOURS, OUR QUEEN AND HEAD.

YOUR NAME IS BLOWN ON EVERY WIND,
YOUR FLAG THRO' AUSTRAL ICE IS BORNE,
AND GLIMMERS TO THE NORTHERN MORN,
AND FLOATS IN EITHER GOLDEN IND.

I GIVE THIS FAULTY BOOK TO YOU,
FOR, THO' THE FAULTS BE THICK AS DUST
IN VACANT CHAMBERS, I CAN TRUST
YOUR WOMAN'S NATURE KIND AND TRUE.

CONTENTS.

LIST OF ILLUSTRATIONS.

PREFACE.

Unpublished Sonnet

(*Written originally as a preface to "Becket"*).

Old ghosts whose day was done ere mine began,
If earth be seen from your conjectured heaven,
Ye know that History is half-dream — ay even
The man's life in the letters of the man.
There lies the letter, but it is not he
As he retires into himself and is:
Sender and sent-to go to make up this,
Their offspring of this union. And on me
Frown not, old ghosts, if I be one of those
Who make you utter things you did not say,
And mould you all awry and mar your worth;
For whatsoever knows us truly, knows
That none can truly write his single day,
And none can write it for him upon earth.

" History is half-dream — ay even
The man's life in the letters of the man ";

but besides the letters of my father and of his friends
there are his poems, and in these we must look for the
innermost sanctuary of his being. For my own part, I
feel strongly that no biographer could so truly give him
as he gives himself in his own works; but this may be
because, having lived my life with him, I see him in every
word which he has written; and it is difficult for me so

far to detach myself from the home circle as to pourtray him for others.   There is also the impossibility of fathoming a great man's mind; his deeper thoughts are hardly ever revealed.   He himself disliked the notion of a long, formal biography, for

> "None can truly write his single day,
> And none can write it for him upon earth."

However he wished that, if I deemed it better, the incidents of his life should be given as shortly as might be without comment, but that my notes should be final and full enough to preclude the chance of further and unauthentic biographies.

For those who cared to know about his literary history he wrote "Merlin and the Gleam."   From his boyhood he had felt the magic of Merlin — that spirit of poetry — which bade him know his power and follow throughout his work a pure and high ideal, with a simple and single devotedness and a desire to ennoble the life of the world, and which helped him through doubts and difficulties to "endure as seeing Him who is invisible."

> Great the Master,
> And sweet the Magic,
> When over the valley,
> In early summers,
> Over the mountain,
> On human faces,
> And all around me,
> Moving to melody,
> Floated the Gleam.

In his youth he sang of the brook flowing through his upland valley, of the "ridgéd wolds" that rose above

his home, of the mountain-glen and snowy summits of
his early dreams, and of the beings, heroes and fairies,
with which his imaginary world was peopled.   Then was
heard the "croak of the raven," the harsh voice of those
who were unsympathetic —

> The light retreated,
> The landskip darken'd,
> The melody deaden'd,
> The Master whisper'd
> "Follow the Gleam."

Still the inward voice told him not to be faint-hearted
but to follow his ideal.   And by the delight in his own
romantic fancy, and by the harmonies of nature, "the
warble of water," and "cataract music of falling torrents,"
the inspiration of the poet was renewed.   His Eclogues
and English Idylls followed, when he sang the songs of
country life and the joys and griefs of country folk,
which he knew through and through.

> Innocent maidens,
> Garrulous children,
> Homestead and harvest,
> Reaper and gleaner,
> And rough-ruddy faces
> Of lowly labour.

By degrees, having learnt somewhat of the real
philosophy of life and of humanity from his own experience, he rose to a melody "stronger and statelier."
He celebrated the glory of "human love and of human
heroism" and of human thought, and began what he had
already devised, his Epic of king Arthur, "typifying
above all things the life of man," wherein he had intended
to represent some of the great religions of the world.
He had purposed that this was to be the chief work

of his manhood. Yet the death of his friend, Arthur
Hallam, and the consequent darkening of the whole
world for him made him almost fail in this purpose; nor
any longer for a while did he rejoice in the splendour of
his spiritual visions, nor in the Gleam that had "waned
to a wintry glimmer."

> Clouds and darkness
> Closed upon Camelot;
> Arthur had vanish'd
> I knew not whither,
> The king who loved me,
> And cannot die.

Here my father united the two Arthurs, the Arthur
of the Idylls and the Arthur "the man he held as half
divine." He himself had fought with death, and had
come out victorious to find "a stronger faith his own,"
and a hope for himself, for all those in sorrow and for
universal humankind, that never forsook him through the
future years.

> And broader and brighter
> The Gleam flying onward,
> Wed to the melody,
> Sang thro' the world.
> *   *   *   *   *
> I saw, whenever
> In passing it glanced upon
> Hamlet or city,
> That under the Crosses
> The dead man's garden,
> The mortal hillock,
> Would break into blossom;
> And so to the land's
> Last limit I came.

Up to the end he faced death with the same earnest and unfailing courage that he had always shown, but with an added sense of the awe and the mystery of the Infinite.

> I can no longer,
> But die rejoicing,
> For thro' the Magic
> Of Him the Mighty,
> Who taught me in childhood,
> There on the border
> Of boundless Ocean,
> And all but in Heaven
> Hovers the Gleam.

That is the reading of the poet's riddle as he gave it to me. He thought that "Merlin and the Gleam" would probably be enough of biography for those friends who urged him to write about himself. However, this has not been their verdict, and I have tried to do what he said that I might do, and have endeavoured to give briefly something of what people naturally wish to know, something about his birth, homes, school, college, friendships, travels, and the leading events of his life, enough to present the sort of insight into his history and pursuits which one wants, if one desires to make a companion of a man. The picture of his early days has been mainly sketched from what he and my mother have told me. My difficulty in arranging the later chapters has been how to choose, and how to throw aside, from the mass of material[1]. I have quoted from many manuscripts never

[1] My thanks are due to Professor Henry Sidgwick and Professor Palgrave, who have helped me to make my selection from upwards of 40,000 letters.

meant for the public eye, many of which I have burnt
according to his instructions.   Among those that I have
collected here, the most interesting to me are my father's
unpublished poems, letters, — and notes on his own life
and work left me for publication after his death, Arthur
Hallam's letters, Edward Fitzgerald's private MS notes [1]
(some of which he gave me, and some of which have
been lent to me by Mr Aldis Wright), and the journal
of our home life.   This last is a simple record of daily
something-nothings.

If there appear, in the Reminiscences kindly contributed by his different friends, to be any discrepancies,
let it be remembered that the many-sided man has
sympathy with many and various minds, and that the
poet may be like the magnetic needle, which, though
it can be moved from without, yet in itself remains true
to the magnetic pole.

According to my father's wish, throughout the
memoir my hand will be as seldom seen as may be, and
this accounts for the occasionally fragmentary character
of my work.   The anecdotes and sayings here related
have been mostly taken down as soon as spoken, and
are hence, I trust, not marred or mended by memory,
which, judging from some anecdotes of him recently
published, is wont to be a register not wholly accurate.
" Fingunt simul creduntque."

Such reviews as I have quoted are chiefly those
which have met with my father's approbation as explanatory commentaries.   For my own part, I have
generally refrained from attempting to pronounce judgment either on his poems or on his personal qualities and
characteristics; although more than any living man I

---

[1] Generally signed E. F. G. throughout this work.

have had reason to appreciate his splendid truth and trustfulness, his varied creative imagination, and love of beauty, his rich humour, his strength of purpose, the largeness of his nature, and the wide range of his genius. If I may venture to speak of his special influence over the world, my conviction is, that its main and enduring factors are his power of expression, the perfection of his workmanship, his strong common sense, the high purport of his life and work, his humility, and his open-hearted and helpful sympathy —

"Fortezza, ed umilitade, e largo core."

CHRONOLOGY OF THE BOOKS OF POEMS.

1827.—POEMS BY TWO BROTHERS. London: Printed for W. Simpkin and R. Marshall, Stationers'-Hall-Court; and J. and J. Jackson. Louth: 1827. Published in two sizes.

1829.—TIMBUCTOO. A Poem which obtained the Chancellor's Medal at the Cambridge Commencement, 1829. By A. Tennyson, of Trinity College. 8vo.

1830.—POEMS, CHIEFLY LYRICAL. By Alfred Tennyson. London: Effingham Wilson, Royal Exchange, Cornhill, 1830. 12mo.

1832.—POEMS, BY ALFRED TENNYSON. London: Edward Moxon, 64 New Bond Street (dated 1833). 12mo.

1833.—THE LOVER'S TALE, privately printed in London.

1842.—POEMS, BY ALFRED TENNYSON. London: Edward Moxon, Dover Street, 1842. 2 vols., 12mo.

1843.—THE SAME. Second edition. London: 1843. 2 vols., 12mo.

1845.—THE SAME. Third edition. London: 1845. 2 vols., 12mo.

1846.—THE SAME. Fourth edition. London: 1846. 2 vols., 12mo.

1847.—THE PRINCESS. A Medley. By Alfred Tennyson. London: Edward Moxon, Dover Street, 1847. 12mo.

1848.—THE SAME. Second edition. London: 1848 (with addition of dedication to Henry Lushington).

1848.—POEMS, BY ALFRED TENNYSON. Fifth edition. London: Edward Moxon, Dover Street, 1848. 12mo.

1850.—IN MEMORIAM. London: Edward Moxon, Dover Street, 1850. 12mo. (Appointed Poet-laureate Nov. 19.)

1850.—THE PRINCESS. Third edition (altered, with songs added). London : Edward Moxon, Dover Street, 1850. 12mo.

1850.—POEMS, BY ALFRED TENNYSON. Sixth edition. London : 1850. 12mo. (*After reading a Life and Letters* included.)

1851.—POEMS, BY ALFRED TENNYSON. Seventh edition. London : 1851. 12mo. (*Come not when I am dead, Edwin Morris, The Eagle*, and the dedication *To the Queen* included.)

1851.—THE PRINCESS. Fourth edition. London : 1851. 12mo. *This edition first has the passages describing the Prince's weird seizures.*

1851.—IN MEMORIAM. Fourth edition. London : 1851. 12mo. (*O Sorrow, wilt thou live with me ?* added.)

1852.—ODE ON THE DEATH OF THE DUKE OF WELLINGTON. By Alfred Tennyson, Poet-laureate. London : Edward Moxon, Dover Street, 1852. 8vo.

1853.—POEMS, BY ALFRED TENNYSON. Eighth edition. London : 1853. 12mo. (With an alteration in the *Dream of Fair Women*, and lines *To E. L.* added.)

1853.—THE PRINCESS. Fifth edition (the final text). London : 1853. 12mo.

1854.—CHARGE OF THE LIGHT BRIGADE, published in the *Examiner*, Dec. 9th, 1854, then printed for the soldiers before Sebastopol, August, 1855.

1855.—MAUD, AND OTHER POEMS. By Alfred Tennyson, D.C.L., Poet-laureate. London : Edward Moxon, 1855. 12mo.

1857.—POEMS BY ALFRED TENNYSON. Illustrations by D. G. Rossetti, J. E. Millais, and others. Edward Moxon. Royal 8vo.

1859.—IDYLLS OF THE KING. By Alfred Tennyson, D.C.L., Poet-laureate. London : Edward Moxon & Co., Dover Street, 1859. 12mo.

1861.—THE SAILOR BOY. London : Emily Faithfull & Co., Victoria Press.

1862.—IDYLLS OF THE KING. A new edition. London : 1862. 12mo. (with Dedication to the Prince Consort).

1862.—ODE : MAY THE FIRST, 1862, FOR THE OPENING OF THE INTERNATIONAL EXHIBITION. London : Edward Moxon & Co. (published also in *Fraser*, June, 1862).

1863.—WELCOME TO ALEXANDRA. 4 pages. London : Edward Moxon & Co.

1864.—ENOCH ARDEN, ETC. By Alfred Tennyson, D.C.L., Poet-laureate. London: Edward Moxon & Co., Dover Street, 1864. 12mo.

1865.—SELECTIONS from the works of Alfred Tennyson, D.C.L., Poet-laureate. London: Edward Moxon & Co., Dover Street, 1865. 16mo.

This was published in Moxon's Miniature Poets, and contains six new poems, viz.: ' The Captain,' 'On a Mourner,' 'Home They Brought Him Slain with Spears,' and three 'Sonnets to a Coquette.'

1867.—THE VICTIM.   } Printed by Sir Ivor Guest (Lord Wimborne), THE WINDOW. } set to music by Sir Arthur Sullivan.

1869.—THE HOLY GRAIL, AND OTHER POEMS. By Alfred Tennyson, D.C.L., Poet-laureate. London: Strahan & Co., Publishers, 56 Ludgate Hill, 1869. 12mo.

1870.—THE WINDOW, OR THE SONG OF THE WRENS. With music by Arthur Sullivan. London: Strahan, 1871 (Dec. 1870).

1871.—MINIATURE EDITION OF COMPLETE WORKS. London: Strahan & Co.

1871.—THE LAST TOURNAMENT. *Contemporary Review*, December.

1872.—GARETH AND LYNETTE, ETC. By Alfred Tennyson, D.C.L., Poet-laureate. London: Strahan & Co., 56 Ludgate Hill, 1872. 12mo.

1872.—THE LIBRARY EDITION OF THE COMPLETE WORKS. In seven volumes. London: Strahan & Co., 1872. Large 8vo. (The Idylls of the King in sequence with Epilogue to the Queen.)

1874.—A WELCOME TO THE DUCHESS OF EDINBURGH. H. S. King & Co.

1874.—THE CABINET EDITION (H. S. King & Co.) contained: *In the Garden at Swainston, The Voice and the Peak, England and America.*

1875.—QUEEN MARY. A Drama, by Alfred Tennyson. London: Henry S. King & Co., 1875. 12mo.

1876.—QUEEN MARY, produced at the Lyceum Theatre.

1876.—HAROLD. A Drama, by Alfred Tennyson. London: Henry S. King & Co. (dated 1877). 12mo.

1879.—THE LOVER'S TALE. By Alfred Tennyson. London: C. Kegan Paul & Co., 1 Paternoster Square, 1879. 12mo.

1879.—THE FALCON, produced at the St. James' Theatre.

1880.—COLLECTED SONNETS. By Charles Tennyson Turner with memorial lines by Alfred Tennyson. Edited (with a short preface) by Hallam Tennyson. London: C. Kegan Paul. 12mo.

1880.—BALLADS AND OTHER POEMS. By Alfred Tennyson. London: C. Kegan Paul & Co., 1 Paternoster Square, 1880. 12mo.

1881.—THE CUP, produced at the Lyceum Theatre.

1882.—THE PROMISE OF MAY, produced at the Globe Theatre.

1884.—THE CUP AND THE FALCON. By Alfred Lord Tennyson, Poet-laureate. London: Macmillan & Co., 1884. 12mo.

1884.—A NEW SINGLE-VOLUME EDITION OF WORKS. Revised by the Author with corrections. Macmillan & Co.

1884.—BECKET. By Alfred Lord Tennyson, Poet-laureate. London: Macmillan & Co., 1884. Crown 8vo.

1885.—TIRESIAS, AND OTHER POEMS (including *Once more the Heavenly Power*, published in *The Youth's Companion*, Boston, U.S.A., 1884). By Alfred Lord Tennyson, D.C.L., Poet-laureate. London: Macmillan & Co., 1885. 12mo.

1886.—A NEW LIBRARY EDITION OF COMPLETE WORKS. In ten volumes (revised, with additions by the author). London: Macmillan & Co. (Also a new single-volume Edition, with slight alterations. Macmillan & Co.)

1886.—LOCKSLEY HALL SIXTY YEARS AFTER, ETC. By Alfred Lord Tennyson, D.C.L., Poet-laureate. London and New York: Macmillan & Co., 1886. 12mo.

1887.—CARMEN SAECULARE. An ode in honour of the Jubilee of Queen Victoria. *Macmillan's Magazine*, April.

1889.—DEMETER AND OTHER POEMS. Macmillan & Co., London and New York. 12mo. (20,000 copies sold in first week.)

1889.—A NEW AND REVISED SINGLE-VOLUME EDITION OF WORKS (with many additions). Macmillan & Co.

1892.—THE FORESTERS, ROBIN HOOD AND MAID MARIAN. London and New York: Macmillan & Co. 12mo. Produced at Daly's Theatre in New York, March 17.

1892.—THE SILENT VOICES. Order of Service in Westminster Abbey, Oct. 12th. Printed for copyright purposes. London and New York: Macmillan & Co.

1892.—Oct. 28th. THE DEATH OF ŒNONE, AKBAR'S DREAM AND OTHER POEMS. London and New York: Macmillan & Co. 12mo. Also large paper Edition with five steel portraits.

1893.—BECKET, AS ARRANGED FOR THE STAGE BY HENRY IRVING (revised by Alfred Lord Tennyson). Macmillan & Co.

1894.—THE COMPLETE SINGLE-VOLUME EDITION OF THE WORKS, with last alterations, etc. London : Macmillan & Co.

In Rowe's *Coming of Arthur*, and *Passing of Arthur;* G.C. Macaulay's *Gareth and Lynette*, and *Marriage of Geraint*, and *Geraint and Enid;* Ainger's *Tennyson for the Young;* Rowe's *Aylmer's Field;* Rowe's *Selections from Tennyson;* Palgrave's Golden Treasury Selection of *Lyrical Poems;* Dawson's *Princess;* Rolfe's *Enoch Arden, and Selections*, whenever there was any doubtful point in the notes, I referred it to my father: so that in the later editions of these annotated volumes the commentaries may be considered tolerably accurate.

POEMS PUBLISHED IN THE " NINETEENTH CENTURY."

My father contributed the following poems to the *Nineteenth Century:* in 1877, " Prefatory Sonnet " (March), and " Montenegro " (May), and " To Victor Hugo " (June), and " Achilles over the Trench " (August) ; and in March, 1878, he contributed " The Revenge " ; in April, 1879, " The Defence of Lucknow, with a Dedicatory Poem to Princess Alice " ; in May, 1880, " De Profundis " ; in November, 1881, " Despair " ; in September, 1882, " To Virgil " ; in March, 1883, " Frater ave atque vale " ; in February, 1892, " On the death of the Duke of Clarence and Avondale."

George Pitt of Strathfieldsaye = Lady Jane Pitt[1]

Jane = Christopher Hildeyard
Dorothy = George Clayton of Grimsby

Ralph Tennyson, of Barton and of Wrawby, 1672-1735 = Dorothy Chapman

Michael Tennyson, of Preston, York, Stainton = Elizabeth Clayton and Lincoln, 1721-1796

George Tennyson, M.P., of = Mary Turner, of Caistor, 1775, Bayons Manor, 1750-1835 | 1753-1825

Mary = John Bourne of Dalby

Rev. George Clayton Tennyson, = Elizabeth Fytche, M.A., LL.D., of Somersby, of Louth, 1778-1831 | 1781-1865

The Right Hon. Charles Tennyson d'Eyncourt, M.P., of Bayons Manor, 1784-1861

Elizabeth = Matthew Russell, M.P. of Brancepeth Castle

George, May, 1806-1806, born at Tealby
Frederick, June, 1807, " Louth = Maria Giuliotti
Charles, July, 1808-1879 " Somersby = Louisa Sellwood 13th June, 1850

ALFRED, Aug. 6th, 1809-1892 " Somersby = EMILY SARAH SELLWOOD, 1813-1896 daughter of Henry Sellwood, Esq., of Berks.

Mary, Sept., 1810-1884 " = Alan Ker, Judge of High Court of Jamaica
Emilia, Oct., 1811-1889 " = Capt. Jesse, R.N.
Engaged to A. H. Hallam, d. 1833
Edward, Jan., 1813-1890, born at Somersby
Arthur, May, 1814- " = 1st Harriet West, 2nd Louisa Maynard
Septimus, Sept., 1815-1866 "
Matilda, Sept., 1816- "
Cecilia, Oct., 1817- " = Prof. Edmund Law Lushington, D.C.L., of Park House, Maidstone
Horatio, Sept., 1819- " = 1st Charlotte d. of Dudley Cary Elwes, 2nd Catharine West

Lionel Tennyson = Eleanor Locker, 1878
1854-1886

Hallam Tennyson = Audrey Boyle, 1884
1852-

Michael Sellwood 1883-

Alfred Browning Stanley 1878-

Charles Bruce Locker 1879-

Harold Courtenay 1896-

Alfred Aubrey 1891-

Lionel Hallam 1889-

[1] Daughter of John Earl Rivers and Catherine daughter of William Lord Morley.

CHAPTER I.

BOYHOOD.

1809–1827.

The Tennysons may probably in their origin have been Danes, and they appear to have first settled north of the Humber, in Holderness. The earliest notice of the family that can be found is that in 1343 one John Tenison charged certain persons with forcibly taking away his goods and chattels at Paulfleet to the amount of £40. In 1528 John Tennyson of Ryall directs that his body should be buried in the kirk-garthe of All Hallows at Skekelinge. To Margaret his wife he devises one ox-yard of land and half a close called Stockett Croft during her widowhood. Bequests are also made to his several children. One of them named William, who was possibly a Mayor, afterwards leaves to John, his son, his "best mace, and to Paul Church, twenty pence." He desires to be buried in the same kirk-garthe of All Hallows. From these Tennysons, through a Lancelot Tennyson of Preston, and Ralph Tennyson, who raised a troop of horse to support William III., descends Michael of Lincoln, my father's great-grandfather. Michael was remembered by my grandfather, the Rev. Dr George Clayton Tennyson, as taking him into his bed and talking to him about the stars.

Half-way between Horncastle and Spilsby, in a land

of quiet villages, large fields, gray hillsides and noble
tall-towered churches, on the lower slope of a Lincolnshire
wold, the pastoral hamlet of Somersby nestles, embosomed
in trees.

Here, on the 6th of August, 1809, was born, in his
father's rectory, Alfred Tennyson. He was the fourth
of twelve children, eight sons and four daughters, most
of them more or less true poets, and of whom all except
two have lived to 70 and upward. Dr Tennyson bap-
tized the boy two days after he was born, following the
Prayer-book instruction that people " defer not the Baptism of their children longer than the first or second
Sunday next after their birth."

" Here's a leg for a babe of a week! " says doctor; and
    he would be bound,
  There was not his like that year in twenty parishes
    round [1],

was said of him; nevertheless during his infancy three
times after convulsions he was thought to be dead.

In 1892 I visited the old home, and when I returned,
told my father that the trees had grown up obscur-
ing the view from the Rectory, and that the house
itself looked very desolate. All he answered was, " Poor
little place! " He always spoke of it with an affectionate
remembrance; of the woodbine that climbed into the bay
window of his nursery; of the Gothic vaulted dining-
room with stained glass windows, making, as my uncle
Charles Turner used to say, "butterfly souls" on the
walls; of the beautiful stone chimney-piece carved by
his father; of the pleasant little drawing-room lined
with book-shelves, and furnished with yellow curtains,
sofas and chairs, and looking out on the lawn.
This lawn was overshadowed on one side by wych-
elms, and on the other by larch and sycamore trees.

[1] See " The Grandmother."

Here, my father said, he made his early song "A spirit haunts the year's last hours." Beyond the path, bounding the green sward to the south, ran in the old days a deep border of lilies and roses, backed by hollyhocks and sunflowers. Beyond that was

> A garden bower'd close
> With plaited alleys of the trailing rose,
> Long alleys falling down to twilight grots,
> Or opening upon level plots
> Of crowned lilies, standing near
> Purple-spiked lavender —

sloping in a gradual descent to the parson's field, at the foot of which flows, by "lawn and lea," the swift, steep-banked brook, where are "brambley wildernesses," and "sweet forget-me-nots," and in which the "long mosses sway." The charm and beauty of this brook,

> That loves
> To purl o'er matted cress and ribbed sand,
> Or dimple in the dark of rushy coves,
> And swerves to left and right thro' meadowy curves
> That feed the mothers of the flock [1],

haunted him through life.

Near Somersby the stream joins another from Holy-well, and their confluence may be referred to in the lines:

> By that old bridge, which, half in ruins then,
> Still makes a hoary eyebrow for the gleam
> Beyond it, where the waters marry.

"Flow down, cold rivulet, to the sea" was the poem more especially dedicated to the Somersby stream, and not, as some have supposed, "The Brook," which designed to be a brook of the imagination.

The orchard on the right of the lawn forms a sunny

---

[1] "Ode to Memory," which he considered one of the best among his very early and peculiarly concentrated Nature-poems.

little spot that awoke in his mind pleasant memories.
" How often," he said, " have I risen in the early dawn
to see the golden globes lying in the dewy grass among
those apple trees." He delighted too to recall the
rare richness of the bowery lanes: the ancient Norman
cross standing in the churchyard, close to the door of the
quaint little church: the wooded hollow of Holywell:
the cold springs flowing from under the sandstone rocks:
the flowers, the mosses, and the ferns. When there I
looked in vain for the words " Byron is dead," which
he had carved on a rock when he was fourteen, on
hearing of Byron's death (April 19th, 1824), "a day
when the whole world seemed to be darkened for me."

Like other children, the Tennysons had their imaginative games; they were knights and jousted in mock
tournaments, or they were "champions and warriors,
defending a field, or a stone-heap, or again they would
set up opposing camps with a king in the midst of
each. The king was a willow-wand stuck into the
ground, with an outer circle of immortals, to defend
him, of firmer, stiffer sticks. Then each party would
come with stones, hurling at each other's king and trying
to overthrow him[1]." Stories are told too about their
boyish pranks in the old red-bricked house with em-
battled parapet (Baumber's Farm), said to have been
built by Vanbrugh, which adjoins the Rectory garden,
and is erroneously called by some " The Moated Grange."
" At all events, whatever may have happened," my father
writes, " The Moated Grange is an imaginary house in
the fen; I never so much as dreamed of Baumber's farm[2]
as the abode of Mariana, and the character of Baumber
was so ludicrously unlike the Northern Farmer, that

[1] Taken from the account which my father gave Mrs Thackeray Ritchie.
[2] The localities of my father's subject-poems are wholly imaginary,
although he has done for general Mid-Lincolnshire scenery what Virgil
did for Mantua.

u my remarks. The first scene is
Sampson, which possesses much pat
  This passage,

houghts, that like a deadly swarm
ts arm'd, no sooner found alone,
upon me thronging, and present
st, what once I was, and what am now,
nd of that in Dante, which Lord By
his " Corsair," " Nessun maggior dol
i del tempo felice, Nella miseria."
is blindness is particularly beautiful,
f sight, of thee I most complain!
nong enemies! O worse than chains,
a or beggary, or decrepit age!
he prime work of God, to me is extinct,
her various objects of delight
d, which might in part my grief have eas
to the vilest now become
or worm; the vilest here excel me:
eep, yet see; I, dark in light, exposed
y fraud, contempt, abuse, and wrong,
    *   *   *   *   *   *   *
half I seem to live, dead more than half.
, dark, dark, amid the blaze of noon,
erably dark, total eclipse
t all hope of day!
created beam, and thou great Word,
here be light!" and light was over all.—
his is beautiful, particularly
ark, dark, dark, amid the blaze of noon.
long lamentation of Sampson, the C
ng these words :
this is he. Softly awhile;
s not break in upon him:
nge beyond report, thought, or belief!
ow he lies at random, carelessly *diffused*.
into Bp. Newton's notes, you will fin
you that " This beautiful application

it really makes me wonder how any one can have the face to invent such stories." I think that their childhood, despite the home circumstances which will be presently noticed, could not have been in the main unhappy. Their imaginative natures gave them many sources of amusement. One of these lasted a long time : the writing of tales in letter form, to be put under the vegetable dishes at dinner, and read aloud when it was over. I have heard from my uncles and aunts that my father's tales were very various in theme, some of them humorous and some savagely dramatic; and that they looked to him as their most thrilling story-teller. Among historical events the doings of Wellington and Napoleon were the themes of story and verse. Yet Somersby was so far out of the world that the elder children say they did not hear of the battle of Waterloo at the time. They had however an early memory that " the coach drove through Somersby, the horses decorated with flowers and ribbons, and this might have been in honour of Wellington's great victory."

My aunt Cecilia (Mrs Lushington) narrates how in the winter evenings by the firelight little Alfred would take her on his knee, with Arthur and Matilda leaning against him on either side, the baby Horatio between his legs; and how he would fascinate this group of young hero-worshippers, who listened open-eared and openmouthed to legends of knights and heroes among untravelled forests rescuing distressed damsels, or on gigantic mountains fighting with dragons, or to his tales about Indians, or demons, or witches. The brothers and sisters would sometimes act one of the old English plays ; and the elder members of the family thought that my father, from his dramatic rendering of his parts and his musical voice, would turn out an actor.

When he was seven years old he was asked, " Will

you go to sea or to school?" He said, "To school,"
thinking that school was a kind of paradise; so he
was taken to the house of his grandmother at Louth.
His mother had been born in that town, being daughter
of the vicar, the Rev. Stephen Fytche[1]; and he was
sent to the Grammar School there, then under the
Rev. J. Waite, a tempestuous, flogging master of the
old stamp. He remembered to his dying day sitting
on the stone steps of the school on a cold winter's
morning, and crying bitterly after a big lad had brutally
cuffed him on the head because he was a new boy. I
still have the books which he used there, his *Ovid,
Delectus, Analecta Græca Minora*, and the old *Eton
Latin Grammar*, originally put together by Erasmus,
Lilly and Colet.

Among the incidents in his school life he would
recall that of walking in a procession of boys, decked
with ribbons, at the proclamation of the Coronation of
George IV., and how the old women said that "The
boys made the prettiest part of the show." Later
in school life, he one day stood on a wall and made a
political speech to his school-fellows, but was promptly
ordered down by an usher, who asked him whether he
wished to be the parish beadle.

Two facts that his grandmother told him at this time
impressed him. One was that she had become blind
from cataract, and then had a dream that she saw; and
that, although couching for cataract was not common
in those days, owing to this dream she had gone to

[1] George Clayton Tennyson of Tealby, clerk, and Elizabeth Fytche of
Louth, spinster, were married in Louth Church by license on the 6th August,
1805 by Wolley Jolland, Vicar, in the presence of John Fytche and Charles
Tennyson. The Fytches were a county family of old descent. The first
name on the Fytche pedigree is John Fitch of Fitch Castle in the North,
who died in the 25th year of Edward I. His descendant Thomas Fitch was
knighted by Charles II. 1679, served the office of High Sheriff in Kent,
and was created baronet, Sept. 7th, 1688.

London, and had been operated
second was that she remembered
widow[1], dressed in white, on her
(her body afterwards to be bu
husband.

A few years ago the present
gave a holiday in my father's ho
gratified him; yet he said,
school! The only good I ev
memory of the words, 'sonus
an old wall covered with wild
windows. I wrote an Englis
the Jacksons; the only line I r
heroes lie along the shore[2].'"

In 1820 he left Louth and
his father.

When twelve years old
ary epistle (the earliest of
aunt Marianne Fytche.

MY DEAR AUNT MARIA

When I was a
that you should be oblig
you and give you my re
I shall now fulfil the prom
Going into the library this
Agonistes," on which (as

[1] "Women who were found g
other offences comprised unde
publicly burnt, by a law which
or eleven feet high was planted
near the top, and from it the cu
under her feet. The law enjo
practice the sentence was usu
the fire touched her body."

Lecky's *Engla*

[2] See Professor J. W. Hal
Magazine, Dec. 1892. See A

I shall
lament
and su

puts m
has pre
Che ri
complai

O
Bl
Du
Li
An
An
Inf
Of
Th
To

Sca
O d
Irre
Wit
O fi
"Le

I think
O

After
enters, say

This,
Let u
O cha
See h

If you look
he informs

word 'diffused' is borrowed from the Latin." It has the
same meaning as " temere " in one of the Odes of Horace,
Book the second,

> Sic temere, et rosâ
> Canos odorati capillos,

of which this is a free translation, " Why lie we not at
random, under the shade of the plantain (sub platano),
having our hoary head perfumed with rose water?" To
an English reader the metre of the Chorus may seem
unusual, but the difficulty will vanish, when I inform
him that it is taken from the Greek. In line 133
there is this expression, " Chalybean tempered steel."
The Chalybes were a nation among the ancients very
famous for the making of steel, hence the expression
" Chalybean," or peculiar to the Chalybes: in line 147
"the Gates of Azzar"; this probably, as Bp. Newton
observes, was to avoid too great an alliteration, which
the " Gates of Gaza " would have caused, though (in
my opinion) it would have rendered it more beautiful :
and (though I do not affirm it as a fact) perhaps Milton
gave it that name for the sake of novelty, as all the
world knows he was a great pedant. I have not, at
present, time to write any more: perhaps I may continue my remarks in another letter to you : but (as I am
very volatile and fickle) you must not depend upon me,
for I think you do not know any one who is so fickle as

Your affectionate nephew,

A. TENNYSON.

P.S. Frederick informed me that grandmamma was
quite growing dissipated, going out to parties every night.
The Russels and grandmamma are to be at Dalby on
Tuesday the 23rd, and I also hope to be taken by papa
and mamma who are invited. Frederick made mamma
promise to write him an account of the visit, but if I go,
I shall take the trouble from mamma.

His second earliest letter is a piece of nonsense with
which he favoured his sisters' governess.

LA MANCHA.

MY DEAR DULCINEA,

Pursuant to your request and the honour of
Knight-errantry, and in conformity to my bump of conscientiousness (which has grown so enormous since my
visit to you that I can scarce put on my helmet), I now
intend, as far as lies in my power, to fulfil that promise
which the lustre of your charms extorted from me. Know
then, most adorable mistress of my heart, that the manuscripts which your angelic goodness and perfection were
pleased to commend are not with me. If however my
memory, assisted by the peerless radiance of your divine
favour, avail me aught, I will endeavour to illume the
darkness of my imagination with the recollection of your
glorious excellence, till I produce a species of artificial
memory unequalled by the *Memoria Technica* of Mr
Gray. Who would not remember when thus requested?
It would cause a dead idiot to start afresh to life and
intellect. Accept then, soul of my soul, these effusions,
in which no Ossianic, Miltonic, Byronic, Milmanic,
Moorish, Crabbic, Coleridgic etc. fire is contained.

The first is a review of death :

Why should we weep for those who die ? etc.

The second is a comparison :

Je fais naître la lumière
Du sein de l'obscurité. (Rousseau.)

How gaily sinks the gorgeous sun, etc.
And now farewell, my incomparable Dulcinea. In the
truest spirit of knight-errantry,

Yours ever, DON QUIXOTE.

As to his earliest attempts at poetry, he wrote the
following note for me in 1890 :

"According to the best of my recollection, when I was about eight years old, I covered two sides of a slate with Thomsonian blank verse in praise of flowers for my brother Charles, who was a year older than I was, Thomson then being the only poet I knew. Before I could read, I was in the habit on a stormy day of spreading my arms to the wind, and crying out 'I hear a voice that's speaking in the wind,' and the words 'far, far away' had always a strange charm for me. About ten or eleven Pope's *Homer's Iliad* became a favourite of mine and I wrote hundreds and hundreds of lines in the regular Popeian metre, nay even could improvise them, so could my two elder brothers, for my father was a poet and could write regular metre very skilfully."

[I give one example:

> Can I forget thee? In the festive hall,
> Where wit and beauty reign and minstrelsy,
> My heart still fondly shall recur to thee,
> Thine image still recall.
>
> Can I forget thee? In the gloomy hour,
> When wave on wave tempestuous passions roll,
> Thou, loved ideal, still shalt soothe my soul,
> And health and peace restore.
>
> Farewell, my choicest blessings round thee wait,
> And kindred angels guard thine angel form,
> Guide and protect thee in life's rudest storm,
> And every blast of fate[1]!]

[1] These lines are copied from my grandfather's scrapbook, a book which with others in his library he bound in leather with his own hands. His sister Mrs Matthew Russell also dabbled in poetry, and Dr Tennyson writes to her about some of her compositions in 1825: "You do wrong to confess you are long in making verses, for no one would conceive it from the peculiar ease of the metre. You are not however singular: Gray hammer'd at his verses with great difficulty, and yet they have immortalized his name. Æschylus, the great Greek tragedian, with great difficulty once composed three verses in three days: a poetaster came to Æschylus, and boasted that he had composed three thousand in the same time. 'Your three thousand verses,' said Æschylus, 'will last only for three days, whereas my three verses will last for ever.' Your soliloquy is very beautiful, and so beautiful that I have transcribed it amongst my choice selections."

The note continues — " My father once said to me,
' Don't write so rhythmically, break your lines occasionally for the sake of variety.'

' Artist first, then Poet,' some writer said of me.
I should answer, ' Poeta nascitur non fit '; indeed, ' Poeta
nascitur et fit.' I suppose I was nearer thirty than twenty
before I was anything of an artist.

At about twelve and onward I wrote an epic of six
thousand lines à la Walter Scott, — full of battles, dealing too with sea and mountain scenery, — with Scott's
regularity of octo-syllables and his occasional varieties.
Though the performance was very likely worth nothing
I never felt myself more truly inspired.   I wrote as much
as seventy lines at one time, and used to go shouting
them about the fields in the dark.   All these early efforts
have been destroyed, only my brother-in-law Edmund
Lushington begged for a page or two of the Scott poem.
Somewhat later (at fourteen) I wrote a Drama in blank
verse, which I have still, and other things.   It seems to
me, I wrote them all in perfect metre."

These poems made my grandfather say with pardon-
able pride, " If Alfred die, one of our greatest poets will
have gone ": and at another time, " I should not wonder
if Alfred were to revive the greatness of his relative,
William Pitt[1]."

His grandmother, the sister of the Reverend Samuel
Turner, would assert: " Alfred's poetry all comes
from me."   My father remembered her reading to him,
when a boy, " The Prisoner of Chillon " very tenderly.
Sam Turner, on the contrary, smashed the bottom out
of his glass of rum and water on the dinner table, as
he inveighed against " this new-fangled Byron."

When at his grandfather's desire my father wrote a
poem on his grandmother's death, the old gentleman gave

him half a guinea with these words, " Here is half a guinea
for you, the first you have ever earned by poetry, and take
my word for it, the last." He himself was not a great
hand at versification. Two lines of his are extant, describing the crest of the Boynes, a goat drinking out of a
stream. His younger son had previously made these lines,

> On yonder bank a goat is stood,
> He seems to sip the silver flood,

which were corrected by the old gentleman as follows,

> On yonder bank a goat I spy,
> To sip the flood he seems to try.

Owing to a caprice of my great-grandfather's,
my grandfather, who was the elder son, was disinherited in favour of his only brother, Charles (Tennyson
d'Eyncourt [1]), and so deprived of a position for which he
would seem to have been well fitted. A neighbouring
squire, being told by my great-grandfather of his intention, remonstrated, " George, if you do this you'll
certainly be damned, you will indeed"; but, in spite of
the remonstrance and the risk, the estate was left away
from the elder son.

As compensation for being disinherited, my grandfather was appointed not only Rector of Somersby and
Wood Enderby, but also Incumbent of Benniworth and
Vicar of Great Grimsby, for those were the days of
pluralists. Not that he could have been a grasping man,
for on one occasion a wealthy land-owner (whose heir
was a remote relation and a poor farm-labourer) announced his intention of leaving all his property to
Dr Tennyson. But this my grandfather felt was unjust,
and accordingly took the first opportunity of offending

---

[1] Charles took the name of d'Eyncourt because, according to Burke and
other heralds, the Tennysons represent the two branches of the old Norman
family of d'Eyncourt.

his would-be benefactor in order that he might change his mind. The ruse was successful, as the sequel proved, for the estate devolved upon the rightful heir.

Undoubtedly the disinheritance of my grandfather created a feeling of injustice in his mind which descended to his sons, though my father used to reflect in later years how little this early trial personally affected them and the d'Eyncourt sons; the cousins were always good friends.

My grandfather had no real calling for the ministry of the Church, yet he faithfully strove to do his duty. He was a man of great ability, and considerably in advance of his age in his theological tenets, although in his sermons he could not escape the academic style of his time; for example: " The benevolent genius of Christianity affords the strongest presumption of its verity. The Almighty, so infinitely benevolent, can only wish to ensure the happiness of His creatures in the truths which He communicates, in the laws which He imposes, and in the doctrines which He promulgates. This indeed is so self-evident that it might be laid down as a rule that if any religion have not a benevolent tendency, this very circumstance is a sufficient refutation of its proceeding from God. What is revealed to us by Christianity but the Redemption of the whole human race by the merits of a crucified Saviour, and the glorious assurance of a future state of existence? "

The Lincolnshire folk among whom he lived were in the early part of this century apt to be uncouth and mannerless. A type of rough independence was my grandfather's coachman, who, blamed for not keeping the harness clean, rushed into the drawing-room, flung the whole harness on the floor and roared out: "Clean it yourself then." It was perhaps the same man, who at the time of the Reform Bill said, " I

suppose, Master Awlfred, your aunt Mrs Bourne will
be going up to London before they begin *to kill the
quality.*"

(This aunt was a rigid Calvinist, who would weep for
hours because God was so infinitely good. " Has He not
damned," she cried, "most of my friends? But *me, me*
He has picked out for eternal salvation, *me* who am no
better than my neighbours." One day she said to her
nephew, " Alfred, Alfred, when I look at you, I think of
the words of Holy Scripture — ' Depart from me, ye
cursed, into everlasting fire.'")

Again the Somersby cook was a decided character,
and " Master Awlfred" heard her in some rage against
her master and mistress exclaim : " If you raäked out
Hell with a smaäll-tooth coämb you weän't find their
likes," a phrase which long lingered in his memory.

Yet notwithstanding their roughness the poor were
fond of the "stern Doctor," as they called him, and
would "do anything for him." Here perhaps I should
mention that the sense of his father's unkindness and
injustice preyed upon his nerves and his health, and
caused him at times to be terribly despondent. More
than once Alfred, scared by his father's fits of despondency, went out through the black night, and threw
himself on a grave in the churchyard, praying to be
beneath the sod himself[1].

---

[1] In one of his books I have found this unfinished prayer, composed by
him, and written in his boyish hand ; it begins thus :

"O Lord God Almighty, high above all height, Omniscient and Omnipresent, Whose lifetime is eternity, wilt Thou condescend to behold from the
throne of Thy inexpressible Majesty the work of Thine own Hands kneeling
before thee? Thou art the God of Heaven and of Earth. Thou hast created
the immeasurable sea. Thou hast laid the foundations of the world that it
should not be moved for ever. Thou givest and Thou takest life, Thou
destroyest and Thou renewest. Blessed be Thy name for ever and ever."

The prayer continues with an appeal for pity to Christ — " Who did leave
the right hand of the Father to endure the agonies of the crown of thorns,"
and " of the Cross."

No doubt the children profited by the dominating force of their father's intellect. A Hebrew and Syriac scholar, he perfected himself in Greek, in order that he might teach his sons. All that they learnt of languages, of the fine arts, of mathematics, and natural science, until they went to Cambridge, was learnt from him. My father said that he himself received a good but not a regular classical education. At any rate he became an accurate scholar, the author "thoroughly drummed" into him being Horace; whom he disliked in proportion. He would lament, "They use *me* as a lesson-book at schools, and they will call me 'that horrible Tennyson.' It was not till many years after boyhood that I could like Horace. Byron expressed what I felt, 'Then farewell Horace whom I hated so.' Indeed I was so over-dosed with Horace that I hardly do him justice even now that I am old."

The boys had one great advantage, the run of their father's excellent library. Amongst the authors most read by them were Shakespeare, Milton, Burke, Goldsmith, Rabelais, Sir William Jones, Addison, Swift, Defoe, Cervantes, Bunyan and Buffon.

Dr Tennyson's social powers were famous throughout the country side. The tradition lingered long among old barristers that, as young men, when they came to Spilsby on circuit, they were always anxious to persuade Dr Tennyson to dine with them because of his geniality and brilliant conversation.

To this sketch of my grandfather, my uncle Arthur adds a few words.

A scene comes before me of Frederick, Charles and Alfred having a regular scrimmage with lesson-books, and of my father suddenly coming round the corner. I didn't wait to see what happened, but bolted; our father's tall form appearing was generally at such moments the signal for a regular "scatter," but, although very severe, he had great tenderness of heart. I can well recollect him by my bedside, almost weeping, when I had a bad paroxysm of croup. Alfred had the same tenderness in spite of his somewhat gruff manner: he was notable among his brothers for strength and independence of character. His was a very gentle nature and I never remember quarrelling with him. He was very kind to us who were younger than he was, and I remember his tremendous excitement when he got hold of Bewick for the first time: how he paced up and down the lawn for hours studying him, and how he kept rushing in to us in the schoolroom to show us some of the marvellous wood-cuts, and to let us have a share in this new pleasure of his. Indeed he was always a great reader; and if he went alone he would take his book with him on his walk. One day in the winter, the snow being deep, he did not hear the Louth mail coming up behind. Suddenly "Ho! ho!" from the coachman roused him. He looked up, and found a horse's nose and eyes over his shoulder, as if reading his book. Like my father, Alfred had a great head, so that when I put on his hat it came down over my face. He too like my father[1] had a powerful frame, a splendid physique, and we used to have gymnastics over the large beam in his attic den, which was in the gable looking westward. Alfred and I often took long rambles together, and on one particular afternoon, when we were in the home fields talking of our respective futures, he said most emphatically, "Well, Arthur, I mean to be famous." (From his earliest years he felt that he was a poet, and earnestly trained himself to be worthy of his vocation.) For our less active amusements we carved in wood and moulded with clay, and one of my earliest recollections of Alfred is watching him form with clay a Gothic archway in the bole of an old tree.

In the poem of "Isabel" my father more or less described his mother, who was a "remarkable and saintly woman." "One of the most innocent and tender-hearted ladies I ever saw," wrote Edward Fitzgerald.

---

[1] He stood six feet two, and was strong and energetic. Tim Green, the Somersby rat-catcher, a great ally of the young Tennysons, said, "I remember the oud Doctor. What a clip he used to goä betweeän them chooörches o' Somersby an' Enderby!"

She devoted herself entirely to her husband and her children.

> The world hath not another
> (Tho' all her fairest forms are types of thee,
> And thou of God in thy great charity)
> Of such a finish'd chasten'd purity.

She had been among the beauties of the county. When she was almost eighty, a daughter, under cover of her deafness, ventured to mention the number of offers of marriage which had been made to her mother, naming twenty-four. Suddenly, to the amusement of all present, the old lady said emphatically, and quite simply, as for truth's sake, " No, my dear, twenty-five." She had a great sense of humour, which made her room a paradise for the children. They inherited her love of animals[1] and her pity "for all wounded wings." And my father was even then a keen observer of the habits of birds and beasts and ants and bees; was " wise in winged things, and knew the ways of Nature," of which he had the true poet's love. In later life this led to an earnest study of science.

As a boy he would reel off hundreds of lines such as these:

> When winds are east and violets blow,
> And slowly stalks the parson crow.

And

> The quick-wing'd gnat doth make a boat
> Of his old husk wherewith to float
> To a new life! all low things range
> To higher! but I cannot change.

---

[1] The boys of a neighbouring village used to bring their dogs to my grandmother's windows and beat them in order to be bribed to leave off, or to induce her to buy them.

To the aggravation of the neighbouring gamekeepers he would spring all their traps, and more than one of them threatened that, if they caught "that there young gentleman who was for ever springing the gins," they would duck him in the pond.

He liked to tell of an owl and a monkey of famous memory. Sitting at night by the open window in his own particular little attic (now used as a store-room for apples and lumber), he heard the cry of a young owl and answered it. The owl came nestling up to him, fed out of his hand, and finally took up its permanent abode with the family. Sometimes it would perch on my grandmother's head, and was so constantly with her that her pet monkey was made jealous. The monkey was a droll fellow: he would imitate the housemaid scrubbing the floor, and his prime luxury was to singe the hair of his back at a candle. One luckless day he was sitting in a corner of the sill outside the attic window, the owl in the opposite corner. The monkey glared at the owl; the owl watched the monkey with solemn round eyes, — the monkey, advancing and retiring, and gibbering like a little Frenchman all the while. The little Frenchman at last plucked up courage, rushed at his solemn opponent, took him by the leg, and hurled him to the ground. "One of the most comical scenes," my father said, "that I have ever witnessed." The owl was eventually drowned in the well; dying, it is supposed, a Narcissus death of vanity.

"Like Wordsworth on the mountains," said Fitzgerald, "Alfred too, when a lad abroad on the wold, sometimes of a night with the shepherd, watched not only the flock on the greensward, but also

the fleecy star that bears
Andromeda far off Atlantic seas":

Two of Alfred's earliest lines were:

The rays of many a rolling central star,
Aye flashing earthwards, have not reach'd us yet.

There is a story current in the family that Frederick,
when an Eton school-boy, was shy of going to a neighbouring dinner-party to which he had been invited.
"Fred," said his younger brother, "think of Herschel's
great star-patches, and you will soon get over all that."

Of the few families in the neighbourhood the Tennysons were most intimate with the Rawnsleys. Mr
Rawnsley, who was Rector of Halton, was appointed by
Dr Tennyson one of the guardians of his children. For
his son Drummond my father had a strong friendship
which lasted through life, having been first attracted
to him by a certain unworldliness of nature.

In the summer-time Dr and Mrs Tennyson took
their holiday by the seaside, mostly at Mablethorpe.
From his boyhood my father had a passion for the sea,
and especially for the North Sea in wild weather—

The hollow ocean-ridges roaring into cataracts:

and for the glorious sunsets over the flats—

The wide-wing'd sunset of the misty marsh.

The cottage[1] to which the family resorted was close
under the sea bank, "the long low line of tussocked dunes."
"I used to stand on this sand-built ridge," my father
said, "and think that it was the spine-bone of the world."
From the top of this, the immense sweep of marsh inland[1]
and the whole weird strangeness of the place greatly

[1] Or even a lowly cottage whence we see
Stretch'd wide and wild the waste enormous marsh,
Where from the frequent bridge,
Like emblems of infinity,
The trenchéd waters run from sky to sky.
"Ode to Memory."

moved him. On the other side of the bank at
low tide there is an immeasurable waste of sand and
clay. "Nottingham and Lincoln foälk moästly coom
'ere," one of the Mablethorpe fishermen grumbled, "a
vast sight of 'em, soom taime (time), but they saäys it
is a mighty dool plaäce with a deäl o' sand, becos there
isn't naw band nor pier like: but howsoomever, the wind
blaws the poor things a bit, an' they weshes their bodies
i' the waäves." At night on the shore, when the tide
is full, the sound is amazing. All around there is a
low murmur of seething foam,

Like armies whispering where great echoes be.

"Nowhere," wrote Drummond Rawnsley, "are the
waves in a storm higher than in the North Sea": nowhere have the breakers a more thunderous roar than
on this Lincolnshire coast: and sometimes at half-tide
the clap of the wave falling on the flat shore can be
heard for miles, and is accurately described in "The
Last Tournament":

As the crest of some slow-arching wave,
Heard in dead night along that table-shore,
Drops flat, and after the great waters break
Whitening for half a league, and thin themselves,
Far over sands marbled with moon and cloud,
From less and less to nothing.

Fitzgerald writes: "I used to say Alfred never
should have left old Lincolnshire, where there were not
only such good seas, but also such fine Hill and Dale
among 'The Wolds,' which he was brought up in, as
people in general scarce thought on."

In 1827 my uncle Frederick went from Eton, where
he was captain of the school, to Trinity College, Cambridge: and in March of this year *Poems by Two Brothers*

was published by Jackson of Louth.   When these poems were written, my uncle Charles was between sixteen and eighteen, and my father between fifteen and seventeen.

The brothers were promised the liberal sum of £20, having however to take more than half of this in books out of Jackson's shop.   According to the fashion of the day, quotations from various authors were freely interspersed throughout the little volume, and the motto at the beginning was " Haec nos novimus esse nihil."   Their preface states, " We have passed the Rubicon and we leave the rest to fate, though its edict may create a fruitless regret that we ever emerged ' from the shade ' and courted notoriety."

As an outburst of youthful poetic enthusiasm, the book is not wanting in interest and a certain charm, although full of the boyish imitation of other poets. Unlike Swift, who exclaimed on re-reading his early work, " What a genius I had when I wrote that ! " my father could hardly tolerate what he called his " early rot."   But latterly he said, " Some of it is better than I thought it was ! "   In consequence of the unearthing of this MS by Messrs Jackson it fell to me to publish the second edition, sixty years after the publication of the first, and to endeavour to initial the poems.   Yet I cannot be sure of the authorship of each, even though the original manuscript has been in my hands, for the poems are not always copied out by their respective authors.   But the initials which I gave received the sanction and authority of my uncle Frederick, as far as his memory served him.   He himself was the author of four of the poems, that had generally been attributed to Charles.

The only contemporary criticism is in the *Literary Chronicle* (May 1827):

This little volume exhibits a pleasing union of kindred tastes, and contains several little pieces of considerable merit.

My uncle Charles would say that, on the afternoon of publication, my father and he hired a carriage with some of the money earned; and driving away fourteen miles, over the wolds and the marsh, to Mablethorpe, their favourite waste sea-shore, "shared their triumph with the winds and waves."

Unpublished Poems of Boyhood.

(Fragments written at 14 or 15 years of age.)

I showed the following early fragments to the late Master of Balliol and by his advice I publish them. He said, "They are most original, and it is wonderful how the whelp could have known such things." They were omitted from the *Poems by Two Brothers*, being thought too much out of the common for the public taste.

(*A scene, written at* 14.)

Act 1, Sc. 1 (In Spain).

DRAMATIS PERSONÆ.

Carlos (a spirited stripling with a spice of suspicion and a preponderance of pride).
Michael (his old attendant).

Moonlight.

Carl. Hear you the sound of wheels?
Mich.   No, faith, not I.
Carl. Methinks they tarry somewhat. What's the
            clock?
Mich. Half way toward midnight.
Carl.   Why, they should be here.
Mich. 'Tis a clear night, they will be here anon.
Carl. Hist! what was that?

Mich.   The night gale in those trees.
Carl.   How beautifully looks the moonbeam through
      The knotted boughs of this long avenue
      Of thick dark oaks, that arch their arms above,
      Coeval with the battlemented towers
      Of my old ancestors !
      I never look upon them but I glow
      With an enthusiastic love of them.
      Methinks an oak-tree never should be planted
      But near the dwelling of some noble race ;
      For it were almost mockery to hang it
      O'er the thatch'd cottage, or the snug brick box
      Of some sleek citizen.
      Ye proud aristocrats whose lordly shadows,
      Chequer'd with moonlight's variation,
      Richly and darkly girdle these gray walls, —
      I and my son's sons and our offspring, all
      Shall perish, and their monuments, with forms
      Of the unfading marble carved upon them,
      Which speak of us to other centuries,
      Shall perish also, but ye still shall flourish
      In your high pomp of shade, and make beneath
      Ambrosial gloom. Thou dost remember, Michael,
      How, when a boy, I joy'd to place me on
      The hollow-stemm'd and well-nigh leafless oak
      Which towers above the lake that ripples out
      In the clear moonshine.
Mich.   You were wont to call it
      Your throne.
Carl.   I was so, Michael.
Mich.   You'd sit there
      From dawn till sunset looking far away
      On the blue mountains, and most joyful when
      The wanton wind came singing lustily
      Among the moss-grown branches, and threw back
      Your floating hair.

Carl.   Ha! Ha! Why even then
My Spanish blood ran proudly in my veins.
Mich. Ay, Ay, I warrant you, and when I came
And would have call'd you down to break your
        fast,
You would look down and knit your baby brows
Into your father's frown, and beckon me
Away.
Carl.   Ha! Ha! 'twas laughable, and yet
It show'd the seeds of innate dignity
That were within me; did it not, good Michael?
Mich. And when your age had somewhat riper grown,
And I was wont to dandle you upon
My knee, and ask you whether you would be
A great man in your time,
You'd weave your waxen fingers in these locks
(They are gray now) and tell me you were great
Already in your birth.
Carl.   Ha! by St James
Mine was no vulgar mind in infancy,
Ev'n then the force of nature and high birth
Had writ nobility upon my brow.
Hark! they are coming.

Extract from a Play also written at 14

(according to an entry made by my grandfather at the beginning
of the MS).

THE DEVIL (speaks)

(*going to the timepiece*).

Half after midnight! these mute moralizers,
Pointing to the unheeded lapse of hours,
Become a tacit eloquent reproach

Unto the dissipation of this Earth.
There is a clock in Pandemonium,
Hard by the burning throne of my great grandsire,
The slow vibrations of whose pendulum,
With click-clack alternation to and fro,
Sound " Ever, Never " thro' the courts of Hell,
Piercing the wrung ears of the damn'd that writhe
Upon their beds of flame, and whensoe'er
There may be short cessation of their wails,
Through all that boundless depth of fires is heard
The shrill and solemn warning " Ever, Never ":
Then bitterly I trow they turn and toss
And shriek and shout to drown the thrilling noise.
Half after midnight !   (*Looking again at the timepiece.*)
              Wherefore stand I here?
Methinks my tongue runs twenty knots an hour :
I must unto mine office.
                            (*Exit abruptly.*)

After reading the *Bride of Lammermoor* he wrote
the following:

THE BRIDAL.*

The lamps were bright and gay
    On the merry bridal-day,
When the merry bridegroom
    Bore the bride away!
A merry, merry bridal,
    A merry bridal-day!
And the chapel's vaulted gloom
    Was misted with perfume.
" Now, tell me, mother, pray,
    Why the bride is white as clay,
Although the merry bridegroom
    Bears the bride away,

On a merry, merry bridal,
   A merry bridal-day?
And why her black eyes burn
   With a light so wild and stern?"
"They revel as they may,"
   That skinny witch did say,
"For — now the merry bridegroom
   Hath borne the bride away —
Her thoughts have found their wings
   In the dreaming of past things:
And though girt in glad array,
   Yet her own deep soul says nay:
For tho' the merry bridegroom
   Hath borne the bride away,
A dark form glances quick
   Thro' her worn brain, hot and sick."
And so she said her say —
   This was her roundelay —
That tho' the merry bridegroom
   Might lead the bride away,
Dim grief did wait upon her,
   In glory and in honour.

    *   *   *   *   *

In the hall, at close of day,
   Did the people dance and play,
For now the merry bridegroom
   Hath borne the bride away.
He from the dance hath gone
   But the revel still goes on.
Then a scream of wild dismay
   Thro' the deep hall forced its way,
Altho' the merry bridegroom
   Hath borne the bride away;
And, staring as in trance,
   They were shaken from the dance. —

Then they found him where he lay
　　Whom the wedded wife did slay,
Tho' he a merry bridegroom
　　Had borne the bride away,
And they saw *her* standing by,
　　With a laughing crazed eye,
On the bitter, bitter bridal,
　　The bitter bridal-day.

THE COACH OF DEATH.*

(A fragment.)

Far off in the dun, dark occident,
　　Behind the burning Sun:
Where his gilding ray is never sent,
　　And his hot steeds never run:

There lies a land of chilling storms,
　　A region void of light,
A land of thin faces and shadowy forms,
　　Of vapours, and mist, and night.

There never green thing will gaily spring
　　In that unwholesome air,
But the rickety blast runs shrilly and fast
　　Thro' the bony branches there.

When the shadow of night's eternal wings
　　Envelopes the gloomy whole,
And the mutter of deep-mouth'd thunderings
　　Shakes all the starless pole,

Thick sobs and short shrill screams arise
　　Along the sunless waste,
And the things of past days with their horrible eyes
　　Look out from the cloudy vast.

* Copyright, 1897, by The Macmillan Company.

And the earth is dry, tho' the pall of the sky
  Leave never an inch of blue;
And the moaning wind before it drives
  Thick wreaths of cloudy dew.

Whoever walks that bitter ground
  His limbs beneath him fail;
His heart throbs thick, his brain reels sick:
  His brow is clammy and pale.

But some have hearts that in them burn
  With power and promise high,
To draw strange comfort from the earth,
  Strange beauties from the sky.

Dark was the night, and loud the roar
  Of wind and mingled shower,
When there stood a dark coach at an old Inn door
  At the solemn midnight hour.

That Inn was built at the birth of Time:
  The walls of lava rose,
Cemented with the burning slime
  Which from Asphaltus flows.

No sound of joy, no revelling tones
  Of carouse were heard within:
But the rusty sign of a skull and cross-bones
  Swung creaking before the Inn.

No taper's light look'd out on the night,
  But ever and anon
Strange fiery eyes glared fiercely thro'
  The windows of shaven bone.

And the host came forth, and stood alone
  And still in the dark doorway:
There was not a tinge on each high cheek bone,
  But his face was a yellow gray.

The skin hung lax on his long thin hands;
   No jolly host was he;
For his shanks were shrunken to willow wands
   And his name was Atrophy!

Dimly the travellers look'd thro' the glooms,
   Worn and wan was their gaze, I trow,
As the shrivell'd forms of the shadowy grooms
   Yoked the skeleton horses to.

They lifted their eyes to the dead, pale skies,
   And above the barkless trees
They saw the green verge of the pleasant earth,
   And heard the roar of her seas.

They see the light of their blest firesides,
   They hear each household voice:
The whisper'd love of the fair young wives;
   And the laugh of their rose-lipp'd boys.

The summer plains with their shining leaves,
   The summer hills they see;
The dark vine leaves round the rustling eaves,
   And the forests, fair and free.

There came a gaunt man from the dark Inn door,
   A dreadnought coat had he:
His bones crack'd loud, as he stept thro' the crowd,
   And his boots creak'd heavily.

Before his eyes so grim and calm
   The tingling blood grew chill,
As each put a farthing into his palm,
   To drive them where he will.

His sockets were eyeless, but in them slept
   A red infernal glow;
As the cockroach crept, and the white fly leapt
   About his hairless brow.

They mounted slow in their long black cloaks,
  The tears bedimm'd their sight:
The grim old coachee strode to the box,
  And the guard gasp'd out "All's right."

The leaders bounded, the guard's horn sounded:
  Far away thro' the night ran the lengthen'd tones:
As the quick wheels brush'd, and threw up the dust
  Of dead men's pulverised bones.

Whose blood in its liveliest course would not pause
  At the strife of the shadowy wheels,
The chattering of the fleshless jaws,
  And the beat of the horny heels?

Deep dells of snow sunk on each side below
  The highway, broad and flat,
As the coach ran on, and the sallow lights shone
  Dimly and blurly with simmering fat.

Vast wastes of starless glooms were spread
  Around in the chilling air,
And heads without bodies and shapes without heads
  Went leaping here and there.

O Coachee, Coachee, what lights approach
  With heavenly melodies?
Oh! those are the lights of the Paradise coach,
  That so gaily meet their eyes!

With pleasant hymns they soothe the air
  Of death, with songs of pride:
With sackbut, and with dulcimer,
  With psaltery they ride.

These fear not the mists of unwholesome damps
  That through that region rove,
For all wreath'd with green bays were the gorgeous
    lamps,
  And a bright archangel drove.

They pass'd (an inner spirit fed
　　Their ever-burning fires,)
With a solemn burst of thrilling light,
　　And a sound of stringéd lyres.

With a silver sound the wheels went round,
　　The wheels of burning flame;
Of beryl, and of amethyst
　　Was the spiritual frame.

Their steeds were strong exceedingly:
　　And rich was their attire:
Before them flow'd a fiery stream;
　　They broke the ground with hoofs of fire.

They glitter'd with a stedfast light,
　　The happy spirits within;
As stars they shone, in raiment white,
　　And free from taint of sin.

CHAPTER II.*

CAMBRIDGE.

1828–1830.

I past beside the reverend walls
  In which of old I wore the gown;
  I roved at random thro' the town,
And saw the tumult of the halls;

And heard once more in College fanes
  The storm their high-built organs make,
  And thunder-music, rolling, shake
The prophets blazon'd on the panes:

And caught once more the distant shout,
  The measured pulse of racing oars
  Among the willows; paced the shores
And many a bridge, and all about

The same gray flats again, and felt
  The same, but not the same; and last
  Up that long walk of limes I past
To see the rooms in which *he* dwelt.

Another name was on the door:
  I linger'd; all within was noise
  Of songs, and clapping hands, and boys
That crash'd the glass, and beat the floor;

Where once we held debate, a band
  Of youthful friends, on mind and art,
  And labour, and the changing mart,
And all the framework of the land.

On February 20th, 1828, my father and my uncle
Charles matriculated at Trinity College, Cambridge,
where their elder brother Frederick was already a distinguished scholar, and had won the University medal
for the best Greek ode on the Pyramids.

* Copyright, 1897, by The Macmillan Company.

Of their entrance into Cambridge, — my father told me that they had left the coach and were walking down Trumpington Street in the dusk of the evening, when a proctor addressed him, "What are you doing without your cap and gown, sir, at this time of night?" To which, not being aware of the dignity of the personage who addressed him, he promptly retorted, "I should like to know what business it can be of yours, sir."

They first occupied rooms at No. 12 Rose Crescent, moving afterwards to Trumpington Street, No. 57 Corpus Buildings. Although they knew but few men when beginning their University career, and were shy and reserved, they soon joined themselves to a set of friends who were all more or less remarkable. At first my father writes to his aunt, Mrs Russell: "I am sitting owl-like and solitary in my rooms (nothing between me and the stars but a stratum of tiles). The hoof of the steed, the roll of the wheel, the shouts of drunken Gown and drunken Town come up from below with a sea-like murmur. I wish to Heaven I had Prince Hussain's fairy carpet to transport me along the deeps of air to your coterie. Nay, I would even take up with his brother Aboul-something's glass for the mere pleasure of a peep. What a pity it is that the golden days of Faerie are over! What a misery not to be able to consolidate our gossamer dreams into reality! When, my dearest Aunt, may I hope to see you again? I know not how it is, but I feel isolated here in the midst of society. The country is so disgustingly level, the revelry of the place so monotonous, the studies of the University so uninteresting, so much matter of fact. None but dry-headed, calculating, angular little gentlemen can take much delight in them.

I have been seeking 'Falkland' for a long time without success. Those beautiful extracts from it, which you showed me at Tealby, haunt me incessantly; but wishes, I think, like telescopes reversed, seem to set their objects at a greater distance."

" I can tell you nothing of his college days," writes
Edward Fitzgerald to a friend, " for I did not know him
till they were over, tho' I had seen him two or three
times before : I remember him well, a sort of Hyperion."

With his poetic nature, and warmth of heart, he soon
made his way. Fanny Kemble, who used to visit her
brother John, said of him when at College, " Alfred
Tennyson was our hero, the great hero of our day."
Another friend describes him as " Six feet high, broad-
chested, strong-limbed, his face Shakespearian, with deep
eyelids, his forehead ample, crowned with dark wavy
hair, his head finely poised, his hand the admiration of
sculptors, long fingers with square tips, soft as a child's
but of great size and strength. What struck one most
about him was the union of strength with refinement."
On seeing him first come into the Hall at Trinity,
Thompson[1] said at once, " That man must be a poet."
Arthur Hallam " looked up to him as to a great poet
and an elder brother[2]."

Hallam said to Trench in 1832 : " Alfred's mind is
what it always was, or rather, brighter, and more vigorous.
I regret, with you, that you have never had the opportunity of knowing more of him. His nervous temperament and habits of solitude give an appearance of
affectation to his manner, which is no interpreter of the
man, and wears off on further knowledge. Perhaps you
would never become very intimate, for certainly your
bents of mind are not the same, and at some points they
intersect ; yet I think you would hardly fail to see much
for love, as well as for admiration." Blakesley described
Alfred as " Truly one of the mighty of the earth."

The friends among whom he lived were Spedding
(author of the Life of Bacon), Milnes (afterwards Lord
Houghton), Trench (afterwards Archbishop of Dublin),

[1] Afterwards Master of Trinity.
[2] A. H. Hallam was born on February 1st, 1811.

Alford (afterwards Dean of Canterbury), Brookfield, Blakesley (afterwards Dean of Lincoln), Thompson, Stephen Spring Rice, Merivale (afterwards Dean of Ely), J. M. Kemble, Heath (Senior Wrangler 1832), Charles Buller, R. Monteith, Tennant, and above all Hallam. Some summers ago my father and I went to see Hallam's rooms, at No. 3, G, New Court, in which with these friends he had spent so many happy hours. Of this band of men Lord Houghton spoke in 1866 at the opening of the New Cambridge Union: "I am inclined to believe that the members of that generation were, for the wealth of their promise, a rare body of men such as this University has seldom contained." They were a genial, high-spirited, poetical[1] set, full of speculation and of enthusiasm for the great literature of the past, and for the modern schools of thought, and despised rhetoric and sentimentalism. Fitzgerald comments thus in one of his unpublished MS notes:

The German School, with Coleridge, Julius Hare, etc. to expound, came to reform all our notions. I remember that Livy and Jeremy Taylor were the greatest poets next to Shakespeare. I am not sure if you were not startled at hearing that Eutropius was the greatest lyric poet except Pindar. You hadn't known he was a poet at all. I remember A. T. quoting Hallam (the great historian) as pronouncing Shakespeare "the greatest man." I thought such dicta rather peremptory for a philosopher. "Well," said A. T., "the man one would wish perhaps to show as a sample of mankind to those in another planet." He used sometimes to quote Milton as the sublimest of all poets, and his two similes, one about the "gunpowder ore," and the other about "the fleet," as the grandest of all similes. He thought that "'Lycidas' was a touchstone of poetic taste." Of Dryden, "I don't know how it is, but Dryden always seems greater than he shows himself to be."

---

[1] The modern poets in the ascendant among them were Wordsworth, Coleridge, Shelley, Keats; but Byron's "comet blaze" was evidently on the wane.

His friends noted that my father had from the first a deep insight into character, and would often turn upon them with a sudden terse criticism when they thought him far away in the clouds [1].

Fitzgerald remembered that of someone suddenly pronouncing a dogma he said, " That's the swift decision of one who sees only half the truth ";

And of a very different character, somewhat apologetic, " There's a want of central dignity in him."

A few of his Cambridge contemporaries have been drawn in verse by him [2].

The then well-known Cambridge orator S— was partly described in the poem, " A Character." He was " a very plausible, parliament-like, self-satisfied speaker at the Union Debating Society."

Another verse-portrait my father quoted to me, which he remembered with pleasure that Hallam had praised:

[1] "We were looking one day at the portrait of an elderly politician in his bland, family aspect: A. T. (with his eye-glass), 'It looks rather like a retired panther.' So true!" MS Note, E. F. G.

[2] Of Brookfield he wrote in 1875 for Lord Lyttelton's preface to " Sermons, by the late Rev. William Henry Brookfield ":

> Old Brooks, who loved so well to mouth my rhymes,
> How oft we two have heard St Mary's chimes!
> How oft the Cantab supper, host and guest,
> Would echo helpless laughter to your jest!
> How oft with him we paced that walk of limes,
> Him, the lost light of those dawn-golden times.

(It was of him that the late Dr Thompson wrote: — "He was far the most amusing man I ever met, or shall meet. At my age it is not likely that I shall ever again see a whole party lying on the floor for purposes of unrestrained laughter, while one of their number is pouring forth, with a perfectly grave face, a succession of imaginary dialogues between characters, real and fictitious, one exceeding another in humour and drollery.")

Of Kemble my father said in a sonnet published in 1830:

> My hope and heart is with thee — thou wilt be
> A latter Luther and a soldier priest.

(*Unpublished.*)

Thy soul is like a landskip, friend,
 Steeple, and stream, and forest lawn,
 Most delicately overdrawn
With the first twilight of the even,
Clear-edged, and showing every bend
 Of each dark hill against the Heaven,
Nor wanting many a sombre mound,
 Stately and mild, and all between
Valleys full of solemn sound,
 And hoary holts on uplands green,
And somewhat loftier antient heights
Touch'd with Heaven's latest lights.

Of Blakesley he said, " He ought to be Lord Chancellor, for he is a subtle and powerful reasoner, and an honest man." Blakesley, he observed another time, was honestly indignant at gaining the Chancellor's Medal, which, he asserted, " ought to have gone to young Kennedy."

Later, of James Spedding he remarked, " He was the Pope among us young men — the wisest man I know."

Of Hallam himself, " He would have been known, if he had lived, as a great man but not as a great poet; he was as near perfection as mortal man could be[1]."

Whewell, who was his tutor, he called " the lion-like man," and had for him a great respect. It is reported that Whewell, recognizing his genius, tolerated in him certain informalities which he would not have overlooked in other men. Thus, " Mr Tennyson, what's the compound interest of a penny put out at the Christian era up to the present time ? " was Whewell's good-natured call to

[1] " And over those ethereal eyes
The bar of Michael Angelo.

These lines I wrote from what Arthur Hallam said after reading of the prominent ridge of bone over the eyes of Michael Angelo: 'Alfred, look over my eyes; surely I have the bar of Michael Angelo!'" A. T.

attention in the Lecture Room while my father was
reading Virgil under the desk.

Once, when Whewell had made himself unpopular, a
tumult arose among the undergraduates, who lined the
street from the Senate House to Trinity Gate and hooted
him, shouting "Billy Whistle!" (Whewell's nickname).
As he passed between them, Hallam, Spring Rice, and
my father, raised a cheer for him.   He saw my father and
bade him come instantly to his rooms. Whewell began, " I
was sorry to see, Mr Tennyson, that you were at the head
of that very disorderly mob outside the Senate House."
" But," answered my father, " my friends and I were not
heading the mob, we were cheering you!"   Whereat
Whewell said nothing, but smiled grimly to himself with
evident pleasure, inviting him to breakfast next morning.

Another Cambridge story about Whewell, but perhaps
of later date, my father would tell somewhat in this way.
At 12 o'clock one night, horns and trumpets and bugles and
drums began to play from all the windows round Trinity
New Court, and a man, who had been expelled that day,
strummed on a piano which had been set in the middle
of the lawn; and there was the fiend's own row.   Presently
Whewell, who lived in Nevile's Court, next to the New
Court, was heard thundering at his door which had been
tied with a rope; 'τρὶς μὲν ὀρέξατ᾽ ἰὼν' and at the third
charge he broke through, rushed out, found all the
windows closed, lights extinguished, dead silence everywhere, only the expelled man standing immovable by the
piano under a cold round moon.   Whewell strode to the
piano, the expelled man ran for his life round and round
the colonnades of Nevile's Court; thrice he ran round,
Whewell pursuing.   At last Whewell caught him.   " Do
you know who I am, sir?" said Whewell, panting.   " Yes,"
was the answer, " Old Whistle, who made that mistake
in his *Dynamics*."   Thereupon Whewell, seeing that he
was the man who had been expelled, took him by the

scruff of the neck, carried him to the great gate, and shot him out like bad rubbish.

As a young man my father's friends have often described him to me as having Johnsonian common sense and a rare power of expression, very genial, full of enjoyment, full of sensitiveness and full of humour, though with the passionate heart of a poet, and sometimes feeling the melancholy of life. He passed through "moods of misery unutterable," but he eventually shook them off. He remembered how, when in London almost for the first time, one of these moods came over him, as he realized that "in a few years all its inhabitants would be lying horizontal, stark and stiff in their coffins."

Despite such passages of gloom he worked on at his poems, wrote Latin and Greek odes[1], read his classics

[1] Before he had left Somersby for Cambridge, he had written in Greek hexameters an Homeric book on the Seven against Thebes, and an Ovidian poem about the death of a young girl who had died for love of the Apollo Belvedere.

In his note-book, mixed up with translations of Aristophanes, and of Greek philosophers, and with astronomical diagrams, I find this fragment, mainly of value as showing at what an early date physical science began to penetrate his verse:

The Moon.   (Unpublished fragment.)

*   *   *   *   *   *

Deep glens I found, and sunless gulfs,
   Set round with many a toppling spire,
And monstrous rocks from craggy snouts
   Disploding globes of roaring fire.

Large as a human eye the sun
   Drew down the West his feeble lights;
And then a night, all moons, confused
   The shadows from the icy heights.

["A night, all moons," means that when seen from the airless moon all the principal stars and planets would be very large and bright in the black heavens, and strike the eye there as the moon strikes the eye here.]

and history and natural science [1].   He also took a lively
interest in politics.   He was among the young supporters
of the Anti-slavery Convention, and advocated the
Measure for abolishing subscription to the Thirty-nine
Articles, while admiring as statesmen Canning, Peel, and
the Duke of Wellington.   England was in a state of ferment with the hope or dread of the Reform Bill.   Farms
were fired, ricks were burnt, and "sanguine Lazarus
felt a vacant hand Fill" with the rich man's purse.
In the poem addressed to Mary Boyle my father tells
how he helped to "hand the bucket from the well," and to
quench a conflagration in a homestead near Cambridge.

At one of these farm fires he heard a countryman
saying, "Now we shall get our taters cheaper."   "You
fools," said my father, although he largely sympathized
with the labourers in their demands, "you are all going
the way to make taters dearer."   Some undergraduates
with over-zeal began to pull down the farmer's house in
order to help him to preserve the materials from fire.
The poor man held them back, comically but naturally
remonstrating, "Leave me, sirs, I pray you, the little
property that the fire has spared!"

My father's note-book contains these unpublished
lines:

I, loving Freedom for herself,
    And much of that which is her form,
Wed to no faction in the state,
    A voice before the storm,
I mourn in spirit when I think
    The year, that comes, may come with shame,
Lured by the cuckoo-voice that loves
    To babble its own name.

That "deep chord which Hampden smote" pulsed

----

[1] "I kept a tame snake in my rooms.   I liked to watch his wonderful sinu-
osities on the carpet."   A. T.

through the life of the young men of the day. These
riots of the poorer classes filled my father with an earnest
desire to do something to help those who lived in misery
among the " warrens of the poor." Indeed from first to
last he always preached the onward progress of liberty,
while steadily opposed to revolutionary license —

> Freedom free to slay herself, and dying while they
> shout her name.

Asked what politics he held: " I am of the same
politics as Shakespeare [1], Bacon, and every sane man."

Carlyle's account of Sterling best describes, as far as
I can gather, the typical intellectual undergraduate of my
father's set: who hated the narrow and ignorant Toryism
to be found in country districts: who loathed parties and
sects: who reverenced the great traditions and the great
men of past ages, and eagerly sympathized with the misfortunes and disabilities of his fellow-men.

He tells how Sterling, famous already for the
brilliance of his talk, had at Cambridge "a wide and
rather genial circle of comrades." They had among
them a society called the " Apostles ": of which my
father was an early member. " On stated evenings,"
Carlyle goes on, " was much logic, and other spiritual
fencing, and ingenuous collision — probably of a really
superior quality in that kind; for not a few of the
then disputants have since proved themselves men of
parts, and attained distinction in the intellectual walks
of life."

It is of the " Apostles " that Sterling writes to Trench:
" Pray let me see you as soon as you reach London, and

---

[1] " Some critics," he said to me more than once, "object to Shakespeare's
aristocratic view of his clowns, because he makes them talk such poor stuff,
but they forget that his clowns occasionally speak as real truths as Hamlet,
and that sometimes they utter very profound sayings. That is the glory of
Shakespeare, he can give you the incongruity of things."

in the mean time commend me to the brethren, who, I trust, are waxing daily in religion and radicalism."

Arthur Hallam, in a letter to Gladstone, says of Frederick Maurice: "The effects which he has produced on the minds of many at Cambridge by the single creation of that society of 'Apostles' (for the spirit though not the form was created by him) is far greater than I can dare to calculate, and will be felt, both directly and indirectly, in the age that is upon us."

There were regular meetings of the society as distinguished from the almost daily gatherings in one or another man's rooms, at all of which much coffee was drunk, much tobacco smoked. The Apostle who proposed the subject for discussion, generally stood before the mantelpiece, and said his say. Douglas Heath writes that the image he has carried away of my father is of one "sitting in front of the fire, smoking and meditating, and now and then mingling in the conversation." With one short phrase he was wont to sum up the issue of the arguments. Heath continues: "I cannot satisfy myself as to the time when I became an Apostle, or when I made acquaintance with A. T. My belief is that he had already become an honorary member extraordinary. In the usual course a member had to read essays in regular succession, or give a dinner in default during a certain period, after which he became honorary. But A. T. was, I suppose, bored by this, and the society was content to receive him, his poetry and wisdom unfettered." "Ghosts" was the subject of an essay written by my father for the Society, but he was too shy to deliver it. The preface alone has survived [1].

These friends not only debated on politics but read their Hobbes, Locke, Berkeley, Butler, Hume, Bentham, Descartes and Kant, and discussed such questions as the Origin of Evil, the Derivation of Moral Senti-

[1] For the prologue of "Ghosts" see Appendix, p. 497.

ments, Prayer and the Personality of God[1]. Among
the Cambridge papers I find a remarkable sentence on
"Prayer" by Arthur Hallam.

With respect to prayer, you ask how am I to distinguish the
operations of God in me from motions in my own heart? Why
should you distinguish them or how do you know there is any
distinction? Is God less God because He acts by general laws
when He deals with the common elements of nature?...That
fatal mistake which has embarrassed the philosophy of mind
with infinite confusion, the mistake of setting value on a thing's
origin rather than on its character, of assuming that *composite*
must be less excellent than simple, has not been slow to extend
its deleterious influence over the field of practical religion.

My father seems to have propounded in some college
discussion the theory, that the "development of the
human body might possibly be traced from the radiated,
vermicular, molluscous and vertebrate organisms." The
question of surprise put to him on this proposition was
"Do you mean that the human brain is at first like a
madrepore's, then like a worm's, etc.? but this cannot be
for they have no brain[2]."

At this time, with one or two of his more literary
friends, he took great interest in the work which Hallam
had undertaken, a translation from the *Vita Nuova* of

---

[1] Three questions discussed by the Society were: (1) Have Shelley's
poems an immoral tendency? Tennyson votes "No." (2) Is an intelligible
First Cause deducible from the phenomena of the Universe? Tennyson
votes "No." (3) Is there any rule of moral action beyond general
expediency? Tennyson votes "Aye."

I have a note to my father from Tennant saying: "Last Saturday we
had an Apostolic dinner when we had the honour, among other things, of
drinking your health. Edmund Lushington and I went away tolerably
early; but most of them stayed till past two. John Heath volunteered a
song; Kemble got into a passion about nothing but quickly jumped out
again; Blakesley was afraid the Proctor might come in; and Thompson
poured large quantities of salt upon Douglas Heath's head because he talked
nonsense."

[2] Letter from A. H. Hallam. Most of his philosophical and religious
letters to my father have been lost.

Dante, with notes and prefaces. For this task Hallam, who in 1827 had been in Italy with his parents and had drunk deep of the older Italian literature, says that he was perfecting himself in German and Spanish, and was proposing to plunge into the Florentine historians and the medieval Schoolmen. He writes to my father: " I expect to glean a good deal of knowledge from you concerning metres which may be serviceable, as well for my philosophy in the notes as for my actual handiwork in the text. I purpose to discuss considerably about poetry in general, and about the ethical character of Dante's poetry."

My father said of his friend: " Arthur Hallam could take in the most abstruse ideas with the utmost rapidity and insight, and had a marvellous power of work and thought, and a wide range of knowledge. On one occasion, I remember, he mastered a difficult book of Descartes at a single sitting."

On June 6th, 1829, the announcement was made that my father had won the prize medal for his poem in blank verse on " Timbuctoo[1]." To win the prize in anything

---

[1] From Somersby, after his father's death (1831 probably), he wrote to the printer Metcalfe, who had asked permission to include " Timbuctoo " in a collection of Cambridge Prize Poems:

SOMERSBY.

SIR, As you intend to reprint the Cambridge Prize Poems, it would seem odd to leave mine out, tho' for my own part I had much rather you had not thought of it. Prize Poems (without any exception even in favour of Mr. Milman's " Belvedere ") are not properly speaking " Poems " at all, and ought to be forgotten as soon as recited. I could have wished that poor " Timbuctoo " might have been suffered to slide quietly off, with all its errors, into forgetfulness: however as I do not expect to turn you from your purpose of republishing the p^e p^s, I suppose mine must be printed along with them: only for " cones of Pyramids," which is nonsense (p. 10), I will thank you to substitute " peaks of Pyramids."

I am, Sir, yours truly,
ALFRED TENNYSON.

(As the poem is now published this is the sole correction. My father would say, " ' The Lover's Tale ' and ' Timbuctoo ' are in no way imitative of

but rhymed heroics was an innovation.   My grandfather had desired him to compete, so unwillingly he patched up an old poem on " The Battle of Armageddon," and came out prizeman over Milnes, Hallam and others.

Charles Wordsworth (afterwards Bishop of St Andrews) writes to his brother Christopher Wordsworth, Sept. 4th, 1829 (see *Annals of my Early Life*, C. Wordsworth, 1890):

What do you think of Tennyson's Prize poem ("Timbuctoo")? If such an exercise had been sent up at Oxford, the author would have had a better chance of being rusticated, with the view of his passing a few months at a Lunatic Asylum, than of obtaining the prize.   It is certainly a wonderful production ; and if it had come out with Lord Byron's name, it would have been thought as fine as anything he ever wrote.

Arthur Hallam writes, Sept. 14th, 1829, to W. E. Gladstone :

I am glad you liked my queer piece about Timbuctoo.   I wrote it in a sovereign vein of poetic scorn for anybody's opinion, who did not value Plato and Milton just as much as I did.   The natural consequence was that ten people out of twelve laughed or opened large eyes; and the other two set about praising highly, what was plainly addressed to them, not to people in general.   So my vanity would fain persuade me, that, like some of my betters, I "fit audience found, tho' few."   My friend Tennyson's poem, which got the prize, will be thought by the ten sober persons afore-mentioned twice as absurd as mine; and to say the truth, by striking out his prose argument, the Examiners have done all in their power to verify the concluding words, " All was night."   The splendid imaginative power that pervades it will be seen through all hindrances.   I consider Tennyson as promising fair to be the greatest poet of our generation, perhaps of our century.

any poet, and, as far as I know, nothing of mine after the date of ' Timbuctoo ' was imitative.   As for being original, nothing can be said which has not been said in some form or another before.")

I asked Dean Merivale, last survivor, except Douglas Heath, of that Cambridge set, to give me his recollections. He answered:

Believe me that I have not written a letter for several months, but you will, I am sure, allow me to make this exception to your very kind note. I only wish I could give you any accurate recollection of your honoured father which would be worthy of your acceptance on such an occasion. You have seen, no doubt, the many contemporary diaries of those who rejoice to set down their reminiscences of so great and so loveable a member of their set....May I be excused for recording a recollection of which I was proud — that of being allowed or enjoined by the Vice-Chancellor to declaim his "Timbuctoo[1]" in the Senate House in the summer of 1829, which he declined to do from the modesty which too often beset him?

The Dean also enclosed the following letter, written, my father said, "under a horror of publicity" which made him "feel as Cowper did."

July 29th, 1829.

My dear Merivale,

Will you write and tell me whether you can read my poem at Commencement or not, since I must come up to Cambridge if you cannot? I hope you found my letter sufficiently clear relatively to corrections. The Vice-Chancellor observed to me, "We cannot do these things quite so well by proxy as with the person himself, to whom several of my objections might have been stated and answered immediately." I hope you have somewhat recovered from the shock of your grandmother's sudden death. I consider it as rather remarkable that on the morning when we were at Hampstead I seemed to myself to have some presentiment of it, and could not shake the idea from my mind, though I could not give utterance to

[1] Matthew Arnold told G. L. Craik that when, as a youth, he first read "Timbuctoo" he prophesied the greatness of Tennyson.

it; you remember my asking you whether either of your grandmothers was dead, and telling you that both mine were.

　　　Believe me, dear Merivale,
　　　　　　　Yours most truly, A. TENNYSON.

In 1829 my uncle Charles won a Bell Scholarship by the beauty of his translations. One sentence survived in my father's memory:

　　"And the ruddy grape shall droop from the desert thorn."

The brothers Charles and Alfred would humorously describe how *Much Ado about Nothing* was played by their friends in March, 1830. Kemble as Dogberry, Hallam as Verges, Milnes as Beatrice. When Beatrice sat down, her weight was such that she crashed through the couch, and sank on the floor, nothing to be seen but a heap of petticoats, much to the discomfiture of the players and the immeasurable laughter of the spectators. The incident used to remind my father by contrast of Kemble's observation to someone who was playing the part of Falstaff, " Pooh, you should see my sister: she does Falstaff better than any man living." My father, I may add, was famous in some parts of Shakespeare, especially in Malvolio.

In certain College rooms he was often asked to declaim the many ballads which he knew by heart, " Clerke Saunders," " Helen of Kirkconnel," " May Margaret," and others: and also his own poems "The Hesperides," " The Lover's Tale " (written 1827), " The Coach of Death "; and he would improvise verses by the score full of lyrical passion. I quote again from Edward Fitzgerald : " ' Oriana ' Tennyson used to repeat in a way not to be forgotten at Cambridge tables."

For his exercise he either rowed, or fenced, or took

long walks, and would go any distance to see "a bubbling brook." " Somehow," he would say, " water is the element I love best of all the four."

His first volume, *Poems, chiefly Lyrical,* was published in 1830 by Effingham Wilson, also the publisher of Robert Browning's *Paracelsus.* Favourable reviews appeared by Sir John Bowring in the *Westminster,* by Leigh Hunt in the *Tatler,* and by Arthur Hallam in the *Englishman's Magazine.*

The *Westminster* article (January 1831) contained this prophetic notice of " The Poet ":

If our estimate of Mr Tennyson be correct, he too is a poet; and many years hence may he read his juvenile description of that character with the proud consciousness that it has become the description and history of his own work.

Arthur Hallam's enthusiasm was worthy of his true and unselfish friendship, and helped my father through the years of darkness and disparagement that were soon to come.

There is a strange earnestness in his worship of beauty which throws a charm over his impassioned song, more easily felt than described, and not to be escaped by those who have once felt it....The features of original genius are clearly and strongly marked. The author imitates no one; we recognize the spirit of his age, but not the individual form of this or that writer. His thoughts bear no more resemblance to Byron or Scott, Shelley or Coleridge, than to Homer or Calderon, Firdusi or Calidasa. We have remarked five distinctive excellencies of his own manner. First, his luxuriance of imagination, and at the same time his control over it. Secondly, his power of embodying himself in ideal characters, or rather moods of character, with such accuracy of adjustment that the circumstances of the narrative seem to have a natural correspondence with the predominant feeling and, as it were, to be evolved from it by assimilative force. Thirdly, his vivid, picturesque delineation of objects, and the peculiar skill with which he holds all of them *fused*, to borrow a metaphor from science, in a medium of strong emotion. Fourthly, the variety of his lyrical measures and the exquisite modulation of harmonious words and cadences to the swell and fall of the feelings expressed. Fifthly, the elevated habits of thought, implied in these compositions, and importing a mellow soberness of tone, more impressive to our minds than if the author had drawn up a set of opinions in verse, and sought to instruct the understanding rather than to communicate the love of beauty to the heart.

Coleridge[1], indeed, for whose prose my father never much cared, but to whose poetry, especially " Kubla Khan," " The Ancient Mariner," and "Christabel," he was devoted, was more reserved in his praise about the first two ventures:

I have not read through all Mr Tennyson's poems, which have been sent to me; but I think there are some things of a good deal of beauty in what I have seen. The misfortune is, that he has begun to write verses without very well understanding what metre is[2].

" The first ' Mariana ' and the ' Arabian Nights ' were the two poems that marked the volume (1830) as something to be thought about." " The affectation " (in

[1] Arthur Hallam visited Coleridge at Highgate and wrote about him in his poem of " Timbuctoo ":

> " Methought I saw a face whose every line
> Wore the pale cast of thought, a good old man,
> Most eloquent, who spake of things divine.
> Around him youths were gather'd, who did scan
> His countenance so grand and mild, and drank
> The sweet sad tears of wisdom."

[2] Concerning this criticism my father said in 1890: " Coleridge did not know much about my poems, for he confounded Charles and me. From what I have heard he may have read *Glen-river* in ' above the loud Glenriver,' and *tendril-twine* in the line ' mantled with flowering tendriltwine' dactylically; because I had an absurd antipathy to hyphens, and put two words together as one word. If that was the case, he might well have wished that I had more sense of metre. But so I, an old man, who get a poem or poems every day, might cast a casual glance at a book, and seeing something which I could not scan or understand, might possibly decide against the book without further consideration."

the volume), E. F. G. adds, "was not of *the man*; but
of the time and society he lived in, and from which he
had not yet emerged to his proper and distinct altitude.
Two years afterwards he took his ground with 'The
Miller's Daughter,' 'Palace of Art,' 'Dream of Fair
Women,' etc."

On the appearance of the poems Hallam wrote the
following letter to my grandmother:

MY DEAR MADAM,

As I have at last the pleasure of sending to Alfred
his long-expected book, I take this opportunity of begging that
you will accept from me a copy of some poems which I originally
intended to have published in the same volume. To this joint
publication, as a sort of seal of our friendship, I had long looked
forward with a delight which I believe was no way selfish. But
there are reasons which have obliged me to change my intention,
and withdraw my own share of the work from the Press. One
of these was the growing conviction of the exceeding crudeness
of style which characterized all my earlier attempts....I have
little reason to apprehend your wasting much time over that
book, when I send you along with it such a treasure in your
son's poetry. He is a true and thorough poet, if ever there was
one; and tho' I fear his book is far too good to be popular, yet
I have full faith that he has thrown out sparks that will kindle
somewhere, and will vivify young generous hearts in the days that
are coming to a clearer perception of what is beautiful and good.

Believe me yours very sincerely,

A. H. HALLAM.

During the summer my father joined Arthur Hallam,
and both started off for the Pyrenees, with money for the
insurgent allies of Torrijos, — a noble, accomplished, truthful man, worthy to be a leader. He it was who had
raised the standard of revolt against the Inquisition and
the tyranny of Ferdinand, King of Spain. Alfred and

Arthur held a secret meeting with the heads of the conspiracy on the Spanish border, and were not heard of by their friends for some weeks[1].

John Frere and James Spedding wrote to my uncle Charles inquiring about them, and about my grandfather who was also abroad, and he answers:

To John Frere.

SOMERSBY, *July* 27*th*, 1830.

From Hallam I heard just now: he complains rather of the heat, and says Alfred is delighted with his journey, though regretting the impermanence of his impressions in the hurry of travel. My father has returned from his tour and I am much surprised to see him so well after the neck-break adventures he has encountered. On one occasion, proceeding along in a small carriage over the mountains, he was hurled down a precipice and stunned, but saved himself from certain death by convulsively grasping a pine that grew out of a ledge: while the driver, carriage and horse were dashed to atoms thousands of feet below him. Again, at the Carnival in Rome, a man was stilettoed in his arms, drawing first suspicion and then violence on his person: the excess of which he prevented by exclaiming that he was an Englishman and had not done the deed. Again, he was suddenly seized with giddiness on the verge of a precipice, and only preserved by the presence of mind of a person near him. At another (time) he was near being buried alive.

To James Spedding.

I expect the travellers home every day; I heard twice from Hallam, who mentioned the middle of September as the most probable period of their return, but a dozen counter-resolutions may come athwart their homeward intention even yet for what I know. Hallam's last letter was dated from Cauteretz, Dép[t]. des Hautes Pyrénées, but from what he there intimated of return about this time, it would be foolish in you to hazard your good things in an epistle directed thither. The said Hallam or one of

---

[1] No further information upon this business has been preserved.

his fellow-travellers, it should seem, wrote a letter to Tennant with full intention, I guess, of its getting further than Perpignan; but Tennant a short time back informed me that he had received a communication from les Administrateurs de la Poste, advertising him of a letter which had taken up its abode at Perpignan on account of its not being paid to the coast. What news it contained "no one dreameth," or whether it was written previous or subsequent to my last receipts from the Continent. Kemble is said to be at Gibraltar. Trench either on the way thither or arrived, and Hallam expressed some apprehensions on the score of their safety, but I hope with you there is not much fear in the present posture of things. Thank you for sending Southey my sonnets, thank you for cheering my heart with the worthy man's good opinion, and thank you for your letter and address.

Before going further it may be as well to pick up the threads of the story of this Spanish insurrection. Torrijos the leader had hoped to restore such a measure of freedom as the Cortes had secured for Spain, in the Constitution which had been framed after the Peninsular War. This was the Constitution to which Ferdinand had sworn when he returned from his long captivity in Bayonne, but which he speedily renounced, dissolving the Cortes and restoring the Inquisition. In 1820, revolution having followed revolution, the Cortes met again, under protection of part of the army, and the Inquisition was abolished. This state of things did not last. In 1823 Ferdinand was, by help of the Duc d'Angoulême, proclaimed absolute King. Again despotism prevailed. Many Liberals fled to England. Of these Carlyle gives a pathetic description as they were seen, chiefly about Euston Square and the new Church of St Pancras — "stately tragic figures, in proud threadbare cloaks," who had acknowledged General Torrijos as their chief. A fiery sympathy had been kindled in the hearts of many of the "Apostles" by this romantic band: some of whom had, after seven years' banishment, "got shipping as private passengers in one craft or the other; and, by degrees or at once, arrived all at Gibraltar; — Boyd (Sterling's cousin), one or two young democrats of Regent Street, the fifty picked Spaniards, and Torrijos[1]."

Among the Pyrenean revolutionists met by Arthur Hallam and my father the chief man was one Señor Ojeda, who informed them that he desired "couper la gorge à tous les curés," then clapping his hand on his heart murmured "mais vous connaissez mon cœur" — "and a pretty black one it is," thought my father.

After the travellers had returned, a report reached Somersby that John Kemble, who had joined the insurgents in the South, had been caught and was to be tried for his life. Away my father posted for miles in the early dawn to try and find someone of authority at Lincoln or elsewhere, who knew the Consul at Cadiz and would help him to save his friend. The report turned out to be untrue and Kemble came back safe and sound.

But on the last night of November, 1831, Torrijos and his gallant companions left Gibraltar in two small vessels; the British Governor, on occasion of the fresh rising of General Mina against Spanish despotism, having intimated that Gibraltar must not shelter rebels against Spain.

They set sail for Malaga, were chased by Spanish guardships, and ran ashore at Fuengirola near Malaga. They barricaded themselves in a farm-house, were surrounded by vastly superior forces and compelled to surrender.

All the fifty-six (Boyd among them) perished by military execution on the Esplanade of Malaga[2].

My father returned from the expedition in improved health. From this time forward the lonely Pyrenean

[1] Carlyle's *John Sterling*, p. 64 (ed. 1871).
[2] Carlyle's *John Sterling*, p. 77.

peaks, the mountains with " their streaks of virgin snow,"
like the Maladetta, mountain "lawns and meadow-
ledges midway down," and the "long brook falling
thro' the clov'n ravine," were a continual source of
inspiration; he had written part of "Œnone" in the
valley of Cauteretz. His sojourn there was also commemorated one and thirty years afterwards in "All
along the Valley."

He came home impressed with the "lightheartedness"
of the French; but, infinitely preferring the freer air
of England," he writes: "Someone says that nothing
strikes a traveller more on returning from the Continent
than the look of an English country town. Houses not
so big, nor such rows of them as abroad, but each man's
house little or big distinct from one another, his own
castle, built according to his own means and fancy, and
so indicating the Englishman's free individual humour.
I am struck on returning from France with the look of
good sense in the London people[1]."

Unpublished Poem, 1828.

By a Brook.

Townsmen, or of the hamlet, young or old,
Whithersoever you may wander now,
Where'er you roam from, would you waste an hour,
Or sleep thro' one brief dream upon the grass,
Pause here. The murmurs of the rivulet,
Rippling by cressy isles or bars of sand,
Are pleasant from the early Spring to when,
Full fields of barley shifting tearful lights
On growing spears, by fits the lady ash
With twinkling finger sweeps her yellow keys.

---

[1] Quoted from MS by E. F. G. (date of letter uncertain).

UNPUBLISHED POEMS, WRITTEN (1828–1831) AT CAMBRIDGE.*

Anacaona.

[My father liked this poem but did not publish it, because the natural history and the rhymes did not satisfy him. He evidently chose words which sounded well, and gave a tropical air to the whole, and he did not then care, as in his later poems, for absolute accuracy.]

I

A dark Indian maiden,
   Warbling in the bloom'd liana,
Stepping lightly flower-laden,
   By the crimson-eyed anana,
Wantoning in orange groves
   Naked, and dark-limb'd, and gay,
Bathing in the slumbrous coves,
In the cocoa-shadow'd coves,
   Of sunbright Xaraguay,
Who was so happy as Anacaona,
   The beauty of Espagnola,
   The golden flower of Hayti?

2

All her loving childhood
   Breezes from the palm and canna
Fann'd this queen of the green wildwood,
   Lady of the green Savannah:
All day long with laughing eyes,
   Dancing by a palmy bay,
In the wooded paradise,
The cedar-wooded paradise
   Of still Xaraguay:
None were so happy as Anacaona,
   The beauty of Espagnola,
   The golden flower of Hayti!

3

In the purple island,
   Crown'd with garlands of cinchona,
Lady over wood and highland,
   The Indiañ queen, Anacaona,
Dancing on the blossomy plain
   To a woodland melody:
Playing with the scarlet crane[1],
The dragon-fly and scarlet crane,
   Beneath the papao tree!
Happy, happy was Anacaona,
   The beauty of Espagnola,
   The golden flower of Hayti!

4

The white man's white sail, bringing
   To happy Hayti the new-comer,
Over the dark sea-marge springing,
   Floated in the silent summer:
Then she brought the guava fruit,
   With her maidens to the bay;
She gave them the yuccaroot,
Maizebread and the yuccaroot,
   Of sweet Xaraguay:
Happy, happy Anacaona,
   The beauty of Espagnola,
   The golden flower of Hayti!

5

Naked, without fear, moving
   To her Areyto's mellow ditty,
Waving a palm branch, wondering, loving,
   Carolling " Happy, happy Hayti!"
She gave the white men welcome all,
   With her damsels by the bay;

[1] Perhaps the scarlet ibis, *guava rubra*, not now known to visit Hayti.

For they were fair-faced and tall,
They were more fair-faced and tall,
    Than the men of Xaraguay,
And they smiled on Anacaona,
    The beauty of Espagnola,
    The golden flower of Hayti!

6

Following her wild carol
    She led them down the pleasant places,
For they were kingly in apparel,
    Loftily stepping with fair faces.
But never more upon the shore
    Dancing at the break of day,
In the deep wood no more, —
By the deep sea no more, —
    No more in Xaraguay
Wander'd happy Anacaona,
    The beauty of Espagnola,
    The golden flower of Hayti!

The Lark.

Full light aloft doth the laverock spring
    From under the deep, sweet corn,
And chants in the golden wakening
    Athwart the bloomy morn.
What aileth thee, O bird divine,
    That thou singest with main and with might?
Is thy mad brain drunk with the merry, red wine,
    At the very break of light?
It is not good to drink strong wine
    Ere the day be well-nigh done;
But thou hast drunk of the merry, sweet wine,
    At the rising of the sun.

Some verses of "Sir Launcelot and Queen Guinevere" were handed about at Cambridge among my father's contemporaries. The following unpublished lines were among them, and kept by Edward Fitzgerald:

Life of the Life within my blood,
    Light of the Light within mine eyes,
The May begins to breathe and bud,
    And softly blow the balmy skies;
Bathe with me in the fiery flood,
    And mingle kisses, tears, and sighs,
Life of the Life within my blood,
    Light of the Light within mine eyes.

Life.

Why suffer human life so soon eclipse?
For I could burst into a psalm of praise,
Seeing the heart so wondrous in her ways,
E'en scorn looks beautiful on human lips!
Would I could pile fresh life on life, and dull
The sharp desire of knowledge still with knowing!
Art, Science, Nature, everything is full,
As my own soul is full, to overflowing —
Millions of forms, and hues, and shades, that give
The difference of all things to the sense,
And all the likeness in the difference.
I thank thee, God, that thou hast made me live:
I reck not for the sorrow or the strife:
One only joy I know, the joy of life.

To Poesy.

O God, make this age great that we may be
    As giants in Thy praise! and raise up Mind,
Whose trumpet-tongued, aerial melody
    May blow alarum loud to every wind,
    And startle the dull ears of human kind!
Methinks I see the world's renewed youth
    A long day's dawn, when Poesy shall bind
Falsehood beneath the altar of great Truth:
The clouds are sunder'd toward the morning-rise;
    Slumber not now, gird up thy loins for fight,
And get thee forth to conquer. I, even I,
Am large in hope that these expectant eyes
Shall drink the fulness of thy victory,
    Tho' thou art all unconscious of thy Might.

To —.

Thou may'st remember what I said
When thine own spirit was at strife
With thine own spirit. "From the tomb
And charnel-place of purpose dead,
Thro' spiritual dark we come
Into the light of spiritual life."
God walk'd the waters of thy soul,
And still'd them. When from change to change,
Led silently by power divine,
Thy thought did scale a purer range
Of prospect up to self-control,
My joy was only less than thine.

The Hesperides.*

[Published and suppressed by my father, and republished by me here
(with accents written by him) in consequence of a talk that I had with
him, in which he regretted that he had done away with it from among
his "Juvenilia."]

> Hesperus and his daughters three
> That sing about the golden tree. *Comus.*

The North wind fall'n, in the new-starréd night
Zidonian Hanno, wandering beyond
The hoary promontory of Soloë,
Past Thymiaterion in calméd bays
Between the southern and the western Horn,
Heard neither warbling of the nightingale,
Nor melody of the Libyan Lotus-flute
Blown seaward from the shore; but from a slope
That ran bloom-bright into the Atlantic blue,
Beneath a highland leaning down a weight
Of cliffs, and zoned below with cedar-shade,
Came voices like the voices in a dream
Continuous; till he reach'd the outer sea:—

Song of the Three Sisters.

I

The Golden Apple, the Golden Apple, the hallow'd
    fruit,
Guard it well, guard it warily,
Singing airily,
Standing about the charméd root.
Round about all is mute,
As the snowfield on the mountain-peaks,
As the sandfield at the mountain-foot.
Crocodiles in briny creeks
Sleep and stir not: all is mute.

* Copyright, 1897, by The Macmillan Company.

If ye sing not, if ye make false measure,
We shall lose eternal pleasure,
Worth eternal want of rest.
Laugh not loudly: watch the treasure
Of the wisdom of the West.
In a corner wisdom whispers. Five and three
(Let it not be preach'd abroad) make an awful mystery:
For the blossom unto threefold music bloweth;
Evermore it is born anew,
And the sap to threefold music floweth,
From the root,
Drawn in the dark,
Up to the fruit,
Creeping under the fragrant bark,
Líquid góld, hóneyswéet thró and thró.

(slow movement)

Keen-eyed Sisters, singing airily,
Looking warily
Every way,
Guard the apple night and day,
Lest one from the East come and take it away.

II

Father Hesper, Father Hesper, Watch, watch, ever.
    and aye,
Looking under silver hair with a silver eye.
Father, twinkle not thy stedfast sight:
Kingdoms lapse, and climates change, and races die;
Honour comes with mystery;
Hoarded wisdom brings delight.
Number, tell them over, and number
How many the mystic fruit-tree holds,
Lest the red-comb'd dragon slumber
Roll'd together in purple folds.

Look to him, father, lest he wink, and the golden apple be stol'n away,
For his ancient heart is drunk with overwatchings night and day
Round about the hallow'd fruit-tree curl'd —
Sing awáy, sing aloúd evermóre in the wínd without stóp, (*Anapæst*)
Lest his sealéd eyelid drop,
For he is older than the world.
If *hé* waken, *wé* waken,
Rapidly levelling eager eyes.
If *hé* sleep, *wé* sleep,
Dropping the eyelid over our eyes.
If the golden apple be taken
The world will be overwise.
Five links, a golden chain are we,
Hesper, the Dragon, and Sisters three
Bound about the golden tree.

III

Father Hesper, Father Hesper, Watch, watch, night and day,
Lest the old wound of the world be healéd,
The glory unsealéd,
The golden apple stol'n away,
And the ancient secret revealéd.
Look from West to East along:
Father, old Himala weakens, Caucasus is bold and strong.
Wandering waters unto wandering waters call;
Let them clash together, foam and fall.
Out of watchings, out of wiles,
Comes the bliss of secret smiles.
All things are not told to all,

Half-round the mantling night is drawn.
Purplefringéd with even and dawn
Hesper hateth Phosphor, evening hateth morn.

IV

Every flower and every fruit the redolent breath
  Of the warm seawind ripeneth,
    Arching the billow in his sleep:
  But the land-wind wandereth,
    Broken by the highland steep,
    Two streams upon the violet deep.
  For the Western Sun, and the Western Star,
  And the low west-wind, breathing afar,
    The end of day and beginning of night,
    Keep the apple Holy and Bright;
Holy and Bright, round and full, bright and blest,
    Mellow'd in a land of rest:
    Watch it warily night and day;
    All good things are in the West.
Till mid-noon the cool East light
Is shut out by the round of the tall hill brow,
  But, when the full-faced Sunset yellowly
  Stays on the flowerful arch of the bough,
  The luscious fruitage clustereth mellowly,
    Golden-kernell'd, Golden-cored,
  Sunset-ripen'd above on the tree.
  The world is wasted with fire and sword,
  But the Apple of gold hangs over the Sea!
  Five links — a Golden chain are we —
  Hesper, the Dragon, and Sisters three,
              Daughters three,
              Round about,
              All round about
  The gnarl'd bole of the charméd tree.

The Golden Apple, The Golden Apple, The hallow'd
   fruit,
           Guard it well,
           Guard it warily,
           Watch it warily,
           Singing airily,
Standing about the charméd root.

Lasting Sorrow.

(Republished from *Friendship's Offering*—an album published by
Smith and Elder 1832.)

Me my own Fate to lasting sorrow doometh:
Thy woes are birds of passage, transitory:
Thy spirit, circled with a living glory,
In summer still a summer joy resumeth.
Alone my hopeless melancholy gloometh,
Like a lone cypress, thro' the twilight hoary,
From an old garden where no flower bloometh,
One cypress on an inland promontory;
But yet my lonely spirit follows thine,
As round the rolling earth night follows day;
But yet thy lights on my horizon shine
Into my night, when thou art far away;
I am so dark, alas! and thou so bright,
When we two meet there's never perfect light.

Another sonnet, " There are three things which fill
my heart with sighs," he contributed (1832) to the
Yorkshire Literary Annual.

CHAPTER III.

CAMBRIDGE, SOMERSBY AND ARTHUR HALLAM.

1830–31.

To Alfred Tennyson (at Somersby) (unpublished).

Those Gothic windows are before me now,
  Which long have shone dim-lighted in my mind;
  That slope of softest green, the brook below,
  Old musty stalls, and tedded hay behind —
All have I seen; and simple tho' they be,
  A mighty awe steals with them on my heart,
  For they have grown and lasted as a part
  Of thy dear self, up-building thine and thee:
From yon tall fir, weathering the April rain,
  Came influence rare, that deepen'd into song,
  Beauty lurk'd for thee in the long gray fields,
  By tufted knolls, and, Alfred, made thee strong!
  Hence are the weapons which thy spirit wields,
  Musical thoughts of unexampled strain.   A. H. H.

As Sterling had been deeply moved "by the opinions and feelings which pervaded the age," and had instituted a crusade against the cold selfishness of the time; so the narrowness and dryness of the ordinary course of study at Cambridge, the lethargy there, and absence of any teaching that grappled with the ideas of the age and stimulated and guided thought on the subjects of deepest human interest, had stirred my father to wrath[1]. He cried aloud for some "soldier-priest, no sabbath-drawler of old saws," to set the world right. But however

[1] Macaulay had written of the Cambridge of his day: "We see men of four and five-and-twenty, loaded with academical honours and rewards—scholarships, fellowships, whole cabinets of medals, whole shelves of prize-books, enter into life with their education still to begin; unacquainted with the first principles of the laws under which they live,

gloomy his own view and that of his contemporaries was then as to the present, my father clearly saw the " Day-beam, New-risen o'er awaken'd Albion." Indeed now, as always, he was one of those " on the look-out for every new idea, and for every old idea with a new application, which may tend to meet the growing requirements of society"; one of those who are "like men standing on a watch-tower, to whom others apply and say, not 'What of the night?' but 'What of the morning and of the coming day[1]?'"

At the request of Aubrey de Vere, he consented that the following denunciatory lines, written in his undergraduate days, should be published among my notes.

Lines on Cambridge of 1830.

Therefore your Halls, your ancient Colleges,
Your portals statued with old kings and queens,
Your gardens, myriad-volumed libraries,
Wax-lighted chapels, and rich carven screens,
Your doctors, and your proctors, and your deans,
Shall not avail you, when the Day-beam sports
New-risen o'er awaken'd Albion.　No!
Nor yet your solemn organ-pipes that blow
Melodious thunders thro' your vacant courts
At noon and eve, because your manner sorts
Not with this age wherefrom ye stand apart,
Because the lips of little children preach
Against you, you that do profess to teach
And teach us nothing, feeding not the heart.

In after years a great change came over Cambridge,

---

unacquainted with the very rudiments of moral and political science." And when Whewell in 1838 was elected to the chair of Moral Philosophy, he began his introductory address by elaborately justifying the innovation of delivering public lectures on the subject committed to his charge.

[1] Speech of the Duke of Argyll in the House of Lords, Aug. 13th, 1894.

and he was sorry that he had spoken so bitterly, for he always looked back with affection to those "dawn-golden times" passed with his friends at Trinity.   He honoured the University for the way it had adapted itself to modern requirements; and he especially approved of the University Extension movement, for spreading higher education throughout local centres in Great Britain. Every vacation after his marriage University men visited him, so that he kept level with such movements.

What impressed him most, when he went to Cambridge in 1872, was the change in the relations between don and undergraduate.   While he was keeping his terms (1828–1831) there was "a great gulf fixed" between the teacher and the taught[1], but in 1872 he found a constant personal intercourse and interchange of ideas between them.   And, as the "living word" is to each man more than the mere lecture-room exposition, this change, he thought, could not fail to have the best influence on the enlargement of the views, sympathies and aspirations of the generations to come.

A letter from Blakesley indicates an intellectual attitude somewhat similar to my father's in relation to the prevailing habits of thought in Cambridge and in society at large.

BLACKHEATH, 1830.

DEAR TENNYSON,

The present race of monstrous opinions and feelings which pervade the age require the arm of a strong Iconoclast. A volume of poetry written in a proper spirit, a spirit like that which a vigorous mind indues by the study of Wordsworth and Shelley, would be, at the present juncture, the greatest benefit the world could receive.   And more benefit would accrue from it than from all the exertions of the Jeremy Benthamites and Millians, if they were to continue for ever and a day.   I have seen Sterling two or three times since I have been in these parts, and had some conversation with him.

[1] He said to Dr Butler, "There was a want of love in Cambridge then."

Sterling, and all of his class, who have been hawked at by the mousing owls of Cambridge, suffer from the narrow-mindedness of criticism. He saw the abuses of the present system of things, which is upheld by the strong hand of power and custom, and he attacked them accordingly. For this conduct he was dubbed a radical. He soon saw that the reforms proposed by that party were totally inadequate to the end which they proposed: that if carried to their fullest effect they would only remove the symptoms and not the cause of evil; that this cause was the selfish spirit which pervades the whole frame of society at present, and that to counterbalance the effects the cause of them must be removed. This end, he at first probably thought with Shelley, might be effected by lopping off those institutions in which that selfish spirit exhibits itself, without any more effort. He afterwards saw, with Wordsworth, that this was not the true method; but that we must implant another principle with which selfishness cannot co-exist, and trust that this plant as it grows up will absorb the nourishment of the weed, in which case those wickednesses and miseries, which are only the forms in which the latter developes itself, will of their own accord die away, as soon as their principle of vegetation is withered and dried up.

Hallam has gone back to Cambridge. He was not well while he was in London; moreover, he was submitting himself to the influences of the outer world more than (I think) a man of his genius ought to do.

I shall be in Cambridge, God willing (which, considering the depth of the snow is not quite clear), to-morrow evening. I hope soon to see you there.

Believe me your affectionate friend,

J. W. BLAKESLEY.

On October 4th, 1830, Arthur Hallam wrote from Forest House, Leyton, Essex:

I am sorry, dear Alfred, that I have left your note so long unanswered; but I don't doubt you have found already that to return to one's native land is to throw oneself into the jaws of all kinds of importunate people, from creditors upwards or downwards, who leave one no time for pleasant things. Yet this excuse lies arrantly, I discover upon second thoughts. I am living here in a very pleasant place, an old country mansion, in the depths of the Forest, with cedars in the garden, the seed of which is vouched to have been brought from Lebanon, and a billiard-table within doors, by dint of which I demolish time pretty well. I have been studious too, partly after my fashion, and partly after my father's; i.e. I read six books of Herodotus with him, and I take occasional plunges into David Hartley, and Buhle's *Philosophie Moderne* for my own gratification. I cannot find that my adventures have produced quite the favourable impression on my father's mind that his letter gave me to expect. I don't mean that he blames me at all; but his old notions about the University begin to revive, and he does not seem quite to comprehend, that after helping to revolutionize kingdoms, one is still less inclined than before to trouble one's head about scholarships, degree and such gear. Sometimes I sigh to be again in the ferment of minds, and stir of events which is now the portion of other countries. I wish I could be useful; but to be a fly on that great wheel would be something. Spanish affairs, you will have seen by the papers, go on slowly: not therefore, I trust, less surely; but I wish something was done. Sterling has had little direct news for a while, and Perina never wrote to me. Sterling has been unwell, and is going to be married. I am glad he does not go out of the Apostolic family, for his lady is to be Susan Barton, of whom you may often have heard Blakesley rave. I had a letter from Spedding the other day, full of pleasant scoffs. I found one on my return from Leighton, dated two months ago, and extolling your book above sun, moon and stars: I have written to him, but as he has not answered, he has probably quitted Upfield Lodge. I cannot make out that you have been reviewed anywhere, but I have seen no magazines, and a letter from Garden, also of very old date, gives hope of *Blackwood*. Effingham of course I shun, as I would "whipping to death, pressing and hanging." Moxon very civilly sent me two copies of Lamb's Album verses, one for you; the book is weak as water. What think you of Belgium? The opinion of everybody here seems against them; yet I cannot well conceive their present resolution, and increasing unanimity, unless the grounds of their aversion to the Dutch were stronger than it is the fashion to represent them. At all events, now blood has flowed in torrents, all union is rendered impracticable.   The chances of a general war in Europe are great; the iniquitous prudence of the Allied Wolves, who struck the Lion down, has guaranteed the possession of Belgium to the Dutch crown, and should the insurgents, as is very likely, declare they never can submit to the government of a Thing who has made war upon them, the inevitable consequence will be that the Prussians will interfere to preserve the sanctity of the guarantee, and the French to maintain the principle, that the allegiance of a people depends on its consent, not on the autocratic transfer of another power.   'Twas a very pretty little revolution in Saxony, and a respectable one at Brunswick.   I am surprised you have not heard of Frederick; have you not written to the Hôtel de Lille? You really ought, for he may be in distress, and Templeton has very likely left Paris. I beg your pardon for this stupid note, and rest in expectation of your promised letter, which I hope will explain your intentions for the future, and the details of things as they are at Somersby.   Remember me most kindly to your mother and sisters, and tell Charles to write.

Affectionately yours, A. H. H.

It may be as well to say here that all the letters from my father to Arthur Hallam were destroyed by his father after Arthur's death: a great loss, as these particular letters probably revealed his inner self more truly than anything outside his poems.

In February 1831 my father left Cambridge, for my grandfather was somewhat ailing and wished that he should return to help his mother.

On the night of leaving he gave a supper in his rooms, Corpus Buildings, and after supper he and his friends all danced a quadrille.   As he drove away in the coach his last sight in Trumpington Street was "Thompson's handsome face under the light of a street lamp."

After he had gone down, the Cambridge friends forwarded him his *Alfieri*, which one of them had borrowed from him and for which he had been making constant demands, and they also told him of the poet Wordsworth's visit to Trinity. They told how Spedding gave him coffee in his rooms; how Wordsworth was in good talking mood but furiously alarmist, nothing but revolutions, reigns of terror; how he had said he wished that Coleridge had not written the second part of " Christabel " because this required the tale to be finished, and asserted that the conclusion of Part I., " It was a lovely sight to see," was too much laboured : how he defended " Passive Obedience " by quoting Scripture. Upon the whole, although he " said nothing very profound or original," yet the young men enjoyed his talk till one o'clock in the morning; he also was pleased with his hearers.

My father's comment on such criticism about a poet whom he loved was : " How can you expect a great man to say anything 'very profound' when he *knows* it is expected of him ? "

On a Wednesday of this March, shortly after 11 o'clock in the morning, my grandfather was found leaning back in his study chair, having passed away peacefully —

> Once thro' mine own doors Death did pass,
> One went, who never hath return'd.
> He will not smile — not speak to me
> Once more.

After Arthur Hallam's death these lines were written in " In Memoriam," referring to the double loss of his father and of his friend :

> As down the garden-walks I move,
> Two spirits of a diverse love
> Contend for loving masterdom.

My father told me that within a week after his father's death he slept in the dead man's bed, earnestly desiring

---

[1] Wordsworth, according to Milnes, heard Hallam deliver his Declamation in Trinity College Chapel. " It was splendid," he writes, " to see the poet Wordsworth's face kindle as Hallam proceeded with it."

to see his ghost, but no ghost came. "You see," he said, "ghosts do not generally come to imaginative people." In a letter to his friend John Frere, my uncle Charles describes what happened:

SOMERSBY, *March 23rd*, 1831.

* * * * * *

John, a melancholy change has taken place in our house since I saw you last. My poor father, all his life *a man of sorrow and acquainted with grief*, has gone to "that bourne from whence no traveller returns." After an illness of about a month's continuance, he died last Wednesday at eleven o'clock in the day. He suffered little, and after death his countenance, which was strikingly lofty and peaceful, was I trust an image of the condition of his soul, which on earth was daily racked by bitter fancies, and tossed about by strong troubles. We are not certain whether we shall be permitted to remain much longer in this place. We must abide the pleasure of Robinson, the next Incumbent, &c. &c.

If...I pay him a rent by which he will be a gainer, I think we are likely to be less under obligations to him than he to us. But as my father's revenues are now sequestrated we are left entirely at the will of my grandfather, who may have a house of his own to put us into.

Charles Tennyson (d'Eyncourt)[1], Dr Tennyson's brother, also writes to the co-trustee of my grandfather's property, Mr Rawnsley of Halton:

This morning's post brought me the afflicting news from Somersby. You will guess my feelings, for you know that I valued my dear brother for his thousand admirable qualities of

---

[1] The Right Hon. Charles Tennyson d'Eyncourt represented in Parliament successively Grimsby, Bletchingley, Stamford, and Lambeth. On his death in 1861, he was succeeded by his son George Hildeyard T. d'Eyncourt, who died in 1871. The Tennyson estates then passed to his brother, Admiral Edwin Tennyson d'Eyncourt, C.B., who had served with distinction in China, and in the Gulf of Finland during the Crimean War. Under an arrangement made with the Admiral, Edmund d'Eyncourt, son of Louis T. d'Eyncourt (long known as Senior Metropolitan Magistrate), now holds the property.

heart, which would have contributed to his own happiness and that of those around him if he had not given way to failings arising out of a nervous temperament. I knew him to be excellent in intention, to be naturally full of worth and goodness, and I respected and loved him. I believe he also depended on my fraternal feelings towards him, and I will, as far as I can, endeavour to justify his good opinion of me. I transmit to you his will and a codicil....I was unable to get down to Somersby, 'my official business requiring my presence in town. I would however have broken through all, if I could have been of use or comfort to my poor brother's widow.

From Arthur Hallam to Emily Tennyson.

1831.

I cannot help thinking that if the name of Tennyson should pass from that little region, which all your life long has been to you home, that blessed little region, "bosomed in a kindlier air, Than the outer realm of care And dole," the very fields and lanes will feel a sorrow, as if part of their appointed being had been reft from them. Yet, after all, a consecration has come upon them from the dwellers at Somersby, which, I think, is not of the things that fail. Many years perhaps, or shall I say many ages, after we all have been laid in dust, young lovers of the beautiful and the true may seek in faithful pilgrimage the spot where Alfred's mind was moulded in silent sympathy with the everlasting forms of nature. Legends will perhaps be attached to the places that are near it. Some Mariana, it will be said, lived wretched and alone in a dreary house on the top of the opposite hill. Some Isabel may with more truth be sought nearer yet. The belfry, in which the white owl sat "warming his five wits," will be shown, for six-pence, to such travellers as have lost their own. Critic after critic will track the wanderings of the brook, or mark the groupings of elm and poplar, in order to verify the "Ode to Memory" in its minutest particulars. I send down, along with this note, some numbers of the *Tatler*, containing a review of Alfred and Charles by Leigh Hunt. You will be amused with the odd style of his observations, and the frank familiarity with which he calls them by their Christian names, just as if he had supped with them a hundred times. His general remarks are nonsensical enough, but being a poet he has a keen eye for true beauty, and the judgments of his taste are worth having. Charles will be proud of this review because it is the first notice which the Press (our new despot, the Kehama, under whom the world now groans, already nearly almighty and omnipresent, but, alas! as far as ever from all-wise) has deigned to take of his "humble plot of ground." But he has had better suffrages: voices have come to him from the Lakes, and the old man of Highgate has rejoiced over him[1]. I am looking forward with eagerness to seeing Charles; would that Alfred were with him! but that will not be, and perhaps ought not to be; "the days are awa" that we have seen.

The upshot of the various transactions as to Somersby was, that the new Incumbent was willing that the Tennysons should live on at the Rectory, where they remained till 1837.

Arthur Hallam had been attached to my aunt Emily since 1829. After the first year, when Mr Hallam thought it desirable that the lovers should be separated for a time, he stayed at Somersby as often as he could spare leisure from his work; and whenever he came, he cheered all with his "bright, angelic spirit and his gentle, chivalrous manner[2]."

"I am," wrote Hallam to Trench, "now at Somersby, not only as the friend of Alfred Tennyson, but as the lover of his sister. An attachment on my part of nearly two years' standing and a mutual engagement of one year are, I fervently hope, only the commencement of a

---

[1] S. T. Coleridge.

[2] Witch-elms that counterchange the floor
    Of this flat lawn with dusk and bright;
    And thou, with all thy breadth and height
Of foliage, towering sycamore;

How often, hither wandering down,
    My Arthur found your shadows fair,
    And shook to all the liberal air
The dust and din and steam of town.

union which circumstances may not impair, and the grave itself may not conclude."

My aunt Emily had eyes "with depths on depths," and "a profile like that on a coin," "testa Romana," as an old Italian said of her. All the Tennyson sons and daughters except Frederick had the colouring of Italy or the south of France with dark eyes and hair. This foreign colouring may possibly have been derived from a Huguenot ancestor, a relation of Madame de Maintenon. On the Continent my father was never taken for an Englishman, and even in Ireland in 1848, when he was at Valentia, an Irishman rose up from among the fern and heather, and said, " From France, your honour?" thinking, as he confessed, that he was a Frenchman come to head a revolution.

While Hallam was at Somersby, after the morning's work the Tennysons and he would generally go for long walks together beyond the "bounding hill." Not only was my father fond of walking, but of "putting the stone" and other athletic feats. Mrs Lloyd of Louth writes: " In proof of his strong muscular power, when showing us a little pet pony on the lawn at Somersby one day he surprised us by taking it up and carrying it." Brook-field remarked: " It is not fair, Alfred, that you should be Hercules as well as Apollo." Fitzgerald notes: " Alfred could hurl the crowbar further than any of the neighbouring clowns, whose humours, as well as those of their betters, knight, squire, landlord and lieutenant, he took quiet note of, like Chaucer himself." Yet as he wandered over the wold, or by the brook, he often seemed to be in dreamland, so that one who often saw him then called him " a mysterious being, seemingly lifted high above other mortals, and having a power of intercourse with the spirit-world not granted to others."

In the evening he lived much in his attic den, but now and then came down and listened to the singing and playing of his sisters. He had a love for the simple style of Mozart, and for our own national airs and ballads, and played himself a little on the flute, but only "cared for complicated music as suggesting echoes of winds and waves." The sisters were all very musical, my aunt Mary playing the harp and accompanying the brothers and sisters who sang. Fitzgerald speaks of music in College days, and says:

A. T. was not thought to have an ear for music; I remember little of his execution in the line except humming over "the weary pund o' tow," which was more because of the weary moral, I think, than for any music's sake. Carlyle once said, "The man must have music dormant in him, revealing itself in *verse*." I remember A. T.'s speaking of Haydn's "Chaos," which he had heard at some Oratorio. He said, "The violins *spoke* of *light*." Carlyle, who was apt to look on poetry as a waste of talents which ought to be employed in other heroic work, took at once to A. T.: among other signs of the man, remarking his voice, "like the sound of a pinewood," he said.

In past years many friends of Somersby days have told me of the exceeding consideration and love which my father showed his mother, and how much they were struck by the young man's tender and deferential manner towards her, and how he might often be found in her room reading aloud, with his flexible voice, Shakespeare, Milton, Chaucer, Spenser and Campbell's patriotic ballads. When Arthur Hallam was with them, Dante, Petrarch, Tasso and Ariosto were the favourite poets: and it was he who taught my aunt Emily Italian, and made her a proficient scholar.

Arthur Hallam to Emily Tennyson.

Lady, I bid thee to a sunny dome,
  Ringing with echoes of Italian song ;
  Henceforth to thee these magic halls belong,
And all the pleasant place is like a home :
Hark ! on the right, with full piano tone,
  Old Dante's voice encircles all the air :
  Hark yet again ! like flute tones mingling rare
Comes the keen sweetness of Petrarca's moan.

Pass thou the lintel freely ; without fear
  Feast on the music.   I do better know thee
  Than to suspect this pleasure thou dost owe me
Will wrong thy gentle spirit, or make less dear
  That element whence thou must draw thy life,
  An English maiden and an English wife.

CHAPTER IV.

ARTHUR HALLAM.

1831–1833.

Thy leaf has perish'd in the green,
  And, while we breathe beneath the sun,
  The world which credits what is done
Is cold to all that might have been.

So here shall silence guard thy fame;
  But somewhere, out of human view,
  Whate'er thy hands are set to do
Is wrought with tumult of acclaim.

In the spring of 1831 my father was much distressed about the condition of his eyes and feared that he was going to lose his sight, "a sad thing to barter the universal light even for the power of ' Tiresias and Phineus, prophets old.'" He took to a milk diet for some months, which apparently "did good." At all events his eyesight was strong enough to allow him to study *Don Quixote* in the original. He also records that one night he "saw the moonlight reflected in a nightingale's eye, as she was singing in the hedgerow[1]." He adds that her voice vibrated with such passion that he wrote of

The leaves
That tremble round the nightingale

---

[1] Owing to his extreme short-sight he could see objects at a short distance better than anyone: and at a long distance with his eye-glass or

in "The Gardener's Daughter." Hallam told him at this time that "The nightingale with long and low preamble," in the sonnet which I give, was "worth an estate in Golconda."

> Check every outflash, every ruder sally
> Of thought and speech, speak low, and give up wholly
> Thy spirit to mild-minded Melancholy:
> This is the place. Thro' yonder poplar alley,
> Below, the blue green river windeth slowly,
> But in the middle of the sombre valley,
> The crisped waters whisper musically,
> And all the haunted place is dark and holy.
> The nightingale, with long and low preamble,
> Warbled from yonder knoll of solemn larches,
> And in and out the woodbine's flowery arches
> The summer midges wove their wanton gambol,
> And all the white-stemm'd pinewood slept above,
> When in this valley first I told my love.

My father contributed "Anacreontics," "No More [1]," and "A Fragment," to a literary annual *The Gem*; and Moxon, who had some sparks of poetry in him, and had come into possession of the *Englishman's Magazine*, wished to start with a "flash number," and asked Hallam to persuade my father to forward him a poem which would appear along with contributions from Wordsworth, Southey, and Charles Lamb. Hallam urged him (July 15th, 1831) to send "The Sisters,"

---

spectacles he could see as far as any long-sighted person. At this time he went to see Brodie for his eyes, and began to talk so learnedly about them, that Brodie raised his hand saying: "Wait; remember I *never* see medical students without a fee." His hearing was extraordinarily keen, and this he held to be a compensation for his short-sight: he "could hear the shriek of a bat," which he said was the test of a fine ear.

[1] "No More" is written out in Arthur Hallam's handwriting in a common-place book belonging to Archdeacon Allen, and is dated by Arthur Hallam 1826. Although my father considered the poem crude, it is remarkable for a boy of seventeen.

or "Rosalind," or the "Southern Mariana," and begged
him not to disdain a mode of publication which Schiller
and Goethe chose for their best compositions.   He
pointed out that the fugitive pieces might form part of
a volume hereafter.

Hallam was at Hastings "listening all day to the
song of the larks on the cliffs," and reading *Destiny*
and *Inheritance*. He had no answer from Alfred, or
any of his brothers, so wrote again :

HASTINGS, *July 26th*, 1831.

I have been expecting for some days an answer to my letter
about Moxon; but I shall not delay any longer my reply to
your last, and before this is sent off yours may come.   I, whose
imagination is to yours as Pisgah to Canaan, the point of distant
prospect to the place of actual possession, am not without some
knowledge and experience of your passion for the past.   To
this community of feeling between us, I probably owe your
inestimable friendship, and those blessed hopes which you have
been the indirect occasion of awakening.   But what with you is
universal and all-powerful, absorbing your whole existence,
communicating to you that energy which is so glorious, in me
is checked and counteracted by many other impulses, tending
to deaden the influence of the senses which were already less
vivacious by nature.   When I say the senses, I mean those
employed in the processes of imagination, viz. sight and hearing.
You say pathetically, "Alas for me ! I have more of the
Beautiful than the Good !"   Remember to your comfort that
God has given you to see the difference.   Many a poet has
gone on blindly in his artist pride.   I am very glad you have
been reading Erskine [of Linlathen].   No books have done me
so much good as his, and I always thought you would like them
if they came in your way.   His doctrine may not be the truth,
but it may contain it still, and this is my own view of the
case.   You perhaps will be angry when I tell you that I sent
your sonnet about the "Sombre Valley" to Moxon[1], who is
charmed with it, and has printed it off.   I confess this is a breach
of trust on my part, but I hope for your forgiveness...

A. H. H.

[1] Published in the *Englishman's Magazine* for August.

The two friends, after a tour taken by Hallam in Devon, Cornwall and Yorkshire, met at Sheffield to talk over literary plans for the future. Hallam wrote that he was "in the humbler station of critic," while "Alfred is brimful of subjects and artist thoughts." The "Apostles" and their little band of Cambridge friends expressed themselves warmly as to Hallam's article on the *Poems, chiefly Lyrical.* After his holiday Hallam returned to his reading of law, and enjoyed "the old fellow Blackstone," culling for Alfred poetic words like "foréstal." "The Dream of Fair Women," Hallam was of opinion, should be published soon, for it would establish the poet at once in general reputation. The friends interchanged thoughts on the political state of the world and on Ireland especially, which is "the most volcanic point." They had grave arguments about the Church, and were exercised about the St Simonians, whose opinions on many points "resembled those of Shelley, although they were much more practical." Miss Austen's novels were read and notes compared. My father preferred *Emma* and *Persuasion*, and Hallam wrote, "*Emma* is my first love, and I intend to be constant. The edge of this constancy will soon be tried, for I am promised the reading of *Pride and Prejudice.*"

My father meets Fanny Kemble, whom he holds "supreme in Juliet," and she speaks of him as having "the grandest head of any man whom she has clapt eyes on." Adelaide Kemble copies out "The Sisters," "raving about it at intervals in the most Siddonian tone," and Fanny has set the ballad to music; "she inclines however to think it too painful, and to wish such things should not be written." Her "enthusiasm is high" over some of the manuscript poems in the forthcoming 1832 volume, especially "The Lady of Shalott."

Her own play, *Francis I.*, runs for several nights
(March 1832). "It is a remarkable production for
seventeen; the language is very pure, free, elegant
English and strictly dramatic. There is none of that
verbiage which is called mere poetry in it. She must
have nourished her childhood with the strong wine of
our old drama": so writes Hallam, who was more
conversant with that old drama than any of his
Cambridge contemporaries.

The Hunchback is then given, and Hallam writes
that "The scene in the second Act, where Fanny
Kemble plays fine lady, was excellent, but the tragic
parts yet finer: for instance where Clifford comes in
as Secretary, and afterwards where she expostulates with
Master Walter. Her 'Clifford, why don't you speak to
me?' and 'Clifford, is it you?' and her 'Do it,' with
all the accompanying speech, I shall never forget."

Hallam and my father in their rambles through
London, and in their smokes in Hallam's den at the top
of the house in the "long unlovely street," touched on all
imaginable topics. Hallam was busy writing essays on
modern authors; and these and my father's 1832 volume
were frequent subjects of discussion. The unsettled
condition of the country and the misery of the poorer
class weighed upon them. It seemed difficult to young
men, starting in life, to know how to remedy these
evils, but they determined not to lose hold of the Real
in seeking the Ideal. Hallam writes: "Where the ideas
of time and sorrow are not, and sway not the soul with
power, there is no true knowledge in Poetry or Philosophy."

On my father's return to Somersby, the correspondence recommenced. Hallam desires the publication of
"The Lover's Tale," for there are "magnificent passages
in that poem. The present casket, faulty as it is, is yet the
only one in which the precious gems contained therein

can be preserved." The author thinks it too diffuse and will not publish. Hallam answers that, since his is "the only printed copy of the 'Lover's Tale,' he shall make a fortune by lending it out at five shillings a head." One day he reads "Œnone" to his father, who "seems to like Juno's speech, but is called away in the middle of Venus'," so the friends do not obtain the great man's criticism.

Meanwhile the colloquial critic of *Blackwood*, "Christopher North," had delivered his judgment on *Poems, chiefly Lyrical* in a comically aggressive though not wholly unfriendly article [1].

The following two letters were written by Arthur Hallam about this review, and the poems which were to appear in the volume of 1832:

[Undated.]

Professor Wilson has thought fit to have a laugh at you and your critics, amongst whom so humble a thing as myself, has not, as you will perceive, escaped. I suppose one ought to feel very savage at being attacked, but somehow I feel much more amused. He means well I take it, and as he has extracted nearly your whole book, and has in his soberer mood spoken in terms as high as I could have used myself of some of your best poems, I think the review will assist rather than hinder the march of your reputation. They little know the while that you despise the false parts of your volume quite as vehemently as your censors can, and with purer zeal, because with better knowledge.

April 10th, 1832.

I don't know that you ought to publish this spring, but I shall never be easy or secure about your MSS until I see them fairly out of your control. The Ballad of "The Sisters" was very popular at Cambridge. Indeed it is very perfect. Monteith showed his ignorance by wishing the murdering lady

---

[1] For example in the criticism of the song entitled "The Owl," he says, "Alfred is as an owl: all that he wants is to be shot, stuffed and stuck into a glass case, to be made immortal in a museum." (*Blackwood's Mag.* Vol. XXXI.)

to have been originally the rival of the seduced lady, which idea was of course scouted by the wiser listeners, that is, all the rest, as substituting a commonplace melodramatic interest for the very poetic interest arising from your conception of the character. All were anxious for the "Palace of Art," etc., and fierce with me for not bringing more. Venables is a great man (at Cambridge), also Dobson. New customs, new topics, new slang phrases have come into vogue since *my* day, which yet was but yesterday. I don't think I could reside again at Cambridge with any pleasure. I should feel like a melancholy Pterodactyl winging his lonely flight among the linnets, eagles and flying fishes of our degenerate post-Adamic world. I have seen Gaskell, who is in the ninth heaven of happiness, going to be married the end of May. I have taken to my law again, and a little to my other studies. The [first Reform] Bill is now in the second reading, and will pass by a very small majority. The cholera is certainly abating; the preliminary symptoms have been very widely prevalent; disorders which are cured without difficulty in our rank of life turn to malignant cholera in the poor. Casimir Périer has had it but is recovering. The heroes of July are cutting the throats of physicians and wine merchants as you will see by the papers.

The report about Macaulay in Tennant's letter has no great foundation : at least he has not seen your book. I think Mac has some poetic taste, and would appreciate you.

Yours affectionately,
A. H. H.

Spedding wrote from Cambridge to Thompson (May 4th, 1832):

Only think of an "Apostolic" dinner next Friday, 11th inst. ; present, Hallam, Trench, Kemble, Arthur Buller, Martineau, Pickering, Donne I hope, etc. etc. Only think of Heath's essay on Niebuhr the day after ! Only think of the "Palace of Art," of which you may see part of a stanza, horribly misquoted, at what should have been the beginning of this sheet ! Only think of all these things, and others which your own fruitful imagination will readily suggest ! By the way, are you not tired by this time of the monotony and manufacture of your infernal county ? or if you are still wandering on the sea-shore, does not your soul feel very much like

> A still salt pool, lock'd in with bars of sand
> Left on the shore, that hears all night
> The plunging seas draw backward from the land
> Their moon-led waters white?

Do you not begin to sigh for apostolic conversation, and your dear lodgings, and River-Gods of " Mighty Michael Angelo," and the massed chestnut boughs that promise soon to put out their leaves?

Charles Merivale also wrote to Thompson that " A daily divan continued to sit throughout the term," and that the " ' Palace of Art ' was read successively to each man as he came up from the vacation." He continues:

> Though the least eminent of the Tennysonian Rhapsodists, I have converted by my readings both my brother and your friend (or enemy?) Richardson to faith in the " Lotos-eaters." They rather scoff at the former (the " Palace of Art "), and ask whether " The abysmal depths of personality " means the *Times* newspaper?

Spedding wrote again to Thompson, June 21st, 1832:

> We talk out of the " Palace of Art," and the " Legend of Fair Women." The great Alfred is here (in London), i.e. in Southampton Row, smoking all the day, and we went from this house on a pilgrimage to see him, to wit, two Heaths, my brother and myself, and meeting Allen on the way we took him along with us, and when we arrived at the place appointed we found A. T. (Alfred Tennyson), and A. H. H. (Arthur Hallam), and J. M. K. (Kemble), and we made a goodly company, and did as we do at Cambridge, and but that you were not among us, we should have been happy.

And on July 18th, 1832, Spedding writes:

> I say, a new volume by A. T. is in preparation, and will, I suppose, be out in Autumn. In the meantime I have no copy of the " Palace of Art," but shall be happy to repeat it to you when you come; no copy of the " Legend of Fair Women," but

can repeat about a dozen stanzas which are of the finest; no copy of the conclusion of "Œnone," but one in pencil which none but myself can read.

This July my father and Hallam went for a tour on the Rhine.

Arthur Hallam to Emily Tennyson.

NONNENWERTH, *July* 16*th*, 1832.

I expect, as far as I can calculate (but a traveller's calculations are always liable to be deranged by unforeseen chances), to be in England by the end of this month, and then I shall go straight to Somersby. I had better tell you something of what Alfred and I have been doing. My last letter, I think, was from Rotterdam.

We resumed our steam-boat last Wednesday morning, and came on slowly up the Rhine; the banks of which are more uniformly ugly and flat as far as Cologne than any country I ever saw of so great an extent. Really, until yesterday, we had seen nothing in the way of scenery that deserved going a mile to see. Cologne is the paradise of painted glass: the splendour of the windows in the churches would have greatly delighted you. The Cathedral is unfinished, and if completed on the original plan, would be the most stupendous and magnificent in the world. The part completed is very beautiful Gothic. Alfred was in great raptures, only complaining he had so little time to study the place. There is a gallery of pictures quite after my own heart, rich, glorious old German pictures, which Alfred accuses me of preferring to Titian and Raffaelle. In the Cathedral we saw the tomb and relics of the three kings, Gaspar, Melchior, and Balthazar, the patrons of Cologne and very miraculous persons in their day, according to sundry legends. The tomb is nearly all of pure massy gold, studded with rich precious stones.

From Cologne we came on to Bonn, which really bears a sort of family-likeness to Cambridge. Here the Rhine begins to be beautiful; and yesterday we took a luxurious climb up the Drachenfels, looked around at the mild vine-spread hillocks, and "river-sundered champaign clothed with corn," ate cherries under the old castle-wall at the top of the crag, then descended to a village below, and were carried over in a boat to the place from which I am writing. And what is that? Ten years ago it was a large convent of Benedictine nuns; now it is a large and comfortable hotel, still retaining the form of the Convent, the Cloisters, cell-like rooms, etc. It stands on an island in the middle of the river; you will understand the size of the isle, when I tell you it is rather larger, according to Alfred, than that of the Lady of Shalott, and the stream is rather more rapid than our old acquaintance that ran down to Camelot. The prospect from the window and gardens is most beautiful, the mountains, as they are called, Drachenfels being one, on one bank of the river, and Rolandseck towering up on the other, with the hills about Bingen glooming in the distance.

After their return Arthur Hallam writes to Alfred:

1832.

My dear Alfred,

Thanks for your batch of MSS. The lines to J. S. are perfect. James [Spedding], I am sure, will be most grateful. The "Old Year" is excellent. The "Little Room" is mighty pleasant[1].

Remember the maxim of the Persian sage: "εἰ δοιάζεις, ἀπέχου." Your epigram to North is good, but I have scruples whether you should publish it. Perhaps he may like the lines. and you the better for them; but "μερμηρίζω." I think the "Lover's Tale" will be liked, as far as I can remember its old shape. Moxon is in ecstasies with the "May Queen"; he says the volume must make a great sensation. He and your friends are anxious that it should be out before the storm of politics is abroad. The French Fleet has got the start of you, and I fear Antwerp may be taken before your last revise is ready; but still you may be beforehand with the elections, which is more

---

[1] (*Note by my father.*)

As soon as this poem was published, I altered the second line to "All books and pictures ranged aright"; yet "Dear room, the apple of my sight" (which was much abused) is not so bad as

"Do go, dear rain, do go away."

A. T.

important.   There has been some delay this week, owing to
want of types, but the (printer's) devils are full of promise to set
up immediately.   Moxon has sent me the revises of " The Palace,"
with the notes; they are, I believe, correct, yet I would know
whether you altered " pouring glorious scorn" into " frowning,"
etc.   In the course of next week I shall send you two compositions of my own, the one very trifling, an article of three pages
only, in the *Foreign Quarterly*, the other, a pamphlet Moxon has
just published for me on Rossetti's *Disquisizioni sullo spirito
Antipapale*[1].   I hope you will like it; yet I have not forgotten
that the last time I sent you a publication of mine you did not
even deign to read it.   When should I have done the like by
one of yours?   Perhaps you may retort with justice, that this
question is like the American's remark in Mrs Trollope, to an
Englishman, who had never read 'Bryant's poems, " How
illiberal you English are! just let me ask you, what you would
say to one of us that had never read Milton or Shakespeare, or
any of *your* great authors! "   Fare thee well, old trump, poems
are good things but flesh and blood is better.   I only crave a
few words.

Ever yours affectionately, A. H. H.

After staying at Kitlands.

DORKING, *October 10th*, 1832.

MY DEAR ALFRED,

I must snatch a few minutes from the overwhelming
mass of law business which is now on my hands, just to talk with
you about the first-proof.   I had it sent down to me while I was
staying at Heath's.   The weather was miserably rainy, so, after
breakfast, we adjourned to an arbour in the garden, and while
Thompson, who was also staying there, furnished cheroots, I
furnished proof-sheets.   After mature examination, we came, in
full conclave, to some decisions, of which you shall have the
benefit.   We think the type very pretty, but are rather sorry
the book will not bind up with its predecessor.   We admire the
Buonaparte sonnet but we strongly urge the substitution of

---

[1] Among other papers Hallam wrote then were the brief though remarkable memoirs of Petrarch, Burke, and Voltaire, for the *Gallery of Portraits*
published by the Society for the Diffusion of Useful Knowledge.

"dreamer" for "madman." The stanzas "All good things" seem to us perfect. The "Lady" (of Shalott) reads charmingly in print: the more I read it, the more I like it. You were, indeed, happily inspired when the idea of that poem first rose in your imagination. We had a long battle with Mr Heath, a famous lawyer, but no man of letters, about the last stanza in the proof. We flatter ourselves we floored him; to be sure we were three to one, but he fought well. The principal point of attack was "cloud-white"; he said it was absurd to explain a fixed colour as pearl by the most variable hue in the world, that of a cloud. We recovered ourselves with all the grace of practised combatants, and talked learnedly about the context of feeling, and the conformity of the lady's dress to her magical character, till at last our opponent left us in possession of the field, declaring still between his teeth, that, for his part, he thought poetry ought to be sense. In one place a whole line was omitted. Douglas Heath read, "sudden laughters of the Tay" (Jay); without ever suspecting the misprint. I hear Tennant has written to dissuade you from publishing "Kriemhild," "Tarpeia" (in the "Fair Women"). Don't be humbugged, they are very good; you may put a note or two if you will, yet Milton did not to "Paradise Lost." Rogers the poet has been staying here, and speaks of you with admiration. Have you written to Moxon? He is anxious to have the rest of the MSS.

Ever your most affectionate ARTHUR.

My father wrote to Mr Moxon, in consequence of this letter from Arthur Hallam:

20 *Nov.* 1832.

DEAR SIR,

After mature consideration, I have come to a resolution of not publishing the last poem in my little volume, entitled, "Lover's Tale": it is too full of faults and tho' I think it might conduce towards making me popular, yet, to my eye, it spoils the completeness of the book, and is better away; of course whatever expenses may have been incurred in printing the above must devolve on me solely.

The vol. can end with that piece titled to J. S.

We, who live in this corner of the world, only get our letters twice or thrice a week: which has caused considerable delay: but on receipt of this you may begin to dress the volume for its introduction into the world, as soon as you choose.

Believe me, Sir, yours very truly,

ALFRED TENNYSON.

P.S.   The title-page may be simply

POEMS

BY ALFRED TENNYSON

(don't let the printer squire me).

Be so good as to send me five copies.

Among the poems in this volume were "The Lady of Shalott" (so-called from an Italian novelette, "Donna di Scalotta"), "Mariana in the South," "The Miller's Daughter," "Œnone," "The Palace of Art," "The Lotos-Eaters," "The Dream of Fair Women," "The May Queen," and "To James Spedding" on the death of his brother Edward. After its publication Arthur Hallam wrote to my father, referring to a review of the book in the *Quarterly* (No. XLVII. 1833):

[*Undated.*]

Your book continues to sell tolerably and Moxon says the *Quarterly* has done good. Rogers defends you publicly as the most promising genius of the time. Sir Robert Inglis told my father he had heard from unquestionable authority that Alfred Tennyson was an assumed name like Barry Cornwall. I endeavoured to shake his scepticism, I fear without effect. I hear to-day that a question is put up at the Cambridge Union, "Tennyson or Milton, which the greater poet?"

*   *   *   *   *

My father met Milman one day who denies altogether having written the infamous article [in the *Quarterly*]. He says he has

made a rule never to cut up any living poet.   Once he made an
exception in the case of a foreigner, and to his horror when
at Florence he found himself invited to meet him at breakfast.   Rogers thinks the first volume decidedly superior to the
second....I don't quite comprehend this.

From Arthur Hallam.

[*Undated.*]

Ὦ μοι, Διογενὲς Πατρόκλεις, οἷον ἔειπες;

You are very impertinent about my talent of letter-writing; I
never said I composed my letters, now at least; formerly I did in
some sort, when Plancus was consul, and Gaskell my correspondent and hero of romance.   Am I not thereby entitled to say of
myself, as Mrs Langley said of her daughters, "Whatever accom-
plishment I may possess in that way, it is entirely self-taught"?

That labour, if labour it was, was one of love.   It had
nothing of the file.   I composed a letter as I composed a poem.
Heart and mind went into it, and why?—because I couldn't
help it.   I was full of thoughts so new to me that I was afraid
of losing them, and took every way to treasure them: so dear
they were too that I could not rest till those I loved were familiar
with them.

I have been reading Mrs Jameson's *Characteristics*, and I
am so bewildered with similes about groves and violets, and
streams of music, and incense and attar of roses, that I hardly
know what I write.   Bating these little flummeries of style, it
is a good book, showing much appreciation of Shakespeare and
the human heart ἓν διὰ δυοῖν.

I went again to Effingham Wilson's shop to-day; he was
bland and submissive, promising to send me the account as
soon as he should have time to make it out.   I am confident
the £11 [1] will be found a mistake.   A rumour is current that
Mrs Arkwright has set "Oriana" to music!   All the world
loves her music, and "Oriana" has a fair chance of becoming
as stale as the "Captive Knight."   The country is in jeopardy
hourly increasing.   Yesterday I saw (perhaps) the last king of
England go down to open the first assembly of delegates from
a sovereign people.   It is an unmanageable house.   O'Connell

---

[1] The sum my father received for the 1830 volume.

aves. Government menaces. Your uncle [C. Tennyson d'Eyn-ourt] seems to be manœuvring to be chief of the Penultimate Radicals, the Girondists, one might call them from their position, were they not alike destitute of genius and patriotism. But there an be no doubt that, if the Mountain continues unshaken, it must increase, and that more faint-hearted crew to which your uncle belongs will adhere to it. O'Connell's speech is said to have been very effective. He and Sheil on one side; Macaulay and Stanley on the other, there will be some fine spectacles of intellectual combat.

Ever yours affectionately, A. H. H.

My father did not view the political situation so gloomily as did Arthur Hallam. It was the "dead waste and middle of the night" when the news of the passing of the Reform Bill for England and Wales had reached Somersby. This "Firm Bill," as the Lincolnshire people called it, had stirred all hearts; and my father and some of his brothers and sisters at once sallied out into the darkness, and began to ring the church bells madly. The new parson, horrified at hearing his bells rung and not merely rung but furiously clashed without his leave, came rushing into his church, and in the pitch blackness laid hold of the first thing which he could clap hand to, and this happened to be my aunt Cecilia's little dog — which forthwith tried to bite. The Tennysons then disclosed themselves amid much laughter; and the parson, who I suppose was a Tory of the old school, was with difficulty pacified. More than once my father thought of turning this scene into verse as an interesting picture of the times.

The advice as to sensitiveness[1] which Hallam

[1] Jowett writes to me: "Your father was very sensitive and had an honest hatred of being gossiped about. He called the malignant critics and chatterers 'mosquitoes.' He never felt any pleasure at praise (except from his friends), but he felt a great pain at the injustice of censure. It never occurred to him that a new poet in the days of his youth was sure to provoke dangerous hostilities in the 'genus irritabile vatum,' and in the old-fashioned public."

gave my father at this time was wise; since th
Quarterly review could not but disturb the equanimit
of a mind peculiarly liable to be annoyed by captiou
and unintelligent criticism[1].   Hallam urged him to fin
amusement in those hair-splitting critics, " who are th
bane of great art," and to assure himself that even thes
reviews would bring him into notice.   His friends wer
of opinion that even the sneering savage *Quarterl*
attack would be innocuous, for the *Review* was known i
London to be the organ of a party, both in politics an
literature.   They cheered him by telling him that hi
very creative originality and unlikeness to any poet, hi
uncommon power over varied metres and rare harmonie
of sound and sense, needed the creation of a taste fo
his work before he could be appreciated.   " To raise th
many," Hallam wrote, " to his own real point of view
the artist must employ his energies, and create energ
in others : to descend to their position is less noble, bu
practicable with ease."   However the estimation in whic
the *Quarterly* was then held throughout the country wa
given by an old Lincolnshire squire, who assured m
father that " The *Quarterly* was the next book to God'
Bible."

My father's attitude towards his critics is illustrate
in the following letter[2], written by him to " Christophe
North " in reference to a pamphlet by Mr Lake, whic

[1] More than once the writer in the *Quarterly* wilfully misinterprets th
lines and poems.   For instance, in " The Miller's Daughter " my fath
describes the mill-pool, and says :

> A water-rat from off the bank
> Plunged in the stream.

This is explained by the reviewer as the poet "likening the first intrusion
love into the virgin bosom of the miller's daughter to the plunging of
water-rat."

[2] This letter was found in a rag-store in Dundee in September 1895 an
forwarded to me by C. M. Falconer.

he thought " Christopher North " might be disposed to notice.

SOMERSBY, SPILSBY, LINCOLNSHIRE.

SIR,

Tho' I *am* " the star of little Britain," I assure you I do not rise or set there very cordially.   I prefer vegetating in a very quiet garden where I neither see nor hear anything of the great world of literature — not lighting even upon *Maga* once a year.   Nevertheless, in the lack of better things, a composition, mistermed a Satyre, entitled *Criticism and Taste*, and particularly remarkable for the want of either, was forwarded to me, a day or two ago, by the author — with a note; he thinks I ought to promote the circulation of his book for the good of my own, does he ? so then I am to be pioneered — perhaps patronized, by Mr John Lake.   Now, Sir, hew me piecemeal, cut me up any way you will, exhaust all your world of fun and fancy upon me, but do not suspect me — tho' I may have done, written, said foolish things, not excepting a silly squib to Christopher North — do not dream that I can, now or ever, own any one grain of sympathy with the ravings of this unhappy coxcomb.   I would rather request you, if you do not object to meet me on such dirty ground, to shake hands over the puddle he has made.

Five months after it had been printed I saw the critique[1] from which Mr L. has drawn his inspiration. I considered it at the time as somewhat too skittish and petulant, tho' it was redeemed to me by a tone of boisterous and picturesque humour such as I love. My gall might have risen a little — that it could never have contained much bitterness the weakness of my epigram ought, I think, to prove; for I trust that you will give me credit for being able to write a better.

1 The *Blackwood* article by Wilson.

I could wish that some of the poems there broken on your critical wheel were deeper than ever plumme sounded. Written as they were before I had attained my nineteenth year they could not but contain as many faults as words. I never wish to see them or hear of them again — much less to find them dragged forward once more on your boards, if you should condescend to divide Mr L. from his one idea by replying to him. Perhaps you should not use him too harshly — tho' his arrogance deserves reproof; a consideration of the real imbecility of his nature ought to blunt the weapon.

Someone (I think M. in his cups) told a friend of mine that you were the author of an article on me in the *Quarterly*. I do not believe it; for I could not recognise one spark of genius or a single touch of true humour or good feeling. Moreover the man misprints me, which is worse than lying — but now that we have shaken hands (for I trust, we have) I find that you owe me an explanation. Somewhere or other you state " Alfred is a gentleman " — to which I answer with Conrade and Borachio, " Yea, sir, we hope ": you say afterwards, that I have forgotten what was due to myself in that character, because having previously sent you " a copy with a grateful superscription " I had publicly disclaimed much relish for your approbation. Now upon mine honour as a gentleman, I did never send or cause to be sent any such presentation-copy, or write, indite, or cause to be written or indited any superscription, grateful or ungrateful, to any Editor of any Review or Magazine whatsoever.

Apologising for having thus far incroached on your valuable time......[1]

The next decade wrought a marvellous abatement of my father's real fault, which was undoubtedly " the

---

[1] The signature of this letter has been cut off.

tendency, arising from the fulness of a mind which had not yet learned to master its resources freely, to over-crowd his composition with imagery...to which may be added an over-indulgence in the luxuries of the senses, a profusion of splendours, harmonies, perfumes, gorgeous apparel, luscious meats and drinks and 'creature com-forts' which rather pall upon the sense, and make the glories of the outward world a little too obscure and overshadow the world within[1]."

"Alfred continued writing," as Spedding says, "like a crocodile, sideways and onward": and defines one aspect of the poet's work in this sort of way:

(What Thor, armed with his hammer, said to the Bard
before dinner.)

Wherever evil customs thicken,
Break thro' with the hammer of iron rhyme,
Till priest-craft and king-craft sicken,
But pap-meat-pamper not the time
With the flock of the thunder-stricken.
If the world caterwaul, lay harder upon her
Till she clapperclaw no longer,
Bang thy stithy stronger and stronger,
Thy rhyme-hammer *shall* have honour.

Yet a poet cannot live his true life without sympathy, and he fancied that England was an unsympathetic at-mosphere, and half resolved to live abroad in Jersey, in the south of France, or in Italy. He was so far per-suaded that the English people would never care for his poetry, that, had it not been for the intervention of his friends, he declared it not unlikely that after the death of Hallam he would not have continued to write.

---

[1] Spedding's *Reviews and Discussions*.

Spedding wrote [1], as to this second volume: " The reception (of the poems), though far from triumphant, was not inauspicious; for while they gained him many admirers, they were treated, even by those critics whose admiration, like their charity, begins and ends at home, as sufficiently notable to be worth some not unelaborate ridicule. The admiration and the ridicule served alike to bring them into notice...The superiority of his second collection of poems lay not so much in the superior workmanship (it contained perhaps fewer that were equally perfect in their kind) as in the general aim and character. If some of the blossom was gone, it was amply repaid by the more certain promise of fruit. Not only was the aim generally larger, the subjects and interest more substantial, and the endeavour more sustained, but the original and distinctive character of the man appeared more plainly. His genius was manifestly shaping a peculiar course for itself, and finding out its proper business; the moral soul was beginning more and more to assume its due predominance, not in the way of formal preaching (the proper vehicle of which is prose), but in the shape and colour which his creations unconsciously took, and the feelings which they were made insensibly to suggest."

To his aunt, Mrs Russell, my father wrote the two following letters:

SOMERSBY.

DEAREST AUNT,

What think you of the state of affairs in Europe? Burking and cholera have ceased to create much alarm. They are our least evils, but reform and

---

[1] In 1842.

St Simonism are, and will continue to be, subjects of the highest interest. The future is so dark in the prospect that I am ready to cry out with the poet:

> The empty thrones call out for kings,
> But kings are cheap as summer-dust.
> The good old time hath taken wings,
> And with it taken faith and trust,
> And solid hope of better things.

Reform (not the measure, but the instigating spirit of reform, which is likely to subsist among the people long after the measure has past into a law) will bring on the confiscation of Church property, and maybe the downfall of the Church altogether: but the existence of the sect of the St Simonists[1] is at once a proof of the immense mass of evil that is extant in the nineteenth century, and a focus which gathers all its rays. This sect is rapidly spreading in France, Germany and Italy, and they have missionaries in London. But I hope and trust that there are hearts as true and pure as steel in old England, that will never brook the sight of Baal in the sanctuary, and St Simon in the Church of Christ. I should delight in having a line from you or Emma.

Believe me,

Ever yours most affectionately,

A. T.

---

[1] See an interesting account of Saint-Simon and his followers in Lecky's *Democracy and Liberty*, Vol. II. pp. 207–215.

SOMERSBY, *March* 10*th*, 1833.

MY DEAREST AUNT,

I am much grieved to find that your kind-hearted letter to me has been lying so many days unanswered. I was at Mablethorpe, a bathing-place on our bleak, flat Lincolnshire coast, when it arrived at Somersby, and as there is no species of post between the latter and the former place, I have only just now received it together with some others. I have sent Emma's[1] picture to 15 Portland Place. I recollect when I first saw it, thinking that it did not do her justice: it wanted her life and vivacity. I would have forwarded this portrait to you long ago, and likewise visited you by the proxy of a letter, but to me as to Dante, "La diritta via era smarrita," for I knew not where you were. What astrologer can point out the place of any star that moves perpetually under a cloud?

You have been singing too in your solitude, and I should like much to hear some of your melodies, but a malicious fatality always seems to thwart me: the ghost of some ex-amateur, jealous of your notes, thrusts himself between me and any possible piano you may sit down to. My grandfather had lately a very severe fit of the gout, — Mr B.[2] stayed two nights in the house, — but our last accounts are that he is pretty well recovered and rides out, I believe, as usual.

Mary remembers having once met you at Tealby: I wish you knew her better — she is a girl of great feeling

---

[1] Her daughter, Lady Boyne.

[2] Mr B——, the county doctor, would miss out his "h's," and say: "Mr Tennyson, I work 'ard and get up so early that I 'eat my own grate." He was in the habit of riding about at night with a gig-lamp fastened to each foot, for fear of being run over.

and very warm in her attachments to her female friends, and true feeling is all that is really valuable on the windy side of the grave. For myself, I drag on somewhat heavily thro' the ruts of life, sometimes moping to myself like an owl in an ivy-bush, or that *one* sparrow which the Hebrew mentioneth as sitting on the housetop (a passage which used always to make me uncomfortable), and sometimes smoking a pipe with a neighbouring parson and cursing O'Connell for as double-dyed a rascal as ever was dipped in the Styx of political villainy[1]. Last year, however, Hallam and myself steamed up the Rhine as far as Bingen; we had the pleasure of being moored by a muddy island, full of stagnant dykes, in the river Maas, where we performed quarantine for a week, and saw by night the boats, from the cholera vessels stationed in the river, creeping round to the burial-place of the island with a corpse and a lantern. We at last got so enraged that we pulled down the Dutch colours and reversed them, which put the ancient skipper into such indignation that he swore he would hang us at the yard-arm.

We returned by Aix-la-Chapelle and Brussels. My mother, who, as you know, is one of the most angelick natures on God's earth, always doing good as it were by a sort of intuition, continues in tolerable health, though somewhat harassed with the cares incident to so large a family. She sends the essence of all love to you and yours, and begs me to state how happy it would make her to see you at Somersby: indeed this is a wish in which we all cordially join, tho' for my own part I have very faint hopes that you will gratify it. Many thanks for your present and letter.

Love to Emma and compliments to Gustavus[2].   I

---

[1] He softened this opinion when he came to know more about O'Connell.
[2] The baby son is the present Lord Boyne.

hope for his own peace of mind that he will have as
little of the Tennyson about him as possible.

Believe me,

My dearest Aunt,

Ever your most affectionate nephew,

A. T.

During these years the Tennysons seem to have
taken turns in going to London. We hear of my uncle
Charles seeing his Cambridge friends in town. "Brookfield is melancholy and not fancy-free." "John Kemble
is buried in Gothic manuscripts, and will only talk of
Runes and Eddas, and of the brave knight Siegfried."
Arthur Hallam is "as kind as ever," and Charles rides
with him "through the beautiful Norwood country." In
March of this year we are told that Arthur Hallam, Alfred
and Mary enjoyed their sight-seeing in London together.
They visited the Elgin Marbles, the Tower and the
Zoological Gardens. They looked through microscopes
at "moths' wings, gnats' heads, and at all the lions
and tigers which lie perdus in a drop of spring water."
My father would say, on looking through the microscope,
"Strange that these wonders should draw some men
to God and repel others. No more reason in one than
in the other."

In July Arthur Hallam wrote to my father who was
in Scotland:

July 31st, 1833.

I feel to-night what I own has been too uncommon with
me of late, a strong desire to write to you. I do own I feel
the want of you at some times more than at others; a sort of
yearning for dear old Alfred comes upon me, and that without

any particularly apparent reason. I missed you much at Somersby — not for want of additional excitement, I was very happy. I had never been at Somersby before without you. However I hope you are not unpleasantly employed in the land of cakes and broiled fish. I hear that you were charmed with the amiability of the Gardens; I also hear in town that the old Monteiths have been here instead of there. I trust you finished the "Gardener's Daughter," and enriched her with a few additional beauties drawn from the ancient countenance of Monteith's aunt. Have you encountered any Highland girl with "a shower for her dower"? I should like much to hear your adventures, but I daresay it will be difficult to persuade you to write to Vienna, whither I am going on Saturday with tolerable speed. At all events if you have any traveller's tale to tell, do not tell it often enough to get tired of it before we meet. I am going perhaps as far as Buda. I shall present your poetic respects to the Danube and to certain parts of Tyrol. In the parcel which accompanies this you will find a volume of poems by Hartley Coleridge, much of which I think you will agree with me is exquisitely beautiful. Probably Charles and Septimus will like the sonnets more than you will. I desire and peremptorily issue my orders that Emily may not be debarred from full, fair and free reading of that book by any of her brothers.

A. H. H.

My father went with Tennant to London to say farewell to his friend, before he set out abroad. There was a supper at my father's lodgings, and Tennant writes to Septimus Tennyson:

Moxon and Leigh Hunt were there, and we did not separate till half-past four o'clock: Alfred repeated glorious fragments of the "Gardener's Daughter," which seemed to produce proper effect upon Leigh Hunt. Yesterday we went in a troop to see Rogers' (the poet's) gallery of paintings: superb Titian, very beautiful Raphael Madonna, and in fact all art gems[1]. There is a fresco

---

[1] The Titian, presumably *Noli me tangere*, and the (so-called) Giotto, a fragment with two Apostles' heads, as well as the Madonna, which had belonged to the Orleans collection, are now in the National Gallery.

by Giotto. In the library we found Charles' volume but *no*
Alfred's. There were many proofs of the engravings that wil
appear in his (Rogers') forthcoming volume.

Hallam sent as a parting present to Emily Ten
nyson the *Pensées de Pascal*, and *Silvio Pellico.* Ir
August he started with his father for the " Tyrol, anc
Salzburg." " Never have mountains seemed to him sc
sublime." He admired "the independence and self
respect of the Tyrolese." Vienna he compared to Paris
but found the city "more uniformly handsome." He
visited the Treasure Chamber, where he saw "the
largest diamond in the world." The Prater was dismal
"insipid, worse even than the Corso at Milan or the
Cascine at Florence." But he revelled in the picture
gallery and wrote about it as follows:

Sept. 6th, 1833.

The gallery is grand and I longed for you: two rooms ful
of Venetian pictures only; such Giorgiones, Palmas, Bordones
Paul Veroneses! and oh Alfred such Titians! by Heaven, tha
man could paint! I wish you could see his Danaë. Do you
just write as perfect a Danaë! Also there are two fine room
of Rubens, but I know you are an exclusive, and care little fo
Rubens, in which you are wrong: although no doubt Titian's
imagination and style are more analogous to your own thar
those of Rubens or of any other school.

A. H. H.

That is the last letter from Arthur Hallam. Witl
his letters I find these MS lines:

I do but mock me with the questionings.
Dark, dark, irrecoverably dark
Is the soul's eye; yet how it strives and battles
Through the impenetrable gloom to fix
That master light, the secret truth of things,
Which is the body of the Infinite God.

A. H. H.

Ie died at Vienna on Sept. 15th, 1833. When Mr
Iallam returned from his daily walk, he saw Arthur
sleep as he supposed upon the couch; a blood-vessel
ear the brain had suddenly burst: it was not sleep but
eath.

On October 1st a letter from Arthur Hallam's uncle,
Ienry Elton, at Clifton, brought the sorrowful news to
iy father:

At the desire of a most afflicted family, I write to you because
iey are unequal from the grief into which they have fallen to
o it themselves. Your friend, sir, and my much-loved nephew,
Arthur Hallam, is no more. It has pleased God to remove him
rom this, his first scene of existence, to that better world for
which he was created. He died at Vienna, on his return from
Buda, by apoplexy, and I believe his remains come by sea from
Trieste. Mr Hallam arrived this morning in 3 Princes Buildings.
May that Being in whose hands are all the destinies of man, and
who has promised to comfort all that mourn, pour the balm of
onsolation on all the families, who are bowed down by this
inexpected dispensation! I have just seen Mr Hallam, who
egs I will tell you that he will write himself as soon as his
heart will let him. Poor Arthur had a slight attack of ague,
which he had often had, ordered his fire to be lighted, and
alked with as much cheerfulness as usual. He suddenly became
nsensible, and his spirit departed without pain. On examination
t was the general opinion that he could not have lived long.
This was also Dr Holland's opinion. The account I have
endeavoured to give you is merely what I have been able to
gather, but the family of course are in too great distress to enter
nto details.

(*Extract of letter from John M. Kemble to Fanny Kemble*[1].)

It is with feelings of inexpressible pain that I announce to
you the death of poor Arthur Hallam, who expired suddenly
from an attack of apoplexy at Vienna, on the 15th of last

[1] Given me by Miss Cobbe.

month.   Though this was always feared by us as likely to occur, the shock has been a bitter one to bear: and most of all so to the Tennysons, whose sister Emily he was to have married.   I have not yet had the courage to write to Alfred.   This is a loss which will most assuredly be felt by this age, for if ever man was born for great things he was.   Never was a more powerful intellect joined to a purer and holier heart; and the whole illuminated with the richest imagination, with the most sparkling yet the kindest wit.   One cannot lament for him that he is gone to a far better life, but we weep over his coffin and wonder that we cannot be consoled: the Roman epitaph on two young children *Sibimet ipsis dolorem abstulerunt, suis reliquere* (from themselves they took away pain, to their friends they left it!) is alway present to my mind, and somehow the miserable feeling of loneliness comes over one even though one knows that the dead are happier than the living.   His poor father was with him only; they had been travelling together in Hungary and were on their return to England; but there had been nothing whatever to announce the fatal termination of their journey; indeed bating fatigue Arthur had been unusually well.

On December 30th Henry Hallam wrote to my father as follows:

It may remove some anxiety from the minds of yourself and others to know that the mortal part of our dearest Arthur will be interred at Clevedon on Friday.   I leave town to-morrow. My first thought was not to write to you till all was over: but you may have been apprehensive for the safety of the vessel.   I did not expect her arrival so soon.   Use your own discretion about telling your sister.   Mrs H. is very anxious to hear about her; if not too painful to her, Miss Tennyson will have the kindness to write.   Do your utmost, my dear young friend, to support her and yourself.   Give as little way to grief as you may.   But I feel that my own rather increases with time; yet I find also that both occupation and conversation are very serviceable.   I fear the solitary life you both lead in the country is sadly unpropitious.   We are now all well, though my boy[1] is not as vigorous as he should be.   God bless you all.

Affectionately yours, H. H.

[1] Harry Hallam.

In the letters from Arthur Hallam's friends there was a rare unanimity of opinion about his worth. Milnes, writing to his father, says that he had a "very deep respect" for Hallam, and that Thirlwall, in after years the great Bishop, for whom Hallam and my father had a profound affection, was "actually captivated by him." When at Cambridge with Hallam he had written: "He is the only man here of my own standing before whom I bow in conscious inferiority in everything." Alford writes: "Hallam was a man of wonderful mind and knowledge on all subjects, hardly credible at his age.... I long ago set him down for the most wonderful person I ever knew. He was of the most tender, affectionate disposition."

So "those whose eyes must long be dim with tears," Henry Hallam says, "brought him home to rest among his kindred and in his own country": and the burial took place on Jan. 3rd, 1834, in the lonely church which overlooks the Bristol Channel.

On the evening of one of these sad[1] winter days my father had already noted down in his scrap-book some fragmentary lines, which proved to be the germ of "In Memoriam":

> Where is the voice I loved? ah where
> Is that dear hand that I would press?
> Lo! the broad heavens cold and bare,
> The stars that know not my distress!
>
> *　　*　　*　　*　　*
>
> The vapour labours up the sky,
> Uncertain forms are darkly moved!
> Larger than human passes by
> The shadow of the man I loved,
> And clasps his hands, as one that prays!

[1] Francis Garden had written to Trench, Nov. 26th, 1833: "When in London, I saw a letter from poor Alfred Tennyson. Both himself and his family seemed plunged in the deepest affliction."

Later, Henry Hallam writes to my father:

It is my intention to print, for private friends only, a few of those pieces which have already appeared, with some poems and perhaps prose papers that I have in my possession. Several of those printed in 1830, and a certain number that are in manuscript, will be included. It will be necessary to prefix a short memoir. I must rely on his contemporaries and most intimate friends to furnish me with part of my materials; and I should wish to have anything that may be thought most worthy of being mentioned, communicated to me by letter. Perhaps you would do something. I should desire to have the character of his mind, his favourite studies and pursuits, his habits and views delineated. I shall not apply to too many persons; but it has been suggested to me that Spedding will be better able to assist me than any one else. I do not know whether this is the case, nor do I know Mr S.'s direction. It is somewhere in Cumberland. I shall be most happy if you can give me a better account than the last we have had of your sister; we all unite in kindest love to all.

Most truly yours, HENRY HALLAM [1].

To this volume of collected poems and essays, published some time after, Henry Hallam prefixed an introduction, in which he said " Arthur seemed to tread the earth as a spirit from a better world." Arthur's old Eton friend Gladstone wrote: "When much time has elapsed, when most bereavements will be forgotten, he will still be remembered, and his place, I fear, will be felt to be still vacant, singularly as his mind was calculated by its native tendencies to work powerfully and for good, in an age full of import to the nature and destinies of man."

In consequence of her sudden and terrible grief my aunt Emily was ill for many months, and very slowly recovered. "We were waiting for her," writes one of her friends, "in the drawing-room the first day since her

[1] See Appendix, p. 498, for Letters about Arthur Hallam.

loss that she had been able to meet anyone, and she
came at last, dressed in deep mourning, a shadow of her
former self, but with one white rose in her black hair as
her Arthur loved to see her."

"The Two Voices" or "Thoughts of a Suicide" was
begun under the cloud of this overwhelming sorrow,
which, as my father told me, for a while blotted out all
joy from his life, and made him long for death, in spite
of his feeling that he was in some measure a help and
comfort to his sister. But such a first friendship and
such a loss helped to reveal himself to himself, while he
enshrined his sorrow in his song. Tennant writes:
"Alfred although much broken in spirits is yet able to
divert his thoughts from gloomy brooding, and keep his
mind in activity."

In the earliest manuscript of "The Two Voices" a
fine verse is found which was omitted in the published
edition as too dismal (after "under earth").

> From when his baby pulses beat
> To when his hands in their last heat
> Pick at the death-mote in the sheet.

Then in the same manuscript-book come the first
written sections of "In Memoriam," in the following
order:

Fair ship that from the Italian shore.
>   (*written on a stray sheet*)

With trembling fingers did we weave.
When Lazarus left his charnel-cave.
This truth came borne with bier and pall.
It draweth near the birth of Christ.

And between "With trembling fingers" and "When
Lazarus left his charnel-cave" he has written the first
draft of his "Morte d'Arthur."

Unpublished Poems of this Period.

*The Statesman.**

They wrought a work which Time reveres,
  A pure example to the lands,
  Further and further reaching hands
For ever into coming years;

They worshipt Freedom for her sake;
  We faint unless the wanton ear
  Be tickled with the loud "hear, hear,"
To which the slight-built hustings shake;

For where is he, the citizen,
  Deep-hearted, moderate, firm, who sees
  His path before him? not with these,
Shadows of statesmen, clever men!

Uncertain of ourselves we chase
  The clap of hands; we jar like boys:
  And in the hurry and the noise
Great spirits grow akin to base.

A sound of words that change to blows!
  A sound of blows on armed breasts!
  And individual interests
Becoming bands of armed foes!

A noise of hands that disarrange
  The social engine! fears that waste
  The strength of men, lest overhaste
Should fire the many wheels of change!

Ill fares a people passion-wrought,
   A land of many days that cleaves
   In two great halves, when each one leaves
The middle road of sober thought!

Not he that breaks the dams, but he
   That thro' the channels of the state
   Convoys the people's wish, is great;
His name is pure, his fame is free:

He cares, if ancient usage fade,
   To shape, to settle, to repair,
   With seasonable changes fair,
And innovation grade by grade:

Or, if the sense of most require
   A precedent of larger scope,
   Not deals in threats, but works with hope,
And lights at length on his desire:

Knowing those laws are just alone
   That contemplate a mighty plan,
   The frame, the mind, the soul of man,
Like one that cultivates his own.

He, seeing far an end sublime,
   Contends, despising party-rage,
   To hold the Spirit of the Age
Against the Spirit of the Time.

1833.

*Youth.**

I

Youth, lapsing thro' fair solitudes,
  Pour'd by long glades and meadowy mounds,
Crown'd with soft shade her deepening floods
  That wash'd her shores with blissful sounds:

Her silver eddies in their play
  Drove into lines and studs of light
The image of the sun by day,
  The image of the moon by night.

The months, ere they began to rise,
  Sent thro' my blood a prophet voice
Before the first white butterflies,
  And where the secret streams rejoice.

I heard Spring laugh in hidden rills,
  Summer thro' all her sleepy leaves
Murmur'd: a voice ran round the hills
  When corny Lammas bound the sheaves:

A voice, when night had crept on high,
  To snowy crofts and winding scars,
Rang like a trumpet clear and dry,
  And shook the frosty winter stars.

When I was somewhat older grown
  These voices did not cease to cry,
Only they took a sweeter tone,
  But did not sound so joyfully:

Lower and deeper evermore
  They grew, and they began at last
To speak of what had gone before,
  And how all things become the past.

Life, to this wind, turn'd all her vanes,
    Moan'd in her chimneys and her eaves;
I grieved as woods in dripping rains
    Sigh over all their fallen leaves;

Beside my door at morning stood
    The tearful spirit of the time;
He moan'd, " I wander from my good!"
    He chanted some old doleful rhyme.

So lived I without aim or choice,
    Still humming snatches of old song,
Till suddenly a sharper voice
    Cried in the future " Come along."

When to this sound my face I turn'd,
    Intent to follow on the track,
Again the low sweet voices mourn'd
    In distant fields, " Come back, come back."

Confused, and ceasing from my quest,
    I loiter'd in the middle way,
So pausing 'twixt the East and West,
    I found the Present where I stay:

Now idly in my natal bowers,
    Unvext by doubts I cannot solve,
I sit among the scentless flowers
    And see and hear the world revolve:

Yet well I know that nothing stays,
    And I must traverse yonder plain:
Sooner or later from the haze
    The second voice will peal again.

II

A rumour of a mystery,
  A noise of winds that meet and blend,
An energy, an agony,
  A labour working to an end.

Now shall I rest or shall I rise?
  It is the early morning, Hark!
A voice like many voices cries,
  Comes hither throbbing thro' the dark;

Now one faint line of light doth glow,
  I follow to the morning sun,
Behind yon hill the trumpets blow,
  And there is something greatly done:

The voice cries "Come." Upon the brink
  A solitary fortress burns,
And shadows strike and shadows sink,
  And Heaven is dark and bright by turns.

"Come" and I come, the wind is strong:
  Hush! there floats upward from the gulf
A murmur of heroic song,
  A howling of the mountain wolf;

A tempest strikes the craggy walls,
  Faint shouts are heard across the glen,
A moan of many waterfalls,
  And in the pauses groans of men.

"Come" and I come, no more I sleep:
  The thunder cannot make thee dumb;
"Come" and I come, the vale is deep,
  My heart is dark, but yet I come.

Up hither have I found my way,
  The latest thunder-peal hath peal'd,
Down from the summit sweeps the day
  And rushes o'er a boundless field.

Out bursts a rainbow in the sky —
  Away with shadows! On they move!
Beneath those double arches lie
  Fair with green fields the realms of Love.

The whole land glitters after rain,
  Thro' wooded isles the river shines,
The casements sparkle on the plain,
  The towers gleam among the vines;

"Come" and I come, and all comes back
  Which in that early voice was sweet,
Yet am I dizzy in the track,
  A light wind wafts me from my feet.

Warm beats my blood, my spirit thirsts;
  Fast by me flash the cloudy streaks,
And from the golden vapour bursts
  A mountain bright with triple peaks:

With all his groves he bows, he nods,
  The clouds unswathe them from the height,
And there sit figures as of Gods
  Ray'd round with beams of living light.

8—2

CHAPTER V.*

THE 1832 VOLUME (DATED 1833).

SOLITUDE AND WORK (1833–1835).

Mighty the voices of earth, which are dull'd by the voices that say:
"All of us drift into darkness, wherein we shall all pass away!"
Better to pass then at once than seeing the darkness to stay,
But for a mightier Voice which was born of the Dawn of the Day.

It becomes no man to nurse despair,
But in the teeth of clench'd antagonisms
To follow up the worthiest.

Before following further the thread of the life,
must set down here certain notes upon the 1832 volume
by my father and by Edward Fitzgerald, omitted from
the last chapter, in order not to interrupt the sequence of
Arthur Hallam's letters.

Fitzgerald writes on "The Lady of Shalott":

Well I remember this poem, read to me, before I knew the
author, at Cambridge one night in 1832 or 3, and its image
passing across my head, as across the magic mirror, while half
asleep on the mail coach to London "in the creeping dawn"
that followed.[1]

The key to this tale of magic "symbolism" is of deep
human significance, and is to be found in the lines:

[1] MS Note, E. F. G.

Or when the moon was overhead,
    Came two young lovers lately wed;
"I am half sick of shadows," said
    The Lady of Shalott.

Canon Ainger in his *Tennyson for the Young* quotes the following interpretation, given him by my father:

The new-born love for something, for some one in the wide world from which she has been so long secluded, takes her out of the region of shadows into that of realities.

The idea of "Mariana in the South" came to my father as he was travelling between Narbonne and Perpignan[1], and foreign critics have found out and have appreciated this representation of southern France.

The first original manuscript verse of "The Miller's Daughter," which he altered both before and after publication, seemed to Fitzgerald too good to be lost:

I met in all the close green ways,
    While walking with my rod and line,
The miller with his mealy face,
    And long'd to take his hand in mine.
He look'd so jolly and so good —
    While fishing in the milldam-water,
I laugh'd to see him as he stood,
    And dreamt not of the miller's daughter.

"This poem," Fitzgerald writes, "as may be seen, is much altered and enlarged from the first edition of 1832; in some respects, I think, not for the better; losing somewhat of the easy character of 'talk across the walnuts and the wine.'" It shows the poet's especial love of setting his human beings in a landscape which is strictly in harmony with the subject of the poem. "The mill was no particular mill," my father writes; "if

[1] See letter from Arthur Hallam on "Mariana in the South" in Appendix, p. 500.

I thought at all of any mill it was that of Trumpington near Cambridge."

From the volume of 1832 he omitted several stanzas of " The Palace of Art " because he thought that the poem was too full. " The artist is known by his self-limitation " was a favourite adage of his. He allowed me however to print some of them in my notes, otherwise I should have hesitated to quote without his leave lines that he had excised. He " gave the people of his best," and he usually wished that his best should remain without variorum readings, " the chips of the workshop," as he called them. The love of bibliomaniacs for first editions filled him with horror, for the first editions are obviously in many cases the worst editions; and once he said to me:

"Why do they treasure the rubbish I shot from my full-finish'd cantos?

νήπιοι οὐδὲ ἴσασιν ὅσῳ πλέον ἥμισυ παντός."

For himself many passages in Wordsworth and other poets had been entirely spoilt by the modern habit of giving every various reading along with the text. Besides, in his case, very often what is published as the latest edition has been the original version in his first manuscript, so that there is no possibility of really tracing the history of what may seem to be a new word or a new passage. " For instance," he said, " in ' Maud ' a line in the first edition was ' I will bury myself in *my books*, and the Devil may pipe to his own,' which was afterwards altered to ' I will bury myself *in myself*, etc.' : this was highly commended by the critics as an improvement on the *original* reading—but it was actually in the first MS draft of the poem."

In 1890 he wrote the following notes: " Trench said to me, when we were at Trinity together, ' Tennyson we cannot live in art.' " " ' The Palace of Art ' is the

embodiment of my own belief that the Godlike life is
with man and for man, that

> Beauty, Good and Knowledge are three sisters...
> That never can be sunder'd without tears.
> And he that shuts out Love, in turn shall be
> Shut out from Love, and on her threshold lie,
> Howling in outer darkness."

"When I first conceived the plan of the poem, I
intended to have introduced both sculptures and paintings into it, but I only finished two sculptures.

> One was the Tishbite whom the raven fed,
>   As when he stood on Carmel-steeps
> With one arm stretch'd out bare, and mock'd and said,
>   'Come, cry aloud, he sleeps.'

> Tall, eager, lean and strong, his cloak wind-borne
>   Behind, his forehead heavenly bright
> From the clear marble pouring glorious scorn,
>   Lit as with inner light.

> One was Olympias; the floating snake
>   Roll'd round her ankles, round her waist
> Knotted, and folded once about her neck,
>   Her perfect lips to taste,

> Down from the shoulder moved: she seeming blithe
>   Declined her head: on every side
> The dragon's curves melted, and mingled with
>   The woman's youthful pride
> Of rounded limbs —

After the old verse XXVI was

> 'From shape to shape at first within the womb
>   The brain is moulded,' she began,
> 'And thro' all phases of all thought I come
>   Unto the perfect man.

All nature widens upward. Evermore
   The simpler essence lower lies,
More complex is more perfect, owning more
   Discourse, more widely wise.'

In the centre of the four quadrangles of the palace
is a tower.

Hither, when all the deep unsounded skies
   Shudder'd with silent stars, she clomb,
And as with optic glasses her keen eyes
   Pierced thro' the mystic dome,

Regions of lucid matter taking forms,
   Brushes of fire, hazy gleams,
Clusters and beds of worlds, and bee-like swarms
   Of suns, and starry streams.

She saw the snowy poles and Moons of Mars,
   That mystic field of drifted light
In mid Orion, and the married stars.

The ' Moons of Mars ' is the only modern reading
here, all the rest are more than half a century old."

After perusing the "marvellously compressed word-
pictures of this poem," Fitzgerald appends a personal
note to "sat smiling babe in arm."

I remember A. T.[1] admiring the abstracted look of a Murillo
Madonna at Dulwich ; the eyes of which are on you, but seem
" looking at something beyond, beyond the Actual into Abstraction."   This has been noticed of some great men ; it is the trance
of the Seer : I do not remember seeing it in A. T. himself ;
great as he was from top to toe, and his eyes dark, powerful
and serene[2].

He was still afraid of blindness, which his brother Frederick
said might accompany the perception of the inward Sublime as
in Homer and Milton.   The names of Dante and Michael Angelo

[1] Fitzgerald generally calls my father A. T.

[2] Fitzgerald afterwards altered his mind and wrote: "I have seen it in
his (A. T.'s).   Some American spoke of the same in Wordsworth.   I suppose
it may be the same with all *poets*."

in (the original form of) this poem remind me that once looking with A. T. at two busts of Dante and Goethe in a shop window in Regent Street, I said, "What is there wanting in Goethe which the other has?" "The Divine[1]!"

After visiting Italy some twenty years after this poem was written, he told me he had been prepared for Raffaelle but not for Michael Angelo: whose picture at Florence of a Madonna dragging a "ton of a child" over one shoulder almost revolted him at first, but drew him toward itself afterwards, and "would not out of memory." I forget if he saw the Dresden Raffaelle[2], but he would speak of the *Child* in it as "perhaps finer than the whole composition, in so far as one's eyes are more concentrated on the subject. The child seems to me the furthest reach of human art. His attitude is a man's: his countenance a Jupiter's — perhaps too much so." But when A. T. had a babe of his own, he saw it was not "too much so." "I am afraid of him: babies have an expression of grandeur which children lose, a look of awe and wonder. I used to think the old painters overdid the expression and dignity of their infant Christs, but I see they didn't. This morning * * * lay half-an-hour worshipping the bed-post on which the sunlight flickered (pure nature worship)[3]. 'If,' as old Hallam said, 'one could have the history of a babe's mind!'"

The "Dream of Fair Women" began in the first edition of 1832 with some stanzas about a man sailing in a balloon, but my father did not like the "balloon stanzas" so they were cut out. As Edward Fitzgerald said to him, "They make a perfect poem by themselves without affecting the 'dream.'"

As when a man that sails in a balloon,
    Down-looking sees the solid shining ground
Stream from beneath him in the broad blue noon,
    Tilth, hamlet, mead and mound:

[1] To me, he said, "The Divine *intensity*," and possibly the same to Fitzgerald. H. T.

[2] He went to Dresden on purpose to see this great picture.

[3] "Afterwards he took to fetish-worship — the worship of a gilded doll sent him by Lear." A. T.

And takes his flags and waves them to the mob,
  That shout below, all faces turn'd to where
Glows rubylike the far-up crimson globe,
  Fill'd with a finer air:

So, lifted high, the poet at his will
  Lets the great world flit from him, seeing all,
Higher thro' secret splendours mounting still,
  Self-poised, nor fears to fall,

Hearing apart the echoes of his fame.
  While I spoke thus, the seedsman, Memory,
Sow'd my deep-furrow'd thought with many a name
  Whose glory will not die.

From the letters of that time I gather that there was a strong current of depreciation of my father in certain literary quarters. However he kept up his courage, profited by friendly and unfriendly criticism, and in silence, obscurity, and solitude, perfected his art. " First the workman is known for his work, afterwards the work for the workman ": but it is " only the concise and perfect work," he thought, " which will last[1]. "

That the volume of 1832 was partially successful (three hundred copies having been sold) is obvious from the fact that Moxon was eager to publish more by him. Later an appreciative article by John Stuart Mill in the *London Review* (July 1835) was a great encouragement. Friendly critics, like G. S. Venables, wrote that his poems had too much concentrated power and thought, were too imaginative and too largely imbued with the " innermost magic," easily to excite popular interest, or to be read at once by those whom he specially wished to influence. Kemble had said, " In Alfred's mind the materials of the greatest works are heaped in an abundance which is almost confusion." Notwithstanding all

[1] A. T.

ostile criticism, he had impressed himself deeply on a imited number of minds. He now began to base his poetry more on the "broad and common interests of the ime and of universal humanity," although no doubt it was harder to idealize such themes than those that appealed mostly to the imagination. The great Catholic painters could express what was at the same time ideal and real in the minds of the people : but the modern artist has hardly ever found similar objects of high imagination and intense popular feeling for his art to work upon. If, wrote Venables, in a contemporary letter to my father, an artist could only now find out where these objects are, he would be *the* artist of modern times. Venables affirmed they were not to be sought in any transient fashions of thought, but in the " convergent tendencies of many opinions" on religion, art and nature, — of which tendencies he and others believed, he said, that my father, with his commanding intellect, and conspicuous moral courage, ought to be the artistic exponent and unifier. My father pondered all that had been said and — after a period of utter prostration from grief, and many dark fits of blank despondency — his passionate love of truth, of nature, and of humanity, drove him to work again, with a deeper and a fuller insight into the requirements of the age.

> His resolve
> Upbore him and firm faith —
> And beating up thro' all the bitter world,
> Like fountains of sweet water in the sea,
> Kept him a living soul[1].

Two pathetic lines of his written at this time are left :

> O leave not thou thy son forlorn;
> Teach me, great Nature : make me live.

"Perpetual idleness," he would say, "must be one of

---

[1] "Enoch Arden."

the punishments of Hell." Hundreds of lines were,
he expressed it, " blown up the chimney with his pip
smoke, or were written down and thrown into the fi
as not being then perfect enough." "The Brook"
later years was actually rescued from the waste-pap
heap.

He lived for the most part at Somersby, and I give
list of his week's work; which he drew up.

Monday.	History, German.
Tuesday.	Chemistry, German.
Wednesday.	Botany, German.
Thursday.	Electricity, German.
Friday.	Animal Physiology, **German**.
Saturday.	Mechanics.
Sunday.	Theology.
Next Week.	Italian in the afternoon.
Third Week.	Greek. *Evenings.* Poetry.

UNPUBLISHED POEM OF THIS PERIOD.

The Mother's Ghost.

Not a whisper stirs the gloom,
    It will be the dawning soon,
We may glide from room to room,
    In the glimmer of the moon :
Every heart is lain to rest,
    All the house is fast in sleep,
Were I not a spirit blest,
    Sisters, I could almost weep !

In that cradle sleeps my child,
    She whose birth brought on my bliss:
On her forehead undefiled
    I will print an airy kiss:

> See, she dreameth happy dreams,
>   Her hands are folded quietly,
> Like to one of us she seems,
>   One of us my child will be.

Now and then, when he could save up a little hoard,
e went to London or to visit his friends in their homes.
rom the occasional letters to and from them (1832–35)
e can see something of what his life was and the im-
ression which his work was then making.

Brookfield writes from Sheffield:

You and Rob Montgomery are our only brewers now! À
ropos to the latter, Jingling James, his namesake, dined with
s last week. And now for a smack of Boswell.
Brookfield. Glass of wine after your fish? *Montgomery.*
'hank you, sir! *B.* Which vegetable, sir? *M.* A potato, if you
lease! *B.* Another, sir! *M.* That will do, I thank you.
. Talking of potatoes, sir, have you read Alfred Tennyson?
1. Only in the reviews yet, but there are two brothers, aren't
1ere? *B.* Both "rather pretty," but Alfred alone has been
xtracted at any length in the reviews. *M.* He has very
'ealthy and luxurious thought and great beauty of expression,
nd is *a poet.* But there is plenty of room for improvement, and
would have it so. Your trim correct *young* writers seldom
urn out well. A young poet should have a great deal which
e can afford to throw away as he gets older. Tennyson *can*
fford this. But I can say little of one of whom I have seen
o little.

I sent him copies of both you and Charles yesterday, and
1et him in the street this morning. He said he was going out
f town, but we would talk about you when he came back and
ead you. "I read," said he, "twelve of the sonnets last night,
'hich if I had not liked them better than other sonnets I could
ot have done. There are great outbreaks of poetry in them."
)mitting my own interjectional queries, etc., which leave to
emmy's remarks an over-pompous connectedness which they
ad not *vivâ voce*, I give you his words as nearly as I remember.
'hey are not important, but we generally wish to know what

is said of us, whether trivial or not.   At autopsychography I a
not good, if I had any idiopsychology to autopsychographize.
am just about as happy as a fish, neither excited by mirth, n
depressed by sadness.   The Clerk's[1] letter awoke me rather t
morning; if he be yet with you tell him it had been good servi
to have done so two months earlier.   Writing from Somers
where there is so much to prevent one from thinking of a
place else was certainly a meritorious exertion, and it has broug
my pardon.   My love to the wretch, and let him know he sh
expiate his neglect by silence on my part, until I know wheth
his address be your house.   Which information do thou gi
me in a day or two; and tell me all about Frederick a
Charles.   From the former I never could worm a letter yet, b
unless you can coax so much of him without, I shall perha
make one more effort shortly.   My kindest regards to all yo
family.

                      Ever, dearest Alfred, yours,

                              W. H. BROOKFIELD.

    P.S.   I wish very much you would make a sonnet for me
Hallam once did.   I could not value it more, and should n
less, than his.   It may be that I could not make a more borir
request.   But I will incur nine chances of vexing you a
thereby myself for the sake of the tenth of getting what I war

    At this time Tennant shot an arrow: "May yor
success in rhyming vary inversely as the number
letters you write!" and Spedding sent to Somersby h
Union speech on Liberty, which had gained renown i
the University.   The poem "You ask me, why, tho' ill
ease" was not, as is often stated, "an edition of th
speech versified."   My father said to me that he an
Spedding freely interchanged their political views, an
that therefore it was not unlikely that there should be
similarity of thought and language.   He did not thin

----

[1] Charles Turner.

at he had ever read the speech when he wrote the
oem.

He wrote to Spedding, begging him to "commend"
book shortly to be published by an old Louth tutor of
s, Mr Dale:

SOMERSBY,
February 9th (1833[1]?).

MY DEAR JAMES,

I seize upon a halfsheet, the blank half of
printed prospectus of a translation of the "Osman
ultan's campaigns in Western Asia, from Bayezyd
dirim to the death of Murad the Fourth (1389–1640),
om the German of Joseph Von Hammer, by Thomas
quila Dale[2]," indeed mine ancient tutor and paidagogue
times of yore. Which work commend everywhere,
or, I think, he is likely to do it well, and the book will
ontain a map of the countries from Sinope to Tiflis,
nd from Odana to Bagdad. Which map will be three
et and a half by two and a half, and you will grant that
ur literature is marvellously deficient in works of
Oriental History. And as I said before the man is mine
ncient and trusty paidagogue, and moreover a good
an, and one that is publishing at a loss, and one that has
ot two cloaks, wherefore it is reasonable that you should
ommend his book. For your letter I thank you heartily:
y thanks have lost half their natural vigour and beauty;
owever you must recollect that half your epistle was
someone else, indeed you confessed as much in your
. S. Are we not quits then, or in the language of Mrs
ennings, "Does not one shoulder of mutton drive out
nother?" You should not have written to me without
elling me somewhat that was interesting to myself

---

[1] The letters of this time are often undated.
[2] Published by William Straker, West Strand, 1835.

(always the first consideration!) or that bore some refe
ence to you and yours (always the second!), or lastl
without giving me some news of the great world, f
know you not I live so far apart from the bustle
life that news becomes interesting to me? I assur
you that we have a spare bed and the bed is not s
spare either, but a bed both plump and pulpy, and
for "your domeship[1]," whenever you can come and s
us. I express myself very clumsily, but being overawe
by the memory of your calm personal dignity and dom
and melted likewise with the recollection of the mar
intellectual evenings we have spent together in olde
days, while we sat smoking (for you know, James, yo
were ever fond of a pipe), — Speak for me, aposiopesi
or rather do not, for thou art an unhappy figure ar
born dumb and of no earthly use but to cut the thro
of a clause! ——

Write to me now and then, lest I perish. Whe
is Tennant? I have not yet answered him: how sha
I direct to him? You inquire after Charles. We s
little of him: I believe his spirits are pretty good.
Brooks at Cambridge? To him I owe a letter, ar
I mean to pay my debt.

Ever thine, A. T.

From Hon. Stephen Spring Rice.

CAMBRIDGE, November 27th, 1833.

DEAR ALFRED,

When I received your note some days back I was
first inclined to think it a pity that so much good abuse shou
be thrown away. Such a happy facility of assertion combin
with such apparent sincerity in the expression deserved a bett

---

[1] "Domeship" refers to Spedding's head.

e than being uselessly employed on one so steeled to abuse as
self. O king! I hope that you will be sufficiently occupied
the 28th with the "Morte d'Arthur." I send Keightley's
ry Legends and the other books, which it shall be my care to
patch to you to-morrow; Kemble (Anglo-Saxon *Lecturer* to
University) sends you to fill up your leisure hours a folio
xo-Grammaticus.......to be jammed into the bowl of your pipe.
tters are going on here much as usual. I have just written
Peacock's desire to Blakesley to tell him to come here and be
ecturer, a summons which there is no doubt he will obey.
rling is here still, and is to be at the yearly dinner [1] which
es place among "mankind," and which will come to pass
Monday next. Spedding, Alford, Donne, the two Farishes
l Pickering are expected; so much for eating. I have read
ilhelm Meister for the first time, with which I find as many
lts and beauties as every one does. What think you of that
υκύπικρον performance? there is another question to burthen
ir soul with unanswered. If your health is proposed I shall
pose it on the ground of your having been an unworthy
mber of the Society!! I hope that you will not be able to
cipher this scrawl, and so write to ask what it is about. I
ll send the books to-morrow; you ought to know when to
d for them.

Thine ever,

S. E. SPRING RICE.

From J. M. Kemble.

CAMBRIDGE, November, 1833.

DEAREST ALFRED,

I write you a line or two by this parcel to tell you
at I know is no news to you, that I love you heartily and
sh you were with us. There is little stirring here save that we
look with interest for news from you; I wish you could come
d dine with the Apostles on Monday next: I am not sure

---

[1] The "Apostles'" dinner.

that Donne and Trench will not be with us.   We are all prett
well, etc., looking out for more sprigs of the garden (or th
gardener's daughter, for I suppose she was not so imperfect
woman as not to be mother as well as maid and married)?   I
there no gardener's granddaughter ?   " Simeon Stylites " is sai
by the prophane, that is the mathematicians Spring Rice an
Heath, to be not "the watcher on the pillar to the end," but t
the nth; and I think this is an improvement; the more so as
shows your universality off, and marks that you have a touch c
mathematics in you: O Alfred! could you only have made th
height of the pillar a geometrical progression!   Give my affe
tionate remembrances to Charles and Fred.   Write to me, c
what is better yet, come to me.

Ever your most affectionate friend,

J. M. KEMBLE.

To J. M. Kemble.

1833.

MY DEAR JOHN,

I hope this will find you at Cambridg
J. Heath wrote to me that the books should have bee
returned by the 21st and I received his note on th
21st.   I know not what the fine is, and as to applyin
for any information even on Cambridge subjects t
Cambridge men I hold it vanity.   They are so smok
sotted.   Shamefully careless was it to have let thes
books lie for three weeks in Spring Rice's roor
Shameful not to have sent the second volume c
Keightley, and hateful the purloining of my album, whic
I *will* have found.   If the thief be not Douglas himse
it is that luxurious, eye-glass-wearing, unconscienc
fellow S. Rice, whom — fill up the chasm as you choos
if the book be returned, let it be with a blessin
Seriously speaking I am disgusted.   I am heartily gla

you have got *Beowulf* out.　Some thoughts, vague ones, I have, of coming up to Cambridge and attending your lectures next term, always provided they be gratis.　Good bye, dear old Jack.

Thine ever,

A. TENNYSON.

Be so good as to send me the " Morte d'Arthur " again.

P.S.　Perhaps you would use your paternal authority with the undergraduate whom you may suspect of being the thief.　Douglas himself ought not to pass unreproved. What a careless set you are!

From R. M. Milnes.

After an "Apostles'" dinner.

CAMBRIDGE, (*not dated*).

To ALFRED,
　　　　I feel I am getting cross, and as I wish to express in simple sincerity my hope that you will not long defer your promist visit to me, as soon as I return to Yorkshire, which will be in about a fortnight, I shall rock myself on the belief that you will bring or send me something comfortable.

Yours affectionately,

RICHARD M. MILNES.

P.S.　I suppose nobody writes to you because you never write to nobody.　John Heath and many others were full to the brim of enquiries after you, and if you had heard the cheer that followed the health of A. T., the Poet of the Apostles, at our dinner, if you had!

Milnes wrote to him later about his *Memorials of a tour in Greece* which he was about to publish, and received the following answer:

December 3rd, 1833.

MY DEAR MILNES,

A letter from you was like a message from the land of shadows.   It is so long since I have looked upon and conversed with you, that I will not deny but that you had withdrawn a little into the twilight.   Yet you do me a wrong in supposing that I have forgotten you.   I shall not easily forget you, for you have that about you which one remembers with pleasure.   I am rejoiced to hear that you intend to present us with your Grecian impressions.   Your gay and airy mind must have caught as many colours from the landskip you moved through as a flying soap-bubble — a comparison truly somewhat irreverent, yet I meant it not as such; though I care not if you take it in an evil sense, for is it not owed to you for your three years' silence to me whom you professed to love and care for?   And in the second place, for your expression, "clearing one's mind of Greek thoughts and Greek feelings to make way for something better."   It is a sad thing to have a dirty mind full of Greek thoughts and feelings.   What an Augean it must have been before the Greek thoughts got there!   To be done with this idle banter, I hope that in your book you have given us much glowing description and little mysticism.   I know that you can describe richly and vividly.   Give orders to Moxon, and he will take care that the volume is conveyed to me.

Believe me, dear Richard,

Ever thine, A. T.

Spedding writes to Thompson (1834) about William Wordsworth and Alfred Tennyson:

Wordsworth's eyes are better, but not well, nor ever likely to be. Reading inflames them and so does composing. I believe it was a series of Highland sonnets that brought on the last attack, so much worse than he had before. He read me several, that I had not seen nor heard before, many of them admirably good: also a long, romantic wizard and fairy poem, of the time of Merlin and king Arthur, very pretty but not of the first order [1]: but I should not have expected anything so good from him which was so much out of his beat. He has not advanced much in his knowledge of Alfred; but he is very modest in his refusal to praise, attributing his want of admiration to a deficiency in himself, whether from the stiffness of old age which cannot accommodate itself to a new style of beauty, or that the compass of his sympathies has been narrowed by flowing too long and strongly in one direction (N.B. He is not answerable for the English that I am writing). But he doubts not that Alfred's style has its own beauty, though he wants the faculty to enter fully into it, alleging as a parallel case the choruses in "Samson Agonistes," the measure of which he has never been able to enjoy, which comes to perhaps as high a compliment as a negative compliment can. He spoke so wisely and graciously that I had half a mind to try him with a poem or two, but that would have been more perhaps than he meant: and indeed it is always so pleasant to hear a distinguished man unaffectedly disclaiming the office of censor, that I think it fair to take him at his word. I have given a copy of Alfred's second volume to Hartley Coleridge, who, I trust, will make more of it. He had only seen it for a few minutes, and was greatly behind the age, though he admitted that A. T. was undoubtedly a man of genius, and was going to say something sharp about the *Quarterly* in a review of "The Doctor," which he was or is writing for *Blackwood*. I also sent him yesterday a copy of Charles Tennyson, accompanied with one of my most gentlemanly letters.

In June 1834 there was great distress at Somersby among the Tennysons, because the landlord threatened

[1] "The Egyptian Maid, or, The Romance of the Water Lily."

to cut down Enderby Wood and the Fairy Wood in Holywell, where, under the trees, the finest and earliest snowdrops blow. A hope was uttered that the fairies might haunt the desecrators. The Fairy Wood was left unscathed; and my father completed his poem, the "Sleeping Beauty"; and warmed to his work because there had been a favourable review of him lately published in far-off Calcutta.

In July he visited his friend Heath at Kitlands near Dorking, and thence journeyed with him to Worthing. When they arrived at the little seaside town on a beautiful still night, the sea was calm and golden, and there was a Cuyp-like picture of boys bathing in the glowing sunset, and of gray fishing-boats moored out in the distance. Heath tried to persuade my father to go to Brighton, for he said " The town is worth going to see, and moreover the coast is very fine, an infinitely finer place than Worthing." But my father refused, and insisted on returning to his work. He took Kitlands again by the way and had " lonely walks in dark valleys," and by the side of the streams which rise in Leith Hill. In his note-book on one page there is a map of Kitlands and of the surrounding country: on another there is an unpublished fragment on mine host of an ancient hostelry!

Mine Host. (*Unpublished.*)

Yon huddled cloud his motion shifts,
    Where, by the tavern in the dale,
The thirsty horseman, nodding, lifts
    The creaming horn of corny ale!

This tavern is their chief resort,
    For he, whose cellar is his pride,
Gives stouter ale and riper port
    Than any in the country-side.

Mine host is fat, and gray, and wise,
　He strokes his beard before he speaks;
And when he laughs, his little eyes
　Are swallow'd in his pamper'd cheeks.

He brims his beaker to the top,
　With jokes you never heard before,
And sometimes with a twinkling drop,
　" To those who will not taste it more ! "

The following letter reached him at Kitlands from his sister Emily:

SOMERSBY RECTORY, *July 12th*, 1834.

MY DEAREST ALFRED,

I certainly intend to go to Moulsey [1]. Would to God I could begin the journey immediately but it is not in my power. You will be sorry to hear that I have been considerably worse in health since your departure......And once or twice indeed I thought that the chilly hand of death was upon me : however I still exist, tho' reduced again to a great state of weakness. If possible I will journey southward soon. You know, Alfred, the great desire I have to become acquainted with the Hallam family, particularly with Ellen ; she will perhaps be the friend to remove in some degree the horrible feeling of desolation which is ever at my heart. I can no longer continue in this deepening grave of tears...depend upon it I will do all in my power to go to Moulsey. What is life to me ! if I die (which the Tennysons never do) the effort shall be made. The deep unaffected kindness of the Hallams made us all weep...How long do you think of remaining at Kitlands ? It would be pleasant to come while you are there. This however will scarcely be the case considering my journey will commence in about three weeks' time, if by any means I can conjure up resolution....Remember us all to " our Mr Heath " and his brother, and cannot you intimate to the sister how sorry we were not to have been able to avail ourselves, that is Mary and myself, of her kind invitation ? Take

[1] The Hallams' house at the time.

care of thyself that thou mayest return with new health and spirits is the ardent wish of

Thy very affectionate sister, EMILY TENNYSON.

His mother wrote him a letter at the same time:

What kind hearts the Hallams have! I hope poor Emily will be able to go to Moulsey. The pony got out of the stables and she went with one of the servants to catch it (as Harrison had gone to Horncastle), which made her very ill for some hours, but she is now as well as usual. I wish I could have induced her to begin her journey immediately, but she fancies she has something still to do before she can set out. The great lassitude she feels makes her fear she is unequal for such an exertion. I should have liked her so much to be introduced to the Hallams by you; she also considers this as very desirable. Charles is busy at present with his flock whom he is catechising, but I hope he will be able to travel with her in three weeks' time. I have found the books which Mr Heath mentions. Shall I send them by Mr Spedding? I have not heard whether or no he is at Tealby. I hope we shall see him.........Should you hear of anything likely to suit Arthur let me know. Remember me to all your friends.

His sister Mary adds a line entreating him

to lend an attentive ear to any music that may be sung, whether by way of chants, hymns, or songs, and to ascertain if Miss Heath will give the name of one or two that most affect his musical organs.

She goes on:

We were rather surprised to hear that the quaint creature Fred has set off to quaff companionless a "beaker full of the warm South," but I suppose a hot sun, south wind and cloudless sky (which constitute a humming day) and all of which are my aversion are all the world to him. And now I must bid thee adieu, hoping to see thee return as blithe as blithe can be. Remember me kindly to all at Kitlands.

When my father returned to Somersby, he had not only Emily to comfort, but also his friend Tennant, who consulted him about a great sorrow which had befallen him and craved for sympathy.

From R. J. Tennant (after a visit to Somersby).

LONDON UNIVERSITY, *August 4th*, 1834.

MY DEAR ALFRED,

I cannot delay writing to you, and cannot express my earnest gratitude for your friendship....The sight of Somersby, and *your* kindness have overcome the hard-hearted stubbornness that shut up all my feelings. Forgotten friendships have been revived, and correspondences been renewed that had long since dropped, and home feelings aroused that had slept a long sleep. ...Your very kind letter serves me every day instead of a companion; the only way in which it is in my power to show gratitude for the repeated and continued kindness I receive from you, is by following your counsel as far as I am able, and keeping my own mind in peace.

*   *   *   *   *   *

Ever your affectionate R. J. TENNANT.

What strikes me much in this early life of my father is not only his wide power of sympathy, but also his practical good sense, shown especially in the management of home and of family. For example, now that he knew Tennant wanted an interest in life, and was a good scholar, and that his brother Horatio never looked at a book (his time at Louth School being over), it occurred to him that Horatio might be placed at Blackheath under the care of Tennant, then a master in Blackheath School. The proposition was put before Tennant, with a plain statement, that, although Horatio had more than average power, he had grown rusty and his acquirements were less than they ought to be at his age.

If he went from the lonely haunts of Somersby to
Blackheath, it was hoped that it might be " of advantage
to him, for he would see men and he never seemed to
care much about boys; but his observations upon the
men he had seen had been very just and penetrating."
So off to Blackheath by my father's decision Horatio
accordingly went.

The elder brother Frederick was just then in the
midst of music at Milan.   He wrote a few lines urging
my father to publish in the spring.   But he would not and
could not; his health since Hallam's death had been
" variable, and his spirits indifferent."   The chief change
my father had from the monotony of Somersby life was
to drive over to Charles at Tealby, " for Lincolnshire,
a beautiful village."   Their grandfather George Tennyson,
who was beginning to show signs of his approaching end,
had left the Tennyson estate of Bayons Manor and
migrated to a small house on a sandy moor, because
his son Charles Tennyson d'Eyncourt pressed to be in-
stalled in the squiredom.   " One would have supposed that
such a thing," said Frederick, "would have been sufficient
to shake the last sands out of his glass."   However he
lived on his moor comfortably and peaceably: and there
died in 1835.

As for his private occupations, my father was
still reading his Racine, Molière, and Victor Hugo
among other foreign literature; and had also dipped into
Maurice's work *Eustace Conway*, which appears to have
been in great disfavour, and into *Arthur Coningsby* by
John Sterling, " a dreary book"; " 'Tis a pretty piece of
work, would 'twere done!" wrote one of the friends.   In
October 1834, he told Tennant he was busy copying out
his " Morte d'Arthur"; then he posted Spedding some
of the new poems for his opinion and Spedding replied as
follows:

MIRE HOUSE, KESWICK, *September* 19*th*, 1834.

MY DEAR ALFRED,

Such as it is, this letter will I expect come to you in an independent character, by the good aid of Philip van Artevelde (Henry Taylor), to whom I have a decent excuse for writing. I received by Douglas and John Heath divers of your compositions, albeit too few for my appetite: to wit, " Sir Galahad," which enjoys my unlimited admiration. The virgin knight is as beautiful a spirit as Don Quixote in a more beautiful kind, if that could be. Also " Nature, so far as in her lies," one of those pieces which nobody except yourself can write, and I think the most exquisite of an exquisite race. Of the rest I cannot find words to express what and how great is the glory. I have also the alterations of " Oh that 'twere possible," improvements I must admit, tho' I own I did not think that could have been: "Along this glimmering corridor" I had seen before, tho' not as it stands now: and

> Fair is her cottage in its place,
>   Where yon broad water sweetly, slowly glides.
> It *sees itself* from thatch to base
>   *Dream* in the sliding tides —[1]

It is perfectly true; how on earth did you find it out? Last and greatest (tho' not most perfect in its kind) I have received "The Thoughts of a Suicide[2]"; the design is so grand, and the moral, if there is one, so important that I trust you will not spare any elaboration of execution. At all events let me have the rest of it and I will tell you at large what I think; also as many more as you can supply; remembering that double letters or parcels will not distress my circumstances. Since I saw you, I have been cultivating my body to the entire exclusion of my soul, which some say is the better part. I have rolled great stones down mountains, but stirred no hidden principle of thought or deed. I have not done anything good; nor said any good thing. I have written no prose and small verse. Perhaps I was too ambitious, for I endeavoured at nothing lower than Milton's high-learned manner. I sent the small effort to

---

[1] " Requiescat."   [2] "The Two Voices."

Tennant, but that is no reason I should not send it to you, who will laugh at it less and understand it more. After all it is but a fragment of a simile!

> Liker that far significant coach that bears
> The windy artist from his central tower
> Whither the stars come clustering to suggest
> The universal secret, she far off
> Swims on Macadam, etc. etc.

The "far significant coach" is the Cambridge Telegraph, exquisitely described by its property of conveying Professor Airy from the Observatory.

I have not forgotten my promise to write to Charles, but alas how many things are sincerely promised which are nevertheless not faithfully performed.

Ever thine, JAMES SPEDDING.

To James Spedding.

1834.

MY DEAR JAMES,

It may be you have waited some time for a reply, but you haven't waited, so say no more. I have been out or you should have heard from me before this, so, I pray you, make not any little lapse of time that may possibly have slided away into the unrecoverable between the writing of your letter and the receipt of mine precedent for further delay in answering this, for your letters do my moral and intellectual man much good. I am going to town with Emily to-morrow and I expect a token from you on my return. You ask me what I have been doing: I have written several things since I saw you, some emulative of the " ἡδὺ καὶ βραχὺ καὶ μεγαλοπρεπὲς [1] " of Alcaeus, others of the " ἐκλογὴ τῶν ὀνομάτων καὶ τῆς συνθέσεως ἀκρίβεια " of Simonides, one or two epical, but you can scarcely expect me to write

[1] Dion. Hal. v. 421.

them out for you: for I can scarcely bring myself to write them out for myself, and do you think I love you better than myself? I had thought your Paley had taught you better. By a quaint coincidence I received your letter, directed (I suppose) by Philip van Artevelde, with Philip himself (not the man but the book), and I wish to tell you that I think him a noble fellow; I close with him in most that he says of modern poetry, tho' it may be that he does not take sufficiently into consideration the peculiar strength evolved by such writers as Byron and Shelley, who, however mistaken they may be, did yet give the world another heart and new pulses, and so are we kept going. Blessed be those that grease the wheels of the old world, insomuch as to move on is better than to stand still. But "Philip is a famous man" and makes me 'shamed of my own faults. À propos of faults I have corrected much of my last volume, and if you will send me your copy I would insert my corrections. Heaven knows what Douglas brought you: as for some stanzas about a "Corridor[1]," I know not whether there be such a poem; if there be it is very evident you have it not rightly.

I think on second thoughts tho' much against my will I will write thee out a poem, partly because Charles likes it, partly to give a local habitation on this paper and in your brain-piece to what else flies loosely thro' the wind of my own memory like a Sibyl's leaf. Voilà! be merciful.

(Here is copied out)

Love thou thy land with love far brought
etc.

It is said one cannot make a silken purse out of a sow's ear, yet have you made a Miltonian out of the Telegraph. "Cynthius aurem vellit": your far significant

<hr>

[1] See page 146, "The Little Maid."

coach drew the purse of my mouth like a sow's ear, it was not the wrong sow's ear to lay hold on, for I grinned. Kemble would have said "screamed" but I never scream, I leave that to your vivid men. I dare say you are right about the stanza in "Sir Galahad," who was intended for something of a male counterpart to St Agnes. I cannot write the "Suicide[1]" for you, 'tis too long, nor "Morte d'Arthur," which I myself think the best thing I have managed lately, for 'tis likewise too long; nor can I write any more at present, for it is much too late.

Angels guard thee, dear Jimmy,

Ever thine, A. T.

P.S. *Fragment on British Freedom.*

Grave mother of majestic works,
   From her isle-altar gazing down,
Who, God-like, grasps the triple forks,
   And, King-like, wears the crown:

Her open eyes desire the truth,
   The wisdom of a thousand years
Is in them. May perpetual youth
   Keep dry their light from tears!

1835.

From J. M. Heath (the first mention of "In Memoriam").

MY DEAR ALFRED,

I sent Julia, on hearing her fears, a copy of your two companions to "Fair Ship[2]," which have been a great delight to her, and she seems to have communicated them to some others. "The Xmas[2]" is indeed most beautiful, most touching, and the

---

[1] "Two Voices."
[2] The sections of "In Memoriam" which were first written; see page 109.

latter portions of the "Fair Ship" speak to *our* hearts indeed.
That last verse, is it not the expression of each voiceless thought?
But the enjoyment of these will sink deeper yet.   I seem sometimes as if I could not take in more than *one* thought at a time,
I mean such thoughts as the mind loves to dwell on, and feed
upon as it were, etc. etc. etc.   I am doubtful how far I am
justified in having sent you this, but I could not resist.   There
are many more people that take an interest in you than you are
aware of.   Your letter was balm to me, send me more such.   I
hope we shall see you in the summer.

Your very affectionate friend,

J. M. Heath.

P.S.   Thompson cometh, Spedding then, and if you ask
what doeth the Spedding, why marry it is this.   He bade me
say in answer to all such enquiries that he, the said Spedding,
was now waiting till he should grow wiser.

To James Spedding.

Somersby Rectory,
Feb. 15*th*, 1835.   *Midnight.*

My dear James,

I shall never more have such respect for
the lymphatic temperament.   A promise has been broken
by you, a promise generated betwixt two cigars at
Gliddon's, corroborated in Holborn, and repeated in the
archway of the Ball and Crown.   I did write to you and
you have thought me "worthy of sacred silence," but let
that pass.   I have heard much of your wisdom from
Thompson and others, and I confess that, despite of your
transgression, I have an inclination to come and see you,
and if possible to bring you back with me here.   Can I
hear that men are wise and not look them in the face?
I will come to you as Sheba came to Solomon.

She travell'd far from Indian streams,
And he a royal welcome made
In ample chambers overlaid
With Lebanonian cedar-beams.

I forget where I read this, and I do not know whether I shall have a royal welcome; wherefore be no more lymphatic but answer me, for I have sold my medal[1], and made money, and would visit you, and if you answer me not I shall —.

Very affectionately thine

As thou usest me, A. TENNYSON.

To James Spedding.

[*Undated.*]

MY DEAR JAMES,

I am sorry to disappoint myself (and perhaps in some slight measure you also) by postponing my visit. I am going to be from home for some time but not anywhere in your direction. The birds must sing and the furze bloom for you and Fitzgerald alone, " par nobile fratrum." I sincerely hope you have not put off any one else in the expectation of seeing me: tho' I did not state as much in my note, it was only when I first proposed it that I could have come to you. Fortune will perhaps bring me whiter days.

I know not whether you are aware that Charles has become an independent gentleman, living in a big house among chalky wolds at Caistor. His and my great uncle, Sam Turner, to whom he was heir, died some little time ago and left him property, but he complains

---

[1] This, the Chancellor's Medal for "Timbuctoo," was given back to him by his cousin Lewis Fytche in 1835.

that it is at present unavailable, talks of debts to be paid etc. etc.

John Heath writes me word that Mill is going to review me in a new Magazine, to be called the *London Review*, and favourably; but it is the last thing I wish for, and I would that you or some other who may be friends of Mill would hint as much to him. *I do not wish to be dragged forward again in any shape before the reading public at present*, particularly on the score of my old poems, most of which I have so corrected (particularly " Œnone") as to make them much less imperfect, which you who are a wise man would own if you had the corrections. I may very possibly send you these some time.

I am in much haste and obliged to conclude, but absent or present,

   Believe me

     Ever your true friend and admirer, A. T.

Unpublished Poems of this Period (about 1834).

Whispers.

'Tis not alone the warbling woods,
 The starr'd abysses of the sky,
The silent hills, the stormy floods,
 The green that fills the eye —
These only do not move the breast;
 Like some wise artist, Nature gives,
 Thro' all her works, to each that lives
A hint of somewhat unexprest.
Whate'er I see, where'er I move,
 These whispers rise, and fall away,
Something of pain — of bliss — of Love,
 But what, were hard to say.

The Little Maid.

Along this glimmering gallery
  A child she loved to play;
This chamber she was born in!   See,
  The cradle where she lay!

That little garden was her pride,
  With yellow groundsel grown!
Those holly-thickets only hide
  Her grave — a simple stone!

ALFRED TENNYSON

From a Sketch by J. Spedding, made at Mirehouse, April, 1835

CHAPTER VI.

VISITS TO THE LAKES AND ELSEWHERE.

THE "MORTE D'ARTHUR."

1836–37.

To a friend, Mrs Neville, who had lately lost her husband (written between 1830 and 1840, unpublished).

Woman of noble form and noble mind!
Whithersoever thro' the wilderness
Thou bearest from the threshold of thy friends
The sacred sorrows of as pure a heart
As e'er beat time to Nature, take with thee
Our warmest wishes, silent Guardians
But true till Death; and let them go in hope,
Like birds of passage, to return with thee
Some happy Summer morning, when the winds
Are fallen or changed; and, water'd by thy tears,
The two fair lilies growing at thy side
Have slowly prosper'd into stately flowers.

The only Tennyson who, in spite of their grand-father's wish "to make all the brothers parsons[1],"

[1] Alluded to in a letter from Frederick Tennyson to John Frere, April 18th, 1832. "After this long sit however I ought certainly to have some interesting passages to tongue. The foremost that presents itself is a crotchet

became a clergyman, was my uncle Charles. He had been ordained in 1835, and appointed to the curacy of Tealby, the village adjoining Bayons Manor. On May 24th, 1836, he married Louisa Sellwood, my mother's youngest sister.

My mother as a bridesmaid was taken into church by my father. They had rarely been in each other's company since their first meeting in 1830, when the Sellwoods had driven over one spring day from Horncastle, to call at Somersby Rectory. Arthur Hallam was then staying with the Tennysons; and asked Emily Sellwood to walk with him in the Fairy Wood. At a turn of the path they came upon my father, who, at sight of the slender, beautiful girl of seventeen in her simple gray dress, moving "like a light across those woodland ways," suddenly said to her: "Are you a Dryad or an Oread wandering here?" Now, as a bridesmaid, she seemed to him even lovelier:

"O happy bridesmaid, make a happy bride!"
And all at once a pleasant truth I learn'd,
For, while the tender service made thee weep,
I loved thee for the tear thou couldst not hide,
And prest thy hand, and knew the press return'd.

My uncle Arthur says: "It was then I first saw your mother, and she read to me Milton's 'Comus,' which I had not known before and which I have loved ever since."

My uncle Charles and his bride left for their honeymoon on the Rhine, a tour which was alluded to in "In Memoriam," section xcviii.:

of my grandfather's, that we are all to take orders, myself especially, which puts me into a demisemijoram and causes me to lose time. In order to fill up this note I must add that I expect to be ordained in June, without much reason, for hitherto I have made no kind of preparation, and a pretty parson I shall make I'm thinking..."

> You leave us: you will see the Rhine,
>   And those fair hills I sail'd below,
>   When I was there with him; and go
> By summer belts of wheat and vine
>
> To where he breathed his latest breath,
>   That City.

To *that* city my father would never go, and he gave me a most emphatic " no " when I once proposed a tour there with him.

Under the will of Sam Turner of Caistor, my uncle assumed the name of Turner, settling with his wife at the vicarage of Grasby near Caistor.

The painful parting from Somersby took place in 1837. The patron, Mr Burton, and the Incumbent had allowed the Tennysons to continue in the Rectory thus long. My grandmother had understood that her father-in-law would leave her the estate of Usselby, not far from the old home; but this was not to be. Not that my grandmother was destitute; she had her jointure; and my uncle Frederick had been left a property at Grimsby, and all his brothers and sisters had their small " portions." Under these circumstances the family decided that it was best for them to leave the county and live nearer London. My uncle Frederick was in Corfu, and remained there as long as his cousin George d'Eyncourt, who was secretary to Lord Nugent[1], kept his appointment. Afterwards he went to Italy and lived near Florence on the Fiesole Road, in a villa planned by Michael Angelo. There, so report ran, " in a large hall, Frederick Tennyson (who was a great lover of music) used to sit in the midst of his forty fiddlers." Thus, his two elder brothers being away, on my father devolved the care of the family and

---

[1] High Commissioner of the Ionian Islands.

of choosing a new home. The task was by no means easy. The mother "ruled by right of love," but knew nothing of the world. First of all a career had to be found for Horatio, the youngest brother, who wanted to be a soldier. The mother would not hear of this, and he was sent off to try his fortune in Tasmania. High Beech in Epping Forest was the home eventually selected; and there the Tennysons lived till 1840, when they went to Tunbridge Wells. Thence they moved in 1841 to Boxley near Maidstone.

Mrs Procter (Barry Cornwall's wife) once said to me:

I have known three great poets, Wordsworth, Browning and your father, and when they chose they could be more prosaic and practical than anybody on earth.

My father certainly proved his practical turn at this time in furnishing High Beech, for they say that he "did not even forget the kitchen utensils: and that throughout the furniture was pretty and inexpensive." The house and park were pleasant enough. There was a pond in the park on which in winter my father might be seen skating, sailing about on the ice in his long blue cloak.

He liked the nearness of London, whither he resorted to see his friends Spedding, Fitzgerald, Heath, Kemble, Tennant and others: but he writes that he could not often stay in town even for a night, his mother being in such a nervous state that he did not like to leave her. "The light of London flaring like a dreary dawn" was an especial admiration of his, during the evening journeys between London and High Beech. When he could leave home he would often visit in Lincolnshire, and stay both at his brother's vicarage and at the Sellwoods' in Horncastle. My mother and he were then quasi-engaged but were not able to marry owing to want of funds. They were not married until 1850, when his poems brought him a competency.

The study at High Beech, where he worked at his 1842 volume, was not the top attic, according to his usual preference, but a large room over the dining-room, with a bay window, red curtains, and a Clytie on a pedestal in the corner.

The "faithful Fitz[1]" writes that as early as 1835, when he met my father in the Lake Country, at the Speddings' (Mirehouse, by Bassenthwaite Lake), he saw what was to be part of this 1842 volume, the " Morte d'Arthur," " The Day-Dream," " The Lord of Burleigh," " Dora," and " The Gardener's Daughter." They were read out of a MS "in a little red book to him and Spedding of a night, 'when all the house was mute.'" Fitzgerald continues:

Spedding's father and mother were both alive ; and his father, who was of a practical turn, and had seen enough of poets in Shelley and Coleridge (perhaps in Wordsworth also), whom he remembered about the Lakes, rather resented our making so serious a business of verse-making, though he was so wise and charitable as to tolerate everything and everybody, except poetry and poets. He was jealous of his son James applying his great talents, which might have been turned to public and practical use, to such nonsense.

My father read them a great deal of Wordsworth, " the dear old fellow," as he called him. " The Yews of Borrowdale," " The Simplon Pass," the sonnet beginning " Two Voices," " The Solitary Reaper," " Peele Castle," the " Ode on Intimations of Immortality," " The Fountain," were among his favourites. Fitzgerald notes again:

I remember A. T. saying he remembered the time when he could see nothing in " Michael " which he now read us in admiration ; though he thought Wordsworth often clumsy

[1] Edward Fitzgerald.

and diffuse. There was no end of "This Thorn" in the piece that bears the name: "such hammering to set a scene for so small a drama."

My father also read Keats and Milton: saying that "Lycidas" was "a test of any reader's poetic instinct," and that "Keats, with his high spiritual vision, would have been, if he had lived, the greatest of us all (tho' his blank verse was poor), and that there is something magic and of the innermost soul of poetry in almost everything which he wrote." Then, perhaps in his weaker moments he used to think Shakespeare greater in his sonnets than in his plays. "But he soon returned to the thought which is indeed the thought of all the world. He would have seemed to me to be reverting for a moment to the great sorrow of his own mind; and in that peculiar phase of mind he found the sonnets a deeper expression of the never-to-be-forgotten love which he felt, more than any of the many moods of many minds which appear among Shakespeare's dramas [1]."

The three friends went to Ambleside together, but Spedding was obliged to leave Fitzgerald and my father there, and go home on business. Fitzgerald says:

Alfred Tennyson staid with me at Ambleside. I will say no more than that the more I see of him, the more cause I have to think him great. His little humours and grumpinesses were so droll that I was always laughing. I must, however, say further that I felt what Charles Lamb describes, a sense of depression at times from the overshadowing of a so much more lofty intellect than my own.

He adds a note about a row on Windermere with my father:

Resting on our oars one calm day on Windermere, whither we had gone for a week from dear Spedding's (Mirehouse), at the

[1] Jowett.

ALFRED TENNYSON

From a Sketch by Edward Fitzgerald, made at Mirehouse, 1835

end of May 1835, resting on our oars, and looking into the lake
quite unruffled and clear, Alfred quoted from the lines he had
lately read us from the MS of "Morte d'Arthur" about the lonely
lady of the lake and Excalibur —

> Nine years she wrought it, sitting in the deeps
> Upon the hidden bases of the hills.

"Not bad that, Fitz, is it[1]?"

This kind of remark he would make when reading
his own or others' poetry when he came to lines that
he particularly admired, from no vanity but from a pure
feeling of artistic pleasure. "The Lord of Burleigh"
was also read from MS and Fitz writes: "I remember
the author doubting if it were not too familiar, with its

> 'Let us see these handsome houses,'

etc. for public taste. 'But a sister,' A. T. said, 'had
liked it'; we never got it out of our heads from the
first hearing; and now is there a greater favourite where
English is spoken?" My father and Fitzgerald then
had a contest as to who could invent the weakest Words-
worthian line imaginable. Although Fitzgerald claimed
this line, my father declared that he had composed it —

> A Mr Wilkinson, a clergyman.

While my father was in the Lake Country he fell in
with Hartley Coleridge, who discussed Pindar with him,
calling Pindar "The Newmarket poet." "Hartley was
wonderfully eloquent," my father said, "and I suspect
resembled his father in that respect. I liked Hartley,
'Massa' Hartley. I remember that on one occasion
Hartley was asked to dine with the family of a stiff
Presbyterian clergyman, residing in the Lake district.
The party sat a long time in the drawing-room waiting
for dinner. Nobody talked. At last Hartley could

[1] E. F. G., MS Note.

stand it no longer, he jumped up from the sofa, kissed the clergyman's daughter, and bolted out of the house. He was very eccentric, a sun-faced little man. He once went a walking tour with some friends. They suddenly missed him, and could not find him anywhere, and did not see him again for six weeks, when he emerged from some inn. He was a loveable little fellow."

Sonnet to Alfred Tennyson, after meeting him for the first time.

Long have I known thee as thou art in song,
And long enjoyed the perfume that exhales
From thy pure soul, and odour sweet entails
And permanence on thoughts that float along
The stream of life, to join the passive throng
Of shades and echoes that are Memory's being;
Hearing, we hear not, and we see not, seeing,
If Passion, Fancy, Faith, move not among
The never-present moments of reflection.
Long have I viewed thee in the crystal sphere
Of verse, that like the Beryl makes appear
Visions of hope, begot of recollection.
Knowing thee now, a real earth-treading man,
Not less I love thee and no more I can.

HARTLEY COLERIDGE.

Of this visit Spedding wrote to Thompson:

Alfred left us about a week since, homeward bound, b meaning to touch at Brookfield's on his way. The weather h been much finer since he went; certainly, while he was here, o northern sun did not display himself to advantage. Neverthele I think he took in more pleasure and inspiration than any o would have supposed who did not know his almost perso dislike of the present, whatever it may be. Hartley Coleridge mightily taken with him; and after the fourth bottom of g deliberately thanked Heaven (under me, I believe, or me un Heaven, I forget which) for having brought them acquaint

aid Hartley was busy with an article on " Macbeth," to appear
he vegetable spirits permitting) in the next *Blackwood*. He
onfessed to a creed touching Destiny which was new to me;
enying Free-Will (if I understood him right) in toto; but at
ne same time maintaining that man is solely and entirely
nswerable for whatever evil he does, not merely that he is
o suffer for it but that he is *answerable* for it, which I do not.
could not get Alfred to Rydal Mount, he would and would
ot[1] (sulky one), although Wordsworth was hospitably minded
owards him; and would have been more so, had the state of his
nousehold permitted, which I am sorry to say is full of sickness.
..Alfred despises the Citation and Exam. of W. Shakespeare[2].

From Edward Fitzgerald.
(After the visit at the Speddings', Mirehouse.)

LONDON, *July 2nd*, 1835.

DEAR TENNYSON,

I suppose you have heard of the death of James
Spedding's sister-in-law: for my part I only came to know of it
a day or two ago: having till then lived out of communication
with any one who was likely to know of such things. After
leaving you at Ambleside, I stayed a fortnight at Manchester,
and then went to Warwick, where I lived a king for a month.
Warwickshire is a noble shire: and the Spring being so late, I
had the benefit of it through most of the month of June. I
sometimes wished for you, for I think you would have liked
it well....... I have heard you sometimes say that you are bound
by the want of such and such a sum, and I vow to the Lord that
I could not have a greater pleasure than transferring it to you on
such occasions; I should not dare to say such a thing to a small
man: but you are not a small man assuredly: and even if you
do not make use of my offer, you will not be offended but put it
to the right account. It is very difficult to persuade people
in this world that one can part with a banknote without a pang.
It is one of the most simple things I have ever done to talk thus
to you, I believe: but here is an end; and be charitable to me.

---

[1] He said that he did not wish to " obtrude himself on the great man at
Rydal."

[2] This refers to Landor's Essay so named.

Edgeworth[1] is......a wonderful man, but I shall be very seriou
with him lest he should wean you from indulging in quaint an
wonderful imaginations, and screw you up too tightly to mora
purpose.   If this sentence is unintelligible to you, I will consol
you with one that is as clear as daylight.   Your muse ha
penetrated into France : there has been a review of your poem
in a paper called the *Voleur*, in which you are called — gues
what! — " Jeune Enthousiaste de l'école gracieuse de *Thoma
Moore* " — this I think will make you laugh and is worth postage
Now I have told you all that I have in my head : it is fortunat
that the sheet of paper is just spacious enough for my ou
pourings.   The " Morte d'Arthur " has been much in my mouth
audibly : round Warwick.

I am yours very truly, E. Fitzgerald.

P. S.   When I was at Manchester, I bought a small *Dant*
for myself : and, liking it well, the same for you : for I had neve
seen the edition before, and I dare say you have not.   It i
small but very clearly printed : with little explanations at th
foot of each page, very welcome to me : the proper price was te
shillings but I only gave three.

Leigh Hunt writes :

4 Upper Cheyne Road, Chelsea.   1835.

The *Prince Arthur*[2] which I should have brought with me
I will send to-morrow or next day by a messenger ; and the res
shall reach you as quickly as may be.   Meanwhile may
venture to hope that my two non-appearances will not hinder m
from having another invitation some day, or yourself from
coming to see me ?   Carlyle expresses the pleasure he shoul
have in meeting you here some evening....... Shall I hope t
see you at Carlyle's lecture on Monday ?

---

[1] Nephew of Maria Edgeworth, the " Little Frank " of the *Parent*
Assistant.

[2] This copy of Malory I have still in my possession, a small book for th
pocket, published 1816, by Walker and Edwards, and much used by m
father.

From R. M. Milnes.

Your brief was infallibly pleasant. I shall wait for you in December. If you like, we will have "Freezetown" (Fryston) all to ourselves and you may smoke while I play the organ. Now be a good boy and do as you're told. Lord Northampton is getting up a charity book of poetry for the destitute family of a man of letters, born in the dead letter office, and he earnestly prays you to contribute not your mite but your might to it. I have half promised you will give him something pretty considerable, for the fault of the book will be that the contributions are not as great in dimension as in name. He has got original things of Wordsworth, Southey, Miss Bailey, R. M. M. etc. I will love you more and more therefore if you will send some jewels directed to the Marquis of Northampton, Castle Ashby, Northampton, as soon as convenient. Your "St Agnes[1]" looks sunny between Lord Londonderry and Lord W. Lennox, God her aid! I like Brookfield's sonnet eminently.......

Yours affectionately, R. M. MILNES.

P. S. You know your contribution will be at your disposal to do what you like with when the book is sold, i.e. in a year or so.

To R. M. Milnes[2].

December, 1836.

DEAR RICHARD,

As I live eight miles from my post-town and only correspond therewith about once a week, you must not wonder if this reaches you somewhat late. Your former brief I received, though some six days behind time, and stamped with the postmarks of every little market-town in the country, but I did not think it demanded an immediate answer, hence my silence.

[1] "St Agnes," published in the *Keepsake* (1837), pp. 247–48, edited by Lady Emmeline Stuart Wortley.
[2] Quoted in Wemyss Reid's *Life of Lord Houghton*.

That you had promised the Marquis I would write
for him something exceeding the average length of
" Annual compositions "; that you had promised him I
would write at all : I took this for one of those elegant
fictions with which you amuse your aunts of evenings,
before you get into the small hours when dreams are
true.   Three summers back, provoked by the incivility
of editors, I swore an oath that I would never again
have to do with their vapid books, and I brake it in the
sweet face of Heaven when I wrote for Lady What's-her-
name Wortley.   But then her sister wrote to Brookfield
and said she (Lady W.) was beautiful, so I could
not help it.   But whether the Marquis be beautiful
or not, I don't much mind; if he be, let him give God
thanks and make no boast.   To write for people with
prefixes to their names is to milk he-goats; there is
neither honour nor profit.   Up to this moment I have
not even seen *The Keepsake :* not that I care to see it,
for the want of civility decided me not to break mine
oath again for man nor woman, and how should such a
modest man as I see my small name in collocation with
the great ones of Southey, Wordsworth, R. M. M., etc.,
and not feel myself a barndoor fowl among peacocks?
Goodbye.

Believe me always thine,

A. T.

Milnes was angry at the refusal, and my father
answered him banteringly again:

Jan. 10*th,* 1837 [1].

Why what in the name of all the powers, my dear
Richard, makes you run me down in this fashion? Now
is my nose out of joint, now is my tail not only curled

---

[1] Quoted in Wemyss Reid's *Life of Lord Houghton.*

so tight as to lift me off my hind legs like Alfred Crow-
quill's poodle, but fairly between them. Many sticks
are broken about me. I am the ass in Homer. I am
blown. What has so jaundiced your good-natured eyes
as to make them mistake harmless banter for *insolent
irony:* harsh terms applicable only to —— who big as
he is, sits to all posterity astride upon the nipple of
literary dandyism, and "takes her milk for gall"? "Insolent irony" and "piscatory vanity," as if you had
been writing to St Anthony, who converted the soft
souls of salmon; but may St Anthony's fire consume
all misapprehension, the spleen-born mother of five-
fold more evil on our turnip-spheroid than is malice
aforethought.

Had I been writing to a nervous, morbidly-irritable
man, down in the world, stark-spoiled with the staggers
of a mis-managed imagination and quite opprest by
fortune and by the reviews, it is possible that I might
have halted to find expressions more suitable to his
case; but that you, who seem at least to take the world
as it comes, to doff it, and let it pass, that you, a man
every way prosperous and talented, should have taken
pet at my unhappy badinage made me lay down my
pipe and stare at the fire for ten minutes, till the stranger
fluttered up the chimney! You wish that I had never
written that passage. So do I, since it seems to have given
such offence. Perhaps you likewise found a stumbling-
block in the expression "vapid books," as the angry
inversion of four commas seems so intimate. But are
not *Annuals* vapid? Or could I *possibly* mean that what
you or Trench or De Vere chose to write therein must
be vapid? I thought you knew me better than even
to insinuate these things. Had I spoken the same
things to you laughingly in my chair, and with my own
emphasis, you would have seen what they really meant,
but coming to read them peradventure in a fit of indi-

gestion, or with a slight matutinal headache after your Apostolic symposium you subject them to such mis-interpretation as, if I had not sworn to be true friend to you till my latest death-ruckle, would have gone far to make me indignant. But least said soonest mended; which comes with peculiar grace from me after all this verbiage. You judge me rightly in supposing that I would not be backward in doing a really charitable deed. I will either bring or send you something for your *Annual.* It is very problematical whether I shall be able to come and see you as I proposed, so do not return earlier from your tour on my account; and if I come, I should only be able to stop a few days, for, as I and all my people are going to leave this place very shortly never to return, I have much upon my hands. But whether I see you or no,

Believe me always thine affectionately,

A. Tennyson.

I have spoken with Charles. He has promised to contribute to your *Annual*[1]. Frederick will, I daresay, follow his example. See now whether I am not doing my best for you, and whether you had any occasion to threaten me with that black "Anacaona[2]" and her cocoa-shod coves of niggers. I cannot have her strolling about the land in this way. It is neither good for her repu-tation nor mine. When is Lord Northampton's book to be published, and how long may I wait before I send anything by way of contribution?

"O that 'twere possible," afterwards the foundation of "Maud," was sent to Lord Northampton. Fitzgerald also notes that in this year my father wrote a poem on

---

[1] *The Tribute.*   [2] p. 56.

the Queen's accession, "of which the burden was ' Here's
a health to the Queen of the Isles.' " One stanza I have
heard my father repeat:

(*Unpublished.*)

That the voice of a satisfied people may keep
A sound in her ears like the sound of the deep,
Like the sound of the deep when the winds are asleep;
Here's a health to the Queen of the Isles.

A fragment of a poem about Mablethorpe he wrote
then, and gave in 1850 to the *Manchester Athenæum
Album:*

Mablethorpe.

Here often when a child I lay reclined:
   I took delight in this fair strand and free;
Here stood the infant Ilion of the mind,
   And here the Grecian ships all seem'd to be.
And here again I come, and only find
   The drain-cut level of the marshy lea,
Gray sand-banks, and pale sunsets, dreary wind,
   Dim shores, dense rains, and heavy-clouded sea.

The following sonnet was also preserved, which he
wrote at the end of 1837 or the beginning of 1838.

Sonnet. (*Unpublished.*)

To thee with whom my true affections dwell,
That I was harsh to thee, let no one know;
It were, O Heaven, a stranger tale to tell
Than if the vine had borne the bitter sloe.
Tho' I was harsh, my nature is not so:
A momentary cloud upon me fell:
My coldness was mistimed like summer-snow,
Cold words I spoke, yet loved thee warm and well.
Was I so harsh? Ah dear, it could not be.
Seem'd I so cold? what madness moved my blood

To make me thus belie my constant heart
That watch't with love thine earliest infancy,
Slow-ripening to the grace of womanhood,
Thro' every change that made thee what thou art?

It was in the latter part of 1837 or the beginning
of 1838 that he appears to have first become known in
America.   Professor Rolfe, who has kindly interested
himself in the matter, writes to me that R. W. Emerson
somehow made acquaintance with the 1830 and 1832
volumes about that time and delighted in lending them
to his friends.

Emerson suggested a reprint of the volumes, and
Longfellow, brother of the poet, showed Prof. Rolfe
a letter from Messrs C. C. Little & Co. of Boston addressed to the poet and dated April 27th, 1838, stating
that they intended to publish the reprint; but for some
reason this plan was not carried out.

During some months of 1837 my father was deeply
immersed in Pringle's *Travels*, and Lyell's *Geology:* and
from Pringle he got the image of the hungry lion used
in his simile in " Locksley Hall ":

Slowly comes a hungry people, as a lion creeping
    nigher,
Glares at one that nods and winks behind a slowly-
    dying fire.

He received the following letter from Leigh Hunt,
dated July 31st:

My dear Sir

        Many thanks for your kind letter.   It delights me to
think you should find anything to like in my verses, especially
" Paganini."   I always fancy that if ever I write anything worthy
of the name of poetry, it is when I write about music.   Your

communication alas! came too late for the book in question;
but the editor shall know of it, and will doubtless be gratified
that you have written.   I wish to send you a copy of the first
number of the new series of a magazine (the *Monthly Repository*)
of which I myself have become editor; but have not the face to
put you to the expense of receiving it at such a distance.   Will
you drop me a *word* to say whether I can forward it to any
intermediate place of communication, and will you at the same
time look into your desk and see if you can oblige me *with a
few verses and your name to them*, for my new adventure?   You
will see in some verses of mine, in the number I speak of, that I
have taken a liberty with said name, in speaking of a fair and no
unworthy imitator of yours, a Miss Barrett[1], who really has
sparks of the "faculty divine," but what I say, as you will easily
believe, has all due respect and admiration at the bottom of it;
as indeed every one knows who knows anything about you, or
about what I say of you.   Therefore do not hesitate to send me
a Sibylline leaf if you can, and be sure I ask it for your honour
and glory as well as my own advantage.   I want my magazine
to be such a magazine as was never seen before, every article
worth something, though *I* say it that shouldn't, and I believe
you know my gallant wish to be a sort of Robin Hood of an
editor, with not a man in my company that does not beat
his leader.   A sonnet — a fragment — anything will be welcome,
most especially if you put your name to it; and therefore for the
sake of poetry and my love of it, again I say, *oblige me if you
can;* and also send instantly because time begins to press.

Ever truly yours, Leigh Hunt.

P. S.   The magazine shall come away the instant I hear
from you where to send it.

In the following extract from an unpublished letter of
Leigh Hunt's to S. C. Hall an interesting criticism is
given of my father and his brothers Frederick and
Charles:

I do not know the birth, parentage and education of Tennyson.   I am pretty sure however that he is not long come from

---

[1] Afterwards Mrs Barrett Browning.

Trinity College, Cambridge, and I believe him to be nephew of Tennyson d'Eyncourt, the member for Lambeth, and son of a clergyman (the last however I know still more dimly than the rest). He has a brother (Charles) whom you ought to know, if you do not know him already.

I will send you his vol. of Sonnets to-morrow, together with the only vol. which I have at home (I find) of Alfred's. If it is not the one you want, I will see who has got the other. Charles is not equal to Alfred, but still partakes of the genuine faculty. He has a graceful luxury but combining less of the spiritual with it, which, I suppose, is the reason why he has become clergyman! I was fearful of what he would come to by certain misgivings in his poetry and a want of the active poetic faith.

There is also another brother, perhaps less inspired than Charles and who has only put forth a sonnet or so in public, Frederick, but still partaking of the right vein; and I think I have heard there are two of the sisters poetical! Here is a nest of nightingales for you! ***

The materials of the noblest poetry are abundant in him (Alfred), and we trust will not find any too weak corner in the sensitiveness of his nature to oppress him with their very exuberance.

Mr Gladstone, as is well-known, was Arthur Hallam's school friend, and on this account my father had a romantic desire to see him; and so called upon him about this time. I wrote to Mr Gladstone for some details of their early intercourse and he kindly replied:

10 DOWNING STREET, WHITEHALL, *October*, 1892.

MY DEAR HALLAM,

I am afraid that I shall have to adjourn any attempt to record my intercourse with your father until after my resignation of my present office, and even then I fear it might have to compete with the demands of my unfinished work.

I do not think that at any time during the last forty years I have ever found myself able when in office to give continuous thoughts on any subject outside public affairs. I will however allow myself the pleasure of referring to the first occasion on

which I saw him. It was about the year 1837, when he called
on me in Carlton Gardens. This was an unexpected honour,
for I had no other tie with him than having been in earlier life
the friend of his friend, to whom he afterwards erected so
splendid a literary monument. I cannot now remember particulars, but I still retain the liveliest impression of both the
freedom and kindness with which he conversed with me during
a long interview.

I am greatly pleased to hear that you have undertaken the
"Life," — doubtless an arduous task, but one to which your titles
are multiple as well as clear.

Believe me most sincerely yours,

W. E. GLADSTONE.

The years spent in strenuous labour and self-educa-
tion, and his engagement to Emily Sellwood, had again
braced my father for the struggle of life. The current of
his mind no longer ran constantly in the channel of mournful memories and melancholy forebodings. During this
autumn of 1838 he sought out "fresh woods and pastures
new" in Torquay, where he wrote his " Audley Court."
His friends had not yet grasped the change in the tenor
of his thoughts and still tried to cheer him. " Go and live
at Cambridge," said Venables. " You might perceive, if
you had any doubt about it, when you were last there
how great a pleasure it was to us all to see you, and
how little trouble to provide for you. Now you would
be more at home there than you were then after so long
an absence, and you can get books innumerable, and
smoke and talk, or not talk ; and make poetry and
commit it to surer records than the leaves of which so
many are lost. Do not continue to be so *careless of
fame, and of influence.*" Or again he advised my father
to go and work in Prague, where he would receive new
impressions and a new stimulus to the imagination.

" I almost wonder that you with *your love of music
and tobacco* do not go and live in some such place."

Yet my father paid heed to none of these invitations, but went his own way. He had abundant materials now for publication. He had made friends in London, and when he published again he would start as a well-known man, with ·the certainty that he could not be overlooked and that by many he would be appreciated. He was on the whole happy in his life, and looked forward to still better days.

> Hope, a poising eagle, burnt
> Above the unrisen morrow.

He must earn a livelihood on which to marry. He would arrange his material and give as perfect a volume as he could to the world. " I felt certain of one point then," he said: "if I meant to make any mark at all, it must be by shortness, for the men before me had been so diffuse, and most of the big things except ' King Arthur ' had been done." Another fact also began to dawn upon him, that if he never published again, even that which he had published " would be taken out of its napkin and would be given to him who had published ten volumes."

Alfred Tennyson.
Engraved by G. J. Stodart
from a daguerreotype. 1838.

CHAPTER VII.*

EXTRACTS FROM LETTERS TO EMILY SELLWOOD.

[These extracts, that follow chronological order, are made from a series of letters from my father to my mother extending over three years. I have not felt able to include the many passages which would show the intensity of feeling expressed in these letters, but have burnt the correspondence according to my father's directions.]

1838–1840.

1838. I saw from the high road thro' Hagworthingham the tops of the elms on the lawn at Somersby beginning to kindle into green. Do you remember sitting with me there on the iron garden chair one day when I had just come from London? It was earlier in the year than now. I have no reason for asking except that the morning three years back seems fresh and pleasant; and you were in a silk pelisse, and I think I read some book with you.

I dare not tell how high I rate humour, which is generally most fruitful in the highest and most solemn human spirits. Dante is full of it, Shakespeare, Cervantes, and almost all the greatest have been pregnant with this glorious power. You will find it even in the Gospel of Christ.

1839. "The stern daughter of the Voice of God," unclothed with the warmth of the feelings, is as impotent to convert as the old Stoicism.

Wells. The light of this world is too full of refractions for men ever to see one another in their true positions. The world is better than it is called, but wrong and foolish. The whole framework seems wrong, which in the end shall be found right.

Bitterness of any sort becomes not the sons of Adam, still less pride, for they are in that talk of theirs for the most part but as children babbling in the market-place.

High Beech. I have been at this place (High Beech in Epping Forest) all the year, with nothing but that muddy pond in prospect, and those two little sharp-barking dogs.

Perhaps I am coming to the Lincolnshire coast, but I scarcely know. The journey is so expensive and I am so poor.

The far future has been my world always.

I shall never see the Eternal City, nor that dome, the wonder of the world; I do not think I would live there if I could, and I have no money for touring.

Mablethorpe. I am not so able as in old years to commune *alone* with Nature. I am housed at Mr Wildman's, an old friend of mine in these parts: he and his wife are two perfectly honest Methodists. When

I came, I asked her after news, and she replied: "Why, Mr Tennyson, there's only one piece of news that I know, that Christ died for *all* men." And I said to her: "That is old news, and good news, and new news"; wherewith the good woman seemed satisfied. I was half-yesterday reading anecdotes of Methodist ministers, and liking to read them too...and of the teaching of Christ, that purest light of God.

That made me count the less of the sorrows when I caught a glimpse of the sorrowless Eternity.

A good woman is a wondrous creature, cleaving to the right and the good in all change; lovely in her youthful comeliness, lovely all her life long in comeliness of heart.

London. There is no one here but John Kemble with whom I dined twice; he is full of burning indignation against the Russian policy and what he calls the moral barbarism of France: likewise he is striving against what he calls the "mechanic influence of the age and its tendency to crush and overpower the spiritual in man," and indeed what matters it how much man knows and does if he keeps not a reverential looking upward? He is only the subtlest beast in the field.

We must bear or we must die. It is easier perhaps to die, but infinitely less noble. The immortality of man disdains and rejects the thought, the immortality of man to which the cycles and the æons are as hours and as days.

"Why has God created souls knowing they would sin and suffer?" a question unanswerable. Man is greater than all animals because he is capable of moral good and evil, tho' perhaps dogs and elephants, and some of the higher mammalia have a little of this capability. God might have made me a beast; but He thought good to give me power, to set Good and Evil before me that I might shape my own path. The happiness, resulting from this power well exercised, must in the end exceed the mere physical happiness of breathing, eating, and sleeping like an ox. Can we say that God prefers higher happiness in some to a lower happiness in all? It is a hard thing that if I sin and fail I should be sacrificed to the bliss of the Saints. Yet what reasonable creature, if he could have been askt beforehand, would not have said, "Give me the metaphysical power; let me be the lord of my decisions; leave physical quietude and dull pleasure to lower lives." All souls methinks would have answered thus, and so had men suffered by their own choice, as now by the necessity of being born what they are, but there is no answer to these questions except in a great *hope* of universal good: and even then one might ask, why has God made one to suffer more than another, why is it not meted equally to all? Let us be silent, for we know nothing of these things, and we trust there is One who knows all. God cannot be cruel. If he were, the heart could only find relief in the wildest blasphemies, which would cease to be blasphemies. God must be all powerful, else the soul could never deem Him worthy of her highest worship. Let us leave it therefore to God, as to the wisest. Who knows whether revelation be not itself a veil to hide the glory of that Love which we could not look upon without marring our sight, and our onward progress? If it were proclaimed as a truth "No man shall perish: all shall live, after a certain time shall have gone by, in bliss with God" such a truth might tell well with one or two lofty spirits, but would be the hindrance of the world.

High Beech, July 10th. What a thunderstorm we had the other night! I wonder whether it was so bad at H—. It lasted the whole night and part of the previous afternoon. Lewis Fytche, who was with us then, was looking out of my window about half-past 11 o'clock, and saw a large fireball come up the valley from Waltham till it seemed to come quite over our pond: it then according to his account grew on a sudden amazingly large. How large? I askt him: he said, "like a great balloon, and burst with an explosion like fifty batteries of cannon." I was so sorry not to have seen it, for it was a thing to remember; but I had just gone to my mother's room: she was grovelling on the floor in an extremity of fear when the clap came; upon which she cried out, "Oh! I will leave this house: the storms are very bad here," and F— who is here burst out weeping. Such a scene, almost ludicrous in its extremes.

I have been engaged in packing books. I have a good many. I am afraid I shall be obliged to sell them, for I really do not know where to stow them and the house at Tunbridge is too small, a mere mouse-trap.

All life is a school, a preparation, a purpose: nor can we pass current in a higher college, if we do not undergo the tedium of education in this lower one.

Annihilate within yourself these two dreams of Space and Time. To me often the far-off world seems nearer than the present, for in the present is always something unreal and indistinct, but the other seems a good solid planet, rolling round its green hills and paradises to the harmony of more steadfast laws. There steam up from about me mists of weakness, or sin, or despondency, and roll between me and the far planet, but it is there still.

Dim mystic sympathies with tree and hill reaching far back into childhood. A known landskip is to me an old friend, that continually talks to me of my own youth and half-forgotten things, and indeed does more for me than many an old friend that I know. An old park is my delight, and I could tumble about it for ever.

Sculpture is particularly good for the mind: there is a height and divine stillness about it which preaches peace to our stormy passions. Methinks that, in looking upon a great statue like the Theseus (maim'd and defaced as it is), one becomes as it were Godlike, to feel things in the Idea.

There is the glory of being loved, for so have we "laid great bases for Eternity."

Thro' darkness and storm and weariness of mind and of body is there built a passage for His created ones to the gates of light.

That world of perfect chrysolite, a pure and noble heart.

Aberystwith. I cannot say I have seen much worth
the trouble of the journey, always excepting the Welsh-
women's hats which look very comical to an English eye, being in truth men's hats, beavers, with the
brim a little broad, and tied under the chin with a
black ribband. Some faces look very pretty in them.
It is remarkable how fluently the little boys and girls
can speak Welsh, but I have seen no leeks yet, nor shot
any cheeses. This place, the Cambrian Brighton, pleases
me not,...a sea certainly to-day of a most lovely blue,
but with scarce a ripple. Anything more unlike the
old Homeric " much-sounding " sea I never saw. Yet
the bay is said to be tempestuous. O for a good
Mablethorpe breaker! I took up this morning an unhappy book of English verse by a Welshman, and read
therein that all which lies at present swampt fathom-
deep under the bay of Carnarvon was long ago in the
twilight of history a lovely lowland, rich in woods, thick
with cities. One wild night a drunken man, who was
a sort of clerk of the drains and sewers in his time,
opened the dam-gates and let in the sea, and Heaven
knows how many stately palaces have ever since been
filled with polyps and sea-tangle. How many gentlemen
discussing after-dinner politics of that day were surprised
by the precocious entrance of lobster before supper!
How many young ladies playing at their pre-historic
pianos ended some warm love-song of life in a quavering
swan-song of death!

———————

I require quiet, and myself to myself, more than any
man when I write.

———————

Barmouth. Barmouth is a good deal prettier place
than Aberystwith, a flat sand shore, a sea with breakers,
looking Mablethorpelike, and sand hills, and close behind

them huge crags and a long estuary with cloud-capt hills running up as far as Dolgelly, with Cader Idris on one side.

The most beautiful thing I saw this time in Wales — Llanberis lakes. (" Edwin Morris" was written there.)

In *letters*, words too often prove a bar of hindrance instead of a bond of union.

London. My friends have long since ceased to write, knowing me to be so irregular a correspondent. A brief and terse style suits the man, but the woman is well when she deals in words.

So much to do and so much to feel in parting from the house. Such a scene of sobbing and weeping was there on Monday morning among the servants at Beech Hill, and cottagers' daughters, as that cockney residence has seldom witnessed, perhaps never since its stones were cemented and trowelled. There were poor Milnes wringing her hands and howling, Ann Green swallowing her own tears with exclamations of such pathos as would have moved the heart of a whinstone, and other villagers all joining in the chorus, as if for some great public calamity. Finding we had human hearts, though we lived in a big house, they thought it all the harder that they were to lose us so soon. We drove the other day to see a Captain Pellew, who had drawn several sketches of the Himala mountains. Capt. P. said that in the early morning when all the hills were wrapt in blackness, the sharp snow-peaks shine out like rosy lamps hung high up in heaven, and apparently having no connection with

this earth. A man who had just visited the Alps was
with him there, and he said " the Himala was just twice
as magnificent."

Warwick. 1840. I got into the third class of
carriages in the train to Leicester. It is a carriage
entirely open, without seats, nothing but a rail or two
running across it, something like pens of cattle....Tho'
we did not move very quickly, yet it was liker flying than
anything else....I learnt some curious lessons in per-
spective, e.g. the two rails on the road were always
drawn together with the greatest rapidity. I stopt last
night at Leicester, and came on here (to Warwick) this
morning by a slow mail. On driving into Warwick, by
great chance I happened to have my glass in my eye
and perceived my friend, Edward Fitzgerald, taking
his walk on the pavé towards Leamington. I stopt
the coach, and he got up, and we drove to the George
here, and had an evening together. Kenilworth looked
grand in the distance. I think of going over with Fitz
to-morrow. Warwick not to be seen till Saturday as
the family are there. Almost afraid I cannot stop as
long, as it is very expensive being at an inn. Warwick
Castle looked grand and black among its woods from the
bridge this evening, a nightingale was singing, and rooks
were cawing, and there was moreover the noise of a
waterfall.

London. I went thro' Warwick Castle. It is certainly
a noble specimen of old feudalism, and the views from the
windows would be of unrivalled loveliness if the river
were only clearer. I and Fitzgerald also (climbed) up
Guy's tower, and had " large prospect " of the surrounding
country : but nothing pleased me better on the whole than
two paintings I saw in the castle : one, an Admiral van

Tromp by Rembrandt, the other Macchiavelli by Titian, both wonderful pictures, but the last grand beyond all words. We strayed about the gardens....Afterwards we went to Stratford and saw Shakespeare's monument. I should not think it can be a good likeness. That foolish fellow painted it white all over, and served poor Johnny Combe, who lies on a monument near, in the same way. I suppose from a notion that so painted they would look more classic, but the monuments all about were gilded and painted, and so were theirs. By which fancy of Malone we have in all probability lost the colour of Shakespeare's hair and eyes, which perhaps would do the world very little good to know, but would have been a little satis-faction to poor physiognomists like myself. We went also into the room where they say he was born. Every part of it is scribbled over with names. I was seized with a sort of enthusiasm, and wrote mine, tho' I was a little ashamed of it afterwards : yet the feeling was genuine at the time, and I did homage with the rest. I forgot Kenilworth. We tumbled about the ruins for three hours, but I was rather disappointed. I had expected to find them larger and more august. (My father came from Coventry to London and wrote "Godiva." He encloses "a virgin-ballad never yet written down," "Sweet Emma Morland " — " simple enough at any rate," he writes of it.)

After this date all correspondence between Alfred Tennyson and Emily Sellwood was forbidden ; since there seemed to be no prospect of their ever being married, owing to that unfortunately

> " Eternal want of pence
> Which vexes public men."

Letters to and from friends, 1840–1842

This letter to Tennant, without date or address, I have found among the letters received from his friends at this period:

To Reverend R. J. Tennant[1].

MY DEAR ROBERT,

It is about three centuries since I heard from you. I suppose you did not calculate on my sending you any answer, had you written. I think it just possible that I might: however my regard for you has thriven as lustily as ever in the silence, and I have had, now and then, certain memorials of you from different quarters: not indeed altogether grateful, for I am told that your wife has been ill almost the whole time you have been in Italy, also that you had lost great part of your library by shipwreck, also that you hated the land of the sun, where men, according to Alfieri, come up more vigorously than in other latitudes. Often have I intended to come over and pay you a visit, and as often my empty purse has gaped in my face and broken my dream of you and the Pitti palace together. Well, I suppose we shall meet somewhere or other on this side of the grave, and that our friendship at Cambridge has not been only to cease to be. How many puns have we made together! how many walks have we taken arm in arm in the dark streets of the old University and on the Trumpington

[1] Since Cambridge days Tennant had been in an unsettled frame of mind. He had been a frequenter of Coleridge's famous gatherings at Highgate, had been shaken in his belief and had hesitated, like many others then, to take orders. Subsequently he was ordained and became curate to J. C. Hare, at Hurstmonceux (a post afterwards filled by John Sterling), then he lived for several years as English chaplain at Florence, where he died.

road! and how you used to scepticize till we both ran away!

My people are located at a place which is my abomination, viz. Tunbridge Wells in this county; they moved thither from Essex by the advice of a London physician, who said it was the only place in England for the Tennyson constitution: the sequel is that they are half killed by the tenuity of the atmosphere and the presence of steel more or less in earth, air and water. I have sometimes tried to persuade them to live abroad but without effect, and I dare say you in your exile agree with them that there is no place like an English home.

I came over to this place about a fortnight back.

A. T.

To Edward Fitzgerald.

MABLETHORPE, ALFORD, 1841.

DEAR OLD FITZ,

Not on the Western, on the Eastern coast. Mablethorpe near Alford in the fat shire of Lincoln is the place where I am. I walk about the coast, and have it all to myself, sand and sea. You bore me about my book; so does a letter just received from America, threatening, tho' in the civilest terms, that, if I will not publish in England, they will do it for me in that land of freemen. I *may* curse, knowing what they will bring forth. But I don't care. I am in a great haste writing for the muffin-man, my only communication with the world, who comes once a week bringing the produce of his art, also what letters may be stagnating at the Alford post, waits five minutes and then returns.

Always yours, A. T.

To Edmund Lushington.

OTLEY, *September* 19*th*, 1841.

MY DEAR EDMUND,

This is to let you know that I am at present in the classic neighbourhood of Bolton Abbey whither I was led the other day by some half-remembrance of a note to one of Wordsworth's poems, which told with me (to speak the truth) more than the poem itself: said Wordsworth having stated, (as far as I recollect) that everything which the eyes of man could desire in a land-skip was to be found at and about the Abbey aforesaid. I, coming with an imagination inflamed, and working upon this passage, was at first disappointed, but yesterday I took a walk of some seven or eight or, by our Lady, nine miles, to left and right of the Wharfe, and you may conjecture that no ordinary charms of nature could get nine miles walk out of legs (*at present*) more familiar with armchair and settle than rock and greensward, so that I suppose there is something in what Wordsworth asserts, and that something will probably keep me here some time, and whether I shall see you or no before you return to Glasgow is thereby rendered uncertain. I suppose there is no chance of your coming here, is there? that would be a Godsend I have no right to expect, but Harry at High Beech was a Godsend I did not expect. Poor fellow, he was very nervous, very uncomfortable too about his Italian journey, but in that respect I found it hard to sympathize with him.

Ever yours, A. TENNYSON.

To Edmund Lushington.

BOXLEY, *Early in* 1842.

DEAR EDMUND,

I was very glad to hear of the reconvalescence of your " Geschwister " for I had some fancy (as I told you) that all was not right. Your lines[1] I liked. Some doubt I had about " πολυπίδακε " but Venables set me right: not that I believed *you* could be out of your Greek, but the " πολυπίδακος Ἴδης " ran in my head. "Νασμῷ ἐν ἀμφιρύτῳ " is a wrong translation, the rest good. I have no news. I have not yet taken my book to Moxon. Spedding's going to America has a little disheartened me, for some fop will get the start of him in the *Ed. Review* where he promised to put an article and I have had abuse enough. Moreover Spedding was just the man to do it, both as knowing me, and writing from clear conviction. However I intend to get it out shortly, but I cannot say I have been what you professors call " working " at it, that indeed is not my way. I take my pipe and the muse descends in a fume, not like your modern ladies who shriek at a pipe as if they saw a " splacknuck ": do you know what a splacknuck is[2]? I have been once into your grounds, the house looked very unhappy. Charles and I went together: he admired the place much, tho' everything was deep in snow.

Yours ever, A. TENNYSON.

---

[1] A translation of " Œnone " in Greek hexameters.

[2] " His Majesty, a Prince of much Gravity, and austere Countenance, not well observing my shape at first view, asked the Queen after a cold manner, how long it was since she grew fond of a *Splacknuck* ? for such it seems he took me to be, as I lay upon my breast on her Majesty's Right hand." Swift's *Voyage to Brobdingnag*.

From John Sterling.

SOUTH PLACE, KNIGHTSBRIDGE, *Oct. 26th.*

MY DEAR TENNYSON,

Your note afflicted us, and others too. I have long wished to be allowed to see something of you, and now that you would be kind enough to permit it we are both invalids, and I in London only for two or three days. For my part however I will not give the thing up and shall either call on you or write to you again in a day or two. Carlyle was here yesterday evening, growled at having missed you, and said more in your praise than in any one's except Cromwell and an American backwoodsman who has killed thirty or forty people with a bowie knife and since run away to Texas.

I learn from Americans who were also here that a certain Wheeler (known to you I think by name) is dead: whether he has carried your dollars with him and paid them by mistake to Beelzebub or Orpheus I know not.

For the moment farewell.

Believe me truly yours, JOHN STERLING [1].

---

[1] Before his death at Ventnor in September, 1844, Sterling reviewed the 1842 volume favourably in the *Quarterly*, classing my father's poems "among the richest of our recent literature."

CHAPTER VIII.

LONDON LIFE AND THE 1842 VOLUMES.

It is long since we have had so good a lyrist; it will be long before we have his superior. "Godiva" is a noble poem that will tell the legend a thousand years... "Locksley Hall" and "The Two Voices" are meditative poems, which were slowly written to be slowly read. "The Talking Oak," though a little hurt by its wit and ingenuity, is beautiful, and the most poetic of the volume. "Ulysses" belongs to a high class of poetry, destined to be the highest, and to be more cultivated in the next generation. "Œnone" was a sketch of the same kind.

EMERSON.

Tunbridge Wells was not liked by my grandmother, so she and the family migrated to Boxley not far from Maidstone in order to be near the Lushingtons at Park House; Edmund Lushington, the accomplished Greek and German scholar and Egyptologist, having married Miss Cecilia Tennyson. The park round the house is described in the prologue to "The Princess." My father had a particularly high regard not only for Edmund and Franklin Lushington but also for their brother Harry, and would say, "Others may find faults in a poem, but Harry finds *the* fault and tells you how to mend it." He is one of the three [1] friends mentioned in the poem "In the Garden at Swainston." His memory was surprising and his criticism always of the finest. "His taste was perhaps rendered more exquisite by his personal anxiety for the perfection and success of works which could scarce have interested him more if they had been his own composition." At

---

[1] Arthur Hallam, Henry Lushington, Sir John Simeon.

Park House my father met many friends, old and new; Monckton Milnes, Venables, Chapman, Savile Morton, Lear, and William Thomson (now Lord Kelvin). With one of these friends, or more generally by himself, he would take long walks either on the Pilgrim's Road, or to some one of the picturesque villages in the neighbourhood.

From time to time he stayed in town and mingled with all sorts and conditions of men. He always delighted in the "central roar" of London. Whenever he and I went to London, one of the first things we did was to walk to the Strand and Fleet Street. "Instead of the stuccoed houses in the West End, this is the place where I should like to live," he would say. He was also fond of looking at London from the bridges over the Thames, and of going into St Paul's, and into the Abbey. One day in 1842 Fitzgerald records a visit to St Paul's with him when he said, "Merely as an inclosed space in a huge city this is very fine," and when they got out into the open, in the midst of the "central roar," "This is the mind; that is a mood of it."

He writes, "My lodgings are the last house, Norfolk Street, Strand, at the bottom of the street on the left; the name is Edwards which you will see projecting from the door on a brass plate." Generally he would stay at the Temple or in Lincoln's Inn Fields; dining with his friends at The Cock, and other taverns[1].

[1] Savile Morton, for some years the brilliant Paris correspondent of the *Daily News*, wrote of one of these dinners: "Thackeray gave the dinner — Tennyson, Forster (the literary critic of the *Examiner*), Emerson Tennant, M.P., Crowe an author, and Maclise were the party. Lever, the ballad and Irish story man, came at the beginning, and told Alfred he was greatly delighted to meet a *brother-poet*, the cool impudence of which amused the party greatly, at Lever's expense....The largeness of Alfred's proportions, both physical and poetical, were universally the theme of admiration. Maclise admired him excessively, and fell quite in love with him." (*From an unpublished letter (undated) to Mary Brotherton, author of "Rosemary for Remembrance" and "Old Acquaintance."*)

A perfect dinner was a beef-steak, a potato, a cut of cheese, a pint of port, and afterwards a pipe (never a cigar). When joked with by his friends about his liking for cold salt beef and new potatoes, he would answer humorously, "All fine-natured men know what is good to eat." Very genial evenings they were, with plenty of anecdote and wit and "thrust and parry of bright monostich." At good sayings my father would sit laughing away, "laughter often interrupted by fits of sadness." He would take off the voices and expressions of well-known public characters, protesting that "The oddities and angularities of *great* men should never be hawked about," or he would dramatically give parts of Shakespeare or of Molière, or "enact with grim humour Milton's 'So started up in his foul shape the fiend,' from the crouching of the toad to the explosion[1].

He used also to do the sun coming out from a cloud, and retiring into one again, with a gradual opening and shutting of the eyes, and with a great fluffing up of his hair into full wig and elevation of cravat and collar; George IV. in as comical and wonderful a way. 'The plump head-waiter of The Cock,' by Temple Bar, famous for chop and porter, was rather offended when told of the poem ('Will Waterproof'). 'Had Mr Tennyson dined oftener there, he would not have minded it so much,' he said. I think A. T.'s chief dinner resort in these ante-laureate days was Bertolini's at the Newton's Head, close to Leicester Square. We sometimes called it Dirtolini's, but not seriously; for the place was clean as well as very cheap and the cookery good for the price. Bertolini himself, who came to take the money at the end of the feast, was a grave and polite man. He retired with a fortune I think[2]."

My father was a member of the Sterling Club, a literary Society of those days named in Sterling's honour, where he met many of his old fellow "Apostles." He

[1] "Depend upon it," my father said, "Milton shot up into some grim Archangel, Fitz." (1842.)

[2] MS Note, Edward Fitzgerald.

also often saw Carlyle, Rogers, "Barry Cornwall," Thackeray, Dickens, Forster, Savage Landor, Maclise, Leigh Hunt, and Tom Campbell. I have heard that he always showed an eager interest in the events and in the great scientific discoveries and economic inventions and improvements of the time[1]. His talk largely touched upon politics[2], philosophy and theology, and the new speculations rife on every side. Upon the projects of reform, or the great movements of philanthropy he reflected much.

> Yearning for the large excitement that the coming
>   years would yield,
> Eager-hearted as a boy when first he leaves his
>   father's field.

The Chartist and Socialist agitations were then alarming the country. My father thought they should be met not by universal imprisonment and repression, but by a widespread National education, by more of a patriotic and less of a party spirit in the Press, by partial adoption of Free Trade principles, and by an increased energy and sympathy among those who belonged to the different forms of Christianity. He was sometimes described as advancing opposite opinions at different times. This was because from his firm sense of justice he had a dramatic way of representing an opinion adverse to his own in a favourable light, in order that he might give it the most generous interpretation possible.

[1] Alluding to one such improvement he said: "Before the Penny Post a wretched review from the Continent followed me all over England, and I had to pay one pound eight shillings for it."

[2] I have heard him speak of his feelings at that time about the Afghan campaign: he thought that we ought to stand no trifling in Afghanistan; and that the English Cabinet was neglectful of the advice of Polonius: "Beware of entrance to a quarrel, but, being in, bear't that the opposer may beware of thee." Speaking of Canadian affairs, he gloried in the work done by Lord Durham and in the form of Colonial Government initiated by him in Canada.

These indeed were years rich in social and political movement: it may be enough to name Bright and Cobden, Carlyle, Thackeray, and Dickens, each with his exposure of abuses, or efforts for amendment. The atmosphere of the time inspired such lines as the following:

Ah, tho' the times when some new thought can bud
Are but as poets' seasons when they flower,
Yet seas that daily gain upon the shore
Have ebb and flow conditioning their march,
And slow and sure comes up the golden year,
When wealth no more shall rest in mounded heaps,
But smit with freer light shall slowly melt
In many streams to fatten lower lands,
And light shall spread, and man be liker man
Thro' all the season of the golden year.

*   *   *   *   *   *   *

Fly, happy happy sails, and bear the Press;
Fly happy with the mission of the Cross;
Knit land to land, and blowing havenward
With silks, and fruits, and spices, clear of toll,
Enrich the markets of the golden year[1].

Theology, always a deep interest to him, shared in this advance. The Oxford movement had been begun by a band of saintly and devoted churchmen, and the Vice-Chancellor of Oxford with the heads of houses had already censured the author of *Tract No. XC*[2]. Meanwhile Maurice, Kingsley and the Cambridge men were striving to make thought more tolerant, and to impress all men with a sense of brotherhood. Both efforts in a few years effected a mighty change in

[1] "The Golden Year" was first published in 1846 in the *Poems* (4th ed.).
[2] Published February 1841.

the spirit of the National Church by broadening its
borders and deepening its spirituality.

The biographies of friends and acquaintances, recently
published, are full of allusions to my father at this period.
Perhaps the most life-like portrait[1] is that drawn by
Carlyle for Emerson in America.

Alfred is one of the few British and foreign figures (a not
increasing number I think) who are and remain beautiful to
me, a true human soul, or some authentic approximation thereto,
to whom your own soul can say, "Brother!" However, I doubt
he will not come [to see me]; he often skips me, in these brief
visits to town; skips everybody, indeed; being a man solitary and
sad, as certain men are, dwelling in an element of gloom, carrying a bit of Chaos about him, in short, which he is manufacturing
into Cosmos......He had his breeding at Cambridge, as if for
the Law or Church; being master of a small annuity on his
father's decease, he preferred clubbing with his mother and
some sisters, to live unpromoted and write Poems. In this way
he lives still, now here, now there; the family always within
reach of London, never in it; he himself making rare and brief
visits, lodging in some old comrade's rooms. I think he must
be under forty, not much under it. One of the finest looking
men in the world. A great shock of rough dusky dark hair;
bright, laughing, hazel eyes; massive aquiline face, most massive
yet most delicate; of sallow brown complexion, almost Indian
looking, clothes cynically loose, free-and-easy, smokes infinite
tobacco. His voice is musical, metallic, fit for loud laughter
and piercing wail, and all that may lie between; speech and
speculation free and plenteous; I do not meet in these late

[1] On Sept. 5th, 1840, Carlyle had sketched another portrait of my father
for his brother John: "Some weeks ago, one night, the poet Tennyson and
Matthew Allen were discovered here sitting smoking in the garden. Tennyson had been here before, but was still new to Jane, — who was alone for
the first hour or two of it. A fine, large-featured, dim-eyed, bronze-coloured,
shaggy-headed man is Alfred; dusty, smoky, free and easy; who swims,
outwardly and inwardly, with great composure in an articulate element as
of tranquil chaos and tobacco-smoke; great now and then when he does
emerge; a most restful, brotherly, solid-hearted man. Allen looked considerably older; speculative, hopeful, earnest-frothy as from the beginning."
(See for Allen, p. 220.)

decades such company over a pipe! we shall see what he will grow to.

Mrs. Carlyle also gives a characteristic portrait:

Three of the autographs which I send you to-day are first-rate. A Yankee would almost give a dollar apiece for them. Entire characteristic letters from Pickwick, Lytton Bulwer and Alfred Tennyson; the last the greatest genius of the three, though the vulgar public have not as yet recognized him as such. Get his poems if you can, and read the "Ulysses," "Dora," the "Vision of Sin," and you will find that we do not overrate him. Besides, he is a very handsome man, and a noble-hearted one, with something of the gypsy in his appearance, which for me is perfectly charming. Babbie never saw him, unfortunately, or perhaps I should say fortunately, for she must have fallen in love with him on the spot, unless she be made absolutely of ice; and then men of genius have never anything to keep wives upon.

Carlyle did not, I believe, become intimate with my father until after 1842, "being naturally prejudiced against one whom everyone was praising, and praising for a sort of poetry which he despised. But directly he saw and heard the Man, he knew there was a man to deal with and took pains to cultivate him; assiduous in exhorting him to leave Verse and Rhyme, and to apply his genius to Prose[1]." Indeed he told him then that he was "a life-guardsman spoilt by making poetry."

When the 1842 volumes were published the literary world in London accepted them at once, and Milnes[2] and Sterling led the chorus of favourable reviews.

My father's comprehension of human life had grown: and the new poems dealt with an extraordinarily wide range of subjects, chivalry, duty, reverence, self-control, human passion, human love, the love of country, science,

[1] MS Note, Edward Fitzgerald.
[2] *Westminster Review*, October, 1842.

philosophy, simple faith and the many complex moods of the religious nature; whilst they were free from the brooding self-absorption into which modern poetry is liable to lapse, and from what Arthur Hallam called "the habit of seeking relief in idiosyncrasies."

It was the heart of England even more than her imagination that he made his own. It was the Humanities and the truths underlying them that he sang, and he so sang them that any deep-hearted reader was made to feel through his far-reaching thought that those Humanities are spiritual things, and that to touch them is to touch the garment of the Divine. Those who confer so deep a benefit cannot but be remembered. The Heroic is not greatly appreciated in these days; but on this occasion the challenge met with a response[1].

With a selection from the early poems, some of them almost rewritten, appeared a number of English Idyls and Eclogues, pictures of English home and country life, quite original in their form. Upon the sacredness of home life he would maintain that the stability and greatness of a nation largely depend; and one of the secrets of his power over mankind was his true joy in the family duties and affections. Among these new poems were " The Gardener's Daughter," " Dora," " Audley Court," " Walking to the Mail," " The Talking Oak," " Locksley Hall," " Godiva," " Edward Gray," " Lady Clare," " The Lord of Burleigh," " Will Waterproof," and the conclusion of " The May Queen." Then there were the more general poems, " Morte d'Arthur," " St Simeon Stylites," " Love and Duty," " Ulysses," " The Two Voices," " The Day-Dream[2]," " Amphion," " St Agnes' Eve," "Sir Galahad," " Sir

---

[1] Aubrey de Vere (in letter to me).

[2] The Prologue and Epilogue were added after 1835, when we first heard it in Cumberland; I suppose for the same reason that caused the Prologue of the " Morte d'Arthur," giving a reason for telling an old-world tale. MS Note, E. F. G.

In 1842 he had eight of the blank verse poems printed for his private use,

Launcelot and Queen Guinevere," " A Farewell," " The Beggar Maid," " The Vision of Sin," " Move eastward, happy Earth," " Break, Break " (made in a Lincolnshire lane at 5 o'clock in the morning between blossoming hedges), " The Poet's Song," and his three political poems.

On the other side of the Atlantic these volumes were also welcomed; Hawthorne, Margaret Fuller, Emerson, Edgar Allan Poe were notably enthusiastic.

The popular German poet Ferdinand Freiligrath writes to Mary Howitt from Frankfort, Oct. 1842 : " Tennyson is indeed a true poet, though perhaps sometimes a little too transcendental. ' Mariana in the Moated Grange,' and some other of his poems are superb; and breathe such a sweet and dreamy melancholy that I cannot cease to read and admire them[1]."

The most remarkable review of these volumes was by Spedding in the *Edinburgh* for April 1843 (reprinted in *Reviews and Discussions*), from which I subjoin extracts, as these give accurately the growth of his friend's mind.

The decade during which Mr Tennyson has remained silent has wrought a great improvement. The handling in his later pieces is much lighter and freer; the interest deeper and purer; there is more humanity with less image and drapery; a closer adherence to truth; a greater reliance for effect upon the simplicity of Nature. Moral and spiritual traits of character are more dwelt upon, in place of external scenery and circumstance. He addresses himself more to the heart and less to the ear and eye. This change which is felt in its results throughout the second volume, may in the latter half of the first be traced in

because he always liked to see his poems in print some months and sometimes some years before publication, " for," as he said, " poetry looks better, more convincing, in print." This little volume was entitled *Morte d'Arthur ; Dora, and other Idyls.*

[2] From private letter lent by Miss Howitt.

its process. The poems originally published in 1832 are many
of them largely altered ; generally with great judgment, and
always with a view to strip off redundancies, to make the expression simpler and clearer, to substitute thought for imagery
and substance for shadow. "The Lady of Shalott," for instance,
is stripped of all her finery ; her pearl garland, her velvet bed,
her royal apparel and her "blinding diamond bright," are all
gone ; and certainly in the simple white robe which she now
wears, her beauty shows to much greater advantage.

"The Miller's Daughter," again, is much enriched by the
introduction of the mother of the lover ; and the following
beautiful stanzas (which many people, however, will be ill
satisfied to miss) are displaced to make room for beauty of a
much higher order :

> Remember you the clear moonlight
>   That whiten'd all the eastern ridge,
> When o'er the water dancing white
>   I stepp'd upon the old mill bridge ?
> I heard you whisper from above,
>   A lute-toned whisper, "I am here!"
> I murmur'd "Speak again, my love,
>   The stream is loud : I cannot hear!"
>
> I heard, as I have seem'd to hear,
>   When all the under-air was still,
> The low voice of the glad New Year
>   Call to the freshly-flower'd hill.
> I heard, as I have often heard,
>   The nightingale in leafy woods
> Call to its mate when nothing stirr'd
>   To left or right but falling floods.

These, we observe, are away ; and the following graceful and
tender picture, full of the spirit of English rural life, appears in
their place. (The late squire's son, we should premise, is bent
on marrying the daughter of the wealthy miller :)

> And slowly was my mother brought
>   To yield consent to my desire :
>   *   *   *   *   *   *

> And rose, and, with a silent grace
> Approaching, press'd you heart to heart.
>
> Vol. i. p. 109.

Mr Spedding goes on to say that in the song of "The Lotos-Eaters," which "hardly admitted of improvement," my father had added "some touches of deeper significance, indicating the first effects of the physical disease upon the moral and intellectual nature:

> Dear is the memory of our wedded lives,
>
> *   *   *   *   *   *   *
>
> And eyes grown dim with gazing on the pilot stars."
>
> Vol. i. p. 182.

Then at the end of the poem there is found an alteration of a like kind : where for the flow of triumphant enjoyment, in the contemplation of merely sensual ease and luxurious repose, with which it originally closed, a higher strain is substituted, which is meant apparently to show the effect of lotos-eating upon the religious feelings. The gods of the Lotos-eaters, it is worth knowing, are altogether Lucretian.

"The May Queen[1]" too was made "more deeply and tragically interesting" by the third and concluding part. But the four poems, in which "the work is at the highest level," and from which we may gather some hints concerning "his moral theory of life and its issues and of that which constitutes a sound condition of the soul," are "The Palace of Art," the dramatic monologue of "St Simeon Stylites," "The Two Voices," and "The Vision of Sin."

"The Palace of Art" represents allegorically the condition of a mind which, in the love of beauty, and the triumphant consciousness of knowledge, and intellectual supremacy, in the intense enjoyment of its own power and glory, has lost sight

---

[1] "The May Queen" is all Lincolnshire inland, as "Locksley Hall" its sea-board.   MS Note, E. F. G.

of its relation to man and God.   * * *   As "The Palace of Art" represents the pride of voluptuous enjoyment in its noblest form, the "St Simeon Stylites" represents the pride of asceticism in its basest[1].

Of "The Two Voices[2]" Spedding says:

In "The Two Voices" we have a history of the agitations, the suggestions and counter-suggestions of a mind sunk in hopeless despondency, and meditating self-destruction; together with the manner of its recovery to a more healthy condition.... Others would have been content to give the bad voice the worst of the argument; but, unhappily, all moral reasoning must ultimately rest on the internal evidence of the moral sense; and where this is disordered, the most unquestionable logic can conclude nothing, because it is the first principles which are at issue; the *major* is not admitted.   Mr Tennyson's treatment of the case is more scientific.... "The Vision of Sin" touches upon a more awful subject than any of these; the end, here and hereafter, of the merely sensual man.

In conclusion Spedding adds, that these poems show that the author's art is no trick of these versifying times, born of a superficial sensibility to beauty and a turn for setting to music the current doctrines and fashionable feelings of the day; but a genuine growth of nature, having its root deep in the pensive heart, a heart accustomed to meditate earnestly and feel truly upon the prime duties and interests of man.

Some notes on the second volume have been left me by my father, the first of which is on the "Morte d'Arthur." This particular note I wrote down from what

[1] This is one of the poems A. T. would read with grotesque grimness, especially such passages as "coughs, aches, stitches," etc., laughing aloud at times. MS Note, E. F. G.

[2] My father told me, "When I wrote 'The Two Voices' I was so utterly miserable, a burden to myself and to my family, that I said, 'Is life worth anything?' and now that I am old, I fear that I shall only live a year or two, for I have work still to do." The last part, E. F. G. writes, was probably made in the fields about Dulwich.

he said; but he gave it his approval, as expressing his own view correctly.

"How much of history we have in the story of Arthur is doubtful. Let not my readers press too hardly on details whether for history or for allegory. Some think that King Arthur may be taken to typify conscience. He is anyhow meant to be a man who spent himself in the cause of honour, duty and self-sacrifice, who felt and aspired with his nobler knights, though with a stronger and a clearer conscience than any of them, 'reverencing his conscience as his king.' 'There was no such perfect man since Adam' as an old writer says. 'Major præteritis majorque futuris Regibus.'"

Edward Fitzgerald writes:

The "Morte d'Arthur" when read to us from manuscript in 1835 had no introduction or epilogue; which was added to anticipate or excuse the "faint Homeric echoes," etc. (as in the "Day-Dream"), to give a reason for telling an old-world tale.

Again:

Mouthing out his hollow oes and aes, deep-chested music, this is something as A. T. reads, with a broad north country vowel, except the u in such words as "mute," "brute," which he pronounces like the thin French "u." His voice, very deep and deep-chested, but rather murmuring than mouthing, like the sound of a far sea or of a pine-wood, I remember greatly struck Carlyle when he first came to know him. There was no declamatory showing off in A. T.'s recitation of his verse; sometimes broken with a laugh, or a burlesque twist of voice, when something struck him as quaint or grim. Sometimes Spedding would read the poems to us; A. T. once told him he seemed to read too much as if bees were about his mouth, all in good humour as in sincerity. Of the Chivalry Romances he said to me, "I could not read 'Palmerin of England' nor 'Amadis,' nor any other of those Romances through. The 'Morte d'Arthur' is much the best: there are very fine things in it, but all strung together without Art[1]."

[1] MS Note.

In "Locksley Hall" my father annotates the line "Let the great world spin for ever down the ringing grooves of change." "When I went by the first train from Liverpool to Manchester (1830), I thought that the wheels ran in a groove. It was a black night and there was such a vast crowd round the train at the station that we could not see the wheels. Then I made this line."— Further: "'Locksley Hall' is an imaginary place (tho' the coast is Lincolnshire) and the hero is imaginary. The whole poem represents young life, its good side, its deficiencies, and its yearnings. Mr Hallam said to me that the English people liked verse in Trochaics, so I wrote the poem in this metre."

In the first unpublished edition of "Locksley Hall," after "*knots of Paradise*," came the following couplet, which was omitted lest the description should be too long:

All about a summer ocean, leagues on leagues of
    golden calm,
And within melodious waters rolling round the knolls
    of palm.

I remember my father saying that Sir William Jones' prose translation of the *Moâllakât*, the seven Arabic poems (which are a selection from the work of pre-Mahommedan poets) hanging up in the temple of Mecca, gave him the idea of the poem.

When these volumes were published my father was often in the habit of breakfasting with Rogers, for whom he had a real affection, but who "rather bored him with attentions, very generous and amiable from the old poet." Rogers would praise "Locksley Hall," and would say "Shakespeare could not have done it better." "I should have thought," observed my father, "that such a poem as 'Dora' was more in Rogers' line:

perhaps it was too much in his line. ' Dora,' being
the tale of a nobly simple country girl, had to be told in
the simplest possible poetical language, and therefore
was one of the poems which gave most trouble."
" Ulysses," my father said, " was written soon after
Arthur Hallam's death, and gave my feeling about the
need of going forward, and braving the struggle of life
perhaps more simply than anything in ' In Memoriam.'"

My father's note on "Audley Court" runs thus:

" This poem was partially suggested by Abbey Park
at Torquay. Torquay was in old days the loveliest
sea village in England and now is a town. In those
old days I, coming down from the hill over Torquay,
saw a star of phosphorescence made by the buoy appearing and disappearing in the dark sea, and wrote
these lines.

> But ere the night we rose
> And saunter'd home beneath a moon, that, just
> In crescent, dimly rain'd about the leaf
> Twilights of airy silver, till we reach'd
> The limit of the hills; and as we sank
> From rock to rock upon the glooming quay,
> The town was hush'd beneath us: lower down
> The bay was oily calm; the harbour-buoy,
> Sole star of phosphorescence in the calm,
> With one green sparkle ever and anon
> Dipt by itself, and we were glad at heart."

However he never cared greatly for this sea on the
south coast of England, "not a grand sea," he would
say, "only an angry curt sea. It seems to shriek as
it recoils with the pebbles along the shore; the finest
seas I have ever seen are at Valencia, Mablethorpe and
in (West) Cornwall. At Valencia the sea was grand,
without any wind blowing and seemingly without a wave:

but with the momentum of the Atlantic behind, it dashes
up into foam, blue diamonds it looks like, all along the
rocks, like ghosts playing at hide and seek. When
I was in Cornwall it had blown a storm of wind and
rain for days, and all of a sudden fell into perfect calm ;
I was a little inland of the cliffs : when, after a space of
perfect silence, a long roll of thunder, from some wave
rushing into a cavern I suppose, came up from the
distance, and died away. I *never* felt silence like that[1]."

The seas at Mablethorpe he would describe as " interminable waves rolling along interminable shores of
sand."

In working at " The Gardener's Daughter " he said :
" The centre of the poem, that passage describing the
girl, must be full and rich. The poem is so, to a fault,
especially the descriptions of nature, for the lover is an
artist, but, this being so, the central picture must hold
its place.

> One arm aloft —
> Gown'd in pure white, that fitted to the shape —
> Holding the bush, to fix it back, she stood.
> A single stream of all her soft brown hair
> Pour'd on one side : the shadow of the flowers
> Stole all the golden gloss, and, wavering
> Lovingly lower, trembled on her waist —
> Ah, happy shade — and still went wavering down,
> But, ere it touch'd a foot, that might have danced
> The greensward into greener circles, dipt,
> And mix'd with shadows of the common ground !
> But the full day dwelt on her brows, and sunn'd
> Her violet eyes, and all her Hebe bloom,
> And doubled his own warmth against her lips,
> And on the bounteous wave of such a breast
> As never pencil drew."

[1] MS Note by E. F. G.

I remember too my father's telling me that Fitzgerald had said that the autumn landscape, which in the
first edition was described in the lines beginning " Her
beauty grew," was taken from a background of a Titian
(Lord Ellesmere's *Ages of Man*); and that perhaps in
consequence they had been omitted.   They ran thus:

Her beauty grew: *till drawn in narrowing arcs*
The southing Autumn touch'd with sallower gleams
The granges on the fallows.   At that time,
Tired of the noisy town I wander'd there;
The bell toll'd four; and by the time I reach'd
The Wicket-gate, I found her by herself.

The correction of the proofs of this poem and of this volume
took place in Spedding's chambers at 60 Lincoln's Inn Fields,
in the forepart of 1842.   The poems to be printed were nearly
all, I think all, in a foolscap folio parchment-bound blank book
such as accounts are kept in (only not ruled), and which I used
to call " The Butcher's Book."   The poems were written in
A. T.'s very fine hand (he once said, not thinking of himself,
that great men generally wrote " terse " hands) toward one side
of the large page; the unoccupied edges and corners being often
stript down for pipe-lights, taking care to save the MS, as A. T.
once seriously observed.   The pages of MS from the Butcher's
Book were one by one torn out for the printer, and, when
returned with the proofs, were put in the fire.   I reserved two
or three of the leaves; and gave them to the Library of Trinity
College (Cambridge[1]).

I insert here an unpublished poem which was originally intended as a prologue to " The Gardener's Daughter " and was called " The Ante-Chamber."   My father
wished it never to be printed in front of " The Gardener's
Daughter " because this is already full enough.   It is
however too good to be lost.   The portrait in " The

---

[1] E. F. G., MS notes on A. T.

Ante-Chamber" might be himself at the period, — so his
friends say, — but that was by no means his intention[1].

The Ante-Chamber.[*] (Unpublished.)

That is his portrait painted by himself.
Look on those manly curls so glossy dark,
Those thoughtful furrows in the swarthy cheek;
Admire that stalwart shape, those ample brows,
And that large table of the breast dispread,
Between low shoulders; how demure a smile,
How full of wisest humour and of love,
With some half-consciousness of inward power,
Sleeps round those quiet lips; not quite a smile;
And look you what an arch the brain has built
Above the ear! and what a settled mind,
Mature, harbour'd from change, contemplative,
Tempers the peaceful light of hazel eyes,
Observing all things.   This is he I loved,
This is the man of whom you heard me speak.
     My fancy was the more luxurious,
But his was minted in a deeper mould,
And took in more of Nature than mine own:
Nor proved I such delight as he, to mark
The humours of the polling and the wake,
The hubbub of the market and the booths:
How this one smiled, that other waved his arms,
These careful and those candid brows, how each —
Down to his slightest turns and attitudes —
Was something that another could not be,
How every brake and flower spread and rose,
A various world! which he compell'd once more
Thro' his own nature, with well mingled hues,

---

[1] Samuel Laurence painted the earliest portrait of my father about 1838.

Into another shape, born of the first,
As beautiful, but yet another world.

All this so stirr'd him in his hour of joy,
Mix'd with the phantom of his coming fame,
That once he spake: "I lift the eyes of thought,
I look thro' all my glimmering life, I see
At the end, as 'twere athwart a colour'd cloud,
O'er the bow'd shoulder of a bland old Age,
The face of placid Death." Long, Eustace, long
May my strong wish, transgressing the low bound
Of mortal hope, act on Eternity
To keep thee here amongst us! Yet he lives;
His and my friendship have not suffer'd loss,
His fame is equal to his years: his praise
Is neither overdealt, nor idly won.

Step thro' these doors, and I will show to you
Another countenance, one yet more dear,
More dear, for what is lost is made more dear;
"More dear" I will not say, but rather bless
The All-perfect Framer, Him, who made the heart,
Forethinking its twinfold necessity,
Thro' one whole life an overflowing urn,
Capacious both of Friendship and of Love.

CHAPTER IX.

REMINISCENCES OF TENNYSON (ABOUT 1842).

[At this time there seems to have been an almost total cessation of correspondence between my father and his intimate friends; and I accordingly asked Edmund Lushington, the present Dean of Westminster, and
Aubrey de Vere to give me some reminiscences of those days.]

Edmund Lushington writes:

During my first two years at Cambridge I had no acquaintance
with A. T.; the first occasion I can remember of knowing
him by sight was when Arthur Hallam read in the College
Chapel his essay which gained the first declamation prize. The
place where the reader stood was slightly raised above the aisle
of the chapel; A. T. sat on the bench just below, listening intently
to the spoken words.

At this time, and indeed for several years later, copies of numerous poems of his were widely circulated about Cambridge in
MS, and I remember one debate in a Society called the " Fifty,"
on the rank to which his poetry was entitled, in the course of
which numerous passages were quoted from poems as yet not
publicly known— " The Gardener's Daughter " in particular.

I believe the first time he visited me in my own house was
in the summer of 1840 when he came to stay a few days. He
was then habitually residing with his mother and sisters at
Tunbridge Wells, where, beautiful as the neighbourhood was,
the site was found not healthy for all of the family, and they
were wishing to meet with some other place to settle in. A day
or two later I went over with him to pay a short visit to his
mother's house at Tunbridge Wells, where among other nota-
bilities we saw an old lady famous for cherishing memories of

the great Dr Samuel Johnson, whose likeness graced an expansive medallion which she wore about her neck, Miss L.[1] Not long after this visit he came over with his mother and two younger sisters to stay some days at Park House, which they partly spent in looking round the neighbouring country at any such houses as might appear to be suitable for a settled residence in preference to Tunbridge Wells.

They eventually settled before long upon engaging a house belonging to Colonel Best in Boxley Parish, to which they removed before the winter of 1841–42. The house was nearly two miles by the road, rather less by the fields, from our residence at Park House, which is nearer Maidstone. Early in October we drove up in an open phaeton to London by the old coach-road which knew no railways in that time. Whether A. T. went up with us I am not sure: at any rate the next day he was in London and came to take leave of us at the station where we left by train for the north. I remember how some one out of a crowd of lookers on, just before the train was starting, after a long gaze at his dark features uttered an emphatic " foreign."

At Xmas 1841 I went for a few days' holiday from Glasgow to Kent and spent the time mostly at Boxley, where A. T. was now settled with his mother and sisters. We had sometimes dance and song in the evening, where, tho! no one spoke of it, assuredly many a heart was filled " with an awful sense of one mute Shadow watching all," as his own undying words record of an earlier occasion. In the meantime the number of the memorial poems had rapidly increased since I had seen the poet, his book containing many that were new to me. Some I heard him repeat before I had seen them in writing, others I learnt to know first from the book itself which he kindly allowed me to look through without stint. I remember one particular night when we were sitting up together late in his bedroom. He began to recite the poem that stands sixth in " In Memoriam," " One writes, that ' Other friends remain,' " and I do not know that the deep melodious thunder of his voice with all its overwhelming pathos, often and often as I have heard it, ever imprest me more profoundly. On one other occasion he

---

[1] She observed that Dr Johnson " often stirred his lemonade with his finger and that often dirty." My father was very angry with her for relating such a story about a great man, and said, " The dirt is in her own heart."

came and showed me a poem he had just composed, saying he
liked it better than most he had done lately, this was No. LI.,
" Do we indeed desire the dead."

He was present on July 6th, 1842, at a festival of the Maidstone Mechanics' Institute held in our Park, of which he has
introduced a lively description in the beginning of " The
Princess."

In the course of that summer appeared the collection of his
poems published in two vols.; the first contains, with some
exceptions, the poems published under the title *Poems, chiefly
Lyrical*, in 1830, and as a second division, with various changes,
those which first appeared in 1832. The second volume had
all new poems, already known to many in private circulation,
but not as yet openly given to the world.

He went with me once or twice to London to make arrangements such as are required by the law with reference to the
marriage of his youngest sister Cecilia. The marriage ceremony
was performed by his elder brother, the Rev. Charles Tennyson
Turner, who had come to spend some time with his mother and
with whom I then first became acquainted.

*   *   *   *   *   *

In the hottest part of the summer (1845) A. T. had gone
down to Eastbourne, and was lodging in one of two or three
cottages prettily grouped together, bearing the well-deserved
name of Mount Pleasant. A little garden lay in front of the
cottages, beyond that a cornfield extended some way till it was
stopt by a path on the edge of the cliff, which overlooked the
sea, and continued its course on to Holywell. Mount Pleasant
and all in front of it has now vanished through the encroachment
of the sea. Its last vestige I saw many years since as a brick
fragment in the yard of a grand new hotel built just above the
parade to which the present sea-line reaches. I went down there
to see him and remained a few days. He had then completed
many of the cantos in " In Memoriam" and was engaged on
" The Princess," of which I had heard nothing before. He read
or showed me the first part, beyond which it had then hardly
advanced. He said to me, " I have brought in your marriage
at the end of 'In Memoriam,' " and then showed me those poems
of " In Memoriam" which were finished and which were a perfectly novel surprise to me.

The Dean of Westminster writes:

In 1841 and 1842 I paid two visits in the month of August to Park House near Maidstone, the property of your father's brother-in-law Edmund Lushington, who in those days made it his southern residence during the many months of the long vacation that set him free from his laborious work in Scotland. I found there not only a bright, charming and happy group of his brothers and sisters, four sisters and two brothers, the Henry Lushington who died at Malta in the year 1855, and my own friend and contemporary Franklin, but one or two visitors, Mr George Venables, and Mr Chapman, a Fellow I think then of Jesus College, Cambridge. I shall never forget the impression made on me by coming in contact with men so striking at once in character and ability, and yet a circle so wholly, so widely, different from that which had gathered round Arnold at Rugby, or with which I was familiar, so far as was possible for one so young, at my own University. The questions that stirred so deeply our seniors and ourselves at Oxford, the position of J. H. Newman and his friends, the course of the "Oxford movement," the whole Tractarian Controversy, were scarcely mentioned, or, if mentioned, were spoken of as matters of secondary or remote interest: while on the other hand the Lushington brothers, especially the Professor, "uncle Edmund" as I have always heard you term him, seemed as much at home in the language of the Greek dramatists as if it was their native tongue, while of Henry I remember his friend Chapman saying that it was difficult to quote or read a line of Shakespeare, to which he could not at once give the reference and the context. Of Mr Venables and the position which he had long held among his Cambridge friends and which he was already gaining in London literary society, I need not speak. How many of that group, whose wide and varied attainments, unstudied but suggestive conversation, so impressed the young Oxford undergraduate, fresh from so different an atmosphere, have passed beyond the veil!

It was in the midst of these, all his warm friends and associates, that I first saw your father. I feel sure that I saw him during my first visit; on the second occasion he and his mother and sisters had been living for some months in Boxley Hall, the parish in which Park House is situated. The Professor was already engaged to your aunt Cecilia Tennyson, and the wedding followed soon after my return home. Your father was I need hardly say constantly at Park House, and there were few days on which I did not see him. The year was marked by the recent publication of the two-volume edition of his poems. The first volume, a copy of which during my visit was given me by Frank Lushington, is still a treasured possession. The second alas! is lost. I try to look back through the mist of years and see your father as I saw him then; I remember watching him as he sat on a garden seat on the grass, in a brown suit, looking somewhat grave and silent, and wondering whether my friends at Oxford would feel as I did the poems which I had already read, "Mariana," "The Gardener's Daughter," "Œnone," "Locksley Hall," and "The Two Voices." Of his conversation I can only recall one or two fragments. We, the younger members of the party, as well as the older guests and your father, were in the garden employed, some of the party in gathering, some in eating wall-fruit, peaches and apricots. Some one made a remark about the fruit being liable to disagree with himself or others, to which another (it was Chapman) replied with a jocular remark about "the disturbed districts," alluding of course to some disorders apprehended or existing in the centres of industry. I remember being startled by your father's voice and accent, "I can't joke about so grave a question," and thinking to myself that it was exactly what one so different as Dr Arnold, who had died some two months earlier, might have said under similar circumstances.

Again, I was greatly struck by his describing to us on one singularly still starlit evening, how he and his friends had once sat out far into the night having tea at a table on the lawn beneath the stars, and that the candles had burned with steady upright flame, disturbed from time to time by the inrush of a moth or cockchafer, as tho' in a closed room. I do not know whether he had already written, or was perhaps even then shaping, the lines in "In Memoriam," which so many years afterwards brought back to me the incident.

As one looks back to the years previous to 1842 it is curious to notice the immense change caused by the publication of those two volumes. On my return to Oxford in October 1842 his name was on everyone's lips, his poems discussed, criticised, interpreted; portions of them repeatedly set for translation

into Latin or Greek verse at schools and colleges; read and
re-read so habitually that there were many of us who could
repeat page after page from memory.   At one of the earliest
meetings which I remember at a small debating Society,
"The Decade," well known at Oxford in those days, I think it
was in 1844, was a discussion as to the relative merits of Wordsworth and Tennyson, in which I especially recall the speeches
of J. C. Shairp, A. H. Clough, and I think I may add of the
future Chief Justice John Coleridge.

It was a great change; though no doubt a small, I should
think a very small, circle of Oxford residents may have been
more or less acquainted with his published poems at an earlier
date.   In a letter from Arthur Stanley, written from Hurstmonceux Rectory in the September of 1834, he says to his
friend W. C. Lake (afterwards Dean of Durham), still at Rugby,
that Julius Hare, with whom he was staying, "often reads to us
in the evening things quite new to me, for instance (tell it not in
Gath) A. Tennyson's *Poems*," and he goes on to name some
which had greatly pleased him, and to advise his friend to get
the volume and read it.   The expression "tell it not," etc. is no
doubt a reference to the acrid and contemptuous article in the
Quarterly of 1833.

The readings at Hurstmonceux were not forgotten by the
young scholar of Balliol.   In Stanley's very striking prize poem
"The Gipsies," written in 1837, he adapted to the heroic measure
a line from the introduction in blank verse to "The Palace of
Art," and quoted the words without the author's name in a note.

In a paper on John Keble he tells us how as the Professor of
Poetry went thro' the poem before recitation with him, he noticed
the quotation and passed on, saying "Shakespeare I suppose."

In the three or four terms which I had spent at Oxford I
remember also myself translating into Latin Elegiacs in February
1841, from a printed copy, the last three stanzas of the lines to
J. S. beginning with "Words weaker than your grief," etc.   They
were in the possession of my private tutor E. Massey of Wadham,
a distinguished Shrewsbury scholar, whose Cambridge friends
may possibly have suggested their use for such a purpose.
Otherwise I cannot recall anyone at Oxford before the publication of the two volumes ever mentioning your father's poems.
We talked much of Keble on the one hand, Shelley and Byron
on the other, and some of us I need not say were strong Words-

worthians and were half-amused, half-indignant at the tendency
of some of our undergraduate friends to depreciate Milton as a
Puritan poet; but the intense interest called out by the two
volumes seems to me, on looking back, to have taken my young
contemporaries at Oxford as well as the outside world of readers
as it were by storm.   I seem still to hear voices that have long
since been silent repeating line after line, which I can hardly
read even now without recalling the very accent and the faces of
friends of " days that are no more."

Aubrey de Vere writes:

It was in 1841 or 1842 that I first met the Poet[1] on whom
and on whose works my imagination had rested so often during
the preceding ten years; and I lost nothing when the living man
stood before me.   The large dark eyes, generally dreamy but
with an occasional gleam of imaginative alertness, the dusky,
almost Spanish complexion, the high-built head and the massive
abundance of curling hair like the finest and blackest silk, are still
before me, and no less the stalwart form, strong " with the certain
step of man," though some years earlier it might have moved

> Still hither thither idly sway'd
> Like those long mosses in the stream.

Whenever we were both in London, I met him as often as
I could, sometimes at the rooms of James Spedding, or at some
late smoking-party consisting of young men, their intimates at
the University, the well-known Cambridge " Apostles."   That
was a society unvexed by formalities ; and I do not remember
that my new friend and I ever called each other otherwise
than by our Christian names.   He was thus always called by
many of his intimates beside; for their affection for him partook
largely of domestic affection in its character.   He was preeminently a *man*, as well as a genius, but not the least the
man of the world.   He was essentially refined; but convention
fled before his face.   At none of those reunions did I meet any
of his brothers, though in later years I knew Frederick, many
of whose poems were much admired by Henry Taylor as
well as by myself.   Unfortunately I never met his brother

[1] See Appendix, p. 501, for " The Reception of the Early Poems," by
Aubrey de Vere.

Charles, who early published a slender volume of Sonnets warmly praised by Coleridge. My father had greatly admired one on the sea —

"The lightest murmur of its seething foam," etc.

The entire simplicity and unconventionality of Alfred Tennyson was part of the charm which bound his friends to him. No acquaintance, however inferior to him in intellect, could be afraid of him. He felt that he was not in the presence of a critic, but of one who respected human nature wherever he found it free from unworthiness, who would think his own thoughts whether in the society of ordinary or extraordinary men, and who could not but express them plainly if he spoke at all. That perfect transparency of mind, like the clearness of air in the finest climates, when it is nearness not distance that "lends enchantment to the view," I have seen only in three men beside him, Wordsworth, Sir William Rowan Hamilton and one other. His unguardedness, in combination with his unworldliness, made his friends all the more zealous to help him; and perhaps their emulous aid was more useful to him than self-help could have been. His friends' appreciation of his poetry too was an enthusiasm ardent enough to carry with it a healthful infection. It forced others to give his works an earlier attention than would otherwise have been their lot, and consequently an earlier recognition; but it was the genuine merit of his poetry which produced that enthusiasm and prevented it from cooling while the wise were forming their judgments, and the wiseacres were depreciating minor poets and confounding him with them. Friends could but raise the sail high enough to catch what breeze might be stirring. The rest depended on the boat. It seems strange however that his larger fame made way so slowly. For many a year, we, his zealots, were but zealots of a sect. Seventeen years after the publication of his first volume, and five more after that of his third, "The Princess," came out, I wrote a critique in one of our chief *Quarterlies*, and called him a "great poet." The then Editor struck out "great" and substituted "true." He considered that the public would not tolerate so strong an eulogium.

Alfred Tennyson's largeness of mind and of heart was touchingly illustrated by his reverence for Wordsworth's poetry, notwithstanding that the immense merits which he recognised in

it were not, in his opinion, supplemented by a proportionate
amount of artistic skill. He was always glad to show reverence
to the "Old Poet," not then within ten years of the age at
which the then younger one died. "Wordsworth," he said to
me one day, "is staying at Hampstead in the house of his
friend Mr. Hoare; I must go and see him; and you must come
with me; mind you do not tell Rogers, or he will be displeased
at my being in London and not going to see him." We drove
up to Hampstead, and knocked at the door; and the next
minute it was opened by the Poet of the World, at whose side
stood the Poet of the Mountains. Rogers' old face, which had
encountered nearly ninety years, seemed to double the number
of its wrinkles as he said, not angrily but very drily: "Ah, you
did not come up the hill to see me!" During the visit it was
with Tennyson that the Bard of Rydal held discourse, while
the recluse of St James' Place, whom "that angle" especially
delighted, conversed with me. As we walked back to London
through grassy fields not then built over, Tennyson complained
of the old Poet's coldness. He had endeavoured to stimulate
some latent ardours by telling him of a tropical island where
the trees, when they first came into leaf, were a vivid scarlet; —
"Every one of them, I told him, one flush all over the island,
the colour of blood! It would not do. I could not inflame his
imagination in the least!" During the preceding year I had
had the great honour of passing several days at Rydal Mount
with Wordsworth, walking on his mountains and listening to
him at his fireside. I told him that a young poet had lately
risen up. Wordsworth answered that he feared from the little
he had heard that if Crabbe was the driest of poets, the young
aspirant must have the opposite fault. I replied that he should
judge for himself, and without leave given, recited to him two
poems by Tennyson: viz. "You ask me, why, tho' ill at ease,"
and "Of old sat Freedom on the heights." Wordsworth listened
with a gradually deepening attention. After a pause he answered, "I must acknowledge that these two poems are very
solid and noble in thought. Their diction also seems singularly
stately [1]."

[1] Some of the critics state that before these poems appeared, no modern
poet had undertaken the hard task of setting forth with poetic fire and glow
the golden mean of politics. Tennyson's view was that a poet ought to love
his own country, but that he should found his political poems on what was

There was another occasion on which the Poet whose great work was all but finished, and the youthful compeer whose chief labours were yet to come, met in my presence.   It was at a dinner given by Mr Moxon.   The ladies had withdrawn, and Wordsworth soon followed them.   Several times Tennyson said to me in a low voice, "I must go: I cannot wait any longer." At last the cause of his disquiet revealed itself.   It was painful to him to leave the house without expressing to the old Bard his sense of the obligation which all Englishmen owed to him, and yet he was averse to speak his thanks before a large company.   Our host brought Wordsworth back to the dining-room; and Tennyson moved up to him.   He spoke in a low voice, and with a perceptible emotion.   I must not cite his words lest I should mar them; but they were few, simple and touching. The old man looked very much pleased, more so indeed than I ever saw him look on any other occasion; shook hands with him heartily, and thanked him affectionately.   Wordsworth thus records the incident in a letter to his accomplished American friend, Professor Reed: "I saw Tennyson when I was in London several times.   He is decidedly the first of our living poets, and I hope will live to give the world still better things.   You will be pleased to hear that he expressed in the strongest terms his gratitude to my writings.   To this I was far from indifferent[1]."

Our many conversations, in those pleasant years, turned chiefly on Poetry, a subject on which Tennyson could say nothing that was not original.   It was easy to see that to discern the Beautiful in all around us, and to reveal that beauty to others, was his special poetic vocation.   In these conversations he never uttered a word that was disparaging, or tainted with the spirit of rivalship.   One of the Poets least like himself, Crabbe, was among those whose merits he affirmed most unequivocally, especially his gift of a *hard* pathos.   The only poet I heard him criticise roughly or unfairly was himself.   "Compare," he once said to me, "compare the heavy handling of my workmanship with the exquisite lightness of touch in Keats!"   Another time he read aloud a song by one of the chivalrous Poets of Charles the First's time, perhaps Lovelace's "Althea," which Wordsworth also used to *croon* in the woods, and said, "There! I would give

noble and great in the history of all countries, and that his utterances should be outspoken, yet statesmanlike, without any colour of partizanship.

[1] *Prose Works of William Wordsworth*, Vol. III., p. 391.   Dr Grosart.

all my poetry to have made one song like that!" Not less ardent was his enthusiasm for Burns. And here an incident with no small significance recurs to me. "Read the exquisite songs of Burns," he exclaimed. " In shape, each of them has the perfection of the berry; in light the radiance of the dewdrop: you forget for its sake those stupid things, his serious pieces!" The same day I met Wordsworth, and named Burns to him. Wordsworth praised him, even more vehemently than Tennyson had done, as the great genius who had brought Poetry back to Nature; but ended, "Of course I refer to his serious efforts, such as the 'Cotter's Saturday Night'; those foolish little amatory songs of his one has to forget." I told the tale to Henry Taylor that evening; and his answer was: "Burns' exquisite songs and Burns' serious efforts are to me alike tedious, and disagreeable reading!" So much for the infallibility of Poets in their own art!

CHAPTER X.

LETTERS.

1842–1845.

From Samuel Rogers.

ST JAMES' PLACE, *August 17th*, 1842.

MY DEAR TENNYSON,

Every day have I resolved to write and tell you with what delight I have read and read again your two beautiful volumes; but it was my wish to tell you so *face* to *face*. That wish however remains unfulfilled and write I must, for very few things, if any, have ever thrilled me so much.

Yours ever, S. ROGERS.

To Edmund Lushington.

Sept. 8th, 1842.

MY DEAR EDMUND,

*   *   *   *   *

I called on Moxon, not at home, gone to the Pyrenees with W. Wordsworth's two sons. 500 of my books are sold: according to Moxon's brother I have made a sensation! I wish the wood-works[1] would make a sensation! I expect they will. I came here this morning by the Liverpool packet. I go to Limerick

[1] This was Dr Allen's manufactory for carving wood, in which my father had invested all his little money. Full details of this are given on p. 220.

to-night. I hope you are all blooming. What with ruin in the distance and hypochondriacs in the foreground God help all. Pray write to me at P. O.

Love to all yours and mine.

Yours ever, A. T.

From Thomas Carlyle.

CHEYNE ROAD, CHELSEA.
7th Dec. 1842.

DEAR TENNYSON,

Wherever this find you, may it find you well, may it come as a friendly greeting to you. I have just been reading your Poems; I have read certain of them over again, and mean to read them over and over till they become my poems: this fact, with the inferences that lie in it, is of such emphasis in *me*, I cannot keep it to myself, but must needs acquaint you too with it. If you knew what my relation has been to the thing call'd English "Poetry" for many years back, you would think such fact almost surprising! Truly it is long since in any English Book, Poetry or Prose, I have felt the pulse of a real man's heart as I do in this same. A right valiant, true fighting, victorious heart; strong as a lion's, yet gentle, loving and full of music: what I call a genuine singer's heart! there are tones as of the nightingale; low murmurs as of wood-doves at summer noon; everywhere a noble sound as of the free winds and leafy woods. The sunniest glow of Life dwells in that soul, chequered duly with dark streaks from night and Hades: everywhere one feels as if all were fill'd with yellow glowing sunlight, some glorious golden Vapour; from which form after form bodies itself; naturally, *golden* forms. In one word, there seems to be a note of "The Eternal Melodies" in this man; for which let all other men be thankful and joyful! Your "Dora" reminds me of the *Book of Ruth;* in the "Two Voices," which I am told some Reviewer calls "trivial morality," I think of passages in *Job.* For truth is quite *true* in Job's time and Ruth's as now. I know you cannot read German: the more interesting is it to trace in your "Summer Oak" a beautiful kindred to something that is best in Goethe; I mean his "Müllerinn" (Miller's

daughter) chiefly, with whom the very Mill-dam gets in love
tho' she proves a flirt after all and the thing ends in satirica
lines! very strangely too in the "Vision of Sin" I ar
reminded of my friend Jean Paul.   This is not babble, it i
speech; true deposition of a volunteer witness.   And so I sa
let us all rejoice somewhat.   And so let us all smite rhythmically
all in concert, "the sounding furrows"; and sail forward wit
new cheer, "beyond the sunset," whither we are bound—

> It may be that the gulfs will wash us down,
> It may be we shall touch the happy Isles
> And see the great Achilles whom we knew!

These lines do not make me weep, but there is in me wha
would fill whole Lachrymatories as I read.   But do you, whe
you return to London, come down to me and let us smoke
pipe together.   With few words, with many, or with none, i
need not be an ineloquent Pipe!

Farewell, dear Tennyson; may the gods be good to you
With very great sincerity (and in great haste) I subscribe mysel
Yours, T. CARLYLE.

My father tells his sister Emily to copy this lette
and enclose it to my mother.   Emily writes as follows:

I like this letter, dost not thou?   I asked Alfred wha
Carlyle meant by saying he could not read German, and h
said, when the poems he (i.e. Carlyle) alluded to were writter
he knew little or nothing of German.   He must have tol
Carlyle this who has made a jumble.   Moreover Alfred says
"Carlyle is mistaken about the satirical lines, concluding th
'Müllerinn.'   They are in another poem."
Thy very affectionate EMILY.

*From Sara Coleridge[1] to Edward Moxon (enclosed
to my father in a letter from Moxon).*

1842.
MY DEAR SIR,

My husband and I have very often had to thank yo
for additions to our library most kindly made.   Your last gif
is a most acceptable one and supplies me with a rich treat fo

---

[1] The only and highly-gifted daughter of S. T. Coleridge.

days to come, and one which I need not devour too greedily,
but can recur to from time to time with fresh pleasure. It is
a compliment (as far as admiration of mine can be compli-
mentary) to Mr Tennyson, that having laid hold of the first
volume, containing poems which I had read over and over again
a few years ago, I could not part with it for the new productions,
much as my curiosity had been excited about them, but fell to
reading my old favourites with even greater admiration than ever.

What I have read of the second volume will sustain the
author's reputation, which is much to say. The Epic is what
might have been expected, not epical at all but very beautiful,
in Tennyson's old manner.

"The Gardener's Daughter" is most highly wrought and still
more to be admired I think than the "Morte d'Arthur."

Accept best thanks both from Mr Coleridge and myself and
believe me

Very sincerely yours, SARA COLERIDGE.

To the Rev. H. D. Rawnsley.

1842.

MY DEAR RAWNSLEY,

Your note dated the 5th only reached me
last night (eleven days after date) at this place, Torquay,
Devon. Dr Allen did not forward it immediately as he
ought to have done, in fact in the multiplicity of his
business and his 40 letters a day I believe he had quite
forgotten my direction, until I refresht his memory by
sending it. How the wood-scheme goes on you ask.
The concern I believe is going on very well; there are
as many orders as can be executed by our old presses;
we have been modelling presses all this time. They
sent one from Brummagem, wretched thing! split as soon
as put into action (I hear that all Brummagem machinery
is of the worst description: let Brummagem look to it or
she will ruin her reputation), but Wood has succeeded
in making really quite a beautiful press which will do as
much work in the same time as two of the old ones.

And now (as we have it on the pattern) we are going
to have one made a week, till we have enough. We shall
go on swimmingly. The presses have been modelling,
and the men educating up till now, for after all (simple
as it seems) it is a very delicate process to manage
properly, and we want a great many workmen.

I have written in great haste, and I know not whether
your queries are answer'd; if not, write again and ask
me what you wish to know. We have dropt the name
" Pyroglyph " as too full of *meaning* (a singular reason
for rejecting a word!), and call ourselves "The Patent
Decorative Carving and Sculpture Company!" Be *careful!* I told you all about it on the score of old friendship and auld lang syne. Poor Sophy! I am deeply
grieved to hear of her illness.

Drummond's affair [1] is no secret to me for I accused
him of it in your little study and the sort of denial he
made was as good as a confession, and I have since
heard of it from other quarters: these things never are
secrets in the country.

You never heard the word " ivy-tod "; but you have
heard of " tods of wool," and I take it they are the same
words originally, a certain weight or mass of something.

Kindest love to all your party,

Ever yours in great haste, A. T.

TORQUAY, DEVON.

I shall most likely leave this place for town in a few
days. You had better, therefore, if you write again write
to London. Farewell. I have had so little time, I am
afraid I have written a very confused letter.

---

[1] Drummond Rawnsley's engagement to Catherine Franklin, daughter
of Sir Willingham Franklin, and niece of Sir John Franklin.

To Aubrey de Vere.

EASTBOURNE.
Saturday, July 30th, 1842.

MY DEAR AUBREY,

As for dining with your uncle, that, you see, s out of the question, as your note has just been delivered to me at this place, Eastbourne, on the Sussex coast. I shall account myself *highly honoured* in receiving a copy of " Edwin the Fair " from Henry Taylor; these are not empty words: therefore I underscore them: likewise your edited book will, I have no doubt, yield me much pleasure. I shall be about a week longer at this place, and if you send the parcel hither directed 22 Seahouses, Eastbourne, it will go far to relieve the tedium of a watering-place.

Ever yours, A. T.

To Aubrey de Vere.

VICTORIA HOTEL, KILLARNEY.
September, 1842.

MY DEAR AUBREY,

I am sorry you had the fruitless trouble of calling at the Temple[1]. I tried hard to find you out in London but did not succeed. Partly from indisposition and partly from business and that of a nature the most unpleasant[2], I was kept at Boxley far longer than I wished or expected, so long indeed that I have hardly any time left for Ireland, as in a day or two I must again set out for Boxley. I have only just got your letter to me out of the Killarney Post Office. Christie, the member, found it in L.'s rooms, and brought it to Chapman, who sent it to Edmund Lushington, who sent

---

[1] 1 Mitre Court Buildings: F. Lushington's rooms where he often lodged.
[2] When the wood-carving company had begun to fail.

it to my people who sent it to me.   Now if that sentence
has not taken away your breath, make my apologies to
your cousin and beg her not to hate me because I never
seem to accept an invitation of hers.   I suppose you are
yet in Blandford Square, to which accordingly I send
this note.   I do not know that, if you were here, I should
have time to come.

I have been to your Ballybunion caves but could not
get into the finest on account of the weather.   I was
obliged to give Dingle up from want of time, tho'
much wished to see it, and I am afraid I must forgo
Glengarry likewise.

A. T.

I can find no further account of this visit to Ireland
except that my father then made the following lines
which occur in " Merlin and Vivien," within one of the
caves of Ballybunion:

> So dark a forethought roll'd about his brain,
> As on a dull day in an Ocean cave
> The blind wave feeling round his long sea-hall
> In silence.

To James Spedding.

January 25th, 1843.

Dear James,

I send you a sketch of Mablethorpe.   I was
wrong about the muffin-man, he comes o' Saturdays and
I can likewise get letters on Tuesdays, those being
market-days at Alford and churls going.   Don't forget
the *Athenæum*.   I send the sketch to melt your heart
Impart what booksellers' news there may be and re
member me to Fitz, if in town.

Ever yours, A. T.

He also writes to Moxon from Mablethorpe : " There
s nothing here but myself and two starfish ; therefore, if
ou have any stray papers which you do not know what
o do with, as you once told me, they would be manna in
he wilderness to me."

*From Charles Dickens, sent with a copy of
his "Works."*

DEVONSHIRE TERRACE,
March 10*th*, 1843.

MY DEAR TENNYSON,

For the love I bear you as a man whose writings
nlist my whole heart and nature in admiration of their Truth
nd Beauty, set these books upon your shelves ; believing that
ou have no more earnest and sincere homage than mine.

Faithfully and Gratefully your Friend,

CHARLES DICKENS.

To Aubrey de Vere.

ST LEONARD'S, *Sept.* 17*th*, 1843.

MY DEAR AUBREY,

I received your letter, but not in time to
nswer by return of post, and as you purposed setting
ut next day, I do not know whether it were worth
vhile writing to you at all: perhaps you may get my note
omewhere in Italy ; as it contains nothing, you will be
urt at sight of an English postmark on a pithless
crawl. I am sorry to hear of Henry Taylor's ill-health,
ut I have good faith in warm suns and leisure. You
re quite unforgiveable in your perpetual assumption of
ny nonchalance as to whatever you write. Why you do
lways so assume, and what reason I can have given you
or such an error on your part, is to me hidden in black
loud. You should have sent your proofs. It is quite

true that you have heard me say that I was sometimes bored by Mr E—— and others; but why you should be so ultra-humble as to mass yourself along with these, and dream you range no higher in my andrometer, is beyond my following. Peace be with such fancies, that is, I hope they are dead and over them the " hic jacent " of all futurity. Thank you however for the book.

I am down here at St Leonard's with the Lushing-tons; there are smooth seas and hot weather, and I wish you were with me. Good-bye, and don't be angry at this scrapling.

Ever yours, A. TENNYSON.

On July 13th, 1844, Moxon wrote that Tom Campbell had died at Boulogne. My father missed him, for he was a kind-hearted man and a brilliant talker in a tête-à-tête; and very good-natured whenever they met, as not un-frequently chanced, at the different clubs.

That the following letter should be understood, it is necessary to explain why my father had fallen ill Dr Allen, who has been already mentioned, was a physician near Beech Hill, with whom the Tennyson family had become acquainted, and who had either conceived, or had adopted, the idea of wood-carving by machinery. At all events he inspired the Tennysons with so great an enthusiasm for it, that by degrees he persuaded my father to give him the money for which wearied by a careless agent, he had sold his little estate in Grasby, Lincolnshire, and even the £500 left him as a legacy by Arthur Hallam's aunt. Not merely this however, — since, but for my father's intervention ap-parently, all the property of such of the family as were at Beech Hill would have been merged in this philanthropic undertaking; so fascinating was the prospect of oak panels and oak furniture carved by machinery, thus brought by its cheapness within the reach of the multitude.

The confidence my father had placed in the "earnest-frothy" Dr Allen proved to be misplaced. The entire project collapsed: my father's worldly goods were all gone, and a portion of the property of his brothers and sisters. Then followed a season of real hardship, and many trials for my father and mother, since marriage seemed to be further off than ever. So severe a hypochondria set in upon him that his friends despaired of his life. "I have," he writes, "drunk one of those most bitter draughts out of the cup of life, which go near to make men hate the world they move in." My uncle Edmund Lushington in 1844 generously insured Dr Allen's life for part of the debt due to my father; the Doctor died in January 1845.

To Edmund Lushington.

CHELTENHAM, *July 29th*, 1844.

MY DEAR EDMUND,

I ought certainly to have written before, but I don't know how it is, I cannot abide letter writing. Many letters have I conceived to you tho' brought forth none. In the first stages of Hydropathy (under Dr Jephson) I found it quite impossible to write, I could not turn my hand to anything and now I am not much better. I shall have to go into the system again and carry it out to the end. It is true I had ten crisises but I am not cured, tho' I do not doubt of the efficiency of the treatment in most cases, having *seen* most marvellous cures performed. I am going to town to-morrow for two or three days. I want among other things to see the exhibition and this is its last week. I have seen no Art, and my soul thirsts for it, for a year. I fear it would be

too expensive to come on to Eastbourne, and you are not
at Park House, and will not be perhaps for a fortnight
or three weeks.   At any rate I shall hope to see you
at Cheltenham.   Perhaps with Harry's leave I shall try
to get Geraldine to give me a bed in his rooms.   I have
walked thrice up Snowdon which I found much easier to
accomplish than walking on level ground.

London.   I arrived last night at the old Hummums
at 11 o'clock: called on Spedding, to my great disappointment he had left town; called on Chapman, door sported,
no answer to repeated applications at his no-knockered
portal.

Love to Cissy and the rest.

Ever yours, A. T.

During this visit to London Savile Morton wrote
to Mrs Brotherton that he had "come across Alfred
Tennyson." "We looked out some Latin translations of
his poems by Cambridge men, and read some poems of
Leigh Hunt's, and some of Theocritus and Virgil.   It is
delightful to have a passage picked out for one to admire
by him.   Seeing through his eyes much enlarges one's
view.   He has the power of impressing you with the
greatness of what he admires and bringing out its
meaning.   I had no idea Virgil could ever sound so fine
as it did by his reading....Yesterday I went to see him
again.   After some chat we sat down in two separate
rooms to read *Ellen Middleton*, by Lady Georgiana
Fullerton — very highly spoken of."   In another letter
he says: "Seeing Alfred has been a diversion to me....
I never met a heart so large and full of love."

In November my father was again at Cheltenham,
and wrote to Edward Moxon:

I want you to get me a book which I see ad-
vertised in the *Examiner:* it seems to contain many

speculations with which I have been familiar for years, and on which I have written more than one poem. The book is called *Vestiges of the Natural History of Creation*[1], and published by J. Churchill, Princes St. Soho; the price 7s. 6d., but you can get it cheaper.

Another book I long very much to see is that on the superiority of the modern painters to the old ones, and the greatness of Turner as an artist, by an Oxford undergraduate I think[2]. I do not much wish to buy it, it may be dear; perhaps you could borrow it for me out of the London Library, or from Rogers. I saw it lying on his table. I would promise to take care of it, and send it back in due time. At any rate let me have the other. Kind remembrances to Mrs and Miss Moxon and the little one to boot.

To Edward Fitzgerald.

Tuesday Night.

10 St James' Square, Cheltenham,
Jan. 14th, 1845.

My dear Fitz,

I *had* heard the news[3]. No gladness crossed my heart but sorrow and pity: that's not theatrical but the truth; wherefore bear with me, tho' perhaps it may seem a little out of the tide of things. Now will you be at 19 C. S. to-morrow or the day after? I am coming up to see you, and shall arrive most probably between

[1] The sections of "In Memoriam" about Evolution had been read by his friends some years before the publication of the *Vestiges of Creation* in 1844. Of natural selection Romanes writes, "In 'In Memoriam' Tennyson noted the fact, and a few years later Darwin supplied the explanation." *Darwin and after Darwin,* Romanes.

[2] Ruskin's first volume of *Modern Painters*.

[3] The reference in this letter is to the death of Dr Allen.

9 and 10 p.m., when I trust I shall find you well and thriving.

Ever yours, A. T.

From Henry Hallam (enclosing Sir Robert Peel's letter).

WRAXALL LODGE, near BRISTOL.
Sept. 24th, 1845.

MY DEAR TENNYSON,

You will believe that it is with the greatest pleasure I enclose to you the letter I have this day received from Sir R. Peel.

I think you will have no hesitation about answering it to *him*, nothing can be more flattering or delicate.

We want to learn more about Emily *herself*. Can she not ever *write* herself? The last we heard was that she had left Cheltenham, yet this can hardly be.

We have been for some months here and shall continue till the beginning of December; if you ever wander this way, we shall be very glad to give you a dinner and bed; and I have both glades and distant views to show you.

Believe me yours very truly,

H. HALLAM.

From the Right Honourable Sir Robert Peel to Alfred Tennyson.

I rejoice that you have enabled me to fulfil the intentions of Parliament by advising the Crown to confer a mark of Royal Favour [1] on one who has devoted to worthy purposes great intellectual powers.

The Queen has cordially approved of the recommendation which on the receipt of your letter I humbly offered to Her Majesty.

[1] Pension of £200 annually.

I have more than once heard Lord Houghton and my father talk together of Peel as a man and a statesman; and on those occasions Lord Houghton would invariably relate the story of his interview with Carlyle about the pension, given in Wemyss Reid's *Life* and here reprinted.

"Richard Milnes," said Carlyle one day, withdrawing his pipe from his mouth, as they were seated together in the little house in Cheyne Row, "when are you going to get that pension for Alfred Tennyson?"

"My dear Carlyle," responded Milnes, "the thing is not so easy as you seem to suppose. What will my constituents say if I do get the pension for Tennyson? They know nothing about him or his poetry, and they will probably think he is some poor relation of my own, and that the whole affair is a job."

Solemn and emphatic was Carlyle's response. "Richard Milnes, on the Day of Judgment, when the Lord asks you why you didn't get that pension for Alfred Tennyson, it will not do to lay the blame on your constituents; it is *you* that will be damned."

The question arose whether Sheridan Knowles or my father should be placed on the pension list. Peel knew nothing of either of them. Houghton said that he then made Peel read "Ulysses," "whereupon the pension was granted to Tennyson."

My father wrote then to his old friend, Rawnsley:

CHELTENHAM, 1845.

My dear Rawnsley,

I was delighted to see your handwriting again. I thought you had given me up as a bad job, for I remember that I once very flagitiously did not answer a very kind letter of yours long long ago: and truly my love for my friends must not be measured by the quantity of black and white into which I put it: for, however appearances are against me, I *have* a love for old Lincolnshire faces and things which will stick by me as long as I live. As to visiting you I wish I could, but I am engaged to Hallam, who has a country house in the neighbourhood of Bristol, and it is an engagement of some standing, and thither am I going as soon as ever I recover from the worst cold I ever caught since I was a Somersby suckling. It has kept me half-deaf for a month. I got it one wet night at Chelsea, when I went to see Mr. Carlyle. The better half of the Carlyle was then in Scotland. He, by the bye, is about to publish a book which you had better get in your book club — all the letters of Oliver Cromwell that can be got at, connected with a short narration or commentary of his own. Oliver is Carlyle's[1] God, the greatest of great men, and he intends if he can to sweep off all the royalist cobwebs that have hitherto obscured his fair fame.

I am glad to hear of your quadrilling at Horncastle. There is something pleasant in the notion of your figuring in L'Été with all your hood fluttering about you, and I respect a man who can keep his heart green when the snows of Time begin to whiten his head: not that I mean to say your head is white, but the silver hair *may* intrude "obiter," tho' as far as I recollect you had a very stout black crop when I saw you last. I should like to have been amongst you as in old times but

    "The days are awa that we hae seen,"

and I begin to feel an old man myself. I have gone thro' a vast deal of suffering (as to money difficulties in my family etc.) since I saw you last, and would not live it over again for quadruple the pension Peel has given me and on which you congratulate me. Well, I suppose I ought in a manner to be grateful. I have done nothing

---

[1] My father would rally Carlyle on his "might is right" and "one man" theories.

slavish to get it: I never even solicited for it either by myself or thro' others. · It was all done for me without word or hint from me, and Peel tells me I " need not by it be fettered in the public expression of any opinion I choose to take up "; so, if I take a pique against the Queen, or the Court, or Peel himself, I may, if I will, bully them with as much freedom, tho' not perhaps quite so gracefully, as if I were still unpensioned. Something in that word " pension " sticks in my gizzard ; it is only the name, and perhaps would " smell sweeter " by some other. I feel the least bit possible Miss Martineauish about it. You know she refused one, saying she "should be robbing the people who did not make laws for themselves ": however that is nonsense : her non-acceptance of the pension did not save the people a stiver, and meantime (what any one would have thought must have been more offensive to her feelings) her friends subscribed for her and kept her from want. If the people *did* make laws for themselves, if these things went by universal suffrage, what literary man ever would get a lift, it being known that the mass of Englishmen have as much notion of poetry as I of fox-hunting? Meantime there is some meaning in having a gentleman and a classic at the head of affairs, who may now and then direct the stream of public bounty to us, poor devils, whom the Grundyites would not only not remunerate, but kick out of society as barely *respectable ;* for Calliope herself, as I have heard, never kept a *gig* but walks barefoot about the sacred hill, no better than an Irishwoman.

I wish the causelessly bitter against me and mine no worse punishment than that they could read the very flattering letter Peel wrote me ; let us leave them in their limbo

" Non ragionam di lor, ma guarda e passa."

Peel's letter I would send you if I had it, but I have sent it to Hallam, and told him to keep it till I see him. I wrote to Rogers thanking him for his kindness. I thought he must have been mentioning me to Peel. He wrote me back a very pretty answer which I send Sophy for an autograph of the old Bard ; would any one think that pretty little hand was written by a man somewhere between eighty and ninety?

Now, Sophy, if as a matron you do not care for autographs, or intend to lose it or give it away, why let me have it back again for I have some value for it; particularly as the old man and I fell out one wet day in Pall Mall about half a year ago, when I said something that offended him, and his face flushed and he plucked his arm out of mine and told me I was " affecting the smart," and since then I haven't seen him. How is " Mamma," you do not say a word about her health and I want to know, for she was always like a mother to me? I wonder whether she recollects my playing the drunken son at Bristol. Many a pleasant talk have I had with her, and I much regret that I cannot come and see you now. Tell Mundy I retain a lively recollection of his puns ; and remember me to Coltman (George I mean), who always seemed to me a real good fellow. I recollect his sending me, when I lived at Boxley, a book of poems by a friend. I forget now what my answer was, but I hope I said nothing to hurt him or his friend's feelings. If you knew what a nuisance these volumes of verse are ! Rascals send me their's per post from America, and I have more than once been knocked up out of bed to pay three or four shillings for books of which I can't get thro' one page, for of all books the most insipid reading is second-rate verse. Blue books, red books, almanacks, peerages, anything is better. See ! how I keep chattering, just as if I were sitting by your fireside, in the little book-room, pipe in hand.

I shall not be in London in November, for I have only just returned from thence, but do you never by any chance mean to come and visit us? Are we in these days, who live East and West, to be as badly off as if we lived one at each Ind, or in the heart of the eighteenth century? Come and see us, you can do it some time, going to or from the Hallidays, and we shall be at least as glad to see you as they. Why don't you clip a few days from them and let us have the advantage? Here is a handsome town of thirty-five thousand inhabitants, a polka-parson-worshipping place, of which the Rev. Francis Close is Pope, besides pumps and pumprooms, chalybeates, quadrilles (as you have taken to them again), and one of the prettiest countries in Great Britain. My mother would be delighted to see you, and the girls would coax you, and make so much of you, you would feel yourself in a new planet. Edmund Lushington and Cissy have been with us and have just gone on to Glasgow. Their little one looks like a young Jupiter with his head full of Greek: but she, poor thing, was out of health, and dreaded the winter in Glasgow, which does not agree with her.

Tell Edward and Drummond that I expected them to have called on me the day after I met them at Moxon's, and I was very savage. Remember me to them with all kindness and to "Mamma" and Sophy; and not *me* only but all of us here to all of you there (if that's sense).

Now dinner's ready and I must say Good bye.

Ever yours affectionately,

A. TENNYSON.

CHAPTER XI.

SWITZERLAND 1846, AND LETTERS 1846-47.

Journal kept in Manuscript-book of "Princess."

("Come down, O maid, from yonder mountain height" was written
during this tour among the Alps.)

1846. Went on a tour to the Isle of Wight and in
August to Switzerland with Edward Moxon.

August 2nd. Up at 4 to go by " Princess Maude."
Picturesque sunrise from the pier. Bruges. Englishman
with moustache told us of festival at Bruges. I go down
into fore-cabin and get the very worst breakfast I ever
had in my life. Arrival at Ostend. Order from Belgian
king that no passports need be shown. Inhuman
conduct and supererogatory fury of porters. We lose
our presence of mind and run for it, but there is plenty
of time. Arrive at Bruges, walk to Hôtel de Blé,
recommended by moustached Englishman, missing the
conveyance thitherward, which, marked with gilt letters
Fleur de Blé, rolls by us as we near our hotel. Great
rejoicings of the people and hero-worship of Simon

Stevin[1], S on the banners, and names, busts and statues of all the Flanders great men, statesmen, sculptors, poets, etc. in an inner square within the great square. Horsemen riding in a circle for prize. High tower and clock in great square, picturesque groups in Cathedral, motioned from the seats we had taken opposite pulpit, depart to F. de Blé, dinner in salle — affected Englishwoman whom I took for Belge or German opposite, hot nervous night with me. Man "hemmed" overhead enough to shake the walls of Jericho.

August 3rd. Off to Grand Hôtel de Flandre, monkey, pleasant folk, commissionaire, pharmacien and opticien. J. Arteveld's house, town-hall very fine, musée not good, go to Louvain, Hôtel de Suède, new town-hall, old café, row of poplars, nervous night.

August 4th. Off to Liège, two sons of Sir Robert Peel, Hôtel d'Angleterre good, money changed, too soon for rail which came very late, pretty scenery, Chaudefontaine, old man and little boy, railway bordered with young acacias. Cologne, Hôtel de Cologne, rooms overlooking moonlit Rhine, hotel full of light and festival, pillaring its lights in the quiet water, bridge of boats, three steamers lying quietly below windows, not quite four hours' sleep.

August 5th. Woke at 5 or earlier, clash and clang of steamboat departure under me, walk on the quay, Cathedral splendid but to my mind too narrow for its length.

> "Gaspar and Melchior and Balthazar
> Came to Cologne on the broad-breasted Rhine
> And founded there a temple which is yet
> A fragment, but the wonder of the world."

---

[1] Born in the sixteenth century at Bruges, and a great mathematician and mechanic.

Embark, the bore of the Rhine, three Hyde Park drawling snobs, deck very hot, Nonnenwerth and Drach- enfels, sad recollections; Coblentz, horrid row, king of Holland, shuffled off to the Rheinischerhof, stupid hotel. Coblentz as hateful as it was long years before, over the bridge to the Cheval Blanc, coffee there, back again, the bridge opening islanded us in the river.

August 6th. Off again by boat, three drawlers de- parted at Mainz, talk about language with Germans, sad old city of Worms among poplars, reach Mannheim, Hôtel de l'Europe, take a dark walk among shrubberies with M.

August 7th. Early next morning off by rail to Kehl, confusion about the two railways, douane, stop and see Cathedral, nave magnificent, rail to Basle, Three Kings, green swift Rhine roaring against the piers, Swiss fountain.

August 8th. Café in room, off by diligence to Lucerne, vines, agreeable Swiss young lady to whom I quoted Goethe and she spouted *William Tell*, sorry to lose her, see Righi and Pilatus in the distance, walk before diligence but get in again, pass bridge over swift green stream, bureau, go to Schweizerhof, room at top of house, look out in the night and see the lake marbled with clouds, gabble of servants, bad night.

August 9th. Walk up the hill above the town, churchyard, innumerable gilt crosses, go to a villa, lie on the grass, return a different way from M., cross a part of the lake, walk back.

August 10th. Strolled about the painted bridges, M. met his friend, we bought Keller's map, off by 2 o'clock steamer to Weggis, hired a horse up the Righi, looked over and saw the little covers and wooded shores and villages under vast red ribs of rock, very fine, dis- missed my horse at the Bains where we entered with an Englishman and found peasants waltzing, gave two francs to boy who had ordered beds, summit, crowd of people, very feeble sunset, tea, infernal chatter as of innumerable apes.

August 11th. Sunrise, strange look of clouds packed on the lake of Egeri, far off Jungfrau looking as if delicately pencilled. Rossberg, Küssnacht, breakfast, began to descend at 9, strange aspect of hill, cloud, and snow, as if the mountains were on fire, watch the clouds opening and shutting as we go down, and making framed pictures of the lake, etc., long hot descent, dined at Weggis, landlady takes me out to select live fish for dinner, I am too tender-hearted so we go without fish, boat touches, off to Fluelen, very sleepy, carriage road to Italy, Tell's chapel, go in to church, return to Sweizerhof.

August 12th. Lake, guide and boat to Alpnach, hire voiture up the vale of Sarnen, walk a little before, get in, nothing very remarkable, arrive at Lungern, pretty green Alpine " thal " shut in with steep cliffs, one long waterfall, jolly old Radical who abused Dr Arnold, over the hills to Meyringen, home (after having seen Lauterbrunnen and the Bernese Alps, the best things in the tour).

To Edward Fitzgerald.

CHELTENHAM, *Nov. 12th,* 1846.

Well, Moxon went to Switzerland; saw Blanc, he was very sulky, kept his nightcap on, doff'd it one morning when I was knocked up out of bed to look at him at four o'clock, the glance I gave did not by any means repay me for the toil of travelling to see him. Two other things I *did* see in Switzerland, the stateliest bits of landskip

I ever saw, one was a look down on the valley of Lauterbrunnen while we were descending from the Wengern
Alp, the other a view of the Bernese Alps: don't think
that I am going to describe them.   Let it suffice that
I was so satisfied with the size of crags that (Moxon being
gone on before in vertigo and leaning on the arm of the
guide) I *laughed* by myself.   I was satisfied with the size
of crags, but mountains, great mountains disappointed
me.   * * * *   I called on Dickens at Lausanne who
was very hospitable, and gave us biscuits (a rare luxury
on the Continent, not such as are sweet and soft, but
hard and unsweet) and a flask of Liebfraumilch, which
is being interpreted "Virginis lac," as I dare say you
know.

I have just got *Festus;* order it and read.   You will
most likely find it a great bore, but there are really *very
grand* things in *Festus.*

Ever thine, A. T.

*Letters to Mrs Burton (the wife of the patron of
Dr Tennyson's living of Somersby).*

1846.

My DEAR MRS BURTON,

Nothing could be sweeter than Cathy's
Somersby violets, and doubt not but that I shall keep
them as a sacred treasure.   The violets of one's native
place gathered by the hands of a pure innocent child
must needs be precious to me, and indeed I would have
acknowledged the receipt of them and sent her a thousand loves and kisses before now, but there were several

reasons why I did not write which it is of no use troub-
ling you with; only I pray you kiss her for me very
sweetly on lip and cheek and forehead, and assure her
of my gratitude. I love all children, but I loved little
Cathy par excellence by a kind of instinct when I saw
her first. Do as you choose about the miniatures, but
I am told that you have had illness in your house and
it would make me uncomfortable to cause you any kind
of trouble. I am here in London on a visit to a friend
of mine at 6 Michael's Grove, Brompton. People fête
and dine me every day but I am somewhat unwell and
out of spirits: meanwhile I trust that your own health
is improved, and that you are prosperous and happy.
Farewell and believe me

Ever yours truly, A. TENNYSON.

MY DEAR MRS BURTON,

The miniatures which you have sent me we
will treasure as precious memorials of our shortlived
acquaintanceship: not that they do either you or the
child full justice. Nature without doubt has been much
more bountiful to you both than the artist: however the
portraits are not unlike and moreover well-painted. I
am sorry to learn from some fragments of your letter
to Emily, which she read to me, that you are not
altogether satisfied with the world about you. Pray
keep up your spirits in the wilderness of Lincolnshire.
I trust that we shall all meet again, and meanwhile may
your New Year be happy. Truly do I wish it may be
so. You know wise men say that our happiness lies
in our own hands: and therefore do you make the best
of things about you, not only for the sake of husband
and children, but of your friends here, who live in the

hope of re-seeing you, among whom count upon myself
as ever yours truly,

A. TENNYSON.

MY DEAR MRS BURTON,

I am very much grieved that your letter
reached me so late. I had left Umberslade and was
visiting at two or three places in Warwickshire, and as
I had given orders for any letter that came to be forwarded to Cheltenham, I have only just now on arriving
received yours. I shall be very happy to be god-father
to your little one, and so I am sure will Charles; he is
not here but in town, but he shall be written to to-day,
and there is no doubt of his compliance with your kind
and flattering proposal: only you must take his consent
for granted, as it is impossible for us or you to receive
an answer before the time specified: nor for many
reasons can either he or I attend in person: I am sorry
that all this has so happened. Call your child Alfred
if you will: he was born in the same house, perhaps the
same chamber, as myself, and I trust he is destined to
a far happier life than mine has been, poor little fellow!
Give him a kiss for his god-father, and one to Cathy for
her violets which I received and cherished: or if one do
not seem enough, give them by the dozen. I am glad
that you like the miniature. The papers spoke the truth
about Umberslade but they fibbed when they said I was
about to publish. What would be the use of that in a
general election? I am writing in a great hurry to save
the Northern post, so I bid you good-bye,

A. TENNYSON.

2 ST JAMES' ST., BUCKINGHAM GATE.
WEDNESDAY, *May* 17*th*.

MY DEAR MRS BURTON,

I have sent a silver cup for my little godson. I had intended to have sent it many a long month ago, but somehow or other I let the days slip on without doing so; for this I beg his pardon, which he must grant me as soon as he can babble. I trust that you will receive the cup at the same time with this letter. I hope that you are well and happy during this fine weather which makes me wish myself far away out of smoky London. Best love to my dear little violet-girl, and believe me always, dear Mrs Burton,

Yours truly, A. TENNYSON.

Letters to Mrs Howitt.

[1846.]

MY DEAR MRS HOWITT,

The day you mention was at least as pleasant to myself as to you; one, indeed, not easily to be forgotten. Clapton is henceforth to be remembered with higher and other than cockney associations, it is no longer the London suburb but the home of Mary Howitt. As for the morning dresses, did I notice them? if I did, what matter? they were a compliment to myself.

Your book from Longman has not yet arrived; but when it does, since (however you may please to depreciate beforehand) it must have something of you about it, I will give it a hearty welcome and my best attention.

I got your letter yesterday, and I have had so much to do in the interim that I have merely glanced over the extracts. They seem to me to be very clever and full of a noble 19th century-ism (if you will admit such a word), but whether not too fantastic, if considered as an explanation of the Mosaic text, may I think admit of doubt. Meanwhile I hail all such attempts as heralding a grander and more liberal state of opinion, and consequently sweeter and nobler modes of living. There was no more *sea*, says St John in Revelation. I wonder your friend did not quote that: perhaps he does in some other part of his book. I remember reading that when a child, and not being able to reconcile myself to a future when there should be no more sea.

I am going up to Cambridge to-morrow to be present at the commemoration of the founding of Trinity College 300 years ago. There is to be a great dinner in Hall, and as I have got a special invitation from my old Tutor, now the Master, I am going; the 22nd is the dinner-day. I have just left myself time to get there; think of me to-morrow night as passing within two or three miles of you on the Eastern C. R., perhaps not so far, and again sweeping back a day or two after on my return yet not able to stop, divers duties calling me home with voices of undeniable authority. I ought not to go at all but old recollections drag me. However sometime betwixt the death of Spring and the birth of Summer I do hope to see you once more.

I partly guess your mysterious request. Mr Howitt's surprise at the hyacinths is a very pretty household picture. I wish that we Englanders dealt more in such symbols, that we drest our affections up in a little more poetical costume; real warmth of heart would lose nothing, rather gain by it. As it is, our manners are as cold as

the walls of our churches.   Good-bye, dear Mrs Howitt,
say everything kind for me to husband and daughter and
trust me

Yours ever, A. TENNYSON.

10 ST JAMES' SQUARE, CHELTENHAM.
Nov. 19th.

DEAR MRS HOWITT,

Your kind letter gave me very sincere pleasure, and I shall be most happy to meet Mr Dempster
under your roof when I come to town.   I did not hear
the Hutchinsons[1] when they were in England and I
regret it.   I am sure Abby must have sung divinely for
everyone says she did.   I can scarce help fancying that
the female voice is more suited by nature to the singing
of such poems than any man's, but I am wrong, for you
tell me that Mr Dempster sings quite as exquisitely as
Abby.   I should have been in town before now but
several little matters have occurred to hinder me.
Among other things I sent an invitation to the German
poet, Freiligrath: he has translated some of my poems
and he sent me his book thro' my publisher: the letter
to Moxon was dated from Mrs Leigh's, Clapton Pond;
do you know such a person?   I have got no answer and
I am puzzled by his silence.   Perhaps he may not be in
England, after all, but every time the postman knocks I
expect to hear from him and that he is coming.   I will
send you word of my arrival in town.

A. T.

---

[1] American ladies who were noted singers.

Letters to Edward Moxon.

(*After the tour in Switzerland.*)

1846.

My dear Moxon,

I got your parcel and bluebell this morning and a letter from a man who seems deserving and in difficulties; he has asked me to lend him four pounds, which I have promised to *give* him, and referred him to you. So let him have that sum if he calls with my letter: his name is R. C. W.

Ever yours, A. Tennyson[1].

Second visit to Dr Gully's watercure.

Umberslade Hall, Birmingham, 1847.
Tuesday afternoon.

My dear Moxon,

I wish you would make up your mind to come down on Saturday and see me here. You could come down by the express as I did in three hours to Birmingham, and any of the cabs at the station would bring you on: here is a Hall in a pleasant park, and you would be all the better for a Sunday's mouthful of fresh air. We can give you a bed here and you should do just as you like. I want to talk with you. I find it very

[1] Whenever any literary man "deserving and in difficulties" applied to him for money, he always endeavoured to help him. To the day of his death he continued this practice.

difficult to correct proofs under the treatment[1], but you shall have them all back with you on Monday; don't show them to people. I have not at all settled whether I shall publish them now or in the Autumn, yet an Edinburgh paper mentions that I have a poem in the press. Confound the publicities and gabblements of the 19th century! Now, I hope you will come. If you do, bring two copies of my poems with you, two persons in this house want them; if you don't come (but I hope you will) send two. The printers are awful zanies, they print erasures and corrections too, and other sins they commit of the utmost inhumanity. Come! Send a line first.

Yours ever,

A. TENNYSON.

To Rev. H. Rawnsley.

PARK HOUSE, MAIDSTONE.
April 16th, 1847.

MY DEAR RAWNSLEY,

Many thanks for your very kind letter, which was grateful to me as showing that I am not forgotten

---

[1] From Umberslade my father writes to Mrs Russell: "They tell me not to read, not to think; but they might as well tell me not to live. I lack something of the woman's long-enduring patience in these matters. It is a terribly long process, but then what price is too high for health, and health of mind is so involved with health of body... I wish you could find time in the course of the summer to come over and see us. We should be so happy to see you. We expect my mother from Scotland in a few days' time. She comes as far as Birmingham with Cecilia and the Professor (Lushington). The latter go on to Park House, Lushington's seat near Maidstone; and Charles goes to bring my mother here. Of *her* kindness and true-heartedness I am sure you never had any doubt, and therefore I need not say anything of the joyful welcome she would give you. She has been much grieved just now with the loss of her cousin, Mr Wheeldon of Market Street near St Albans. A purer Christian, a better man, never lived. He was like her, for he had not a touch of gall in his whole nature. Peace be with him."

amongst you; not that I wanted any proof of that, but still it is pleasant to have assurance doubly sure. You would have been answered before had I not been away from home, lying sick of more than one ailment at a friend's chamber in the Temple, from whence the other day I came on here partly for change of air and partly because I had promised to pay a farewell visit to my brother-in-law's brother, Harry Lushington. He is going out to Malta as secretary to the Maltese government, a post of (I believe) about £1500 a year and one which he is quite clever enough to occupy with credit to himself; but being a man of feeble stamina he is afraid of the climate and altogether down in the mouth about it, so I came to see the last of him before he went, and do my best to set him up. I am much grieved to hear of your rheumatism. I fear this bitter April is very unfavourable and the east wind which comes sweeping from the sea over your marshes to Halton. H. L. goes some time next week, and till then I must be here, so that I fear that what with this and my illness a journey into Lincolnshire so as to catch all your "clan" in full conclave is quite impossible. Well, I can't help it, I love my old friends as much as ever; recent friendships may be broken thro' but old ones early-made are a part of one's blood and bones. I say my old friendships are as dear as ever, but that you must accept this protestation in lieu of my personal presence and not be hard of faith but believing.

Give my kindest love to each and all of the "old familiar faces," and

Believe me always yours truly,

A. TENNYSON.

To Mrs Russell.

10 ST JAMES' SQUARE, CHELTENHAM.
Saturday evening.   [*Undated.*]

MY DEAREST AUNT,

I have received your welcome note and
cheque and had hoped to have a better account of your
eyes. Those "animals[1]" you mention are very dis-
tressing and mine increase weekly : in fact I almost look
forward with certainty to being blind some of these days.
I have however no sort of inflammation to complain of,
it is all failing nerve. I have no great opinion of the
salubrity of Leamington, and as for this place it is often
as muggy and turbid as London itself. "Much company"
and after-dinner "talk of roads," etc. are not much in
your favour, but why do all English country gentlemen
talk of dogs, horses, roads, crops etc.? It is better after
all than affecting Art and Feeling: they would make a
poor hand of that, though *you* tried to help them out.
I wish they would be a little kinder to the poor. I
would honour them then and they might talk what they
would. But I am rambling and moreover getting personal on the squires, which perhaps I have no business
to do, for, as Hamlet says, "use every man after his
deserts and who shall scape whipping?" With respect
to the non-publication of those poems [2] which you mention,
it is partly occasioned by the considerations you speak
of, and partly by my sense of their present imperfectness ;
perhaps they will not see the light till I have ceased to
be. I cannot tell but I have no wish to send them out
yet. Emily wished us to remember her kindly to you

[1] *Muscæ volitantes.*
[2] Probably " In Memoriam."

when she was here.   She has been visiting the Lushing-
tons in Kent, and is now with the Hallams at Clifton.
I wonder whether you can read this scrawl, my pen is an
old steel one in a state of hopeless splittage and divari-
cation.   You must forgive me for not answering you
before[1].   I have no excuse to offer and I fling myself on
your mercy.   Do you know, I don't write even a note
once in three months.   I never can get myself set down
to write, and I am in arrears of correspondence with all
the world.   Goodbye, dearest Aunt.   Mother, sisters
etc. send lots of love to you and Emma.

> Always affectionately yours,
>
> A. TENNYSON.

P.S.   Have you read Miss Martineau on Mesmerism
in the *Athenæum* (two of them)?   I have got them and
if you like I will send them to you.   They are very
wonderful.

In 1846 the fourth edition of the Poems was published: and, having been bitterly attacked by Lytton
Bulwer because Peel had placed him on the Pension
list, my father contributed to *Punch* the only personal
satire he ever wrote, " The New Timon and the Poets,"
February 28th; followed by an "After-thought[2]," March
7th.   About these poems he left a note:

" I never wrote a line against anyone but Sir Edward
Lytton Bulwer.   His lines did not move me to do so.
But at the very time he was writing or had written these
he was visiting my cousins, the d'Eyncourts, and said to
them, ' How much I should like to know your cousin

---

[1] He said he could not devote himself to his work and write letters also,
so he gave up writing to friends and relations.

[2] Published afterwards under the title of " Literary Squabbles."

Alfred'; and I, going into a book-club in the town where
I was then living, found a newspaper turned up and
folded so that I could not miss, 'See how Sir Edward
tickles up the poetasters and their patrons.' The stupid
insignificant paper, and the purpose with which it had
been set before me, provoked me. I saw afterwards a
letter which he wrote to my friend John Forster.
Moreover, he stated in a note that I belonged to a very
rich family. The younger son, his friend, who had
inherited was rich enough, but the elder branch was shut
out in the cold, and at that time I had scarce anything.
Moreover, I remembered that he had said 'If a man be
attacked, let him attack.'

Wretched work. Odium literarium."

My father added : " I never sent my lines to *Punch*.
John Forster did. They were too bitter. I do not think
that I should ever have published them."

. Then she "let some one sing to us. lightlier move
The minutes fledged with music." & a maid
Of those behind her smote her harp & sang

Tears, idle
~~the foolish~~ Tears, I know not what they mean.
Tears from the depth of some divine despair
Rise in the heart & gather to the eyes
In looking on the happy Autumn fields
And thinking of the days that are no more.

        Fresh as the first beam glittering on a sail
That brings our friends up from the underworld
Sad as the last which reddens over one
That sinks with all we love below the verge
So sad, so fresh the days that are no more

Ah sad & strange as in dark summer-dawns
The earliest pipe of half awaken'd birds
To dying ears when unto dying eyes
The casement slowly grows a glimmering square
So sad, & strange the days that are no more.

        Dear as remember'd kisses after death
And sweet as those by hopeless fancy feign'd
On lips that are for others; deep as love
Deep as first love, & wild with all regret
O death in life, the days that are no more

From the Original MS.

CHAPTER XII.

"THE PRINCESS."

> Maybe wildest dreams
> Are but the needful preludes of the truth.

> O lift your natures up:
> Embrace our aims: work out your freedom!

> There are thousands now
> Such women, but convention beats them down;
> It is but bringing up; no more than that.

> "I say God made the woman for the man,
> And for the good and increase of the world."
> "Parson," said I, "you pitch the pipe too low."

What someone called the "herald-melody" of the higher education of women, "The Princess," mostly written in Lincoln's Inn Fields, was published in 1847, and at this time "The Golden Year" was added to the *Poems*. The subject of "The Princess," my father believed, was original, and certainly the story is full of original incident, humour and fancy[1].

It may have suggested itself when the project of

---

[1] Sir William Rowan Hamilton, the great mathematician, said: "It deeply presses on my reflection how much wiser a book is Tennyson's *Princess* than my *Quaternions*."

a Women's College was in the air[1], or it may have arisen in its mock-heroic form from a Cambridge joke, such as he commemorated in these lines, which I found in one of his old MS books:

The Doctor's Daughter. (*Unpublished.*)

Sweet Kitty Sandilands,
  The daughter of the doctor,
We drest her in the Proctor's bands,
  And past her for the Proctor.

All the men ran from her
  That would have hasten'd to her,
All the men ran from her
  That would have come to woo her.

Up the street we took her
  As far as to the Castle,
Jauntily sat the Proctor's cap
  And from it hung the tassel.

As for the various characters in the poem, they give all possible views of Woman's higher education; and as for the heroine herself, the Princess Ida, the poet who created her considered her as one of the noblest among his women. The stronger the man or woman, the more of the lion or lioness untamed, the greater the man or woman tamed. In the end we see this lioness-like woman subduing the elements of her humanity to that which is highest within her, and recognizing the relation in which she stands towards the order of the world and toward God —

A greater than all knowledge beat her down.

[1] He talked over the plan of the poem with my mother in 1839.

His friends report my father to have said, that the two great social questions impending in England were "the housing and education of the poor man before making him our master, and the higher education of women"; and that the sooner woman finds out, before the great educational movement begins, that "woman is not un-developt man, but diverse," the better it will be for the progress of the world [1].

There have not been wanting those who have deemed the varied characters and imagery of the poem wasted on something of a fairy tale without the fairies [2]. But, in this instance as in others involving the supreme meaning and guidance of life, a parable is perhaps the teacher that can most surely enter in at all doors.

It was no mere dramatic sentiment, but one of my father's strongest convictions of the true relation between man and woman, which impelled him to write:

> Let this proud watchword rest
> Of equal; seeing either sex alone
> Is half itself, and in true marriage lies
> Nor equal, nor unequal: each fulfils
> Defect in each, and always thought in thought,
> Purpose in purpose, will in will, they grow,
> The single pure and perfect animal,
> The two-cell'd heart beating, with one full stroke,
> Life.

[1] Dawson, the Canadian editor of "The Princess," writes: "At the time of the publication of 'The Princess' the surface-thought of England was intent solely upon Irish famines, corn-laws and free-trade. It was only after many years that it became conscious of anything being wrong in the position of women... No doubt such ideas were at the time 'in the air' in England, but the dominant, practical Philistinism scoffed at them as 'ideas' banished to America, that refuge for exploded European absurdities."

[I believe the *Vindication of the Rights of Woman* by Mary (Wollstone-craft) Godwin (1792) first turned the attention of the people of England to the "wrongs of women."]

[2] The following paragraphs are based on what my father said about the poem.

And if woman in her appointed place "stays all the fair young planet in her hands," she may be well content. She has space enough to

> Burgeon out of all
> Within her — let her make herself her own
> To give or keep, to live and learn and be
> All that not harms distinctive womanhood.

She must train herself to do the large work that lies before her, even though she may not be destined to be wife or mother, cultivating her understanding not her memory only, her imagination in its highest phases, her inborn spirituality and her sympathy with all that is pure, noble and beautiful, rather than mere social accomplishments; then and then only will she further the progress of humanity, then and then only men will continue to hold her in reverence.

On the other hand one of the poet's main tests of manhood is "the chivalrous reverence" for womanhood.

> To love one maiden only, cleave to her,
> And worship her by years of noble deeds,
> Until they win her; for indeed I know
> Of no more subtle master under heaven
> Than is the maiden passion for a maid,
> Not only to keep down the base in man,
> But teach high thought and amiable words,
> And courtliness and the desire of fame,
> And love of truth, and all that makes a man.

He would say, "I would pluck my hand from a man even if he were my greatest hero, or dearest friend, if he wronged a woman or told her a lie."

After 1847 "The Princess" underwent considerable alterations. The second edition was published in 1848 with a few amendments, and dedicated to Henry

Lushington, but in 1850 a third edition appeared with omissions and many additions, and notably six songs were introduced, which help to express more clearly the meaning of "the medley."

These songs

> The women sang
> Between the rougher voices of the men,
> Like linnets in the pauses of the wind.

In 1851 the "weird seizures" of the Prince were inserted. His too emotional temperament was intended from an artistic point of view to emphasize his comparative want of power. "Moreover," my father writes, "the words 'dream-shadow,' 'were and were not' doubtless refer to the anachronisms and improbabilities of the story: compare the prologue,

> Seven and yet one, like shadows in a dream,

and v. 466,

> And like a flash the weird affection came,
> *   *   *   *   *   *   *
> I seem'd to move in old memorial tilts,
> And doing battle with forgotten ghosts,
> To dream myself the shadow of a dream."

"It may be remarked that there is scarcely anything in the story which is not prophetically glanced at in the prologue." My father added: "It is true that some of the blank verse in this poem is among the best I ever wrote" — such passages as:

> Not peace she look'd — the Head: but rising up
> Robed in the long night of her deep hair, so
> To the open window moved, remaining there
> Fixt like a beacon-tower above the waves

Of tempest, when the crimson-rolling eye
Glares ruin, and the wild birds on the light
Dash themselves dead. She stretch'd her arms and
  call'd
Across the tumult and the tumult fell;

and as this description of a storm seen from Snowdon:

As one that climbs a peak to gaze
O'er land and main, and sees a great black cloud
Drag inward from the deeps, a wall of night,
Blot out the slope of sea from verge to shore,
And suck the blinding splendour from the sand,
And quenching lake by lake, and tarn by tarn,
Expunge the world;

and as these lines from the last canto:

Look up, and let thy nature strike on mine,
Like yonder morning on the blind half-world;
Approach and fear not; breathe upon my brows;
In that fine air I tremble, all the past
Melts mist-like into this bright hour, and this
Is morn to more, and all the rich to-come
Reels, as the golden Autumn woodland reels
Athwart the smoke of burning weeds. Forgive me,
I waste my heart in signs: let be. My bride,
My wife, my life. O we will walk this world,
Yoked in all exercise of noble end,
And so thro' those dark gates across the wild
That no man knows.

For *simple* rhythm and vowel music he considered
his "Come down, O maid, from yonder mountain height,"
written in Switzerland (chiefly at Lauterbrunnen and
Grindelwald), and descriptive of the waste Alpine heights
and gorges, and of the sweet, rich valleys below, as
amongst his "*most successful work.*" But by this phrase

he meant no more than that he felt he had done his best: there was no tinge of vanity in it. To put his own poetry in favourable comparison with that of others was never in his mind.

He said that "The passion of the past, the abiding in the transient, was expressed in 'Tears, idle Tears,' which was written in the yellowing autumn-tide at Tintern Abbey, full for me of its bygone memories. Few know that it is a blank verse lyric." He thought that my uncle Charles' sonnet of "Time and Twilight" had the same sort of mystic, *dämonisch* feeling.

The only song in "The Princess" approved by Fitzgerald was "Blow, Bugle, Blow," commemorating the echoes at Killarney[1].

"That is one of Fitz's crotchets," Fitzgerald said to me in 1876, "and I am considered a great heretic, because like Carlyle I gave up all hopes of him after 'The Princess.'" He wrote once, and repeated for me in his MS notes, that none of the songs had "the old champagne flavour," adding, "Alfred is the same magnanimous, kindly delightful fellow as ever, uttering by far the finest prose-sayings of anyone." Nothing either by Thackeray or by my father met Fitzgerald's approbation unless he had first seen it in manuscript.

The following notes on "The Princess" were left by my father:

In the Prologue the "Tale from mouth to mouth" was a game which I have more than once played when I was at Trinity College, Cambridge, with my brother undergraduates. Of course, if he "that inherited the tale" had not attended very carefully to his predecessors, there were contradictions; and if the story were historical, occasional anachronisms. In defence of what

---

[1] When my father was last there a boatman said to him, "So you're the gentleman that brought the money to the place?"

some have called the too poetical passages, it should
be recollected that the poet of the party was requested
to " dress the tale up poetically," and he was full of the
" gallant and heroic chronicle."   Some of my remarks
on passages in the " Princess " have been published by
Dawson of Canada, who copied them from a letter
which I wrote to him criticizing his study of the
" Princess [1]."   The child is the link thro' the parts as
shown in the songs which are the best interpreters of
the poem [2].   Before the first edition came out, I deliber-
ated with myself whether I should put songs between
the separate divisions of the poem; again I thought
that the poem would explain itself, but the public did not
see the drift.   The first song I wrote was named " The
Losing of the Child."   The child is sitting on the bank
of the river and playing with flowers; a flood comes
down; a dam has been broken thro' — the child is borne
down by the flood; the whole village distracted; after
a time the flood has subsided; the child is thrown safe
and sound again upon the bank; and there is a chorus
of jubilant women.

[1] The letter is printed on pp. 256–259 of this volume.

[2] " At the end of the first canto, fresh from the description of the female
college, with its professoresses, and hostleresses, and other Utopian monsters,
we turn the page, and —

> As through the land at eve we went.
>
> *   *   *   *   *   *
>
> O there above the little grave,
> We kissed again with tears.

Between the next two cantos intervenes the well-known cradle song, perhaps
the best of all; and at the next interval is the equally well-known bugle-
song, the idea of which is that of twin-labour and twin-fame in a pair of
lovers. In the next the memory of wife and child inspires the soldier on
the field; in the next the sight of the fallen hero's child opens the sluices of
his widow's tears; and in the last,...the poet has succeeded, in the new
edition, in superadding a new form of emotion to a canto in which he
seemed to have exhausted every resource of pathos which his subject
allowed." Charles Kingsley, in *Fraser's Magazine*, September, 1850.

(Unpublished fragment.)

The child was sitting on the bank
   Upon a stormy day,
He loved the river's roaring sound;
The river rose and burst his bound,
Flooded fifty leagues around,
Took the child from off the ground,
   And bore the child away.
O the child so meek and wise,
   Who made *us* wise and mild!

     *   *   *   *   *

Two versions of "Sweet and Low" were made, and were sent to my mother to choose which should be published. She chose the published one in preference to that which follows, because it seemed to her more song-like.

(Unpublished version.)

Bright is the moon on the deep,
Bright are the cliffs in her beam,
   Sleep, my little one, sleep!
Look he smiles, and opens his hands,
He sees his father in distant lands,
And kisses him there in a dream,
   Sleep, sleep.

Father is over the deep,
Father will come to thee soon,
   Sleep, my pretty one, sleep!
Father will come to his babe in the nest,
Silver sails all out of the West,
Under the silver moon,
   Sleep, sleep!

"The notices of "The Princess" that I know interested my father were those by Aubrey de Vere[1], Charles Kingsley, Robertson (the Brighton preacher), and Dawson of Montreal. To the last[2] he wrote a letter (Nov. 21st, 1882) which may be quoted in full:

I thank you for your able and thoughtful essay on "The Princess." You have seen amongst other things that if women ever were to play such freaks, the burlesque and the tragic might go hand in hand. * * * Your explanatory notes are very much to the purpose, and I do not object to your finding parallelisms. They must always occur. A man (a Chinese scholar) some time ago wrote to me saying that in an unknown, untranslated Chinese poem there were two whole lines[3] of mine almost word for word? Why not? Are not human eyes all over the world looking at the same objects, and must there not consequently be coincidences of thought and impressions and expressions? It is scarcely possible for anyone to say or write anything in this late time of the world to which, in the rest of the literature of the world, a parallel could not somewhere be found. But when you say that this passage or that was suggested by

[1] *Edinburgh Review*, No. CLXXXII. October, 1849.

[2] In Dawson's *Study of the Princess* I find that I have written, after a talk with my father *à propos* possibly of the battle at the end of the poem: — "A. T. observed: 'Macpherson's 'Ossian' is poor in most parts, but this is a grand image — After saying that the beam of battle was bright before the spectral warrior, he goes on somehow like this: 'But behind thee was the Shadow of Death, like the darkened half of the moon behind its other half in growing light.'' A. T. talked of 'the beautiful picture that the girl graduates would have made; the long hall glittering like a bed of flowers with daffodil and lilac.' Then he touched on the old religions and the 'old god of war'; 'the Norse mythology,' he said, 'is finer than the Greek with its human gods, though the Greek has more beauty. The Norsemen thought that there was something better in the way of religion that would dawn upon the earth after the Ragnarok or twilight of the gods.'"

[3] The Peak is high, and the stars are high,
And the thought of a man is higher.
"The Voice and the Peak."

Wordsworth or Shelley or another, I demur; and more, I wholly disagree. There was a period in my life when, as an artist, Turner for instance, takes rough sketches of landskip, etc. in order to work them eventually into some great picture, so I was in the habit of chronicling, in four or five words or more, whatever might strike me as picturesque in Nature. I never put these down, and many and many a line has gone away on the north wind, but some remain: e.g.

A full sea glazed with muffled moonlight.

Suggestion.

The sea one night at Torquay, when Torquay was the most lovely sea-village in England, tho' now a smoky town. The sky was covered with thin vapour, and the moon behind it.

A great black cloud
Drags inward from the deep.

Suggestion.

A coming storm seen from the top of Snowdon.

In the " Idylls of the King,"
With all
Its stormy crests that smote against the skies.

Suggestion.

A storm which came upon us in the middle of the North Sea.

As the water-lily starts and slides.

Suggestion.

Water-lilies in my own pond, seen on a gusty day with my own eyes. They did start and slide in the sudden puffs of wind till caught and stayed by the tether of their own stalks, quite as true as Wordsworth's simile and more in detail.

> A wild wind shook, —
> Follow, follow, thou shalt win.

Suggestion.

I was walking in the New Forest. A wind did arise and

> Shake the songs, the whispers and the shrieks
> Of the wild wood together.

The wind I believe was a west wind, but because I wished the Prince to go south, I turned the wind to the south, and naturally the wind said "follow." I believe the resemblance which you note is just a chance one. Shelley's lines are not familiar to me tho' of course, if they occur in the *Prometheus*, I must have read them. I could multiply instances, but I will not bore you, and far indeed am I from asserting that books as well as Nature are not, and ought not to be, suggestive to the poet. I am sure that I myself, and many others, find a peculiar charm in those passages of such great masters as Virgil or Milton where they adopt the creation of a bygone poet, and re-clothe it, more or less, according to their own fancy. But there is, I fear, a prosaic set growing up among us, editors of booklets, book-worms, index-hunters, or men of great memories and no imagination, who *impute themselves* to the poet, and so believe that *he*, too, has no imagination, but is for ever poking his nose between the pages of some old volume in order to see what he can appropriate. They will not allow one to say ' Ring the bell ' without finding that we have taken it from Sir P. Sidney, or even to use such a simple expression as the ocean " roars," without finding out the precise verse in Homer or Horace from which we have plagiarised it (fact!).

I have known an old fish-wife, who had lost two sons
at sea, clench her fist at the advancing tide on a stormy
day, and cry out, "Ay! roar, do! how I hates to see thee
show thy white teeth." Now if I had adopted her ex-
clamation and put it into the mouth of some old woman
in one of my poems, I daresay the critics would have
thought it original enough, but would most likely have
advised me to go to Nature for my old women and not
to my own imagination[1]; and indeed it is a strong figure.

Here is another anecdote about suggestion. When
I was about twenty or twenty-one I went on a tour to
the Pyrenees. Lying among these mountains before a
waterfall[2] that comes down one thousand or twelve
hundred feet I sketched it (according to my custom
then) in these words:

Slow-dropping veils of thinnest lawn.

When I printed this, a critic informed me that "lawn"
was the material used in theatres to imitate a waterfall,
and graciously added, "Mr T. should not go to the
boards of a theatre but to Nature herself for his suggestions." And I *had* gone to Nature herself.

I think it is a moot point whether, if I had known
how that effect was produced on the stage, I should have
ventured to publish the line.

I find that I have written, quite contrary to my
custom, a letter, when I had merely intended to thank
you for your interesting commentary.

Thanking you again for it, I beg you to believe me

Very faithfully yours,

A. TENNYSON.

---

[1] He used to compare with this the Norfolk saying which we heard when
we were staying with the Rev. C. T. Digby at Warham: "The sea is
moaning for the loss of the wind."

[2] In the Cirque de Gavarnie.

Letters after the publication of "The Princess."

To Edward Fitzgerald.

1847.

My dear Fitz,

Ain't I a beast for not answering you before? not that I am going to write now, only to tell you that I have seen Carlyle more than once, and that I have been sojourning at 42 Ebury Street for some twenty days or so, and that I am going to bolt as soon as ever I can, and that I would go to Italy if I could get anybody to go with me which I can't, and so I suppose I shan't go, which makes me hate myself and all the world; for the rest I have been be-dined usque ad nauseam. A pint of pale ale and a chop are things yearned after, not achievable except by way of lunch. However, this night I have sent an excuse to Mrs Procter and here I am alone, and wish you were with me. How are you getting on? Don't grow quite into glebe before I see you again.

My book is out and I hate it, and so no doubt will you.

Never mind, you will like me none the worse, and now good-night. I am knocked up and going to bed.

Ever yours, A. TENNYSON.

To Aubrey de Vere.

1847.

My dear Aubrey,

I have ordered Moxon to send you the new edition[1] of " The Princess." You will find that I have in some measure adopted your suggestions, not entirely.

[1] Not published till 1848.

Many thanks for your critique in the *Edinburgh*. There were only one or two little things in it which I did not like; for instance that about the " dying and the dead " which is quite wide of the mark[1], and you will see that I have inserted a line to guard against such an interpretation in future; however I have every reason to be grateful to you, both for the ability of the article and for the favourable view you take of me in general; too favourable surely. I dare not believe such good things of myself. I have seen no papers for an age, and do not know how your poor are going on. I fear this bitter weather is very hard upon them.

A. T.

To Mrs Howitt.

42 EBURY STREET.

MY DEAR MRS HOWITT,

I got your beautiful book of Ballads the other day at Moxon's. It contains (as far as I have seen it) much that is sweet and good and reminds me of yourself. I have however been myself so much engaged with proof-sheets for the few days since I received it that I have not had leisure to do it justice by a fair perusal. Accept in return a book[2] of mine which I have sent to Longmans' for you. I don't believe you will like it — not at least till after three readings, if you will honour it so far. Best remembrances to husband and daughter, not forgetting the younglings and

Believe me always yours,

A. TENNYSON.

[1] See p. 282.
[2] " The Princess."

For the sisters Brontë my father had the highest admiration. He received the following letter from Currer Bell (Charlotte Brontë):

June 16th, 1847.

Sir,

My relatives, Ellis and Acton Bell, and myself, heedless of the repeated warnings of various respectable publishers, have committed the rash act of printing a volume of poems.

The consequences predicted have of course overtaken us; our book is found to be a drug; no man needs it nor heeds.

In the space of a year the publisher has disposed but of two copies; and by what painful efforts he succeeded in getting rid of these two, himself only knows.

Before transferring the edition to the trunkmakers, we have decided on distributing as presents a few copies of what we cannot sell. We beg to offer you one in acknowledgement of the pleasure and profit we have often and long derived from your works.

I am, Sir, yours very respectfully,

CURRER BELL.

CHAPTER XIII.

CHELTENHAM, LONDON, CORNWALL, SCOTLAND AND IRELAND, 1846–1850.

The headquarters of the Tennysons were now at Cheltenham, Bellevue House in St James' Square. I am indebted to Dr Ker, brother of Judge Alan Ker, who married Miss Mary Tennyson, for some details of my father's life at this time.

From 1846 to 1850 he was often with his mother and family, but cannot be said to have moved in the society of the place: still he made some new acquaintances. The names I can recall are those of Dobson [1], afterwards Principal of Cheltenham College; Boyd, afterwards Dean of Exeter; Foxton, author of *Popular Christianity;* Sydney Dobell, the poet; Dr Acworth; Rashdall, Vicar of Malvern; Reece; and the well-known and "much beloved" Frederick Robertson, then Boyd's curate, afterwards incumbent of Trinity Chapel, Brighton.

There was a little room at the top of the house in St James' Square, not kept in very orderly fashion, for books and papers were to be seen quite as much on the floor and the chairs as upon the table. Here my father, pipe in mouth, discoursed to his friends more unconstrainedly than anywhere else on men and things and what death means. When the talk was on religious

---

[1] Dobson was third classic in the same year that Edmund Lushington was senior classic and Thompson fourth.

questions, which was not often, he spoke confidently of future existence.   Of Christianity he said, " it is ruggin at my heart[1]."

My father would say: "The first time I me Robertson I felt that he expected something notabl from me because I knew that he admired my poem that he wished to pluck the heart from my mystery; s for the life of me from pure nervousness I could talk c nothing but beer."

Dr Ker says:

Sydney Dobell did not see much of your father in Che tenham; but in Malvern, some years after your family le this place, Dobell, as he afterwards told me, saw a good deal c him.   Dobell, as you know, was not a popular poet, and th number of his readers does not increase as the years go on, bu that he was no commonplace poet your father heartily allowec Frederick Foxton could only be brought to speak on one subjec Carlyle, whose companion and caretaker he had been during journey on the Continent.   Rashdall and Dr Acworth were me of cultivation and high social qualities whom your father me occasionally and much liked.

One acquaintance would keep on assuring my fathe that it was the greatest honour of his life to have me him.   My father's answer to such praise was, " Don' talk d—d nonsense."

His chief companion, when in Cheltenham, for th best part of two years, was Dr Ker's brother Alan Both were great walkers, and few near or distant place in this beautiful neighbourhood were left unvisited by them.

A year or two before, my father had lived some weeks in a Hydropathic Establishment at the very primitive village of Prestbury, and the village boys were in the habit of following him and the other inmates whenever they showed themselves on the roads and shouting

[1] Dr Ker, MS Notes.

"Shiver and shake." This made him very nervous at the time, and the thought even of passing through Prestbury revived the feeling.

Dr Ker writes:

Two wishes I used to hear him express; one was to see the West Indies, the other to see the earth from a balloon.

Few things delighted me more than to see the mother and son together. You cannot remember your grandmother, I think. She was a perfect picture, a beautiful specimen of the English gentlewoman, loving and loveable, "no angel but a dearer being," and so sensitive that touch her feelings ever so lightly and the tears rushed to her eyes. Then it was we used to hear your father say, " Dam your eyes, mother, dam your eyes! " and then she smiled and applied the white pocket-handkerchief and shook her head at her son. He often jested with her about Dr Cumming and his "bottles," the bottles being the seven vials of St John's Revelation! You have heard, I dare say, that your grandmother confined her reading at that time to two books, the *Bible* and Dr Cumming's work on *Prophecy*. He used to jest with his mother about her monkey, a clever little black thing that was generally seen in the garden perched on the top of a pole. Your father naturally christened it St Simeon Stylites. I once ventured to ask him whether his mother had not sat for the picture of the Prince's mother in " The Princess," and he allowed that no one else had.

> Happy he
> With such a mother! faith.in womankind
> Beats with his blood, and trust in all things high
> Comes easy to him, and tho' he trip and fall
> He shall not blind his soul with clay.

Your father's estimate of Wordsworth's poetry was a very high one as you must know, and I dare say you know that Wordsworth's opinion of your father was also very high. On one of the occasions of their meeting Wordsworth said to him : " Mr Tennyson, I have been endeavouring all my life to write a pastoral like your ' Dora ' and have not succeeded." That was great praise from one who honestly weighed his words and was by no means lavish of his praise.

From Cheltenham my father made expeditions t
London to see his old friends. One day Savil
Morton writes that he has called on Alfred, and foun
Thackeray there, and "a stack of shag tobacco wit]
Homer and Miss Barrett on the table." " Both Thackera
and Alfred," he adds, "praise Miss Barrett." My fathe
grew to know Thackeray well and would call him
"loveable man." A story which he told illustrates th
character of both the friends. They had been dinin₃
together and my father said, " I love Catullus for hi
perfection in form and for his tenderness, he is tenderes
of Roman poets," and quoted the lines about Quintilia'
death ending with

> " Quo desiderio veteres renovamus amores
> Atque olim amissas flemus amicitias " —

lines which he would translate by four lines from one o
Shakespeare's Sonnets,

> " Then can I drown an eye, unused to flow
> For precious friends hid in death's dateless night,
> And weep afresh Love's long since cancell'd woe,
> And moan the expense of many a vanish'd sight,"

and the stanza from the " Juliæ et Mallii Epithalamium,'

> " Torquatus, volo, parvulus
> Matris e gremio suæ
> Porrigens teneras manus
> Dulce rideat ad patrem,
> Semihiante labello."

Thackeray answered, " I do not rate him highly
I could do better myself." Next morning my fathe₁
received this apology:

My dear Alfred,

I woke at 2 o'clock, and in a sort of terror at a
certain speech I had made about Catullus. When I have dined
sometimes I believe myself to be equal to the greatest painters
and poets. That delusion goes off; and then I know what a

nall fiddle mine is and what small tunes I play upon it. It
as very generous of you to give me an opportunity of recalling a
lly speech : but at the time I thought I was making a perfectly
mple and satisfactory observation. Thus far I must *unbus'm*
yself : though why should I be so uneasy at having made a
nceited speech ? It is conceited not to wish to seem conceited.
Vith which I conclude,

Yours, W. M. T.

" It was impossible," said my father, " to have written
1 a more generous spirit. No one but a noble-hearted
an could have written such a letter."

During the " forties " he was in the habit of walking
ith Carlyle at night, and Carlyle would rail against the
governments of Jackasserie which cared more for
ommerce than for the greatness of our empire "; or
ould rave against the stuccoed houses in London as
acrid putrescence," or against the suburbs as a " black
imble of black cottages where there used to be pleasant
elds "; and they would both agree that it was growing
nto " a strange chaos of odds and ends, this London."
They were not in the least afraid of one another although
nany were afraid of them, and they had long and free
liscussions on every conceivable subject, and once only
lmost quarrelled, when Carlyle asserted that my father
alked of poetry as " high art," which he flatly contra-
licted, " I never in my whole life spoke of ' high art.' "

They had — both of them — lost MSS of their works;
Carlyle his *French Revolution*, my father *Poems, chiefly
Lyrical*. When my father asked Carlyle how he felt
fter the disappearance of his MS, he answered, " Well,
just felt like a man swimming without water."

My uncle Frederick writes :

I am sure I could not perform such a feat as I know Alfred
o have done, any more than raise the dead. The earliest MS
f the *Poems, chiefly Lyrical* he lost out of his great-coat pocket
ne night while returning from a neighbouring market town.

This was enough to reduce an ordinary man to despair, but the invisible ink was made to reappear, all the thoughts and fancies in their orderly series and with their entire drapery of words arose and lived again. I wonder what under such circumstances would become of the "mob of gentlemen who write with ease." Of course it would not much matter as they could easily indite something new.

My father's poems were generally based on some single phrase like "Someone had blundered": and were rolled about, so to speak, in his head, before he wrote them down: and hence they did not easily slip from his memory.

In these London days among his friends were the Kembles, Coventry Patmore, Frederick Pollock, Alfred Wigan, and Macready; and he enjoyed " turning in " at the theatres. Macready he thought not good in " Hamlet " but fine in " Macbeth ": yet said that his " Out, out, brief candle ! " was wrong, " not vexed and harassed as it ought to be, but spoken with lowered voice, and a pathos which I am sure, Shakespeare never intended."

One evening, at Bath House, Milnes wished to introduce my father to the Duke of Wellington. " No," my father said, " why should the great Duke be bothered by a poor poet like me?" He only once saw the Duke when he was riding out of the Horse Guards at White hall: and took off his hat. The Duke instantly made his usual military salute, commemorated in the " Ode on the death of the Duke of Wellington " in the well-known lines :

> No more in soldier fashion will he greet
> With lifted hand the gazer in the street.

Rogers continued to be intimate with my father, and would ask him privately his opinion on literary matters

---

[1] My father asked him why he did not write a sonnet. " I never could dance in fetters," he answered. My father himself preferred the Shakspearian form of sonnet to the Italian, as being less constrained.

At one of the famous breakfasts, wishing to do my father
honour before the company, and expecting praise, Rogers
enquired whether he approved of a particular poem by
himself. My father told him frankly that a certain
emendation would be an improvement. "It shall be
attended to," answered Rogers, but very stiffly. Then,
because my father went to the Water-Cure, Rogers had
an erroneous idea that he "suffered from many infirmities." When I showed my father this statement in
a published letter, he wrote down: "No truer comment
could be made on this than my favourite adage, 'Every
man imputes himself.' My good old friend had many infirmities. What mine were I know not unless short-sight
and occasional hypochondria be infirmities. I used,
from having early read in my father's library a great
number of medical books, to fancy at times that I had
all the diseases in the world, like a medical student. I
dare say old Rogers meant it all for the best. Peace be
with him! often bitter, but very kindly at heart. We
have often talked of death together till I have seen the
tears roll down his cheeks."

About this time there was a dinner given at
Hampstead by a Society of Authors, Sergeant Talfourd
in the chair. My father accepted an invitation to the
dinner on condition that he should not be asked to make
a speech. Many speeches were made, each author
praising every other author. My father seems to have
said to his neighbour, "I wonder which of us will last
500 years?" Upon which Talfourd jumped up and burst
forth into "A speech about Tennyson," affirming that
he was "sure to live." Then Douglas Jerrold seized my
father's hand and said, "I haven't the smallest doubt that
you will outlast us all, and that you are the one who
will live." The subject of these enthusiastic words disclaimed his sureness of lasting, and told his friends
that while thanking them all he felt his inability to make

a speech and so on. Talfourd shouted out, "Why you
making a speech." " Yes," answered my father, "but
upon my legs."

Letters, 1847.

To Mrs Howitt.

[DR GULLY'S.]
May 22nd, [1847?].

MY DEAR MRS HOWITT,

  I got your letter three or four days ago a
if I did not answer immediately you must lay it to t
account of the water-cure which I am undergoing a
which renders letter-writing or anything, except washi
and walking, more difficult than those who have not p
thro' the same ordeal would easily believe.

  At this moment my own family do not know wher
am : I have not written home, nor shall write I dare
for some time; to be sure I am not at any time much
the habit of writing home, and so my people know
ways and forgive them; but to you I feared to se
unkind and forgetful of the pleasant day I spent unc
your roof if I kept silence; so I write to tell you that
visit to Clapton though necessarily postponed will rea
if I live and thrive sometime take place; " sunshin
and "flowers " will go on for a long time yet, and bef
they are all gone I hope to see you and to find y
wholly recovered from the effects of that sad and anxic
winter you speak of; to me it is not permitted to
either sad or anxious if I am to get better.   I mu
like Prince Hal, "doff the world aside and let it pas
so says my doctor tho' he does not quote Shakespe
for it.

Good-bye and give my best remembrances to all yours
hom I know, and

Believe me, my dear Mrs Howitt,

Yours very truly, A. TENNYSON.

To F. Freiligrath.

10 ST JAMES' SQUARE, CHELTENHAM.
Nov. 5th, [1847?].

MY DEAR SIR,

I had long ago heard of you: I knew that you
ere a celebrated German Poet and lover of Liberty:
herefore was my satisfaction great to receive (as I did
his morning) a copy of your works with your own
riendly autograph. I need not say how much I feel
he honour you have done me in translating some of
y poems into your own noble and powerful language.
Vould that my acquaintance were more perfect with
german[1], then would my tribute of approbation be of
ore value and less incur the charge of presumption. I
ave not yet had time and leisure sufficient to read your
ranslations from myself carefully; but from what I have
een and if I may be permitted to judge, I should say
hat they are not dry bones, but seem full of a living
varmth, in fact a *Poet's* translation of Poetry. I could
vish however that you had taken the 2nd edition of
Mariana in the South": the old poem was so imperfect
s to be wholly unworthy your notice.

Accept my friendship and my regrets that I am not
t present able to come up to town and shake you by the
and. How long do you stop in England? Is there
ny hope that you could be prevailed upon to come to

---

[1] He could read German with ease at this time.

Cheltenham?   I should be most happy to see you
Write to me and tell me, and

> Believe me, my dear Sir, ever yours,
>
> A. TENNYSON.

1848–49.

In February the Tennysons received a letter from
Emily in Paris. The Revolution against Louis Philippe
had begun. She had been looking out of her window
and was shot at by one of the Revolutionists, the bullet
missing her and going through the ceiling. The account
continues, written but not signed by her:

31, RUE TRONCHET.
Feb. 25th, 1848.

*   *   *   *   *   *   *   *   *

It would be impossible to attempt any description of the
horrors of yesterday. However, the public events are better
recorded, and will have reached you by means of the paper.
But I will at once satisfy your anxiety as to the safety of myself
and all our friends. Instead of retiring to the Convent as I had
intended on Wednesday, I could not make up my mind to leave
my friends at a moment of such imminent danger, and the only
moment past in which I could have crossed the Bridges. I have
remained the last two nights with Madame Marthion, sleeping
in her room, unable to procure any clothes but those I brought
on my back from the Convent on Tuesday. Yesterday passed
like a fearful dream. In the morning it was hoped the resignation of Guizot would satisfy the people, but their triumph
only made them the more exorbitant, and while the General who had gone to his post at the Tuileries was breakfasting at 11 o'clock, the Deputation came to the King, and
everything was immediately in disorder. The King, after
recommending to the National Guard the safety of the citizens,
started for St Cloud in a carriage, with all his family, except the
Duchess of Orleans and her children. The General was ap-
prised of Sophie's arrival at the Tuileries, and went downstairs
to see her, and on returning to his post by the Duchess

Orleans as quickly as he could, was met by her. "Mon cher Général, suivez-moi" was all she was able to say to him in passing. The poor man was unable to obey, and his feelings can be better understood than described, as he saw her crossing the Tuileries Gardens on foot, escorted by a few friends amidst this infuriated mob to the Chamber of Deputies. There she was at first well received, but some of the mob penetrated and surrounded her, and one man applied a gun to her cheek. This however was happily turned off by a Deputy, and Jules Lasteyre, another of the Opposition Deputies, aided by many of his brother Deputies, defended her and contrived to get her into a fiacre which he drove to the Invalides. She was separated from her children for some time, but at length they joined her in disguise, and she is at this moment not at the Invalides, but in a secret place of safety, of which the General himself is ignorant. After the departure of the King, the Tuileries was thoroughly invaded by the mob, and every article of furniture completely destroyed. The poor General stayed to defend the property of the Duchess as long as he thought he could be of use, and then he with Sophie left the Tuileries, he, almost lifted downstairs by a man whom he had had an opportunity of serving, and his infirmities were respected by the mob, till he got to the Rue du 29 Juillet, towards 2 o'clock; from thence, as soon as he could be removed, to the Rue des Capucines where he is now. Of course his place and position are gone, but you may conceive the anxiety of our minds to know what had become of him and Sophie during the fearful hours they were in the Tuileries, where it was impossible to attempt any communication. * * * You never saw such a set of ruffians as infest the streets, armed with every weapon with which they could furnish themselves, shouting and singing the "Marseillaise," etc. About half an hour ago a gang went by shouting "Au chemin de fer"; and we fear that the passage out of Paris will be completely cut off. The streets are all barricaded so that no carriage can pass, and though Madame Marthion and Sophie consider the wisest plan would be to leave the town we fear it will scarcely now be possible. * * * The Palais Royal is burnt down. * * * We were obliged to illuminate for safety's sake last night, and such a host of villains have taken advantage of this tumult, that you may imagine our rest was scarcely so to be called. The fear of pillage, and the anxiety lest this infuriated mob might even turn against our only security, the National Guard, at a moment of no existing government (for the provisional government could not yesterday come to any measures), kept our minds awake, while our eyes were closed, though fatigue of mind and body overcame our anxiety in a great measure. The situation of the General's house, next to Guizot's, also keeps us in constant alarm. The noise of firing also all night, in the uncertainty of its being merely rejoicing, or with murderous objects, contributed its share to add to our anxiety. * * *

Provisions are growing very scarce, and the cry for bread is now strong. Yesterday half the mob were drunk.

My father's journal of his Tour in Cornwall, 1848 (*when he thought of again taking up the subject of Arthur*).

Tuesday, May 30*th.* Arrived at Bude in dark, askt girl way to sea, she opens the back door...I go out and in a moment go sheer down, upward of six feet, over wall on fanged cobbles[1]. Up again and walked to sea over dark hill.

June 2*nd.* Took a gig to Rev. S. Hawker at Morwenstow, passing Comb valley, fine view over sea, coldest manner of Vicar till I told my name, then all heartiness. Walk on cliff with him, told of shipwreck.

Sunday. Rainy and bad, went and sat in Tintagel ruins, cliff all black and red and yellow, weird looking thing.

---

[1] " At one place," writes Miss Fox, " where he arrived in the evening, he cried, ' Where is the sea? Show me the sea.' So after the sea he went stumbling in the dark, and fell down and hurt his leg so much that he had to be nursed six weeks by a surgeon there, who introduced some friends to him, and thus he got into a class of society totally new to him; and when he left they gave him a series of introductions, so that instead of going to hotels he was passed on from town to town, and abode with little grocers and shopkeepers along his line of travel. He says that he cannot have better got a true impression of the class, and thinks the Cornish very superior to the generality. They all knew about Tennyson, and had read his poems, and one miner hid behind a wall that he might see him. Thus he became familiarized with the thoughts and feelings of all classes of society."

5th. Clomb over Isle, disappointed, went thro' the sea-tunnel-cavern over great blocks. Walls lined with shells, pink or puce jellies. Girls playing about the rocks as in a theatre.

6th. Slate quarries, one great pillar left standing; ship under the cliff loading; dived into a cavern all polished with the waves like dark marble with veins of pink and white. Follow'd up little stream falling thro' the worn slate, smoked a pipe at little inn, dined, walked once more to the old castle darkening in the gloom.

7th. Camelford, Slaughter Bridge, clear brook among alders. Sought for King Arthur's stone, found it at last by a rock under two or three sycamores, walked seaward, came down by churchyard. Song from ship.

8th. Walked seaward. Large crimson clover; sea purple and green like a peacock's neck. " By bays, the peacock's neck in hue."

14th. Read part of *Œdipus Coloneus.*

19th. Finished reading *Fathom* [1]. Set off for Polperro, ripple-mark, queer old narrow-streeted place, back at 9. Turf fires on the hills; jewel-fires in the waves from the oar, which Cornish people call "bryming."

July 1st. Museum. After dinner went to Perranzabuloe. Coast looked gray and grand in the fading light. Went into cave, Rembrandt-like light thro' the opening.

6th. Went to Land's End by Logan rock, leaden-backed mews wailing on cliff, one with two young ones. Mist. Great yellow flare just before sunset. Funeral. Land's End and Life's End.

8th. The Lizard, rocks in sea, two southern eyes of England [2]. Tamarisk hedge in flower. Round Pentreath beach, large crane's bill near Kynance, down to cove. Glorious grass-green monsters of waves. Into caves of Asparagus Island. Sat watching wave-rainbows.

---

[1] Doubtless Smollett's *Ferdinand Count Fathom.*   [2] Lighthouses.

11th. Down to Lizard Cove. Smoked with work-men. Boat to several places. Saw the further ships under Penzance like beads threading the sunny shore.

12th. Polpur. Bathed, ran in and out of cave. Down to Caerthillian, lovely clear water in cove. Lay over Pentreath beach, thunder of waves to west. Pena-luna's *Cornwall*.

13th. Bathed in Polpur Cove. Bewick-like look of trunk, cloak and carpet bag, lying on rock. Sailed, could not land at Kynance. Saw the long green swell heaving on the black cliff, rowed into Pigeonthugo, dismal wailing of mews. To St Ives.

Mrs Rundle Charles[1], who was then Miss Rundle, allowed me to publish the following account, from her private diary, of my father's visit (during this tour) to her uncle's house near Plymouth.

We were staying at Upland, a country house belonging to an uncle of mine four miles from Plymouth. Whilst there we were walking on the Hoe at Plymouth one day, when to my delight we were told that my father was to drive Mr Tennyson from Tavistock to pay us a visit at Upland. The clergyman's wife and other friends came to tea that afternoon, but Mr Ten-nyson did not appear. We went out for a ramble in the wood, were caught in a shower and ran home. Mr Tennyson was there, in the hall, just arrived: my father introduced me to him, and he came into the drawing-room, and said to my mother, "You have a party," which he did not seem to like. My father then called me in to make tea for Mr Tennyson in the dining-room, and we had a quiet talk; a powerful, thoughtful face, kind smile, hearty laugh, extremely near-sighted[2]. He spoke of travelling; Dresden, unsatisfactoriness of picture-gallery seeing; the first time he was in Paris he "went every day for a fortnight to the

[1] Author of *The Schönberg-Cotta Family*; she died in 1896.
[2] He talked then with his friends of Sir Charles Napier and of his battle of Meeanee (1843), about which he half thought of making a poem, and said that Westley the optician had told him that Sir Charles Napier and he were the two most short-sighted men in England.

Louvre, saw only one picture, 'La Maîtresse de Titien,' the second time looked only at 'Narcissus lying by a stream, Echo in the distance and ferocious little Love.'" Mr Ruskin set his own thought against the united admiration of centuries, but he spoke of a " splendid chapter on Clouds " in *Modern Painters*.

Then he turned to Geology, Weald of Kent, Delta of a great river flowing from as far as Newfoundland. "Conceive," he said, "what an era of the world that must have been, great lizards, marshes, gigantic ferns!" Fancied, standing by a railway at night, the engine must be like some great Ichthyosaurus. I replied how beautiful Hugh Miller's descriptions of that time are: he thought so too: then spoke of Peach, the Cornish geologist on the Preventive Service, maintaining a wife and seven children on £100 a year, whilst we in one annual dinner, champagne, turtle, etc. spend £25.

He spoke of the Italians as a great people (it was in 1848, the year of revolutions [1]) "twice matured." He had read a poem of mine on Italy : said he felt "great interest in the Italian movement as in all great movements for freedom"; that perhaps all looked equally disorderly as they arose; that the German revolutions (of 1848) were miserable plagiarisms. We went into the drawing-room, I played Mendelssohn. Mr Tennyson came and talked to me about Schiller, — "Schwärmerisch, yet Schwärmerei better than mere kalter Verstand, not dramatic; knew by heart Goethe's Gedichte 'Summer breathings.' Felt the grand intellectual power of *Faust*, but threw it aside in disgust at the first reading!" Then he spoke of Milton's Latinisms, and delicate play with words, and Shakespeare's play upon words. At supper he spoke of Goethe's *Tasso:* he felt with Tasso, did not care for anything else in the play. "Leonora, discreet, prudential young lady, could not of course care for the poor

---

[1] He used to tell with infinite humour the following story, illustrating the love of a row in the hot-blooded South. "Edward Lear, the painter, had been living at a hotel in a small town in Southern Italy, but had gone on a tour leaving his room locked up. On his return he found the place in the uproar of a mushroom revolution, the inhabitants drunk with *chianti* and shouting *libertà* and *la patria* through the streets. 'Where is my *chiave*,' said he to the waiter, 'of my *camera* to get at my *roba ?*' 'O,' replied the waiter, not liking to be let down from his dream of a golden age, '*O che chiave!* O che camera! O che roba! Non c' è più chiave! Non c' è più camera! Non c' è più roba! Non c' è più niente! Tutto è amore e libertà! O che bella revoluzione!'"

poet — it would not have been the thing, it would not have done:
remembered only these lines:

> 'Es bildet ein Talent sich in der Stille,
> Sich ein Charakter in dem Strom der Welt.'"

Said he had talked of me last night and heard from Dr Beale,
a clergyman of Tavistock, brother-in-law of W. H. Smith, that I
knew Greek, and he said he only disliked *pedantry* in women. He
said, "Wordsworth was great, but too one-sided to be dramatic."
He spoke of the "snobbery of English society." It was getting
late, so my aunt asked him to stay the night, but he said he had
breakfasted alone for a dozen years; then he said to me, "Ich
kann nicht hier schlafen." I said, "Warum?" He said, "Ich kann
nicht rauchen." I translated aloud, he laughed, declared he "had
never been played such a trick before, chose the disguise of an
obscure northern dialect, and was betrayed to everyone"; then
he said, "German has great fine words: every language is really
untranslateable." Then the carriage came to take him into
Plymouth: he asked to take my poems (manuscript) with him, and
said, "Good-night not Good-bye." Next morning (Tuesday, July
25th) Mr Tennyson came again: he talked about lower organisms
feeling less pain than higher, but would not fish: could not comprehend the feeling of animals with ganglia, little scattered knots
of nerves and no brain; spoke of wonderful variety of forms of
life, instinct of plants, etc., told the story of "a Brahmin destroying
a microscope because it showed him animals killing each other
in a drop of water"; "significant, as if we could destroy facts by
refusing to see them." We walked into the garden, sat on chairs
at entrance of avenue; then he laughed about some tremendous
"duty-woman," clergyman's wife, now Low, now High Church,
"always equally vehement, little brains, much conscientiousness;
husband preached one thing in the church, she another in the
parish." He said it was right to "enjoy leisure," spoke of Miss
Martineau's *Eastern Life*, did not like her, said he supposed we
were not Unitarians or Pagans, although it was the fashion with
literary ladies. Then he spoke of my poems, said he liked some
very much, especially some lines on the gentianella: then he
kindly made one or two verbal criticisms in one called "The
Poet's Daily Bread." "Have you printed?" he said. "Do not
publish too early, you cannot retract." I ventured to thank him
for his poems, in which we delighted. "I thank you for yours,"

he said graciously. We went into the kitchen garden, he talked of flowers and cabbages, picked gooseberries, he "used as a boy to lie for hours under a gooseberry bush reading a novel, finishing his gooseberries and novel together "; he liked the kitchen garden, "so wholesome." "I would rather stay with you bright girls than dine with Mr W.," he said. He sent away his fly, then we went into my cousin Helen's garden, and he told us stories of "an African woman, who asked to *be breakfasted upon* (by white men)," etc. etc. Afterwards we drove him into Plymouth. "You would not think me a shy man, but I am always shy with false or conventional people; people are sometimes affected from shyness, and *grow* simple." Then we talked of Carlyle: "You would like him for one day," he said, "but get tired of him, so vehement and destructive"; he gave by way of a specimen of his talk in a deep tragic voice, "For God's sake away with gigs, thousand million gigs in the world, away with them all in God's name, spoke and axle, the world will never be right until they are all swept into the lowest pit of Tophet." He often smokes with Carlyle; "Goethe once Carlyle's hero, now Cromwell his epitome of human excellence. Carlyle spoke once as if he wished poets to be our statesmen; fancy Burns Prime Minister!" Then he said to me, "Do you know the *Odyssey?* I like it better as a whole than the *Iliad:* I should have met you before; why didn't you write? I could teach you Greek in a month, then perhaps (quoting my poem called 'The Poet's Daily Bread') you would scorn me with bitter scorn." I laughed. "I will send you the *Odyssey*, I have two copies in my portmanteau; I will be grave when next I meet you; I vary." In the course of conversation he said, "Some parts of *The Book of Revelation* are finer in English than in Greek, e.g. 'And again they said "Alleluia" and their smoke went up for ever and ever[1],' — magnificent conception, darkness and fire rolling together, for ever and ever."

[1] He would quote the tenth chapter with boundless admiration: "And I saw another mighty angel come down from heaven, clothed with a cloud... and he set his right foot upon the sea, and his left foot on the earth... And the angel which I saw stand upon the sea and upon the earth lifted up his hand to heaven, and sware by him that liveth for ever and ever, who created heaven, and the things that therein are, and the earth, and the things that therein are, and the sea, and the things that are therein, that there should be time no longer," or, as he translated it, "that time should be no more."

Letters, 1848–9.

To Aubrey de Vere (after a visit to Scotland in 1848).

CHELTENHAM, Oct.

MY DEAR AUBREY,

I have just now on my return to Cheltenham got two letters from you, for I am one, as you know, who wander to and fro for months careless of P. O. and correspondences. I am grieved to have occasioned you so much trouble about the article, but let it pass, excuses will not mend it: neither will I mention the money[1] troubles I have had, for they are dead and buried, tho' you bribe with your "great piece of news," which I take it must mean that you are going to be married! is it so? if so, joy to you. I am glad that you have thought of me at Kilkee by the great deeps. The sea is my delight, tho' Mr Chretien in the *Christian Examiner* says that I have no power upon him and always represent him dead asleep. I have seen many fine things in Scotland, and many fine things did I miss seeing, rolled up as they were tenfold in Scotch mists. Loch Awe too, which you call the finest, I saw. It is certainly very grand, tho' the pass disappointed me. I thought of Wordsworth's lines there, and, approving much, disapproved of much in them. What can be worse than to say to old Kilchurn Castle,

"Take then thy seat, vicegerent unreproved"?

Surely, master Aubrey, that is puffed and false. I steamed from Oban to Skye, a splendid voyage, for the whole day, with the exception of three hours in the

---

[1] His friends tried to persuade him to write popular short poems in magazines, but, however poor he might be, he never could or would write a line for money offered.

morning, was blue and sunny; and I think I saw more outlines of hills than ever I saw in my life; and exquisitely shaped are those Skye mountains.   Loch Corusk, said to be the wildest scene in the Highlands, I failed in seeing.   After a fatiguing expedition over the roughest ground on a wet day we arrived at the banks of the loch, and made acquaintance with the extremest tiptoes of the hills, all else being thick wool-white fog.   Dunkeld is lovely, and I delighted in Inverary, tho' there likewise I got drenched to the skin, till my very hat wept tears of ink.   I rejoiced in Killeen, but on the whole perhaps I enjoyed no day more than the one I spent at Kirk Alloway by the monument of poor Burns, and the orchards, and "banks and braes of bonny Doon."   I made a pilgrimage thither out of love for the great peasant; they were gathering in the wheat and the spirit of the man mingled or seemed to mingle with all I saw.   I know you do not care much for him, but I do, and hold that there never was immortal poet if he be not one. Farewell.   Give my best love and remembrances to all yours, and

Believe me ever yours,
A.

To Aubrey de Vere.
[*Undated.*]

My dear Aubrey,

I have just returned to this place whence I think I wrote to you last, and hither your letter after travelling Cheltenhamward and otherwhere followed me. I assure you I experienced a very lively gratification in finding that my recent alterations [1] had met your approval and not your's only but your mother's and sister's.   I am still not quite satisfied with it, and I think that one or two of the ballads might be improved or others substituted, but I have done with it at present.   I gave it up

---

[1] In "The Princess."

to the printer in a rage at last and left London, not having revised the last proofs, and so I see there is a mistake or two, for instance "marbled stairs" which is vile. Don't you think too that the Dedication to Harry Lushington looks very queer, dated " January, '48," the French row taking place in the February following, and such allusions and the subsequent ones made in the Epilogue! Well, I suppose that does not much matter, and I am as I said vastly gratified with your good opinion of the improvements.

I wrote so far — now I am in town for a week or so. Now for your two queries.

I have not the *Edinburgh* with me, and so cannot give you the exact passage in the critique; but I know there is mention made therein of "The Princess" coming out among the dying and the dead. Now I certainly did not mean to kill anyone, and therefore I put this new line into the old king's mouth,

I trust that there is no one hurt to death,

and in the old tourneys it really did happen now and then that there was only a certain amount of bruises and bangs and no death. Perhaps the Editor, not you, inserted the passage. With respect to the "Elegies [1]," I cannot say that I have turned my attention to them lately. I do not know whether I have done anything new in that quarter since you saw them, but I believe I am going to print them, and then I need not tell you that you will be perfectly welcome to a copy, on the condition that when the book is published, this avant-courier of it shall be either sent back to me, or die the death by fire in Curragh Chase. I shall print about twenty-five copies, and let them out among friends under the same condition of either return or cremation. The review in the *Westminster* was not one of "The Princess," but of two or three of the old Poems.

1 " In Memoriam."

I have sent you a most shabby note in return for your long and agreeable one, but pray forgive me: I have such a heap of correspondence just now, half of which will never get answered at all.

Love to your brother and his wife, your mother and sister. I don't know, but I feel quite sorry that Caroline (Standish) is married. She did so well unmarried, and looked so pure and maidenly that I feel it quite a pity that she should have changed her state.

Ever yours, dear Aubrey,

A. TENNYSON.

The following *four* letters refer to what my father called "the highest honour I have yet received."

(1) *From Mrs Gaskell to John Forster.*

MANCHESTER, *Oct. 8th,* 1849.

I want to ask for your kind offices. You know Tennyson, and you know who Samuel Bamford is, a great, gaunt, stalwart Lancashire man, formerly hand-loom weaver, author of *Life of a Radical,* age nearly 70, and living in that state which is exactly decent poverty with his neat little apple-faced wife. They have lost their only child. Bamford is the most hearty (and it's saying a good deal) admirer of Tennyson I know. I dislike recitations exceedingly, but he repeats some of Tennyson's poems in so rapt and yet so simple a manner, utterly forgetting that anyone is by in the delight of the music and the exquisite thoughts, that one can't help liking to hear him. *He* does not care one jot whether people like him or not in his own intense enjoyment. He says when he lies awake at night, as in his old age he often does, and gets sadly thinking of the days that are gone when his child was alive, he soothes himself by repeating T.'s poems. I asked him the other day if he had got them of his own. "No," he said rather mournfully: he had been long looking out for a second-hand copy, but somehow they had not got into the old book-shops, and 14*s.* or 18*s.* (which are they?) was too much for a poor man, and then he brightened up and said, Thank God he had a good memory, and whenever he got into a house where there were Tennyson's poems he learnt as many as he could by heart. He thought he knew better than twelve, and began " Œnone," and then the " Sleeping Beauty." Now I wonder if you catch a glimpse of what I want. I thought at first of giving him the poems this Xmas, but then I thought you would perhaps ask Tennyson if he would give Bamford a copy *from himself*, which would be glorious for the old man. Dear, how he would triumph.

(2) *To John Forster.*

MABLETHORPE, ALFORD,
LINCOLNSHIRE. 1849.

MY DEAR FORSTER,

I got both your notes almost at the same time. I have been flying about from house to house for a long time, and yours was delivered to me at a place called Scremby Hall in this county where I was making a morning call. All that account of Sam. Bamford is very interesting indeed. I reckon his admiration as the highest honour I have yet received. A lady was so charmed with the relation that I gave her the letter. Of course I will give him a copy but I shall not be in town for a fortnight. The first thing I do will be to call at Moxon's and get him one. I am here on this desolate sea-coast. My friends have fêted me in this county so long that I think it high time to move, but they will not let me go yet. How have you been, my dear boy? I trust well. In the hope of seeing you as soon as possible,

I am, yours as ever,

A. TENNYSON[1].

(3) *From Mrs Gaskell to John Forster.*

FRIDAY, *Dec.* 7*th*, 1849.

I have not yet taken my bonnet off after hunting up Bamford. First of all we went to Blakeley to his little white-

[1] He inclosed to Forster for the *Examiner*, March 24th, " You might have won the poet's fame ": reprinted in the *Poems* (sixth ed.), 1850.

washed cottage. His wife was cleaning, and regretted her
"master" was not at home. He had gone into Manchester,
where she did not know. I shan't go into the details of the
hunting of this day. At last we pounced upon the great gray
stalwart man coming out of a little old-fashioned public-house
where Blakeley people put up. When I produced my book he
said, "This is grand." I said, "Look at the title-page," for I saw
he was fairly caught by something he liked in the middle of the
book, and was standing reading it in the street. "Well, I am a
proud man this day!" he exclaimed. Then he turned it up and
down and read a bit (it was a very crowded street) and his gray
face went quite brown-red with pleasure. Suddenly he stopped.
"What must I do for him back again?" "Oh! you must write
to him, and thank him." "I'd rather walk 20 mile than write a
letter any day." "Well, then, suppose you set off this Christmas,
and walk and thank Tennyson." He looked up from his book,
right in my face, quite indignant. "Woman! walking won't
reach him. We're on the earth don't ye see, but he's there, up
above. I can no more reach him by walking than if he were an
eagle or a skylark high above my head." It came fresh, warm,
straight from the heart, without a motion or making a figurative
speech, but as if it were literal truth, and I were a goose for not
being aware of it. Then he dipped down again into his book,
and began reading aloud the "Sleeping Beauty," and in the
middle stopped to look at the writing again. And we left him
in a sort of sleep-walking state, and only trust he will not be run
over.

(4) *From Samuel Bamford to Alfred Tennyson.*

BLAKELEY, *Dec.* 13*th*, 1849.

DEAR SIR,

Mrs Gaskell a few days since presented to me your
poems, with your autograph, in kind terms, and I can only say,
as to the present, that I am very greatly obliged; and that you
could not have done anything that would have pleased me
better. Accept my most sincere thanks.

Your poems, I cannot forget them. I cannot put them away
from my thoughts; the persons and the scenes they represent

haunt me. I have read them all over and over, and I have not awakened once this night without

> Thy heart, my life, my love, my bride

immediately recurring to my thoughts.

Oh! your "Oriana" has started the tears into my eyes, and into those of my dear wife, many a time. It is a deep thing. Your "Locksley Hall" is terribly beautiful; profoundly impressive. The departure of your "Sleeping Palace" is almost my favourite, and your "Gardener's Daughter," ah! it brings early scenes to my mind.

> The story of my early love that haunts me now I'm old,
> And broods within my very heart altho' 'tis well-nigh cold.

My wife, bless her! I never feel my sensibilities gushing over, but when I look I find hers are doing the same. And it has frequently been the case since I was so fortunate as to have your poems.

But your English! why it is almost unlimitedly expressive. This language of ours, what can it not be made to say ? What height, what depth filled with all glorious hues, terrible glooms, and vivid flashes does it not combine and your poems exhibit all?

Are you well?   Are you happy?   I hope you are both. Accept my kindest wishes, and believe me to be

> Yours most truly,
>
> SAMUEL BAMFORD.

To Miss Holloway (of Spilsby) my father wrote about her cousin Miss Jean Ingelow's poems, *A Rhyming Chronicle of Incidents and Feelings.*

My DEAR MISS HOLLOWAY,

Many thanks for your very kind note. I have only just returned to town, and found the *Rhyming Chronicle.* Your Cousin must be worth knowing: there are some very charming things in her book, at least it seems so to me, tho' I do not pique myself on being much of a critic at first sight, and I really have only skimmed a few pages. Yet I think I may venture to pronounce that she need not be ashamed of publishing them. Certain things I saw which I count abomina- tions, tho' I myself in younger days have been guilty of the same, and so was Keats. I would sooner lose a pretty thought than enshrine it in such rhymes as " Eudora " " before her," " vista " " sister." She will get to hate them herself as she grows older, and it would be a pity that she should let her book go forth with these cockneyisms. If the book were not so good I should not care for these specks, but the critics will pounce upon them, and excite a prejudice. I declare I should like to know her.

I have such a heap of correspondence to answer that I must bid you good-bye. What the German lady says is very gratifying. I shall perhaps see you again in the autumn. My best remembrances to each and all of your circle.

Ever yours truly, A. TENNYSON.

P.S. Strange! that I did not see it. I turn to the title-page, and find the book *is* published. I fancied it had only been printed. Forgive my hurry! Well, your cousin will amend, perhaps, the errors I have mentioned, in her next edition.

———————

On the invitation of Aubrey de Vere, my father paid his second visit to Ireland; but he has left no record of his tour. At my request Mr de Vere has kindly written the following account: to which he has added some reminiscences of his first hearing " In Memoriam " read in 1850.

In the year 1848 Alfred Tennyson had felt a craving to make a lonely sojourn at Bude: "I hear," he said, "that there are larger waves there than on any other part of the British coast: and must go thither and be alone with God." I persuaded him to come also to Ireland where the waves are far higher and the cliffs often rise to 800 feet and in one spot, Slieve League, to 2000 : while at the mountain's landward side are still shown the "prayer-stations" of Saint Columbkill.　He passed five weeks with us at Curragh Chase, to us delightful weeks.　The day before our arrival we visited the celebrated "fall" of the Shannon at Castleconnel; over it there hung a full moon, the largest I have ever seen.　The aspect might well have shaken weak nerves.　It looked as if the "centrifugal" force had ceased, and the vast luminary might come down upon the earth in another hour.　That night we slept in my sister's house, and she had the satisfaction of conversing with the Poet whose works she had fed on since her girlhood.

The weeks passed by only too rapidly.　We drove our guest to the old Castles and Abbeys in the neighbourhood : he was shocked at the poverty of the peasantry, and the marks of havock wrought through the country by the great potato-famine : he read in the library; and worked on a new edition of "The Princess," smoking at the same time without hindrance in our most comfortable bedroom, and protected as far as possible from noise; he walked where he pleased alone, or in company through woods in which it was easy to lose oneself, by a cave so deep that Merlin might have slept in it to this day unawakened.　In the evenings he had vocal music from Lady de Vere and her sister, Caroline Standish, and Sonatas of Mozart or Beethoven played by my eldest brother, with a power and pathos rare in an amateur.　Later, he read poetry to us with a voice that doubled its power, commonly choosing pathetic pieces; and on one occasion after finishing "A Sorrowful Tale" by Crabbe, glanced round reproachfully and said, "I do not see that any of you are weeping!"　One night we turned his poem of "The Day-Dream" into an acted charade; a beautiful girl whom he used to call "that stately maid," taking the part of the Sleeping Beauty; and the poet himself that of the Prince who broke the spell of her slumber.　Another night there was a dance which he denounced as a stupid thing, while a brilliant and amusing person, Lady G., who was accustomed to speak her mind to all alike, scolded him sharply.　"How would the world get on if others went about it growling at its amusements in a voice as deep as a lion's ?　I request that you will go upstairs, put on an evening coat, and ask my daughter Sophia to dance."　He did so, and was the gayest of the gay for several hours, turning out moreover an excellent dancer. He was liked all the better for always saying what came into his head. One day a young lady who sat next him at dinner, spoke of a certain marriage just announced, as a very *penniless* one. He rummaged in his pocket, extracted a penny, and slapped it down loudly close to her plate saying, "There, I give you that, for that is the God you worship." The girl was a little frightened, but more amused: they made friends; and he promised to send her a pocket copy of Milton. Some months later she received one from England, beautifully bound.

It was a time of political excitement, and Ireland was on the brink of that silly attempt at rebellion which put back all her serious interests for a quarter of a century. Half Europe was in revolt and the prophets of the day averred that England might any day find herself involved in a general war. Some one remarked that an invasion would be more practicable in these days of steamships than in those of Nelson and Napoleon. Tennyson was a Patriot-poet like Shakespeare, who gave us the glorious dying speech of "Old John of Gaunt, time-honoured Lancaster," the Patriot-prince. His reply was, "Don't let them land on England's coast, or we will shatter them to pieces."

We took care that our guest should see or hear something of Ireland's quaint humours: I must find room for one story which especially amused him, and which he often retold. Returning home recently after a fortnight's absence, I had visited our old Parish Priest, Father Tim, and found him at dinner with his curate. It had been a time of great disturbance: many houses had been attacked by night, many guns borne off in triumph, and much blood shed. In answer to my enquiries he said: "The country has been quiet enough, much as usual, except one disgraceful outrage, such as no one ever heard of before in Ireland. What would you think, Sir, of a girl being carried off by night, and no car sent for her?" It had long been a traditional usage in Ireland, when parents on unreasonable grounds resisted their daughter's marriage, for her lover and his friends to carry her off, apparently by force, but in reality with her connivance. After a few days the parents had to accept what they could not then avert; but the abduction was a ceremonial in which the Sabine Maid was always treated with entire respect. "Sir, I ask you," said Father Tim to his curate, laying down his knife and fork, and his old face flushing up, "as long as you are on the mission, did you ever hear of a girl being carried off, and no car sent for her?" "Never, Sir," was the answer, "and it would not be a common car, but a side-car." "Yes," Father Tim rejoined, "and moreover a woman would be sent for her with the party, to keep her in courage." "To be sure there would," the curate replied; "and a most respectable woman." For several minutes the affirmation and the response were alternated more and more loudly and with stronger gesticulations; "A car would be sent!" "Aye, and a side-car!" "A woman would be sent!" "Aye, and a most respectable woman!" The old priest ended, "I am afraid old Ireland is going to the bad! Well, thank Heaven it did not happen in my parish; but it happened within a hundred yards of it! A girl of the Molonys, one of the old stock!" Neither priest finished his poor dinner of bacon and cabbage that day. This violation of traditional etiquette led to consequences which justified Father Tim's last words, "Well, God is good! it did not happen in my parish!" For more than two years that parish had been the prey of eight marauders who roamed at large, plundering or making the farmers pay black-mail. They defied alike magistrate, police and country-gentlemen; for though everyone knew who they were, no one dared to give information. Not so that daughter of the old stock. The rogues had carried her to the house of an old woman in complicity with the enterprise, but who, on recogniz-ing in the girl a fifth cousin of her aunt's, placed her in her own bed and sent off the adventurers without a glass of whisky. At the risk of her life the girl went to a magistrate, gave infor-mation against the gang, and promised to swear to it in Court, on one condition. It was that one man should not be pro-ceeded against. The other seven, she affirmed, were blackguards, who had not so much as given her time to dress herself "anyway tidy"; and who had dragged her without a shoe on her feet through three muddy fields; but there was one man of a better sort who had "behaved mighty polished" to her, hoisting her up on his shoulders once when they crossed a bog. The "polished" man was forgiven, and probably begged pardon of Father Tim, and returned to his duties: the other seven were transported, and probably made their fortunes in the Colonies; and the parish had peace.

Alfred Tennyson's desire to see cliffs and waves revived, and we sent him to our cousin, Maurice FitzGerald, Knight of Kerry, who lived at Valencia where they are seen at their best. On his way thither he slept at Mount Trenchard, the residence of Lord Monteagle, and I led him to the summit of Knock Patrick, the farthest spot in the South West to which Ireland's Apostle, Patriarch and Patron, advanced. There while from far and near from both sides of the Shannon the people flocked round him, Saint Patrick preached his far-famed sermon and gave his benediction to the Land, its mountains and its plains, its pastures, its forests, its rivers and the sands under the rivers. The sunset was one of extraordinary but minatory beauty. It gave, I remember, a darksome glory to the vast and desolate expanse with all its creeks and inlets from the Shannon, lighted the green islands in the mouth of the Fergus, fired the ruined Castle of Shanid, a stronghold of the Desmonds, one of a hundred which they were said to have possessed. The western clouds hung low, a mass of crimson and gold; while, from the ledge of a nearer one, down plunged a glittering flood empurpled like wine. The scene was a thoroughly Irish one; and gave a stormy welcome to the Sassenach Bard. The next morning he pursued his way alone to Valencia. He soon wrote that he had enjoyed it. He had found there the highest waves that Ireland knows, cliffs that at one spot rise to the height of 600 feet, tamarisks and fuchsias that no sea-winds can intimidate, and the old " Knight of Kerry," who, at the age of nearly 80, preserved the spirits, the grace and the majestic beauty of days gone by — as chivalrous a representative of Desmond's great Norman House as it had ever put forth in those times when it fought side by side with the greatest Gaelic Houses, for Ireland's ancient faith, and the immemorial rights of its Palatinate[1]. Afterwards Tennyson visited Killarney but

[1] On his eighty-second birthday my father received the following letter:

CALVERLEY PARK, TUNBRIDGE WELLS,
August 6th, 1891.

" Long life to your honour," as Irish peasants used to say, and so say I, the man who was working the State quarry, on the Island of Valencia, when you spent a few days there in 1848, Chartist times in London and Fenian times in Ireland. I remember your telling us, not without some glee, how a Valencian Fenian stealthily dogged your footsteps up the

remained there only a few days; yet that visit bequeathed a memorial. The echoes of the bugle at Killarney on that loveliest of lakes inspired the song introduced into the second edition of his " Princess," beginning

The splendour falls on castle walls.

It is but due to Killarney that *both* the parents of that lyric should be remembered in connection with "that fair child between them born"; and through that song, Killarney wîll be recalled to the memory of many who have seen yet half forgotten it. When they read those stanzas, and yet more when they hear them fittingly sung, they will see again, as in a dream, the reach of its violet-coloured waters where they reflect the " Purple Mountain," the "Elfland" of its Black Valley, " Croom-a-doof," the silver river that winds and flashes through wood and rock, connecting the mystic "Upper Lake," and the beetling rock of the " Eagle's Nest" with the two larger and sunnier but not lovelier lakes. Before them again will rise Dinis Island, with its embowered coves and their golden sands, the mountain gardens of Glena haunted by murmurs of the cascade, not distant, but shrouded by the primeval oak-woods. They will look again on that island, majestic at once and mournful, Inisfallen, its grey-stemmed and solemn groves, its undulating lawns,

mountain and coming at last close to your ear, whispered, "Be you from France?"

Your sonorous reading to us after dinner sundry truculent passages in Daniel O'Connell's *History of Ireland*, which happened to be lying on my table, has lingered in my ears ever since. Seeing among my few books all that your friend Carlyle had up to that time published, you told me you thought he had nothing more to say. I was often reminded of this whilst reading his subsequent *Cromwell* and *Frederick* and *Latter Days*, and how near that was to the truth. You will hardly have forgotten the old Knight of Kerry, the owner of the Island, his dignified presence and his redolence of Grattan and Curran and Castlereagh and the Irish Parliament in which he sat for many years. I don't know whether "the rude imperious surge" which lashes the sounding shore of the Island ever drew from you, as I had hoped, some "hoarse rough verse," some of that roar, which tells us, as "music tells us, of what in all our life we have never known, and never will know."

With the "troops of friends" this day wishing you long life, heartily joins the ci-devant quarryman and

Yours truly, BEWICKE BLACKBURNE.

(Now also Octogenarian.)

which embosom the ruins of that Abbey, the shelter from century to century of Ireland's Annalists. They will muse again in the yew-roofed cloister of Muckross, and glide once more by its caverned and fantastic rocks, and promontories fringed by arbutus brakes, with their dark yet shining leaves, their scarlet berries and their waxen flowers. Whatever is fairest in other lakes they will see here combined, as if Nature had amused herself by publishing a volume of poetic selections from all her works. As the vision fades, their eyes will rest long on the far mountains that girdle all that beauty, mountains here and there dark with those yew-forests through which the wild deer of old escaped from the stag-hounds of MacCarthymore. It is marvellous that so many of the chief characteristics of Killarney should have found place in a poem so short.

We met next in London. Few of the hours I spent with Alfred survive with such a pathetic sweetness and nearness in my recollection as those which are associated with that time and with "In Memoriam," which, as he told me, he once thought of entitling "Fragments of an Elegy." Soon after this he published the poem.

I went to him very late each night, and he read many of the poems to me or discussed them with me till the early hours of the morning. The tears often ran down his face as he read, without the slightest apparent consciousness of them on his part. The pathos and grandeur of these poems were to me greatly increased by the voice which rather intoned than recited them, and which, as was obvious, could not possibly have given them utterance in any manner not thus musical. Sometimes towards the close of a stanza his voice dropped; but I avoided the chance of thus losing any part of the meaning by sitting beside him, and glancing at the pieces he read. They were written in a long and narrow manuscript book, which assisted him to arrange the poems in due order by bringing many of them at once before his eye. As I walked home alone in the early mornings, the noises had ceased in each "long unlovely street"; and the deep voice which had so long charmed me followed me still, and seemed to waft me along as if I had glided onward half-asleep in a gondola. I have ever regarded "In Memoriam" as the finest of the Poet's works. As in the case of Dante, a great sorrow had been the harbinger of a song greater still: Dante had vowed to celebrate Beatrice as no other woman had ever been celebrated; and he kept that vow. The Northern Poet had also in early youth lost his chief friend, and after the lapse of seventeen years commended him to a fame such as neither "Lycidas" nor "Adonais" had ever inherited. Many of Tennyson's poems are " of imagination all compact." In " In Memoriam" imagination claims less, comparatively, to win more. In this work each successive feeling and thought ascend from the depths of the Poet's heart, as the fountain's bubbles mount from the gold sands beneath it, and pass thence through the imagination, in progress to the sympathies of mankind. Natural description is here too invested with its finest function, for throughout it blends itself most subtly with the human affections, now adding to their sorrow, and now assuaging it: and here Poetic Art finds its aptest opportunities, for each of the pieces, while it constitutes part of a great whole, is itself so brief that it admits of the highest, most palpable perfection of shape. Tennyson was a true artist because he was not an artist only. He understood the relations in which Art stands to Nature and to fact. An incident will illustrate this remark. It had often seemed to me that though " In Memoriam" had been designed by its author chiefly as a monument raised to his friend, it was also regarded by him as a work which carried a spiritual teaching with it: it taught that the history of a great sorrow is the history of a soul; and that a soul which passes bravely through the dark shadow of the planet of grief must, on emerging thence, meet the sunrise at its remoter side. Long after the publication of " In Memoriam" I reminded him of what he had let fall on that subject, and added that such a scheme of poetic thought if carried out to the full, would create, in a lyrical form, a work not without much analogy to Dante's *Divina Commedia*, the first part of which is all woe, though the latter cantos of the second part, the " Purgatorio," abound in consolation and peace; while the third part, the " Paradiso," is the song of triumph and of joy. I remarked that many of the later pieces in the second part of " In Memoriam" were also songs of consolation and peace, and suggested that perhaps he might at some later time give to the whole work its third part, or Paradise. The poet's answer was this: " I have written what I have felt and known; and I will never write anything else."

Break, break, break
  On thy cold gray stones, O Sea!
And I would that my tongue could utter
  The thoughts that arise in me!

O well for the fisherman's boy,
  That he shouts with his sister at play!
O well for the sailor lad,
  That he sings in his boat on the bay!

And the stately ships go on
  To their haven under the hill—
But O for the touch of a vanished hand,
  And the sound of a voice that is still!

Break, break, break,
  At the foot of thy crags O Sea—
But the tender grace of a day that is dead
  Will never come back to me. A Tennyson

From an Original MS.

CHAPTER XIV.*

"IN MEMORIAM."

Break, break, break,
    On thy cold gray stones, O Sea!
And I would that my tongue could utter
    The thoughts that arise in ·me.

O well for the fisherman's boy,
    That he shouts with his sister at play!
O well for the sailor lad,
    That he sings in his boat on the bay!

And the stately ships go on
    To their haven under the hill;
But O for the touch of a vanish'd hand,
    And the sound of a voice that is still!

Break, break, break,
    At the foot of thy crags, O Sea!
But the tender grace of a day that is dead
    Will never come back to me.

Half a mile to the south of Clevedon in Somerset-shire, on a lonely hill, stands Clevedon Church, "obscure and solitary," overlooking a wide expanse of water, where the Severn flows into the Bristol Channel. It is dedicated to St Andrew, the chancel being the original fishermen's chapel.

From the graveyard you can hear the music of the tide as it washes against the low cliffs not a hundred· yards away. In the manor aisle of the church, under

---

which is the vault of the Hallams, may be read this epitaph to Arthur Hallam, written by his father:

TO

THE MEMORY OF

ARTHUR HENRY HALLAM

ELDEST SON OF HENRY HALLAM ESQUIRE
AND OF JULIA MARIA HIS WIFE
DAUGHTER OF SIR ABRAHAM ELTON BARONET
OF CLEVEDON COURT

WHO WAS SNATCHED AWAY BY SUDDEN DEATH
AT VIENNA ON SEPTEMBER 15TH 1833
IN THE TWENTY-THIRD YEAR OF HIS AGE
AND NOW IN THIS OBSCURE AND SOLITARY CHURCH
REPOSE THE MORTAL REMAINS OF
ONE TOO EARLY LOST FOR PUBLIC FAME
BUT ALREADY CONSPICUOUS AMONG HIS CONTEMPORARIES
FOR THE BRIGHTNESS OF HIS GENIUS
THE DEPTH OF HIS UNDERSTANDING
THE NOBLENESS OF HIS DISPOSITION
THE FERVOUR OF HIS PIETY
AND THE PURITY OF HIS LIFE

VALE DULCISSIME
VALE DELECTISSIME DESIDERATISSIME
REQUIESCAS IN PACE
PATER AC MATER HIC POSTHAC REQUIESCAMUS TECUM
USQUE AD TUBAM

In this part of the church there is also another tablet to the memory of Henry Hallam, the epitaph written by my father: who thought the simpler the epitaph, the better it would become the simple and noble man, whose work speaks for him:

HERE WITH HIS WIFE AND CHILDREN RESTS

HENRY HALLAM THE HISTORIAN

It was not until May 1850 that "In Memoriam" was printed and given to a few friends.   Shortly afterwards it was published, first of all anonymously, but the authorship was soon discovered.

The earliest jottings, begun in 1833, of the "Elegies" as they were then called, were nearly lost in a London lodging, for my father was always careless about his manuscripts.

Mr Coventry Patmore wrote to me about this :

The letter from your father concerning the MS of "In Memoriam" I gave to the late Sir John Simeon, thinking that he ought to have it, as he had the MS[1] itself. This letter asked me to visit the lodging in Mornington Place, Hampstead Road, which he had occupied two or three weeks before, and to try to recover the MS, which he had left in a closet where he was used to keep some of his provisions. The landlady said that no such book had been left, but I insisted on looking for it myself, and found it where your father said it was.

The letter alluded to is given below :

BONCHURCH, I. W.,
Feb. 28*th*, 1850.

MY DEAR COVENTRY,

I went up to my room yesterday to get my book of Elegies : you know what I mean, a long, butcher-ledger-like book.   I was going to read one or two to an artist here : I could not find it.   I have some obscure remembrance of having lent it to you.   If so, all is well, if not, will you go to my old chambers and institute a vigorous inquiry?   I was coming up to-day on purpose to look after it, but as the weather is so furious I have yielded to the wishes of my friends here to stop till to-morrow.   I shall be, I expect, in town to-morrow at 25 M. P. when I shall be glad to see you.   At 9.10 p.m. the train in which I come gets into London.   I shall be

---

[1] This MS, given to Sir John Simeon by my father, has been generously returned to me by Lady Simeon.

in Mornington Place about 10 o'clock I suppose. Perhaps
you would in your walk Museum-ward call on Mrs
Lloyd and tell her to prepare for me.   With best remembrances to Mrs Patmore,

Believe me ever yours,

A. TENNYSON.

At first the reviews of the volume were not on the
whole sympathetic.   One critic in a leading journal, for
instance, considered that " a great deal of poetic feeling
had been wasted," and "much shallow art spent on the
tenderness shown to an Amaryllis of the Chancery
Bar."   Another referred to the poem as follows : " These
touching lines evidently come from the full heart of the
widow of a military man."   However, men like Maurice
and Robertson thought that the author had made a definite step towards the unification of the highest religion
and philosophy with the progressive science of the day ;
and that he was the one poet who " through almost the
agonies of a death-struggle " had made an effective
stand against his own doubts and difficulties and those
of the time, "on behalf of those first principles which
underlie all creeds, which belong to our earliest childhood, and on which the wisest and best have rested
through all ages ; that all is right ; that darkness shall be
clear ; that God and Time are the only interpreters ; that
Love is King ; that the Immortal is in us ; that, which
is the keynote of the whole, 'All is well, tho' Faith and
Form be sundered in the night of Fear[1].' "   Scientific
leaders like Herschel, Owen, Sedgwick and Tyndall
regarded him as a champion of Science, and cheered

---

[1] Robertson goes so far as to say : " To my mind and heart the *most*
satisfactory things that have been ever said on the future state are contained in this poem."

The best analysis of "In Memoriam " is by Miss Chapman (Macmillan
and Co.).

him with words of genuine admiration for his love of
Nature, for the eagerness with which he welcomed
all the latest scientific discoveries, and for his trust
in truth. Science indeed in his opinion was one of the
main forces tending to disperse the superstition that
still darkens the world. A review which he thought
one of the ablest was that by Mr Gladstone. From
this review I quote the following to show that in Gladstone's opinion my father had not over-estimated Arthur
Hallam.

In 1850 Mr Tennyson gave to the world under the title of
"In Memoriam," perhaps the richest oblation ever offered by the
affection of friendship at the tomb of the departed. The memory
of Arthur Henry Hallam, who died suddenly in 1833, at the age
of twenty-two, will doubtless live chiefly in connection with this
volume. But he is well known to have been one who, if the
term of his days had been prolonged, would have needed no
aid from a friendly hand, would have built his own enduring
monument, and would have bequeathed to his country a name
in all likelihood greater than that of his very distinguished
father. The writer of this paper was, more than half a century
ago, in a condition to say

"I marked him
As a far Alp ; and loved to watch the sunrise
Dawn on his ample brow [1]."

There perhaps was no one among those who were blessed
with his friendship, nay, as we see, not even Mr Tennyson [2], who
did not feel at once bound closely to him by commanding
affection, and left far behind by the rapid, full and rich development of his ever-searching mind; by his

"All-comprehensive tenderness,
All-subtilising intellect."

It would be easy to show what in the varied forms of human
excellence, he might, had life been granted him, have accomplished; much more difficult to point the finger and to say, "This

[1] De Vere's *Mary Tudor* IV. I.
[2] See "In Memoriam," CIX., CX., CXI., CXII., CXIII.

he never could have done." Enough remains from among his early efforts, to accredit whatever mournful witness may now be borne of him. But what can be a nobler tribute than this, that for seventeen years after his death a poet, fast rising towards the lofty summits of his art, found that young fading image the richest source of his inspiration, and of thoughts that gave him buoyancy for a flight such as he had not hitherto attained[1].

Bishop Westcott and Professor Henry Sidgwick have written me interesting letters which respectively give the impressions the poem made on Cambridge men in 1850, and in 1860, and I quote them *in extenso.*

The Bishop writes:

When "In Memoriam" appeared, I felt (as I feel if possible more strongly now) that the hope of man lies in the historic realization of the Gospel. I rejoiced in the Introduction, which appeared to me to be the mature summing up after an interval of the many strains of thought in the "Elegies." Now the stress of controversy is over, I think so still. As I look at my original copy of "In Memoriam," I recognise that what impressed me most was your father's splendid faith (in the face of the frankest acknowledgment of every difficulty) in the growing purpose of the sum of life, and in the noble destiny of the individual man as he offers himself for the fulfilment of his little part (LIV., LXXXI., LXXXII. and the closing stanzas). This faith has now largely entered into our common life, and it seems to me to express a lesson of the Gospel which the circumstances of all time encourage us to master.

Professor Sidgwick writes:

After thinking over the matter, it has seemed to me better to write to you a somewhat different kind of letter from that which I originally designed: a letter not primarily intended for publication, though I wish you to feel at liberty to print any part of it which you may find suitable, but primarily intended to serve rather as a "document" on which you may base any statements you may wish to make as to the impression produced by "In Memoriam." I have decided to adopt this course:

[1] Gladstone's *Gleanings of Past Years,* Vol. II., pp. 136–37.

because I want to write with rather more frank egotism than I should otherwise like to show. I want to do this, because in describing the impression made on me by the poem, I ought to make clear the point of view from which I approached it, and the attitude of thought which I retained under its influence. In what follows I shall be describing chiefly my own experiences : but I shall allow myself sometimes to say " we " rather than " I," meaning by " we " my generation, as known to me, through converse with intimate friends.

To begin, then : our views on religious matters were not, at any rate after a year or two of the discussion started in 1860 by *Essays and Reviews*, really in harmony with those which we found suggested by " In Memoriam." They were more sceptical and less Christian, in any strict sense of the word : certainly this was the case with myself : I remember feeling that Clough *represented* my individual habits of thought and sentiment more than your father, although as a poet he *moved* me less. And this more sceptical attitude has remained mine through life ; while at the same time I feel that the beliefs in God and in immortality are vital to human well-being.

Hence the most important influence of " In Memoriam " on my thought, apart from its poetic charm as an expression of personal emotion, opened in a region, if I may so say, deeper down than the difference between Theism and Christianity : it lay in the unparalleled combination of intensity of feeling with comprehensiveness of view and balance of judgment, shown in presenting the *deepest* needs and perplexities of humanity. And this influence, I find, has increased rather than diminished as years have gone on, and as the great issues between Agnostic Science and Faith have become continually more prominent. In the sixties I should say that these deeper issues were somewhat obscured by the discussions on Christian dogma, and Inspiration of Scripture, etc. You may remember Browning's reference to this period —

> " The Essays and Reviews debate
> Begins to tell on the public mind
> And Colenso's words have weight."

During these years we were absorbed in struggling for freedom of thought in the trammels of a historical religion : and perhaps what we sympathize with most in " In Memoriam " at this time, apart from the personal feeling, was the defence of "honest doubt," the reconciliation of knowledge and faith in the introductory poem, and the hopeful trump^t-ring of the lines on the New Year —

> Ring out the thousand wars of old,
> Ring in the thousand years of peace,

and generally the *forward* movement of the thought.

Well, the years pass, the struggle with what Carlyle used to call "Hebrew old clothes" is over, Freedom is won, and what does Freedom bring us to? It brings us face to face with atheistic science: the faith in God and Immortality, which we had been struggling to clear from superstition, suddenly seems to be *in the air:* and in seeking for a firm basis for this faith we find ourselves in the midst of the "fight with death" which "In Memoriam" so powerfully presents.

What "In Memoriam" did for us, for me at least, in this struggle was to impress on us the ineffaceable and ineradicable conviction that *humanity* will not and cannot acquiesce in a godless world: the "man in men" will not do this, whatever individual men may do, whatever they may temporarily feel themselves driven to do, by following methods which they cannot abandon to the conclusions to which these methods at present seem to lead.

The force with which it impressed this conviction was not due to the *mere intensity* of its expression of the feelings which Atheism outrages and Agnosticism ignores: but rather to its expression of them along with a reverent docility to the lessons of science which also belongs to the essence of the thought of our age.

I remember being struck with a note in *Nature*, at the time of your father's death, which dwelt on this last-mentioned aspect of his work, and regarded him as preeminently the Poet of Science. I have always felt this characteristic important in estimating his effect on his generation. Wordsworth's attitude towards Nature was one that, so to say, left Science unregarded: the Nature for which Wordsworth stirred our feelings was Nature as known by simple observation and interpreted by religious and sympathetic intuition. But for your father the physical world is always the world as known to us through physical science: the scientific view of it dominates his thoughts about it; and his general acceptance of this view is real and sincere, even when he utters the intensest feeling of its inadequacy to satisfy our deepest needs. Had it been otherwise, had he met the atheistic tendencies of modern Science with more confident defiance, more confident assertion of an Intuitive Faculty of theological knowledge, overriding the results laboriously reached by empirical science, I think his antagonism to these tendencies would have been far less impressive.

I always feel this strongly in reading the memorable lines:

"If e'er, when faith had fallen asleep" down to "I have felt[1]."

At this point, if the stanzas had stopped here, we should have shaken our heads and said, "Feeling must not usurp the function of Reason. Feeling is not knowing. It is the duty of a rational being to follow truth wherever it leads."

But the poet's instinct knows this; he knows that this usurpation by Feeling of the function of Reason is too bold and confident; accordingly in the next stanza he gives the turn to humility in the protest of Feeling which is required (I think) to win the assent of the "man in men" at this stage of human thought.

These lines I can never read without tears. I feel in them the indestructible and inalienable minimum of faith which humanity cannot give up because it is necessary for life; and which I know that I, at least so far as the man in me is deeper than the methodical thinker, cannot give up.

If the possibility of a "godless world" is excluded, the faith thus restored is, for the poet, unquestionably a form of Christian faith: there seems to him then no reason for doubting that the

Sinless years
That breathed beneath the Syrian blue,

and the marvel of the life continued after the bodily death, were a manifestation of the "immortal love" which by faith we embrace as the essence of the Divine nature. "If the dead rise not, Christ is not risen": but if we may believe that they rise, then it seems to him, we may and must believe the main drift of the Gospel story; though we may transiently

[1] See pp. 314–15.

wonder why the risen Lord told his disciples only of life, and nothing of " what it is to die[1]."

From this point of view the note of Christian faith struck in the introductory stanzas is in harmony with all that follows. And yet I have always felt that in a certain sense the effect of the introduction does not quite represent the effect of the poem. Faith, in the introduction, is too completely triumphant. I think this is inevitable, because so far as the thought-debate presented by the poem is summed up, it must be summed up on the side of Faith. Faith must give the last word : but the last word is not the whole utterance of the truth : the whole truth is that assurance and doubt must alternate in the moral world in which we at present live, somewhat as night and day alternate in the physical world. The revealing visions come and go ; when they come we *feel* that we *know:* but in the intervals we must pass through states in which all is dark, and in which we can only struggle to hold the conviction that

> Power is with us in the night
> Which makes the darkness and the light
> And dwells not in the light alone.

" It must be remembered," writes my father, " that this is a poem, *not* an actual biography. It is founded on our friendship, on the engagement of Arthur Hallam to my sister, on his sudden death at Vienna, just before the time fixed for their marriage, and on his burial at Clevedon Church. The poem concludes with the marriage of my youngest sister Cecilia. It was meant to be a kind of *Divina Commedia*, ending with happiness. The sections were written at many different places, and as the phases of our intercourse came to my memory and suggested them. I did not write them with any view of weaving them into a whole, or for publica- tion, until I found that I had written so many. The different moods of sorrow as in a drama are dramatically given, and my conviction that fear, doubts, and suffering

[1] See Browning's " Epistle containing the Strange Medical Experience of Karshish."

will find answer and relief only through Faith in a
God of Love. ' I ' is not always the author speaking
of himself, but the voice of the human race speaking
thro' him. After the Death of A. H. H., the divisions
of the poem are made by First Xmas Eve (Section
XXVIII.), Second Xmas (LXXVIII.[1]), Third Xmas Eve
(CIV. and CV. etc.). I myself did not see Clevedon till
years after the burial of A. H. H. Jan. 3rd, 1834, and
then in later editions of ' In Memoriam ' I altered the
word ' chancel,' which was the word used by Mr Hallam
in his Memoir, to ' dark church.' As to the localities in
which the poems were written, some were written in
Lincolnshire, some in London, Essex, Gloucestershire,
Wales, anywhere where I happened to be[2]."

"And as for the metre of ' In Memoriam ' I had no
notion till 1880 that Lord Herbert of Cherbury had

---

[1] No. LXXII. refers to the first anniversary of the death Sept. 15th, 1833.
No. C. to the farewell of the family to Somersby in 1837.

[2] In a letter to Mr Malan written at the same time as the above note,
in reply to enquiries as to whether, in "In Memoriam," he has copied
Statius, or Ovid's " Epicedion," or the " Sorrow of Arcadius Etruscus," or
" Spring Stanzas to Domitian," etc. etc. my father writes :

Nov. 14th, 1883.

DEAR SIR,

    I am sorry that your letter has gone so long unanswered, but my
eyes are so bad, and I have such a large correspondence that I find it
impossible to answer everybody. It is news to me that the remains of
A. H. H. were landed at Dover. I had always believed that the ship which
brought them put in at Bristol. As to his being buried in the chancel,
Mr Hallam in a printed memoir of his son, states that it was so. * * * * I
can assure you I am innocent as far as I am aware of knowing one line of
Statius ; and of Ovid's "Epicedion " I never heard. I have searched for it
in vain in a little three volume edition of Ovid which I have here, but that
does not contain this poem ; nor have I ever heard of the " Sorrow of
Arcadius Etruscus," nor of the " Spring Stanzas to Domitian." The memoir
of his son by Mr Hallam, to which I allude, was printed merely for private
circulation : and whether he repeated the statement of the chancel burial in
the published Memoir I do not know.

Yours very truly,
A. TENNYSON.

written his occasional verses in the same metre. I
believed myself the originator of the metre, until after
'In Memoriam' came out, when some one told me that
Ben Jonson and Sir Philip Sidney had used it. The
following poems were omitted from 'In Memoriam'
when I published, because I thought them redundant[1]."

The Grave (originally No. LVII.). *(Unpublished.)*

I keep no more a lone distress,
　　The crowd have come to see thy grave,
　　Small thanks or credit shall I have,
But these shall see it none the less.

The happy maiden's tears are free
　　And she will weep and give them way;
　　Yet one unschool'd in want will say
"The dead are dead and let them be."

Another whispers sick with loss:
　　"O let the simple slab remain!
　　The 'Mercy Jesu' in the rain!
The 'Miserere' in the moss!"

"I love the daisy weeping dew,
　　I hate the trim-set plots of art!"
　　My friend, thou speakest from the heart,
But look, for these are nature too.

––––––––––

To A. H. H. (originally No. CVIII.). *(Unpublished.)*

Young is the grief I entertain,
　　And ever new the tale she tells,
　　And ever young the face that dwells
With reason cloister'd in the brain:

[1] "O Sorrow, wilt thou live with me" was added in 1851.

Yet grief deserves a nobler name:
  She spurs an imitative will;
  'Tis shame to fail so far, and still
My failing shall be less my shame:

Considering what mine eyes have seen,
  And all the sweetness which thou wast
  In thy beginnings in the past,
And all the strength thou wouldst have been:

A master mind with master minds,
  An orb repulsive of all hate,
  A will concentric with all fate,
A life four-square to all the winds.

———————

The Victor Hours (originally No. cxxvii.).
(*Unpublished.*)

Are those the far-famed Victor Hours
  That ride to death the griefs of men?
  I fear not; if I fear'd them, then
Is this blind flight the winged Powers.

Behold, ye cannot bring but good,
  And see, ye dare not touch the truth,
  Nor Sorrow beauteous in her youth,
Nor Love that holds a constant mood.

Ye must be wiser than your looks,
  Or wise yourselves, or wisdom-led,
  Else this wild whisper round my head
Were idler than a flight of rooks.

Go forward! crumble down a throne,
  Dissolve a world, condense a star,
  Unsocket all the joints of war,
And fuse the peoples into one.

———————

That my father was a student of the Bible, those who have read " In Memoriam " know. He also eagerly read all notable works within his reach relating to the Bible, and traced with deep interest such fundamental truths as underlie the great religions of the world. He hoped that the Bible [1] would be more and more studied by all ranks of people, and expounded simply by their teachers ; for he maintained that the religion of a people could never be founded on mere moral philosophy : and that it could only come home to them in the simple, noble thoughts and facts of a Scripture like ours [2].

Soon after his marriage he took to reading different systems of philosophy [3], yet none particularly influenced him. The result I think is shown in a more ordered arrangement of religious, metaphysical and scientific thought throughout the " Idylls " and his later works. " In Poems like ' De Profundis ' and the 'Ancient Sage,' " Jowett said, " he often brings up metaphysical truths from the deepest depths." But as a rule he knew that poetry must touch on metaphysical topics rather by allusion than systematically. In the following pages I shall not give any of his subtler arguments; but only attempt to illustrate from " In Memoriam," with some of the other poems, and from his conversation, the *general* everyday attitude of his mind toward the highest problems that confront us. In dealing with these none was readier in the discovery of fallacies, none was more resolute in proclaiming what seemed to him realities.

His creed, he always said, he would not formulate, for people would not understand him if he did ; but he

---

[1] He also said : " The Bible ought to be read, were it only for the sake of the grand English in which it is written, an education in itself."

[2] See Nos. XXXVI., LII., LXXXIV. last stanza but one.

[3] Spinoza, Berkeley, Kant, Schlegel, Fichte, Hegel, Ferrier, were among the books added to his library.

considered that his poems expressed the principles at the foundation of his faith.

He thought, with Arthur Hallam, "that the essential feelings of religion subsist in the utmost diversity of forms," that "different language does not always imply different opinions, nor different opinions any difference in *real* faith." "It is impossible," he said, "to imagine that the Almighty will ask you, when you come before Him in the next life what your particular form of creed was: but the question will rather be, 'Have you been true to yourself, and given in My Name a cup of cold water to one of these little ones?'"

"This is a terrible age of unfaith," he would say. "I hate utter unfaith, I cannot endure that men should sacrifice everything at the cold altar of what with their imperfect knowledge they choose to call truth and reason. One can easily lose all belief, through giving up the continual thought and care for spiritual things."

And again, "In this vale of Time the hills of Time often shut out the mountains of Eternity."

My father's friend, the Bishop of Ripon, writes:

With those who are impatient of *all* spiritual truth he had no sympathy whatever; but he had a sympathy with those who were impatient of the formal statement of truth, only because he felt that all formal statements of truth must of necessity fall below the greatness and the grandeur of the truth itself. There is a reverent impatience of forms, and there is an irreverent impatience of them. An irreverent impatience of formal dogma means impatience of all spiritual truth; but a reverent impatience of formal dogma may be but the expression of the feeling that the truth must be larger, purer, nobler than any mere human expression or definition of it. With this latter attitude of mind he had sympathy, and he expressed that sympathy in song; he could understand those who seemed

> To have reach'd a purer air,
> Whose faith has centre everywhere,
> Nor cares to fix itself to form.

He urged men to "cling to faith, beyond the forms of faith[1]." But while he did this he also recognised clearly the importance and the value of definitions of truth, and his counsel to the very man who prided himself upon his emancipation from forms was:

Leave thou thy sister when she prays,
    Her early Heaven, her happy views;
    Nor thou with shadow'd hint confuse
A life that leads melodious days.

Her faith thro' form is pure as thine,
    Her hands are quicker unto good:
    Oh, sacred be the flesh and blood
To which she links a truth divine[2]!

He warned the man proud of his emancipation from formal faith, that in a world of so many confusions he might meet with ruin, "Ev'n for want of such a type." And we are not surprised, knowing how insidious are the evil influences which gather round us:

Hold thou the good; define it well,
    For fear Divine Philosophy
    Should push beyond her mark, and be
Procuress to the lords of Hell.

And thus he had sympathy with those who feel that faith is larger and nobler than form, and at the same time he had tenderness and appreciation for those who find their faith helped by form. To him, as to so many, truth is so infinitely great that all we can do with our poor human utterances is to try and clothe it in such language as will make it clear to ourselves,

[1] Cf. Vol. II. chap. XXIII. 1st paragraph.

[2] Jowett wrote about my father's "defence of honest doubt" as compared with this passage: "Can we find any reconciliation of these varying utterances of the same mind? I think that we may. For we may argue that truth kept back is the greatest source of doubt and suspicion: that faith cannot survive without enquiry, and that the doubt which is raised may be the step upward to a higher faith. And so we arrive at the conclusion that truth is good, and to be received thankfully and fearlessly by all who are capable of receiving it. But on the other hand it is not always to be imparted in its entirety to those who cannot understand it, and whose minds would be puzzled and overwhelmed by it."

and clear to those to whom God sends us with a message, but meanwhile, above us and our thoughts — above our broken lights — God in His mercy, God in His love, God in His infinite nature is greater than all.

Assuredly Religion was no nebulous abstraction for him. He consistently emphasized his own belief in what he called the Eternal Truths; in an Omnipotent, Omnipresent and All-loving God, Who has revealed Himself through the human attribute of the highest self-sacrificing love; in the freedom of the human will; and in the immortality of the soul. But he asserted that "Nothing worthy proving can be proven," and that even as to the great laws which are the basis of Science, "We have but faith, we cannot know." He dreaded the dogmatism of sects and rash definitions of God. "I dare hardly name His Name" he would say, and accordingly he named Him in "The Ancient Sage" the "Nameless." "But take away belief in the self-conscious personality of God," he said, "and you take away the backbone of the world." "On God and God-like men we build our trust." A week before his death I was sitting by him, and he talked long of the Personality and of the Love of God, "That God, Whose eyes consider the poor," "Who catereth even for the sparrow." "I should," he said, "infinitely rather feel myself the most miserable wretch on the face of the earth with a God above, than the highest type of man standing alone." He would allow that God is unknowable in "his whole world-self, and all-in-all," and that therefore there was some force in the objection made by some people to the word "Personality," as being "anthropomorphic," and that perhaps "Self-consciousness" or "Mind" might be clearer to them: but at the same time he insisted that, although "man is like a thing of nought" in "the boundless plan," our highest view of God must be more or less anthropomorphic: and that

"Personality," as far as our intelligence goes, is the widest definition and includes "Mind," "Self-consciousness [1]," "Will," "Love" and other attributes of the Real, the Supreme, "the High and Lofty One that inhabiteth Eternity Whose name is Holy."

Jowett asked him to write an anthem about God for Balliol Chapel and he wrote "The Human Cry":

We feel we are nothing — for all is Thou and in Thee;
We feel we are something — *that* also has come from Thee;
We know we are nothing — but Thou wilt help us to be.
Hallowed be Thy name — Hallelujah!

When his last book was in proof, we spoke together of the ultimate expression of his own calm faith at the end of his life:

That Love which is and was
My Father and my Brother and my God [2].

Everywhere throughout the Universe he saw the glory and greatness of God, and the science of Nature was particularly dear to him. Every new fact which came within his range was carefully weighed. As he exulted in the wilder aspects of Nature (see for instance sect. xv.) and revelled in the thunderstorm; so he felt a joy in her orderliness; he felt a rest in her steadfastness, patient progress and hopefulness; the same seasons ever returned; the same stars wheeled in their courses;

---

[1] "A. T. thinks it ridiculous to believe in a God and deny his consciousness, and was amused at someone who said of him that he had versified Hegelianism." Jowett, MS Note.

[2] To enquiries as to the meaning of the words "Immortal Love" in the Introduction to "In Memoriam," he explained that he had used "Love" in the same sense as St John (1 John, chap. iv.). "The Word" also in No. xxxvi. was "The Word" as used by St John, the Revelation of the Eternal Thought of the Universe.

the flowers[1] and trees blossomed and the birds sang yearly in their appointed months; and he had a triumphant appreciation of her ever-new revelations of beauty. One of the "In Memoriam" poems, written at Barmouth[2], gives preeminently his sense of the joyous peace in Nature, and he would quote it in this context along with his Spring and Bird songs:

> Sweet after showers, ambrosial air,
>   That rollest from the gorgeous gloom
>   Of evening over brake and bloom
> And meadow, slowly breathing bare
>
> The round of space, and rapt below
>   Thro' all the dewy-tassell'd wood,
>   And shadowing down the horned flood
> In ripples, fan my brows and blow
>
> The fever from my cheek, and sigh
>   The full new life that feeds thy breath
>   Throughout my frame, till Doubt and Death,
> Ill brethren, let the fancy fly
>
> From belt to belt of crimson seas
>   On leagues of odour streaming far,
>   To where in yonder orient star
> A hundred spirits whisper "Peace[3]."

But he was occasionally much troubled with the intellectual problem of the apparent profusion and waste of life and by the vast amount of sin and suffering throughout the world, for these seemed to militate against the idea of the Omnipotent and All-loving Father.

No doubt in such moments he might possibly have

---

[1] Picking up a daisy as we walked, and looking close to its crimson-tipt leaves he said: "Does not this look like a thinking Artificer, one who wishes to ornament?" MS Note, E. F. G.

[2] He notes this in his own hand.

[3] See also Nos. LXXXVIII., LXXXIX., XCI., CXV., CXVI., CXXI., CXXII.

been heard to say what I myself have heard him say:
"An Omnipotent Creator Who could make such a painful world is to me *sometimes* as hard to believe in as to
believe in blind matter behind everything. The lavish
profusion too in the natural world appals me, from the
growths of the tropical forest to the capacity of man to
multiply, the torrent of babies."

" I can almost understand some of the Gnostic here-
sies, which only after all put the difficulty one step further
back ":

> O me! for why is all around us here
> As if some lesser god had made the world,
> But had not force to shape it as he would,
> Till the High God behold it from beyond
> And enter it, and make it beautiful?[1]

After one of these moods in the summer of 1892
he exclaimed: " Yet God *is* love, transcendent, all-
pervading! We do not get *this* faith from Nature or
the world. If we look at Nature alone, full of perfection
and imperfection, she tells us that God is disease, murder
and rapine. We get this faith from ourselves, from
what is highest within us, which recognizes that there
is not one fruitless pang, just as there is not one lost
good."

> That which we dare invoke to bless;
>   Our dearest faith; our ghastliest doubt;
>   He, They, One, All; within, without;
> The Power in darkness whom we guess;
>
> I found Him not in world or sun,
>   Or eagle's wing, or insect's eye;
>   Nor thro' the questions men may try,
> The petty cobwebs we have spun:

[1] He would sometimes put forward the old theory that " The world is
part of an infinite plan, incomplete because it is a part. We cannot therefore
read the riddle."

If e'er when faith had fall'n asleep,
  I heard a voice "believe no more"
  And heard an ever-breaking shore
That tumbled in the Godless deep;

A warmth within the heart would melt
  The freezing reason's colder part,
  And like a man in wrath the heart
Stood up and answer'd "I have felt."

No, like a child in doubt and fear;
  But that blind clamour made me wise;
  Then was I as a child that cries,
But, crying, knows his father near;

And what I am beheld again
  What is, and no man understands;
  And out of darkness came the hands
That reach thro' nature, moulding men.

He had been reading the eighth chapter of Romans,
and said that he thought that St Paul fully recognized
in the sorrows of Nature and in the miseries of the world
a stumbling-block to the divine idea of God, but that
they are the preludes necessary as things are to the
higher good[1]. "For myself," he said, "the world is
the shadow of God," and then he referred to Jowett's
commentary on this chapter:

As we turn from ourselves to the world around us, the
prospect on which we cast our eyes seems to reflect the tone and
colour of our own minds, and to share our joy and sorrow. To
the religious mind it seems also to reflect our sins. We cannot
indeed speak of the misery of the brute creation, of whose
constitution we know so little; nor do we pretend to discover
in the loveliest spots of earth indications of a fallen world. But
when we look at the vices and diseases of mankind, at the life of
labour in which animals are our partners, at the aspect in modern

[1] Cf. St John xvi. 21, 22.

times of our large towns, as in ancient, of a world given to
idolatry, we see enough to explain the Apostle's meaning, and to
understand how he could say that " The whole creation groaneth
and travaileth till now."   He is not speaking, of course, of the
conscious feeling of degradation, but of the world, as it seemed
to the eye of faith ; not as it appeared to itself, but as we may
imagine it to appear in the sight of God when compared with
the divine idea....   But the Spirit helps us, and God has chosen
us according to his purpose, and in all things God is working
with us for good [1].

My father invariably believed that humility [2] is the
only true attitude of the human soul, and therefore
spoke with the greatest reserve of what he called " these
unfathomable mysteries," as befitting one who did not
dogmatise, but who knew that the Finite can by no
means grasp the Infinite: " Dark is the world to thee [3],
thyself is the reason why "; and yet, he had a profound
trust that when all is seen face to face, all will be seen
as the best.   " Fear not thou the hidden purpose of that
Power which alone is great."   " Who knows whether
Revelation be not itself a veil to hide the Glory of that
Love which we could not look upon, without marring the
sight and our onward progress ? "
This faith was to him the breath of life, and never,
I feel, really failed him, or life itself would have failed.
Free-will and its relation to the meaning of human
life and to circumstance was latterly one of his most
common subjects of conversation.   Free-will was un-
doubtedly, he said, the " main miracle, apparently an act
of self-limitation by the Infinite, and yet a revelation by

---

[1] Jowett, *Epistle to the Romans.*

[2] " Almost the finest summing up of Religion is 'to do justice, to love
mercy, and to walk humbly with God.'"   A. T.

He often quoted Newton's saying that we are like children picking up
pebbles on the shore of the Infinite Ocean.

[3] The real mysteries to him were Time, life, and " finite-infinite " space :
and so he talks of the soul " being born and banish'd into mystery."

Himself of Himself." "Take away the sense of individual responsibility and men sink into pessimism and
madness." He wrote at the end of the poem "Despair":
"In my boyhood I came across the Calvinist Creed,
and assuredly however unfathomable the mystery, if one
cannot believe in the freedom of the human will as of
the Divine, life is hardly worth having." The lines that
he oftenest repeated about Free-will were,

> This main miracle that thou art thou
> With power on thine own act and on the world.

Then he would enlarge upon man's consequent moral
obligations, upon the Law which claims a free obedience,
and upon the pursuit of moral perfection (in imitation of
the Divine) to which man is called.

> οὐ γὰρ ἔχω ἔγωγε οὐδὲν οὕτω μοι ἐναργὲς ὄν, ὡς τοῦτο,
> τὸ εἶναι ὡς οἷόν τε μάλιστα καλόν τε καὶ ἀγαθόν.

"For I hold nothing so clear as this, that I must be as
good and noble as a man can be."

I cannot refrain from setting down the drift of his
talk to a young man who was going to the University. —
"If a man is merely to be a bundle of sensations,
he had better not exist at all. He should embark on
his career in the spirit of selfless and adventurous
heroism; should develop his true self by not shirking
responsibility, by casting aside all maudlin and intro-
spective morbidities, and by using his powers cheerfully
in accordance with the obvious dictates of his moral
consciousness, and so, as far as possible, in harmony
with what he feels to be the Absolute Right.

> Self-reverence, self-knowledge, self-control,
> These three alone lead life to sovereign power.
> Yet not for power (power of herself
> Would come uncall'd for) but to live by *law*,

> *Acting* the law we live by without fear;
> And, because right is right, to follow right
> Were wisdom in the scorn of consequence.

It is motive, it is the great purpose which consecrates life[1]. The real test of a man is not what he knows, but what he is in himself and in his relation to others. For instance, can he battle against his own bad inherited instincts, or brave public opinion in the cause of truth? The love of God is the true basis of duty, truth, reverence, loyalty, love, virtue and work. I believe in these although I feel the emptiness and hollowness of much of life. ' Be ye perfect as your Father in heaven is perfect.'" Then he added characteristically: " But don't be a prig. Most young men with anything in them make fools of themselves at some time or other."

One of the last passages I heard him recite about Free-will was:

> But ill for him who, bettering not with time,
> Corrupts the strength of Heaven-descended Will,
> And ever weaker grows thro' acted crime,
> Or seeming-genial venial fault,
> Recurring and suggesting still!
> He seems as one whose footsteps halt,
> Toiling in immeasurable sand,
> And o'er a weary sultry land,
> Far beneath a blazing vault,
> Sown in a wrinkle of the monstrous hill,
> The city sparkles like a grain of salt.

And he wrote for me as to man's will being free but only within certain limits: " Man's Free-will is but a bird in a cage; he can stop at the lower perch, or he can

[1] St Paul's expression "The temple of the Holy Ghost" he thought had had a powerful effect on the Christian appreciation of the meaning of life.

mount to a higher.   Then that which is and knows will enlarge his cage, give him a higher and a higher perch, and at last break off the top of his cage, and let him out to be one with the Free-will of the Universe."   Then he said earnestly: "If the absorption into the divine in the after-life be the creed of some, let them at all events allow us many existences of individuality before this absorption; since this short-lived individuality seems to be but too short a preparation for so mighty a union[1]."

> Death's truer name
> Is "Onward," no discordance in the roll
> And march of that Eternal Harmony
> Whereto the worlds beat time.

In the same way, "O living will that shalt endure" he explained as that which we know as Free-will, the higher and enduring part of man.   He held that there was an intimate connexion between the human and the divine, and that each individual will had a spiritual and eternal significance with relation to other individual wills as well as to the Supreme and Eternal Will.

Throughout his life he had a constant feeling of a spiritual harmony existing between ourselves and the outward visible Universe, and of the actual Immanence of God in the infinitesimal atom as in the vastest system[2]. "If God," he would say, "were to withdraw Himself for one single instant from this Universe, everything would vanish into nothingness."   When speaking on that subject he said to me: "My most passionate desire is to

[1] "In Memoriam," No. XLVII.

[2] He would point out the difficulties of materialism, and would propound to us, when we were boys, the old puzzle: "Look at the mystery of a grain of sand; you can divide it for ever and for ever. You cannot conceive anything material of which you cannot conceive the half." He disliked the Atomic theory: and was taken by the theory of *aboriginal centres of force*.

have a clearer and fuller vision of God.   The soul seems
to me one with God, how I cannot tell.   I can sympathize with God in my poor little way."   In some
phases of thought and feeling his idealism tended more
decidedly to mysticism.   He wrote : "A kind of waking
trance I have frequently had, quite up from boyhood,
when I have been all alone.   This has generally come
upon me thro' repeating my own name two or three
times to myself silently, till all at once, as it were out
of the intensity of the consciousness of individuality,
the individuality itself seemed to dissolve and fade away
into boundless being, and this not a confused state, but
the clearest of the clearest, the surest of the surest, the
weirdest of the weirdest, utterly beyond words, where
death was an almost laughable impossibility, the loss of
personality (if so it were) seeming no extinction but the
only true life[1]."   "This might," he said, "be the state
which St Paul describes, 'Whether in the body I cannot
tell, or whether out of the body I cannot tell.'"

He continued: "I am ashamed of my feeble description.   Have I not said the state is utterly beyond
words?   But in a moment, when I come back to my
normal state of 'sanity,' I am ready to fight for *mein
liebes Ich*, and hold that it will last for æons of æons."

In the same way he said that there might be a more
intimate communion than we could dream of between the
living and the dead, at all events for a time.

May all love,
His love, unseen but felt, o'ershadow Thee,
Till God's love set Thee at his side again!

---

[1] Cf. "The Ancient Sage," and the smaller partial anticipation in "In
Memoriam," xcv. st. 9.
"Yet it appeared that he distinguished himself from external things."
Jowett, MS Note.

And —

> The ghost in Man, the ghost that once was Man,
> But cannot wholly free itself from Man,
> Are calling to each other through a dawn
> Stranger than earth has ever seen; the veil
> Is rending, and the Voices of the day
> Are heard across the Voices of the dark.

I need not enlarge upon his faith in the Immortality of the Soul as he has dwelt upon that so fully in his poems[1]. " I can hardly understand," he said, " how any great, imaginative man, who has deeply lived, suffered, thought and wrought, can doubt of the Soul's continuous progress in the after-life." His poem of " Wages " he liked to quote on this subject.

He more than once said what he has expressed in " Vastness ": " Hast Thou made all this for naught! Is all this trouble of life worth undergoing if we only end in our own corpse-coffins at last? If you allow a God, and God allows this strong instinct and universal yearning for another life, surely that is in a measure a presumption of its truth. We cannot give up the mighty hopes that make us men."

> My own dim life should teach me this,
>   That life shall live for evermore,
>   Else earth is darkness at the core,
> And dust and ashes all that is.
> What then were God to such as I?

I have heard him even say that he " would rather know that he was to be lost eternally than not know that the whole human race was to live eternally "; and when he speaks of " faintly trusting the larger hope " he means by " the larger hope " that the whole human race would

---

[1] He said to Bishop Lightfoot: " The cardinal point of Christianity is the Life after Death " (2 Tim. chap. i.).

through, perhaps, ages of suffering, be at length purified and saved, even those who now "better not with time"; so that at the end of "The Vision of Sin" we read

> God made Himself an awful rose of dawn.

One day towards the end of his life he bade me look into the Revised Version and see how the Revisers had translated the passage "Depart from me, ye cursed, into everlasting fire." His disappointment was keen when he found that the translators had not altered "everlasting" into "æonian[1]" or some such word: for he never would believe that Christ could preach "everlasting punishment."

> "Fecemi la divina potestate
> La somma sapienza, e 'l primo amore,"

were words which he was fond of quoting in this relation, as if they were a kind of unconscious confession by Dante that Love must conquer at the last.

Letters were not unfrequently addressed to him asking what his opinions were about Evolution, about Prayer, and about Christ.

Of Evolution he said: "That makes no difference to me, even if the Darwinians did not, as they do, exaggerate Darwinism. To God all is present. He sees present, past, and future as one."

> To your question now
> Which touches on the workman and his work.
> "Let there be light and there was light": 'tis so:
> For was and is and will be are but is:
> And all creation is one act at once,
> The birth of light; but we that are not all,
> As parts, can see but parts, now this, now that,
> And live perforce from thought to thought, and make
> The act a phantom of succession: there
> Our weakness somehow shapes the shadow, Time.

---

[1] "Eternal" in R. V.

In the poem " By an Evolutionist," written in 1888 when he was dangerously ill, he defined his position; he conceived that the further science progressed, the more the Unity of Nature, and the purpose hidden behind the cosmic process of matter in motion and changing forms of life, would be apparent. Someone asked him whether it was not hard to account for genius by Evolution. He put aside the question, for he believed that genius was the greatest mystery to itself[1].

To Tyndall he once said, " No evolutionist is able to explain the mind of Man or how any possible physiological change of tissue can produce conscious thought[2]." Yet he was inclined to think that the theory of Evolution caused the world to regard more clearly the " Life of Nature as a lower stage in the manifestation of a principle which is more fully manifested in the spiritual life of man, with the idea that in this process of Evolution the lower is to be regarded as a means to the higher[3]."

[1] " People," he once said, " do not consider that every human being is a vanful of human beings, of those who have gone before him, and of those who form part of his life."

[2] Cf. Tyndall's *Scientific Materialism* : " But the passage from the physics of the brain to the corresponding facts of consciousness is unthinkable, granted that a definite thought and a definite molecular action in the brain occur simultaneously; we do not possess the intellectual organ, nor apparently any rudiment of the organ, which would enable us to pass, by a process of reasoning, from the one to the other. They appear together, but we do not know why."

[3] In a letter from the present Master of Balliol to me.

And in " In Memoriam " he had written thus:

They say,
The solid earth whereon we tread

In tracts of fluent heat began,
And grew to seeming-random forms,
The seeming prey of cyclic storms,
Till at the last arose the man;

Who throve and branch'd from clime to clime
The herald of a higher race,

In " Maud " he spoke of the making of man:

As nine months go to the shaping an infant ripe for
  his birth,
So many a million of ages have gone to the making
  of man:
He now is first, but is he the last?

The answer he would give to this query was: " No,
mankind is as yet on one of the lowest rungs of the
ladder [1], although every man has and has had from
everlasting his true and perfect being in the Divine
Consciousness."

About prayer he said: " The reason why men find it
hard to regard prayer in the same light in which it was
formerly regarded is, that *we* seem to know more of the
unchangeableness of Law: but I believe that God
reveals Himself in each individual soul. Prayer is, to
take a mundane simile, like opening a sluice between the
great ocean and our little channels when the great sea
gathers itself together and flows in at full tide."

  " Prayer on our part is the highest aspiration of the
soul."

  And of himself in higher place,
  If so he type this work of time

  Within himself, from more to more;
    Or, crown'd with attributes of woe
    Like glories, move his course, and show
  That life is not an idle ore,

  But iron dug from central gloom,
    And heated hot with burning fears,
    And dipt in baths of hissing tears,
  And batter'd with the shocks of doom

  To shape and use. Arise and fly
    The reeling Faun, the sensual feast;
    Move upward, working out the beast,
  And let the ape and tiger die.

        [1] " The herald of a higher race."

A breath that fleets beyond this iron world
And touches Him who made it.

And

Speak to Him thou for He hears, and Spirit with
  Spirit can meet —
Closer is He than breathing, and nearer than hands
  and feet.

And
            More things are wrought by prayer
Than this world dreams of.

He said that "O Thou Infinite, Amen," was the
form of prayer which he himself used in the time of
trouble and sorrow: and that it was better to suffer
than to lose the power of suffering.

When questions were written to him about Christ,
he would say to me: "Answer for me that I have given
my belief in ' In Memoriam [1].' "

As the Master of Balliol wrote:

The "In Memoriam" records most of his inner nature. It
was the higher and prevailing temper of his mind. He used to
regard it as having said what he had to say on religion.

The main testimony to Christianity he found not in
miracles but in that eternal witness, the revelation of
what might be called "The Mind of God," in the
Christian morality, and its correlation with the divine
in man.

He had a measureless admiration for the Sermon on
the Mount; and for the Parables — "perfection, beyond
compare," he called them. I heard a talk on these between him and Browning, and Browning fully agreed with
my father in his admiration. Moreover my father expressed
his conviction that " Christianity with its divine Morality

[1] "In Memoriam," XXXVI.

but without the central figure of Christ, *the* Son of Man, would become cold[1], and that it is fatal for religion to lose its warmth"; that "*The* Son of Man" was the most tremendous title possible; that the forms of Christian religion would alter; but that the spirit of Christ would still grow from more to more "in the roll of the ages."

> Till each man find his own in all men's good,
> And all men work in noble brotherhood.

"This is one of my meanings," he said, "of

> Ring in the Christ that is to be:

when Christianity without bigotry will triumph, when the controversies of creeds shall have vanished, and

> Shall bear false witness, each of each, no more,
> But find their limits by that larger light,
> And overstep them, moving easily
> Thro' after-ages in the Love of Truth,
> The truth of Love[2]."

"The most pathetic utterance in all history," he said, "is that of Christ on the Cross, 'It is finished,' after that passionate cry, 'My God, My God, why hast Thou forsaken Me?'" Nevertheless he also recognized the note of triumph in "It is finish'd[3]." "I am always amazed when I read the New Testament at the splendour of Christ's purity and holiness and at His infinite pity[4]." He disliked discussion on the Nature of Christ, "seeing that such discussion was mostly unprofitable, for none knoweth the Son but the Father." "He went about doing good" he would say: and one of the

---

[1] "He did not preach His opinions; He preached Himself." Renan's *Vie de Jésus*. "The spiritual character of Christ," my father would say, "is more wonderful than the greatest miracle."

[2] "Akbar's Dream."

[3] See *The Death of Œnone, and other Poems*, p. 80. Westcott writes: "I always think that the tense ἐγκατέλιπες marks the crisis as past."

[4] What he called "the man-woman" in Christ, the union of tenderness and strength.

traditional and unwritten sayings of Christ which oftenest came home to him was, " He that is near Me is near the fire," the baptism of the fire of inspiration. For in " In Memoriam " the soul, after grappling with anguish and darkness, doubt and death, emerges with the inspiration of a strong and steadfast faith in the Love of God for man, and in the oneness of man with God, and of man with man in Him —

> That God, which ever lives and loves,
>   One God, one law, one element,
>   And one far-off divine event,
> To which the whole creation moves.

I cannot end this chapter on " In Memoriam " more fitly than by quoting Henry Hallam's letter on receiving in 1850 what he calls " the precious book."

I know not how to express what I have felt. My first sentiment was surprise, for, though I now find that you had mentioned the intention to my daughter, Julia, she had never told me of the poems. I do not speak as another would to praise and admire : few of them indeed I have as yet been capable of reading, the grief they express is too much akin to that they revive. It is better than any monument which could be raised to the memory of my beloved son, it is a more lively and enduring testimony to his great virtues and talents that the world should know the friendship which existed between you, that posterity should associate his name with that of Alfred Tennyson.

CHAPTER XV.

MARRIAGE (1850–51).

Like perfect music unto noble words.

My father and mother had met in the spring of 1850 at Shiplake on the Thames; where they had both stayed with the Rawnsleys, Mrs Rawnsley being my mother's cousin.

If "In Memoriam" were published, Moxon had promised a small yearly royalty on this and on the other poems, and so my father had decided that he could now honourably offer my mother a home.

Accordingly after ten years of separation their engagement was renewed.

Early in those ten years my grandmother had suggested dividing her jointure with them, so that they might marry, but this, of course, they could not allow. Moxon now advanced £300 — so my Uncle Charles told a friend, — at all events £300 were in my father's bank in his name; and with this and their united small incomes, and all household furniture given them by my mother's father, they decided that they could brave life together and that the marriage should take place at Shiplake on the 13th of June, the month which saw the publication of "In Memoriam."

Of the Vicarage with its terraced garden, and of
ιe fine old church Miss Mitford gives the following
cturesque description:

A few miles further, and a turn to the right conducts us to one
the grand old village churches, which give so much of character
English landscape. A large and beautiful pile it is. The tower,
ιlf clothed with ivy, stands with its charming vicarage and
, pretty vicarage-garden on a high eminence, overhanging one
the finest bends of the great river. A woody lane leads from
e church to the bottom of the chalk-cliff, one side of which
ands out from the road below, like a promontory, surmounted
ʳ the laurel hedges and flowery cedar of Lebanon. This is
ιiplake church, famed far and near for its magnificent oak
ιrving, and the rich painted glass of its windows, collected, long
:fore such adornments were fashionable, by the fine taste of the
te vicar, and therefore filled with the very choicest specimens
ʹ mediæval art, chiefly obtained from the remains of the
:lebrated Abbey of St Bertin near St Omer, sacked during the
·st French Revolution. In this church Alfred Tennyson was
arried.

The wedding was of the quietest (even the cake and
resses arriving too late), which made my father say, to
ιe amusement of those who were present, that it was
the nicest wedding" he had ever been at. In after-life
e said: "The peace of God came into my life before the
ltar when I wedded her."

The marriage party consisted of the bride's father[1],
lenry Sellwood, Edmund and Cecilia Lushington,
Charles Weld, husband of Anne, one of the Sellwood
ιsters, and Mr Greville Phillimore. The two child
ridesmaids were Mary and Margaret Rawnsley.

[1] He was a stately, courteous gentleman, kindly, cultivated, unaffected,
ιd above all a good friend. His family had come in old days from
omersetshire into Berkshire. He himself was a solicitor at Horncastle.
·reatly to his honour he had taken up this profession when his family was
n the road to ruin. In 1812 he had married Sarah Franklin, sister of the
heroic sailor" Sir John Franklin, but she had died in 1816, aged 28, leaving
ιree daughters, Emily, Anne, and Louisa.

My uncle Charles and Louisa Tennyson Turner coul
not join the party, and my uncle wrote accordingly:

Oh what a queer world it is! I hope however it has don
a brace of amiable and remarkable people some genuine goo
whirligig as it is — this time at least. Well! The thing is t
come off on the 13th, daddy says. Good wishes in crowds fro
me. I despatch a dove's wing to you. I am going to kee
pigeons, would they were carrier pigeons! then would I troubl
their wings with missives of congratulation to arrive mo
swiftly than the railroad.

      Coo! coo! coo! Your affectionate brother,

                         CHARLES.

My father made and repeated the following poem, a
my mother and he drove from Shiplake to Pangbourn
enclosing it to Drummond Rawnsley through M
Rawnsley.

MY DEAR KATE,

      You managed it all very well yesterda
Many thanks.

                Ever yours, A. T.

P.S. Dubbie's[1] fees must be come at as he can be
manage. The clerk and shirts are owing.

The poem would be more perfect without the thi
stanza, but I do not think you would like to miss it.

To the Vicar of Shiplake. (Unpublished.)

Vicar of this pleasant spot
    Where it was my chance to marry,
Happy, happy be your lot
    In the Vicarage by the quarry.
You were he that knit the knot!

        [1] Short for *Drummond.*

Walker & Boutall Ph Sc.

Mrs Tennyson.

from the portrait at Aldworth, painted by G. F. Watts. R.A.

Sweetly, smoothly flow your life.
  Never tithe unpaid perplex you,
Parish feud, or party strife,
  All things please you, nothing vex you,
You have given me such a wife!

Live and prosper! Day by day
  Watch your standard roses blowing,
And your three young things at play,
  And your triple terrace growing
Green and greener every May!

Sweetly flow your life with Kate's,
  Glancing off from all things evil,
Smooth as Thames below your gates,
  Thames along the silent level,
Streaming thro' his osier'd aits!

And let me say here — although, as a son, I cannot
allow myself full utterance about her whom I loved as
perfect mother and "very woman of very woman," —
such a wife" and true helpmate she proved herself.
It was she who became my father's adviser in literary
matters; "I am proud of her intellect," he wrote. With
her he always discussed what he was working at; she
transcribed his poems: to her and to no one else he
referred for a final criticism before publishing. She,
with her "tender, spiritual nature [1]," and instinctive nobility of thought, was always by his side, a ready, cheerful,
courageous, wise, and sympathetic counsellor. It was she
who shielded his sensitive spirit from the annoyances and
trials of life, answering (for example) the innumerable
letters addressed to him from all parts of the world. By
her quiet sense of humour, by her selfless devotion, by
her faith as clear as the heights of the June-blue
heaven," she helped him also to the utmost in the hours

[1] My father's words.

of his depression and of his sorrow; and to her he wrote two of the most beautiful of his shorter lyrics, "Dear, near and true," and the dedicatory lines which prefaced his last volume, *The Death of Œnone.*

The day after the wedding they went to Weston-super-Mare, on their way to Clevedon. "It seemed a kind of consecration to go there." They saw Arthur Hallam's resting-place, and were received by Sir Abraham Elton in the beautiful old Manor House, Clevedon Court; and thence they went to Lynton. In that country, more solitary then than now, they enjoyed long rambles through the woods and over the heather and rode to the Valley of Rocks and Exmoor, in spite of "the weeping Devonshire climate."

Glastonbury, one of the reputed "island valleys of Avilion," followed: where they lunched in what had been the Refectory of the old Hospital for Pilgrims, built by an Abbot, John de Selwode, of the same name and race as my mother. This Abbot alone, as they were told, is buried beside the tomb of King Arthur, in the chancel of that famous Abbey, — once the wonder of the world, now but a few ruins in a garden. My father was greatly interested by the legend that Joseph of Arimathea came there in 63 A.D. and founded the first Christian colony in England:

> From our old books I know
> That Joseph came of old to Glastonbury,
> And there the heathen Prince, Arviragus,
> Gave him an isle of marsh whereon to build;
> And there he built with wattles from the marsh
> A little lonely church in days of yore.

Clifton was the next halting-place; thence they went to Bath, and on to Cheltenham to visit his mother. Many honeymoon houses were offered; among others Brancepeth by his cousins, Fryston by R. M. Milnes.

Tent Lodge, Coniston, by Mrs James Marshall, a sister of my father's college friend, Stephen Spring Rice. They selected Tent Lodge, and set off for Patterdale and Ullswater, then to "the little villa on Coniston water." On their arrival my father writes to Mrs Russell:

DEAREST AUNT,

Have you yet received the bound copy of "In Memoriam" which I purposed for you? If not, will you or Emma drop me a line to this place, and I will take care that you have it immediately? We have been making a little tour about these lakes, and have spent the last few days with my friends the Speddings at Bassenthwaite Water. We only arrived here last night. Mr Marshall's park looked as lovely as the Garden of Eden, as we descended the hill to this place. We have a very beautiful view from our drawing-room windows, crag, mountain, woods and lake, which look especially fine as the sun is dropping behind the hills. I wish you could see it. The Marshalls themselves are not here but expected daily. We found the seat of a Marshall on almost every lake we came to, for it seems there are several brothers who have all either bought or been left estates in this country; and they are all, report says, as wealthy as Crœsus. I send you this little note just to tell you where we are, and how much your bounty has enabled us to enjoy ourselves among the mountains. We have been on the whole fortunate in weather, tho' this climate has a bad name. I do not know whether you are at Cheltenham or Burwarton, but wherever you are, dearest aunt, God bless and preserve you from all ill. My wife desires her kindest love to you. Good-bye.

Ever yours affectionately,
A. TENNYSON.

The drives and walks over the mountains, the boating on the lake among the water-lilies and by the islands where the herons built, he rowing, she steering, are noted in their diary.

Here for the first time my mother saw Carlyle, who was staying with the Marshalls. The meeting was characteristic; he slowly scanned her from head to foot, then gave her a hearty shake of the hand. Next day he called at Tent Lodge; and, hearing her cough, "with his invariable kindness" stole round, while the others were talking, and shut the window which was open behind her[1].

One evening Mr Venables and Mr de Vere called. They talked for about an hour with my father — my mother having already retired to rest. At last, after puffing at his pipe for some moments in silence, my father spoke "like one thinking aloud": "I have known many women who were excellent, one in one way, another in another way, but this woman is the noblest woman I have ever known[2]." As Aubrey de Vere writes to me: "No friend who had then heard him could have felt any further anxiety as to his domestic happiness."

The Marshalls offered my father and mother Tent Lodge as a permanent home, and the Ashburtons a house near Croydon, but these kind offers they thought it best to decline and went for a time to Park House, to find a residence of their own.

On November 19th my father was appointed Poet Laureate, owing chiefly to Prince Albert's admiration for " In Memoriam." Wordsworth had been now dead

---

[1] Another story of his concern for others my father would tell. "Having heard that Henry Taylor was ill, Carlyle rushed off from London to Sheen with a bottle of medicine, which had done Mrs Carlyle good, without in the least knowing what was ailing Henry Taylor, or for what the medicine was useful."

[2] MS, Aubrey de Vere.

some months; and my father, as he has assured me, had not any expectation of the Laureateship, or any thought upon the subject: it seemed to him therefore a very curious coincidence, that the night before the offer reached him he dreamt that Prince Albert came and kissed him on the cheek, and that he said in his dream, " Very kind, but very German."

In the morning this letter about the Laureateship was brought to his bedroom:

WINDSOR CASTLE, *Nov.* 5*th*, 1850.

By the death of the late lamented Wm. Wordsworth the Office of Poet Laureate to the Queen became at Her Majesty's disposal.

The ancient duties of this Office, which consisted in laudatory Odes to the Sovereign, have been long, as you are probably aware, in abeyance, and have never been called for during the Reign of Her present Majesty. The Queen however has been anxious that the Office should be maintained; first on account of its antiquity, and secondly because it establishes a connection, through Her Household, between Her Majesty and the poets of this country as a body.

To make however the continuance of this Office in harmony with public opinion, the Queen feels that it is necessary that it should be limited to a name bearing such distinction in the literary world as to do credit to the appointment, and it was under this feeling, that Her Majesty in the first instance offered the appointment to Mr Rogers, who stated to Her Majesty, in his reply, that the only reason which compelled him gratefully to decline Her Majesty's gracious intention, was, that his great age rendered him unfit to receive any new office.

It is under the same desire that the name of the poet appointed should adorn the Office, that I have received the commands of the Queen to offer this post to you, as a mark of Her Majesty's appreciation of your literary distinction.

I have the honour to be, Sir,

Your obedient humble servant,

C. B. PHIPPS.

He took the whole day to consider and at the last wrote two letters, one accepting, one refusing, and determined to make up his mind after a consultation with his friends at dinner. He would joke and say, " In the end I accepted the honour, because during dinner Venables told me, that, if I became Poet Laureate, I should always when I dined out be offered the liver-wing of a fowl.'

After accepting the Laureateship he writes to the Rev. H. Rawnsley:

MY DEAR RAWNSLEY,

You do ill to seem as though you blamed me for forgetfulness of you and yours; you know it is not so, and can never be so, but I confess that in the matter of letter-writing I am in arrear to everybody. I have dozens of letters to write this afternoon, and I cannot help wishing that I could hire the electric telegraph once a month, and so work off my scores with the wires at whatever expense. This old-world, slow pen and ink operation is behind the age. I thank you for your congratulations touching the Laureateship. I was advised by my friends not to decline it * * *. I have no passion for courts, but a great love of privacy. It is, I believe, scarce £100 a year, and my friend R. M. Milnes tells me that the price of the patent and court dress will swallow up all the first year's income. I have mislaid your letter, and so cannot tell whether you asked me any questions. Let me ask *you* one. I have been looking out for an unfurnished house, with good rooms, for £60 a year or thereabouts: do you know of any such near you? If you do, please communicate with me and I will come and see it. I expect an heir to nothing about next March or April. I suppose I must lay by the Laureate's hire for him as Southey did. Pray give

my kindest love to Mrs R. and my best remembrances
to all friends, particularly G. Coltman, and

Believe me yours affectionately,

A. TENNYSON.

The immediate result of becoming Poet Laureate
was that poems and letters poured in, and my father
writes: " I get such shoals of poems that I am almost
crazed with them; the two hundred million poets of
Great Britain deluge me daily with poems: truly the
Laureateship is no sinecure. If any good soul would
just by way of a diversion send me a tome of prose!"
In answer to an appeal from Moxon for a fresh volume
of new poems, he said, "We are correcting all the
volumes for new editions[1]."

My parents' first venture in the choice of a home
was not encouraging. The house that they took was at
Warninglid in Sussex, pleasant and sunny, with large
airy rooms from which there was a Copley-Fielding-
like view of the South Downs. "The full song of the
birds delighted us as we drove up to the door," and the
home seemed at first in every way suitable. But one night
soon after their arrival a tremendous storm blew down
part of the wall in their bedroom, and through the gap
the wind raved and the water rushed. Then they learnt
that their dining-room and bedroom had been a Roman
Catholic Chapel, that a baby was buried somewhere on
the premises, and later that one of a notorious gang of
thieves and murderers known as " The Cuckfield Gang "
had lived in their very lodge.

Besides they discovered that no postman came near

---

[1] In the *Keepsake* for 1851 were published:

What time I wasted youthful hours,

and

Come not when I am dead.

This last poem, " Edwin Morris," " The Eagle," and the Dedication
" To the Queen," were included in the *Poems*, seventh edition, 1851.

the house, that the nearest doctor and butcher lived at
Horsham, seven miles off; and that there was not even
a carrier who passed anywhere within hail.   Altogether
everything was so uncanny and so uncomfortable, that
they took a speedy departure, my father drawing my
mother in a Bath chair over a very rough road to
Cuckfield.

Finally, by the kind aid of Mrs Henry Taylor, they
took up their abode at Chapel House, Montpelier Row,
Twickenham; a house which overlooked the parks of
General Peel and of the Duc d'Aumale.   It was entered
through a square hall, and on the fine old staircase
stood the carved figure of a mitred bishop "as if to
bless the passers by."

On the 21st February their diary says: "We read
Alton Locke, drove about in search of a Court dress for
Levée, could not find one and had to give up Levée
on the 26th.   Rogers, hearing of this, offer'd his own
dress, which had been also worn by Wordsworth and
had been promised to the Wordsworth family as an
heirloom.   The coat did well enough, but about other
parts of the dress there was some anxiety felt for the
Levée on March 6th, as they had not been tried on."

He was meditating his first Laureate poem, " To the
Queen," and was especially thinking of a stanza in which
" the empire of Wordsworth should be asserted : for he
was a representative Poet Laureate, such a poet as kings
should honour, and such an one as would do honour to
kings ; — making the period of a reign famous by the
utterance of memorable words concerning that period."
Spedding wrote to my father: " Those potentates stand
highest in the estimation of succeeding ages, not who
have been best praised in their own time, but who have
in their own time done honour and given aid and encouragement to that which remains great and memorable
in all time."

Later in March he stayed at Sir Alexander Duff Gordon's; and whilst there, at an evening party given by Lord John Russell, was introduced to Bunsen and to the Duke of Argyll. The Duke in after days and to the end of my father's life was one of his most valued friends.

On April 5th he received from Mr Macready a letter of thanks for the sonnet addressed to him on leaving the stage.

Farewell, Macready, since to-night we part;
    Full-handed thunders often have confessed
    Thy power, well used to move the public breast.
We thank thee with our voice, and from the heart.
Farewell, Macready, since this night we part,
    Go, take thine honours home; rank with the best,
    Garrick and statelier Kemble, and the rest,
Who made a nation purer thro' their art.
Thine is it that our drama did not die,
    Nor flicker down to brainless pantomime,
And those gilt gauds men-children swarm to see.
    Farewell, Macready; moral, grave, sublime;
Our Shakespeare's bland and universal eye
Dwells pleased, thro' twice a hundred years, on thee.

From W. C. Macready.

SHERBORNE, DORSET, *April 4th*, 1851.

MY DEAR MR TENNYSON,

If I had obeyed the impulse of my feelings, I should have written to you long since, when our friend Forster first communicated to me the kindness you had shown me in honouring my name with the glory of your verse. This was some days before the publication of your lines, and he may have told you that the emotion they excited in me was a manifestation of my grateful appreciation beyond what words can render you.

You have indeed embalmed my perishable name, which will not so soon be lost in the long night, as "carens vate sacro," and I may truly assure you, of no testimony have I felt more proud, and on none have I reflected with more grateful pleasure, than on that which bears your name.

I remain, dear Mr Tennyson,

Always and sincerely yours,

W. C. MACREADY.

On the 20th of April my parents' first child, a boy, was born, and, owing to my mother's having fallen down a step, died in the birth. At the time my father wrote:

"It was Easter Sunday and at his birth I heard the great roll of the organ, of the uplifted psalm (in the Chapel adjoining the house).... Dead as he was I felt proud of him. To-day when I write this down, the remembrance of it rather overcomes me; but I am glad that I have seen him, dear little nameless one that hast lived tho' thou hast never breathed, I, thy father, love thee and weep over thee, tho' thou hast no place in the Universe. Who knows? It may be that thou hast...... God's Will be done."

In the summer they met the Carlyles again. About this time he described my father to Sir J. Simeon as "sitting on a dung-heap among innumerable dead dogs." Carlyle meant that he was apt to brood over old-world subjects for his poems. Once many years after, when we called upon him, my father teazed him about this utterance, and Carlyle replied, "Eh! that was not a very luminous description of you."

This was the year of the first great Exhibition, and what seems to have most delighted my father was the building itself and the great glass fountain.

On July 15th they left for Boulogne on their way to Italy. "The Daisy" gives the journey better than any prose of mine can give it. Jowett writes, "He always had a living vision of Italy, Greece and the Mediterranean." He was proud of the metre of " The Daisy " which he called a far-off echo of the Horatian Alcaic[1]. Among the many metres he invented, this he ranked among his best, together with some of the anapæstic movements in " Maud," and the long-rolling rhythm of his " Ode to Virgil." On their journey he took with him his usual travelling companions, Shakespeare, Milton, Homer, Virgil, Horace, Pindar, Theocritus, and probably the *Divina Commedia* and Goethe's *Gedichte*.

Italy was in such a disturbed state that they did not go to Rome as they had intended. The fever was prevalent in Venice, so this had also to be given up. They stayed three weeks at the Baths of Lucca in the house of one Giorgio Basantino, opposite a wood where they would sit watching the green lizards at play. There were delightful evening drives over the mountains; and they rejoiced in " the glorious violet colouring of the Apennines, and the picturesqueness of the peasants beating out their flax or spinning with their distaffs at their cottage doors." Thence they journeyed to Florence to stay with my uncle Frederick at the Villa Torregiani, which had been for many years his home. On September 24th they left Florence, returning by way of the "snowy Splügen" to Paris. Here the Brownings called on them at their hotel. Mr Browning, already my father's friend, was affectionate as ever. Mrs Browning was "fragile-looking, with great spirit eyes," and met my mother "as if she had been her own sister." Savile Morton came too, and the diary says: " His wild laugh sounded through the corridors. The Brownings gave us, before parting, two beautiful Paris nosegays (the flowers arranged in a sort of Grecian

---

[1] He was pleased with the slightly different effect of (substantially) the same metre in the invitation " To the Rev. F. D. Maurice," gained by the dactyl which in those verses begins each fourth line (see p. 429).

pattern) and both alike." On their return home to Chapel House, my father quotes Catullus as he enters the door:

> "O, quid solutis est beatius curis!
> Cum mens onus reponit, ac peregrino
> Labore fessi venimus larem ad nostrum,
> Desideratoque acquiescimus lecto.
> Hoc est, quod unum est pro laboribus tantis!"

Soon after he wrote the following letter to his old friends Mr and Mrs Brookfield, who were on their way to Madeira:

MY DEAR WILLIAM AND JANE,

I have only just got back to England and heard of you in calling on Mrs Taylor at Mortlake. Grieved I was to hear so ill an account, that you are forced to leave England and that I may not see you again for a long time; yet I do not know why I should write except to tell you that my sympathies go with you and to wish that you, William, may soon be better and that God's blessing may be with you on the winter seas, and in the fair island which I have so often longed to see. If my wife could stand the sea nothing would have pleased me better than to have accompanied you thither, but I hear that one friend at least has preceded you, and is there now, Stephen Spring Rice. That we may soon see you back in renewed health is the wish and prayer of

Yours affectionately,

A. TENNYSON.

Spedding was consulted as to some "National Songs for Englishmen" published in the *Examiner* in 1852, "since

> Easy patrons of their kin
> Have left the last free race with naked coasts."

He replies:

I will send £ 5 to Coventry Patmore for the Rifles, thinking that the more noise we make in that way the better, and the more we practise the less likely are we to be called upon to perform. I answered your summons to the Thatched House and found a room full of people not one of whom I knew; all sufficiently zealous, and at the same time rational, and (so far as the preliminaries went) of one mind. I suppose they know one another, or some know some; and as there seemed to be no want of volunteers for the Committee and Sub-committee to arrange details, I thought I might, without abandoning my country in her extremity, leave that part of the business to them and join some club when it is organized. I think I could hit a Frenchman at 100 yards, if he did not frighten me.

Forster sent for me yesterday to look at the new poems, which I highly approve, and by no means allow of the objection suggested against the stanza[1]. America is our daughter but the men of America are our sons. Forster wants a name for the poet, which I think very desirable; and no great matter what name is chosen so it be short and pronounceable, Alfred, Arthur, Merlin, Tyrtæus, Edward Ball, Britannicus, Honved, Hylax, anything. Amyntor would sound well, is not hackneyed, and is good Greek for defender or protector.

Your note though dated the 2nd did not arrive yesterday till I had gone out.

National Songs (1852).

When " Britons, guard your own," and " Hands all round " were written, my father along with many others regarded France under Napoleon as a serious menace to the peace of Europe. Although a passionate patriot, and a true lover of England, he was not blind to her faults, and was unprejudiced and cosmopolitan in seeing the best side of other nations; and in later years after the Franco-German war, he was filled with admiration at the dignified way in which France was gradually

---

[1] About America (p. 346).

gathering herself together. He rejoiced whenever England and France were in agreement, and worked together harmoniously for the good of the world.

Britons, guard your own.

This version was given to my mother many years afterwards, so that she might publish it with her musical setting.

Rise, Britons, rise, if manhood be not dead;
The world's last tempest darkens overhead:
    All freedom vanish'd —
    The true men banish'd —
He triumphs! maybe we shall stand alone!
        Britons, guard your own.

Call home your ships across Biscayan tides,
To blow the battle from their oaken sides.
    Why waste they yonder
    Their idle thunder?
Why stay they there to guard a foreign throne?
        Seamen, guard your own.

We were the best of marksmen long ago,
We won old battles with our strength, the bow.
    Now practise, yeomen,
    Like those bowmen,
Till your balls fly as their true shafts have flown,
        Yeomen, guard your own.

Should they land here and but one hour prevail,
There must no man go back to bear the tale;
    No man to bear it,
    Swear it! We swear it!
Although we fought the banded world alone,
        We swear to guard our own.

Hands all round[1]*!*

First drink a health, this solemn night,
  A health to England, every guest;
That man's the best cosmopolite,
  Who loves his native country best.
May Freedom's oak for ever live
  With stronger life from day to day;
That man's the true Conservative
  Who lops the moulder'd branch away.
      Hands all round!
      God the tyrant's hope confound!
To this great cause of Freedom drink, my friends,
And the great name of England round and round.

A health to Europe's honest men!
  Heaven guard them from her tyrant jails!
From wrong'd Poerio's noisome den,
  From iron'd limbs and tortured nails!
We curse the crimes of southern kings,
  The Russian whips and Austrian rods,
We, likewise, have our evil things;
  Too much we make our Ledgers Gods,
      Yet hands all round!
      God the tyrant's cause confound!
To Europe's better health we drink, my friends,
And the great name of England round and round.

What health to France, if France be she,
  Whom martial prowess only charms?
Yet tell her — Better to be free
  Than vanquish all the world in arms.

---

[1] Feb. 9th, 1852. I must send you what Landor says in a note this
morning: "'Hands all round! is incomparably the best (convivial) lyric in
the language, though Dryden's 'Drinking Song' is fine."

JOHN FORSTER to MRS TENNYSON.

Her frantic city's flashing heats
　　But fire to blast the hopes of men.
Why change the titles of your streets?
　　You fools, you'll want them all again.
　　　　　Yet hands all round!
　　　God the tyrant's cause confound!
To France, the wiser France, we drink, my friends,
And the great name of England round and round.

Gigantic daughter of the West,
　　We drink to thee across the flood,
We know thee most, we love thee best,
　　For art thou not of British blood?
Should war's mad blast again be blown,
　　Permit not thou the tyrant powers
To fight thy mother here alone,
　　But let thy broadsides roar with ours.
　　　　　Hands all round!
　　　God the tyrant's cause confound!
To our great kinsmen of the West, my friends,
And the great name of England round and round.

O rise, our strong Atlantic sons,
　　When war against our freedom springs!
O speak to Europe thro' your guns!
　　They *can* be understood by kings.
You must not mix our Queen with those
　　That wish to keep their people fools;
Our freedom's foemen are her foes,
　　She comprehends the race she rules.
　　　　　Hands all round!
　　　God the tyrant's cause confound!
To our great kinsmen of the West, my friends,
And the great cause of freedom round and round[1].

---

[1] "The third of February, 1852," is not printed here because it was included in the *Poems* (ed. 1872). Other contributions appeared in the *Examiner*, but my father did not think them good enough to be reprinted.

CHAPTER XVI.

CHELTENHAM AND WHITBY (1852).

My father's letter-diary [1].

Alan Ker has taken four copies of my Ode "My Lords" to send to papers here and there. Mother was delighted beyond measure to see me, making me remorseful that I had not been here before. Alan and Mary seem well and hopeful: they say it is only a fortnight's steam to Jamaica (where he is appointed a judge), and they will not take a large outfit because at any time they can have things from England. Dobson says we could live here much better and cheaper than at Twickenham. I find the air much fresher.

(*Apparently answering a query as to Count D'Orsay* [2].)

Jan. 1852.

Count D'Orsay is a friend of mine, co-godfather to Dickens' child with me. He is Louis Napoleon's

---

[1] This he habitually wrote to my mother when absent from home.

[2] My father said that before this he had dined with Count D'Orsay and other friends at John Forster's. The Count was a glorious, handsome fellow, generally dressed in tight-fitting blue coat with gilt buttons. So carried away by D'Orsay's splendour was Forster that he was heard shouting out above the hubbub of voices to his servant Henry: "Good heavens, sir, butter for the Count's flounders!"

intimate friend and secretary, and moreover I am told a man who has wept over my poems. See how strangely things are connected. Just put the things together. Wonderful are these times, and no one knows what may arise from the smallest things. I the poet of England with the secretary of Louis Napoleon whom I have abused.

CHELTENHAM, *Jan. 22nd.*

A note from Charles Weld this morning. He sent my poem to the *Times*, but the *Times* ignores it. Alan Ker says it is not their custom to put in poems except they are allowed to subscribe the author's name. I have told him to try the *Morning Chronicle:* he seems for *Fraser*, tho' it is so long before *Fraser* comes out that my poem will be half superannuated like the musket. I see that here and there people are really beginning to be awake to their danger * * * *. In this horrible age of blab I can scarce trust aright.

Jan. 23rd.

I have been out every day dining. The readers of the *Examiner* will no doubt guess the authorship from knowing Forster's friendship for me. The military letters in the *Times* are very interesting. The hills here have fine lights on them as seen from my windows. John Rashdall wants us to go and spend three weeks with him at Malvern.

YORK, *July 7th,* 1852.

Slept at Spedding's where I found they expected me. Started this morning 11 a.m. Hay fever atrocious with irritation of railway, nearly drove me crazed, but could not complain, the other only occupant of the carriage having a curiously split shoe for his better ease,

and his eyes and teeth in a glare at me with pain of gout
the whole way, and finally helped out by his servant,
going to drink Harrogate waters. Came here to the
Black Swan, ordered dinner, went out and bought weed,
having left mine at Spedding's with gloves (ay me!).
Enquired of tobacconist state of parties here, " Never
was anything so satisfactory, all purity of Election, no
row, no drunkenness, Mr Vincent will come in without
any bother." While he was yet speaking arose a row, innumerable mob raging, housekeepers all down the street
rushed out with window-shutters to prevent windows being
broken. My dinner waiting for me, I having to plunge
thro' mob to get at it, essayed the fringes of the crowd,
very dense nucleus of enormous brawl somewhere within.
Presently the glazed hats of policemen, like sunshine
striking here and there at the breaking up of a storm,
showed me an issue of hope. I plunged through in the
wake of the bluecoats and got home. To-morrow to
Whitby. Vincent after all not returned. When I got
to Waterloo the roses had snapt off short and lay at the
bottom of the carriage. The porter opened the door,
picked up one, snuffed at it with vast satisfaction, and
never so much as " by your leave."

5, NORTH TERRACE, WEST CLIFF, WHITBY,
July 8th, 1852.

I am set down here for a week at least in lodgings.
It is rather a fine place, a river running into the sea
between precipices, on one side new buildings and a very
handsome royal hotel belonging to Hudson the railway
king, on the other at the very top a gaunt old Abbey,
and older parish Church hanging over the town amid
hundreds of white gravestones that looked to my eye
something like clothes laid out to dry. Moreover there

is the crackiness of an election going on and lots of pink and blue flags, and insane northland boatmen of Danish breed, who meet and bang each other for the love of liberty, foolish fellows. In the midst of the row yesterday came a funeral followed by weeping mourners, a great hearse, plumes nodding and mourning coach, and the gaunt old Abbey looked down with its hollow eyes on the life and death, the drunkenness and the political fury, rather ironically as it seemed to me, only that it was too old to have much feeling left about anything. No bathing men were to be had, so I e'en walked into the sea by myself and had a very decent bathe. Hay fever was much better yesterday and is bad again this morning. I could not write yesterday for I came in after the post had started by a very pretty rail which curves like a common road between great wolds, the Esk, which is the stream that debouches here, running below. Then we really went down a considerable hill with a rope. The same thing I think occurs at Liége, but this seemed to me much steeper. I am told there are very fine views in the neighbourhood, though most probably I shall not get out far enough to see them as it is pestilent hot.

WHITBY, *July* 13*th.*

I want to go to Redcliffe Scar which old Wordsworth once told me of, or perhaps to Bolton Abbey. I think it a great pity that your "Sweet and low" hadn't the start of all these musical jottings. I have had two very good days coasting, I mean walking along on and under the cliffs. Very singular they are with great bivalve shells sticking out of them. They are made of a great dark slate-coloured shale (is it to be called?) that comes showering down ever and anon from a great height; and on the hard flat rock which makes the beach on one side of the town (for on the other side are sands), you see

beautiful little ammonites which you stoop to pick up
but find them part of the solid rock. You know these
are the snakes which St Hilda drove over the cliff and
falling they lost their heads, and she changed them into
stone. I found a strange fish on the shore with rainbows
about its wild staring eyes, enclosed in a sort of sack with
long tentacula beautifully coloured, quite dead, but when
I took it up by the tail it spotted all the sand underneath
with great drops of ink, so I suppose it was a kind of
cuttle-fish. I found too a pale pink orchis on the sea
bank and a pink vetch, a low sort of shrub with here and
there a thorn. I am reading lots of novels. The worst is
they do not last longer than the day. I am such a fierce
reader I think I have had pretty well my quantum suff.:
Venables' anecdotes are very interesting indeed. One
cannot help wishing that such a man as Gladstone may
come to sit on the top branch of the tree.

WHITBY, *July* 19*th.*

I have ordered a carriage and am going to see Lord
Normanby's park near here, tho' I am half afraid of it,
a carriage so excites my hay fever. I met an old
smuggler on the coast yesterday who had been in Lord
N.'s service (not as smuggler of course!), and he took
me for Lord Normanby at first, a likeness I have been
told of more than once before. I got into conversation
with him and I am going to call for him to-day and he
is to show me the caves and holes in the coast where
they used to land their kegs. I am going from here
to-morrow, I think I shall go by the Scarboro' packet
but I am not certain. I shall most likely pop down on
Charles at Grasby, but if I go to Scarboro' I hardly
think I shall go out of my way again to Leeds. I shall
like much to see the Brownings again, Mrs B. particularly. I suppose when I come back the Lushingtons

will want me to spend some days at Park House. I have seen no houses here to be sold, but then I have not looked out for them. A tailor who sewed me on some buttons, told me Whitby was remarkable for longevity, the healthiest place in England except some place (he said) near Cheltenham, he had forgotten the name. I dare say he meant Malvern.

GRASBY, *July 22nd.*

I came by the packet boat to Scarborough where I stopt the night and came on here yesterday. The train only stopt at Moortown, and I was obliged to walk through the fields to Grasby when I admired the deep long-stemmed Lincolnshire wheat which I had not seen for many a day.

I find Charles and Louisa very well, only Charles rather low as it seems to me. It is a nice little place they have and the country really looks pretty at this time of year. I shall stop a few days.

GRASBY, *July 27th.*

Pray take drives every day. The school children have a feast here to-morrow for which I am going to stay. They run in sacks and do all manner of queer things. Our parson-party went off well. Agnes I suppose will be triumphant to-morrow. I think when I leave here I shall go round by Grimsby to see the new docks and perhaps get a bathe at Cleethorpes.

We went over to drink tea the other afternoon with Mr Maclean, the Vicar of Caistor, where I made fun for the children, and saw a young cuckoo which a boy had found in a sparrow's nest, a rather rare circumstance so late in July; but the boy had had him for three weeks and fed him with worms. He was a good deal duskier than the adult cuckoo, and with a white band on his head and very voracious, would have swallowed anything.

Hull, *July 31st.*

I am going out of the way to see Crowland Abbey and maybe shall stop a day or so there. I write this in vast haste at the Mason Arms, Louth. Daddy[1] drove me over last night to Grimsby to see the new dock, truly a great work.

When he reached home, Monckton Milnes asked him to dinner. He wrote:

My dear Milnes,

I have never dined in town (except once with Hallam en famille when I met him by chance in Lear the painter's rooms looking at his picture of the Syracusan Quarries[2], and once or twice with my brother-in-law en famille also) since I dined with you, Heaven knows how long ago, and met Doyle and others. I have given up dining out and am about to retire into utter solitude in some country house, but if you feel aggrieved at sending one invitation after another to me, unaccepted, I will come. You have not mentioned your hour 6? 7? 8? let me know. Do not bother yourself about giving me a bed, I can get one (and my own way too in the matter of smoke) better at Spedding's. Really I am very unwell and, tho' hay fever sometimes lets me alone for a whole day together, yet it sometimes makes me quite unfit to sit at table. Send me a line to say what your hour is and what Maurice's hour is and I will see if I can come in time for Maurice.

Ever yours,

A. Tennyson.

[1] Henry Sellwood.
[2] Now in the drawing-room at Farringford.

To James Spedding.

Dear J. S.

Can you let me have your attic next Saturday night and Sunday? I am going to dine with Milnes on Sunday, he has offered me a bed but I am more at mine ease in mine inn (smoking-room I should say) with you.

*   *   *   *   *

Go and see (and having seen, if you can interest yourself in) Thomas Woolner's design for the W. W.[1] Westminster monument. I am told it is good and I promised to say a good word for him.

Ever yours, A. Tennyson.

[1] Wordsworth, now in the drawing-room at Farringford.

CHAPTER XVII.

TWICKENHAM (1852–53).

Early in 1852 my father and mother went on a visit
to one of his old College friends, Mr. Rashdall the clergyman of Malvern, and met the Carlyles and Sydney
Dobell[1]. Rashdall was a man so beloved by his parish-
ioners, and so simple and direct in his language from the
pulpit, that he had emptied the Dissenting Chapels for
miles round. He would often hold his Church services
in the fields. A flowery record of Spring follows in my
mother's journal, about the beauty of the daffodils, wood
anemones, primroses, and violets; the pear trees throughout the country in bloom "like springing and falling
fountains." While they were there my father read
Dr Wordsworth's *Apocalypse* to my mother. On their
return to Twickenham, he visited the Exhibition, and was
delighted with Millais' "Ophelia" and "The Huguenot,"
but liked "The Huguenot" much the best. They came
to know the Peels at Marble Hill, and Archibald Peel
(the General's son) pointed out the avenue in which Sir
Walter Scott placed the interview between Jeanie Deans
and Queen Caroline. Happy days were spent in the

---

[1] Mr Briton Rivière writes to me: "I asked my brother-in-law, Sydney
Dobell, to describe your father to me, and he said: 'If he were pointed out
to you as the man who had written the *Iliad*, you would answer, "I can well
believe it."'"

little Twickenham garden, my father reading aloud passages of any book which struck him. Layard's *Nineveh* and Herschel's *Astronomy* were read at this time. Numerous friends called from London: Spedding, Venables, Patmore, Edmund and Franklin Lushington, Temple, Palgrave, Jowett, the Welds and others. He writes, "lots of callers, I expect I shall be inundated." The Diary continues, "Hallam born on the 11th of August."

To John Forster.

August 11th, 1852.

MY DEAR JOHN FORSTER,

I did not tell you of my marriage which you took rather in dudgeon. Now I will tell you of the birth of a little son this day. I have seen beautiful things in my life, but I never saw anything more beautiful than the mother's face as she lay by the young child an hour or two after, or heard anything sweeter than the little lamblike bleat of the young one. I had fancied that children after birth had been all shriek and roar; but he gave out a little note of satisfaction every now and then, as he lay by his mother, which was the most pathetic sound in its helplessness I ever listened to. You see I talk almost like a bachelor, yet unused to these things: but you — I don't hear good reports of you. You should have been better by this. Get better quickly if you would have me be as I always am

Yours most truly, A. TENNYSON.

MY DEAR JOHN FORSTER,

I have only time for one word of bulletin. Everything, I believe, is going on well, tho' the mother suffers from an almost total want of sleep, and the little monster does anything but what Hamlet says Osric did in his nursery-days. I found him lying alone on the third day of his life, and, while I was looking at him, I saw him looking at me with such apparently earnest, wide-open eyes, I felt as awe-struck as if I had seen a spirit. I hope you are mending.

God bless you, A. TENNYSON.

To Mrs Browning.

CHAPEL HOUSE, TWICKENHAM,
August 11th, 1852.

MY DEAR MRS BROWNING,

I wrote to you once before this morning. I now write again to tell you what I am sure your woman's and poet's heart will rejoice in, that my wife was delivered of a fine boy at 9.30 a.m. this day, and that both she and the child are doing well. I never saw any face so radiant with all high and sweet expression as hers when I saw her some time after.

Ever yours truly, A. TENNYSON.

Mrs Browning's reply was the first congratulatory letter.

58 WELBECK STREET,
Wednesday night.
August 12th, 1852.

MY DEAR MR TENNYSON,

Thank you and congratulate you indeed from my heart. May God bless you all three.

Robert said, when I was writing the note of enquiry which has gone to the post, "Tell him we will hope still for a joyful meeting," but I had not courage at that moment of crisis to mention a word of "joy."

Now I may, thank God. Will you say to dear Mrs Tennyson

when she is able to think of anything so far off as a friend, how deeply I sympathise in her happiness, with the memory of all that ecstasy as I felt it myself, still thrilling through me?

And there are barbarians in the world who dare to call the new little creatures not pretty, ugly even!!

Will you after a day or two send me a " line of bulletin "? See how I encroach upon your kindness!

Most truly yours,

ELIZABETH BARRETT BROWNING.

P.S. by Robert Browning.

I can't help saying too, how happy I am in your happiness and in the assurance that it is greater than even you can quite know yet. God bless, dear Tennyson, you and all yours.

R. B.

Saturday.

MY DEAR MRS BROWNING,

Here is one word of bulletin as you desired. All is doing as well as can be.

To this one word, let me add another, that is how very grateful your little note and Browning's epilogue made me. I began to read it to my wife but could not get on with it, so I put it away by her bedside, and she shall read it as soon as she reads anything.

Ever yours and your husband's,

A. TENNYSON.

" From the first," my mother writes, "Alfred watched Hallam with interest; some of his acquaintances would have smiled to see him racing up and down stairs and dandling the baby in his arms." The poem " Out of the Deep " was begun then and finished long afterwards. The christening was at Twickenham, the godfathers being Henry Hallam and F. D. Maurice.

From Henry Hallam.

WILTON CRESCENT, *August 25th*, 1852.

MY DEAR ALFRED TENNYSON,

I returned from a three weeks' tour in France late last night. Of your paternal dignity, lately accrued, I had had no information. This is my excuse for delay in acknowledging your letters of the 16th and in expressing at once my sincere congratulations on the event, and my most willing acceptance of the office which you desire me to undertake. That the names of Hallam and Tennyson should be united in the person of this infant will be to me a gratifying reflection for the remainder of my days. You have already made those names indissoluble. I beg you to give my kind regards to Mrs A. Tennyson. My daughter is at her own house at Hayes in Kent; I shall soon go down.

Yours most truly, H. HALLAM.

From Rev. F. D. Maurice.

BODINGTON RECTORY, nr. SHREWSBURY,
August 30th, 1852.

MY DEAR SIR,

I am almost ashamed to confess the pleasure which your note of this morning caused me. It does not look like the proper feeling of responsibility of the office with which the kindness of Mrs Tennyson and you would invest me, to have experienced such delight, and I am afraid you will think very differently and much more truly of my Christianity when you hear of it. But I have so very much to thank you for, especially of late years since I have known your poetry better and I hope I have been somewhat more in a condition to learn from it, that I cannot say how thankful I feel to you for wishing that I should stand in any nearer and more personal relation to you. I beg you to express to Mrs Tennyson how very much I value this proof of her confidence and how much I hope I may not prove utterly unworthy of it.

Very truly yours, F. D. MAURICE.

From Mrs Browning.

58 WELBECK STREET, *Sept.* 1852.

MY DEAR MRS TENNYSON,

It is delightful always to have kind words, most delightful to have them from *you.*

We had resolved on leaving England on the fifth, but you offer us an irresistible motive for staying, in spite of fogs and cold. So you will see us on Tuesday, and we shall come in time for the ceremony : we would not miss the christening for the world.

And I must tell you, a baby has screamed in this house ever since we have been in England, much to my sympathy...only, as the child grows fatter and fatter I have come to consider the screaming to be a sign of prosperity. Still, it is very painful to hear a young child : when he cried I was always near crying myself. Only the fact is that these little creatures *will* make much ado about nothing sometimes, and we are wrong in reading their ills too large through our imagination. I hope to find your darling well and serene on Tuesday, and yourself stronger than you seem to be now.

Let me be (why not ?)

Affectionately yours always,

ELIZABETH BARRETT BROWNING.

From Charles Dickens.

DOVER, *1st Oct.* 1852.

MY DEAR TENNYSON,

I have received your note here only to-day. It would have given me the heartiest pleasure to have welcomed a young Tennyson to this breathing world wherein he is much wanted, on so good an occasion as his christening, but that I have engaged to go to Boulogne on Sunday for a fortnight. I shall drink his health on the fifth.

As your letter bears no address and as I cannot call your address to mind, I send this to Moxon's care.

Ever yours, CHARLES DICKENS.

From Frederick Tennyson.

VILLA TORREGIANI, 1852.

Having duly received the bulletins announcing an autumnal shoot of the old Laurel in the shape of Hallam Tennyson (is this his only name?) I write not only to wish you joy of your new acquisition but to have more particulars from you on that all engrossing subject. Is he to turn out a dove or an eagle? Has he a hawking eye and the aquiline supremacy of the Cæsars in his nose or is there a classical type of head, a Belvederino with strong ideality? Will the pencils of the rays of the ancestral Intellectualities converge into a focus in the concavity of his cranium and be reflected therefrom in redoubled warmth and light, or will they neutralize one another and become common sense, a very good thing? You will probably be better enabled to answer these questions some ten years hence than now, but it is astonishing how early children begin to exhibit distinctive qualities. In my three little girls I fancy I detect strong marks of Individualities.

Your affectionate brother, F. T.

There was some question as to the name, whether it should be Arthur or Hallam. My father called out in a clear voice, that rang through the church, " Hallam," which pleased Henry Hallam, though jokingly he said in London: " They would not name him Alfred lest he should turn out a fool, and so they named him 'Hallam.'" Thinking that in future it would be an interesting link with a former age [1], his parents took him with them to old Samuel Rogers, and Rogers, bowing to my mother, said in his courtly and diplomatic way, " Mrs Tennyson, I made one great mistake in my life, I never married." In November was the burial of the Duke of Wellington. The Ode was published on the morning of

---

[1] Rogers, my father told me, had had his hand on Dr Johnson's knocker, but was too shy to knock and had run away without seeing the great man.

the funeral, but some additions were made to it afterwards [1].

My father wrote: *Nov.* 18*th.* "Have seen the procession at the Duke of Wellington's funeral: very fine;
hope to see the interior of St Paul's before I leave."
To Edward Fitzgerald he observed: "At the funeral I
was struck with the look of sober manhood in the British
soldier." "In the midst of the solemn silence," said my
father, "Magdalene Brookfield whispered to her mother
when she saw the Duke's boots carried by his charger,
'Mama, when I am dead shall I be that?' meaning the
boots."

It is interesting to note that while the Ode was
being abused in all directions by the Press my father
wrote thus to his publishers: "If you lose by the
Ode, I will not consent to accept the whole sum of
£200, which you offered me. I consider it quite a
sufficient loss if you do not gain by it."

Henry Taylor wrote:

MORTLAKE, *Nov.* 17*th*, 1852.

I have read your ode ("Death of the Duke of Wellington"),
and I believe that many thousands at present, and that many
hundreds of thousands in future times, will feel about it as
I do, or with a yet stronger and deeper feeling; and I am sure
that every one will feel about it according to his capacity of
feeling what is great and true. It has a greatness worthy of
its theme and an absolute simplicity and truth, with all the
poetic passion of your nature moving beneath.

And here is my father's reply:

SEAFORD HOUSE, SEAFORD,
Nov. 23*rd*, 1852.

Thanks, thanks! I have just returned from Reading
and found your letter. In the all but universal depre-

---

[1] The Ode was written in the "Green Room," Chapel House, Twickenham.

ciation of my ode by the Press, the prompt and hearty appreciation of it by a man as true as the Duke himself is doubly grateful.

Ever, my dear Taylor, yours,
A. TENNYSON.

This autumn the Twickenham meadows were so much flooded that my father and mother moved to Seaford, Brighton and Farnham. At the last place Charles Kingsley came to see them, fresh and vivacious as ever.

At the beginning of next year (1853) my father was asked whether he would allow himself to be nominated as Rector of the University of Edinburgh. He replied:

To Appleby Stephenson, M.D.

LONDON, March 1st, 1853.

SIR,

Your letter of the twenty-fourth of February has reached me only this morning. I trust that yourself and those other gentlemen, whom you speak of as being willing to give their vote for me as President of your University, will forgive me when I say that however gratefully sensible of the honour intended me, I must beg leave with many thanks to decline it. I could neither undertake to come to Edinboro' nor to deliver an inaugural address at the time specified. You will doubtless find another and worthier than myself to fill this office.

I am, Sir, your obliged and obedient servant,

A. TENNYSON.

My father then went off house-hunting and wrote from Farnham to my mother:

FARNHAM.

" I saw Elstead Lodge yesterday, dry soil but quite flat, with view of distant hills, and one hill very near:

splendid lawn but house looking north. The park here is delicious and the little house to be sold has a large garden...... As for the house, you would find the rooms too low. If I buy, there is plenty of room for building two good additional rooms. I saw the lawyer here and he has given me the refusal. It is quite retired, just under the Bishop's palace. What an air after Twickenham! I walked over to Hale and looked into the old premises [1]."

In the summer my father and mother took a tour to York[2], Whitby, Redcar, Richmond and Grasby. He left her at Richmond to return to Grasby, and went with Palgrave to Glasgow. From Glasgow the change was very pleasant when the travellers found themselves at Carstairs, the home of my father's old college friend, Robert Monteith. "The Daisy" was written in Edinburgh; and "To Edward Lear, on his Travels in Greece" was printed at this time among the collected poems.

Farringford[3].

Later my father paid a visit to Bonchurch. There he heard of Farringford as a place that might possibly be suitable for his home, as it was beautiful and far

[1] Where my grandfather, Henry Sellwood, lived with my mother after leaving Horncastle.

[2] My father wrote from Tait's Hotel, July 29th, 1853: "A Roman epitaph in the Museum at York touched me:

D. M. Simpliciae Florentine
Anime innocentissime
Que vixit menses decem.
Felicius Simplex Pater Fecit.
Leg. VI. V."

[3] The name *Farringford* is old. I have in my possession deeds of the fourteenth century signed by Walter de Ferringford. Prior's Manor, attached to Farringford, belonged to the Abbey of Lyra in Normandy. Many of the fields retain the old names of that time, the Prior's Field, Maiden's Croft (dedicated to the Virgin Mary), the Clerks' Hill, Abraham's Mead, etc.

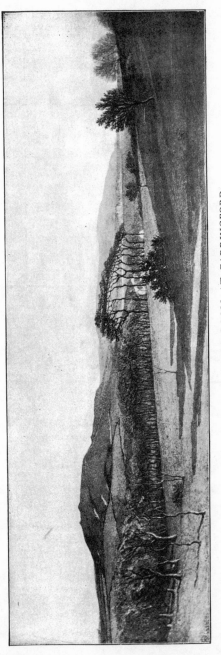

VIEW FROM DRAWING ROOM AT FARRINGFORD

From a Painting by Richard Doyle

from the haunts of men. " If society were what it is not," wrote Lady Taylor to Aubrey de Vere, "it might be well to give up something for it." Society being what it is, he determined to quit Twickenham and to live a country life of earnest work, only seeing his many friends from time to time. When my mother and he went down to look at Farringford, they crossed the Solent in a rowing boat on a still November evening, and " One dark heron flew over the sea, backed by a daffodil sky."

Next day, as they gazed from the drawing-room window out through the distant wreath of trees towards a sea of Mediterranean blue, with rosy capes beyond, the down on the left rising above the foreground of undulating park, golden-leaved elms and chestnuts, and red-stemmed pines, they agreed that they must if possible have that view to live with.

Nov. 14*th*, 1853. My father writes: " I wrote on Friday to accept [1] the house (Farringford), I also wrote to-day to Moxon to advance one thousand pounds, four hundred pounds he owes me, the odd six hundred to be paid if he will in March when I get my moneys in. Why I did it? Because by buying safe debentures in the East Lincolnshire Line for two thousand five hundred pounds, with that and five hundred [2] a year I think we ought to get on...Venables and Chapman agree in the propriety of the investment. Seymour has sent no papers yet. I don't know what is to be done with Laurence: it would be in the highest degree inconvenient for me to come back from the Isle of Wight to sit for him. Fitz would, I have no doubt, let him have his old sketch of me."

Accordingly on November the 24th, having taken the house on trial, they left Twickenham, and on the

[1] To lease the house with the option of buying it.
[2] The sum which since 1850 he had made from his books.

25th entered into possession of Farringford, which was to be a home to them for forty years, and where some of my father's best-known works were written. Mrs Thackeray Ritchie describes the place in her pleasant *Records*, as she saw it when it had become their own.

For the first time I stayed in the Island, and with the people who were dwelling there, and walked with Tennyson along High Down, treading the turf, listening to his talk, while the gulls came sideways, flashing their white breasts against the edge of the cliffs and the Poet's cloak flapped time to the gusts of the west wind. The house at Farringford itself seemed like a charmed palace, with green walls without, and speaking walls within. There hung Dante with his solemn nose and wreath; Italy gleamed over the doorways; friends' faces lined the passages, books filled the shelves, and a glow of crimson was everywhere; the oriel drawing-room window was full of green and golden leaves, of the sound of birds and of the distant sea.

My father and mother settled to a country life at once, looking after their little farm, and tending the poor and sick of the village. In the afternoons they swept up leaves, mowed the grass, gravelled the walks, and he built what he called "a bower of rushes" in the kitchen garden. The primroses and snowdrops and other flowers were a constant delight, and he began a flower dictionary. He also bought spy-glasses through which he might watch the ways and movements of the birds in the ilexes, cedar and fir trees. Geology too he took up, and trudged out with the local geologist, Keeping, on many a long expedition.

He wrote to Charles Kingsley about *Hypatia*:

1853.

MY DEAR KINGSLEY,

I hope your wife got my books which mine ordered Moxon to send. In the conclusion of the "Princess" the compositors have made a slight mistake.

Gray halls alone among their massive groves.

They have printed " their " " the " which somewhat weakens the line.

Hypatia never came; but I cannot afford to be without it. Part of the conclusion seems to me particularly valuable. I mean the talk of the Christianized Jew to the classic boy. Hypatia's mistreatment by the Alexandrians I found almost too horrible. It is very powerful and tragic; but I objected to the word " naked." Pelagia's nakedness has nothing which revolts one... but I really was hurt at having Hypatia stript, tho' I see that it adds to the tragic, and the picture as well as the moral is a fine one.

Will you lay your hand on my Adam Smith and send it per post? I enclose you six Queen's heads for that purpose.

Believe me, dear Kingsley,

Ever yours, A. TENNYSON.

CHAPTER XVIII.

FARRINGFORD (1853-1855).

Throughout the following chapters I have, with my mother's leave, made free use of her private journal. Most of it however has been necessarily compressed; and the numerous anecdotes about our childhood have been eliminated.

Here however I may perhaps be allowed to note my father's attitude toward children. This has best been given in his baby-songs, "Sweet and Low," "What does little birdie say?" "Minnie and Winnie," "Dainty Little Maiden," and his dedicatory poem to "Ally." I will however endeavour to set down briefly what I myself have known of some of his ways with children, and to begin with, what I have heard of his love for them in days before my own.

When he was a young man, living at Somersby, I have been told by those of the family younger than himself that "Alfred was their delight." They would sit upon his knee, or cling about his feet, while he told them stories of his own invention that enthralled them, long stories of hair-breadth escapes, and of travels ranging over all parts of the world. For the boys he would make himself a Colossus of Rhodes, the fun being that they should brave a "thwack" from his open hand, or escape it if they could, while rushing under the archway of his legs.

Of babies he would say: "There is something gigantic about them. The wide-eyed wonder of a babe has a grandeur in it which as children they lose. They seem to me to be prophets of a mightier race."

To his own children he was devoted. From the first he would, when my mother and he were alone, carry me in my bassinet into the drawing-room that he might watch my baby-gestures; and one of the very early things which I remember is that he helped the Master of Balliol to toss my brother and myself in a shawl. Later, he made us, though still very young, as much as possible his little companions. My mother was not strong enough to walk as far as we did, and so my father would harness my brother and myself to her garden carriage, and himself push from behind; and in this fashion we raced up hill and down dale. When the days were warm enough, perhaps we sat together on a bank in one of our home-fields, and he would read to us, or in cold weather would play football with us boys in an old chalk-pit, or build castles of flint on the top of the "Beacon Cliff," and we all then cannonaded from a distance, or he would teach us to shoot with bow and arrow. Some days we went flower-hunting, and on our return home, if the flower was unknown, he would say, " Bring me my Baxter's *Flowering Plants*," to look it out for us.

If it was rainy or stormy, and we were kept indoors, he often built cities for us with bricks, or played battledore and shuttlecock; or sometimes he read Grimm's *Fairy Stories* or repeated ballads to us. I remember his emphatic recitation in those far-off years of

> " Malbrouck s'en va-t'en guerre,
> Mironton, mironton, mirontaine,"

and of

> "Si le roi m'avait donné
> Paris sa grand' ville,"

and of   "Ye Mariners of England,"

and of   " The Burial of Sir John Moore."

On feast days he would blow bubbles and then grow
much excited over the "gorgeous colours and landscapes, and the planets breaking off from their suns,
and the single star becoming a double star," which he
saw in these bubbles; or if it were evening he would
help us to act scenes from some well-known play.
He enjoyed superintending our boy-charades, and if
a prologue had to be written would make the most
amusing part of it.

In the autumn we had frequent brushing up of leaves
from the lawns, and he would employ us in helping to
make new glades through the shrubs or in re-shingling
old paths.   It was a red-letter day when an Italian
organ-grinder came, as he did more years than one, and
was asked to warm himself by our bonfire of leaves and
wood, while my father and he told stories of Savoy,
Piedmont and Lombardy.   My father was always interested in the imaginative views which we children took
of our surroundings.   Of these I may give one instance:
how Lionel had been brought from his bed at night,
wrapt in a blanket, to see the great comet, and suddenly
awaking and looking out at the starry night, asked, " Am
I dead ? "

The chief anxiety of my parents, I remember, was
that we should be strictly truthful, and my father's words,
spoken long ago, still dwell with me, " A truthful man
generally has all virtues."   He was very particular about
our being courteous to the poor.   The severest punishment he ever gave me, though that was, it must be
confessed, slight, was for some want of respect to one of
our servants.

The first Latin I learnt from him was Horace's
O fons Bandusiæ, and the first Greek the beginning of

the *Iliad*.   Before this he liked to make us learn
and repeat ballads, and simple poems about Nature, but
he would never teach us his own poems, or allow us
to get them by heart.

In the summer as children we generally passed
through London to Lincolnshire, and he would take
us for a treat to Westminster Abbey, the Zoological
Gardens, the Tower of London, the Elgin Marbles at
the British Museum, or the National Gallery.   In the
last he much delighted and would point us out the
various excellences of the different masters; he always
led the way first of all to the " Raising of Lazarus "
by Sebastian del Piombo and to Titian's " Bacchus and
Ariadne."

A favourite saying was, " Make the lives of children
as beautiful and as happy as possible."   In the later
years of his life his grandchildren loved a romp with him,
and enjoyed their drives when he would fight them with
newspapers or play " pat-a-cake " with them.   To the end
he liked a "frolic with young things," and when on one
of his last walks he met the village school-children, he
pointed his stick at them, barking like a dog to make
them laugh.   In 1889, after he had turned eighty, he
wrote the lullaby in " Romney's Remorse," partly for his
little grandson Lionel:

> Father and mother will watch you grow,
> And gather the roses whenever they blow,
> And find the white heather wherever you go,
>   My sweet.

These anecdotes about him and his children, as I
read them over, seem trivial enough, yet I preserve them,
as testifying in their way to the " eternal youth of the
poet."

The year 1854 opened with the booming of cannon from Portsmouth, where the artillery were practising for the Crimean war. On March 16th Lionel was born. My father when he heard of the birth was looking through the study window at the planet Mars "as he glowed like a ruddy shield on the Lion's breast," and so determined to give the name Lionel.

After Lionel's birth he writes to Mrs Cameron and to John Forster:

March 22nd, 1854.

MY DEAR MRS CAMERON,

In my first batch of letters, sent off in all directions, when the new babe was born, I omitted to write to you, not willingly, but of necessity, not knowing your "Terrace," and my wife, who did know, not being to be spoken to....But I hope that this day, the sixth from her confinement, will, ere it fade (a very brilliant one over cape and sea), see her well, except for weakness. I have been mesmerizing her, which, she says, has done her a great deal of good. If she could but get a sleepful night, I have no doubt it would be all right by the morrow. As for the little fellow, he is as jolly as can be, and hardly cries at all yet. Little Hallam watches him, awe-struck, cannot make him out, and occasionally wails over him. I daresay that these are phenomena which you have often tenderly watched in your own family. You have not written, which I would far rather impute to the fact of my not having written than to the possibility of your being unwell. Pray Heaven the last be not the case with you; neither has Mary Marshall answered, which makes me anxious about her. God bless you, dear Julia Cameron, and

Believe me affectionately yours,

A. TENNYSON.

FARRINGFORD HOUSE, ISLE OF WIGHT,
March 29th, 1854.

MY DEAR FORSTER,

I understand from Archibald Peel that you are aggrieved at my not writing to you: that is wrong, morbid I think. I almost never write except in answer. Why, if you wished to know of me did you not write to me and you would have heard? Pray don't be distrustful. I love you all the same, tho' I should not write for 100 years.

Now it happens that a letter was half written to you partly to condole with you on the loss of dear good genial Talfourd, partly to announce the birth of another son of mine. I had dozens of letters to indite at that time to female cousins, etc., and I put this by to finish another day, and I cannot find it, or I would send it to prove that you are not forgotten, but you *must* be more trustful of me, or how can we get on? You must at any rate try the effect of a small note addrest to *me* before you find fault with me.

A reason for my not writing much is the bad condition of my right eye which quite suddenly came on as I was reading or trying to read small Persian text. You know perhaps how very minute in some of those Eastern tongues are the differences of letters: a little dot more or less: in a moment, after a three hours' hanging over this scratchy text, my right eye became filled with great masses of floating blackness, and the other eye similarly affected tho' not so badly. I am in a great fear about them, and think of coming up to town about them, for (whatever you may conjecture) I have not been in town for many months, not ever since I came here — did not even pass thro' town on my way here but went by Kingston.

I beseech your and all my friends' most charitable interpretation of whatever I do or may be said to do.

Our post only allows us from 11 o'clock to 1 o'clock to receive and answer letters which is (I think) another reason why I write so few.

I have been correcting my brother Frederick's proofs[1]. I dare say you may have seen notice of their approaching publication. He is a true poet, though his book (I think) ought to have been a shorter one.

Farewell, my dear fellow, God bless you and keep you.

Yours affectionately and unchangingly,

A. TENNYSON.

My wife's kind regards to you: she has been in a great state of suffering and sleeplessness for nine days, but at last I set her right by mesmerizing, — the effect was really wonderful.

In April the diary says that he drew my mother out in her garden chair to see the "wealth of daffodils" and the ruby sheaths of the lime leaves. At this time Edward Fitzgerald stayed at Farringford for a fortnight; he sketched and my father carved in wood. One day Fitzgerald brought home bunches of horned poppies and yellow irises over which like a boy he was ecstatic. In the evenings he played Mozart, or translated Persian Odes for my father, who, as has been said in the letter to Forster, had hurt his eyes by poring over a small-printed Persian Grammar: until this with Hafiz and other Persian books had to be hidden away, for he had seen "the Persian letters stalking like giants round the walls of his room." My father observed that his best working days were "in the early spring, when Nature begins to awaken from her winter sleep."

[1] *Days and Hours.*

To this date belongs the following letter to a friend:

You will not often see anything so sweet as my little, not quite two years old boy, who is toddling up and down the room, and saying, "Da, date," and "dada," meaning "give" in a very respectable Italian lingo, pointing to everything that strikes his fancy. Singularly enough the very day when I despatched my note to you another boy was born at 9 p.m., a lusty young fellow, who strikes the elder one with awe, sometimes into sympathetic tears, sometimes into a kind of mimic bleating, when he hears the younger one's inarticulate cooings. The first we had was born dead (a great grief to us), really the finest boy of the three; and I nearly broke my heart with going to look at him. He lay like a little warrior, having fought the fight, and failed, with his hands clenched, and a frown on his brow....If my latest born were to die to-night, I do not think that I should suffer so much as I did, looking on that noble little fellow who had never seen the light. My wife, who had had a most terrible time lasting near the whole of one Easter Sunday, never saw him. Well for her.

Yours, A. TENNYSON.

In May my father stayed in London and in August visited Glastonbury, Wells and the Cheddar Cliffs.

My father's letter-diary.

May 18th, 1854. 60 *Lincoln's Inn Fields*. I called on Moxon to arrange the "Illustrated Edition of Poems," and we went round to the artist Creswick, a capital broad genial fellow; Mulready, an old man, was full of vivacity and showed me lots of his drawings and one or two of his pictures. Then on to Horsley who was likewise very amiable and said that I was the painter's poet, etc., then on to Millais, who has agreed to come down in a month's time and take little Hallam as an illustration of "Dora." Sir E. Landseer I did not call upon and Holman Hunt was out of town.

Went to Forster's, and am going now to dine with Spedding somewhere, and then going to the Exhibition.

May 21st. Grove called and will be ready to show us the Crystal Palace. On Friday I dine with Frederick Locker, on Saturday with Forster.

May 22nd. I went to the Crystal Palace yesterday with Weld: certainly a marvellous place, but yet all in confusion. I do not think that it will be worth while to go up on the 10th for the opening, as it will be by no means so striking an affair as the last opening, 1851. I was much pleased with the Pompeian house and with the Iguanodons and Ichthyosaurs. I dined with Frank Lushington at the Oxford and Cambridge Club afterwards; Horatio dined with us. Tom Taylor came to Spedding's in the evening and gave me a book of Breton ballads, exceedingly beautiful, many of them.

May 23rd. I called on Hallam yesterday, he looks very well.

August.

I came to Glastonbury after parting from Grant[1], then to Yeovil in a fly, 17 miles, which rather jarred against my paternity when I thought that little Hallam and Lionel had to be educated. I went to the Abbey. As soon as I got there, there rose an awful thunderstorm, and I took shelter over Arimathæan Joseph's bones in

---

[1] Sir Alexander Grant who was first head of the University of Bombay, afterwards Principal of the University of Edinburgh.

the crypt of his chapel for they say (credat Judæus) he lies there.   Only one arch remains.

Walked over to Wells.   To Wookey Hole this morning, a cave; it was not quite what I wanted to see, tho' very grim.   Am at the Swan Hotel, shall go over to Cheddar to-morrow.

Arrived at Cheddar to-day and have just seen a stalactite cavern, a thing I had never seen before.

August 17th.   Corfe Castle, Christchurch, very well worth seeing: Bournemouth fashionable, not at all a place to buy a house in.   We found an old Waterloo soldier on the coast.

When my father had returned to Farringford, he and my mother "saw a great deal of the Simeons, Aubrey de Vere and Baron de Schroeter from Swainston, and lengthy were the discussions on Roman Catholicism." My father was much impressed by the deeply felt religious enthusiasm of the Baron, who was like an old ascetic monk, and anxious to convert my parents.

Of Sir John Simeon's first visits his daughter, Mrs Richard Ward, writes:

On the day of Lionel's christening my father paid his first visit to Farringford, and found the family party just returning from church.   During these early years, it was one of my father's greatest pleasures to ride or drive over from Swainston in the summer afternoons.   He and the Tennysons would go long expeditions through the lanes and over the downs: then back through the soft evening air to dinner and to the long evening of talk and of reading, which knit "that fair companionship" and made it "such a friendship as had mastered time."

It was then that my father worked at "Maud," morning and evening, sitting in his hard high-backed wooden chair in his little room at the top of the house. His "sacred pipes," as he called them, were half an hour after breakfast, and half an hour after dinner, when no one was allowed to be with him, for then his best thoughts came to him. As he made the different poems he would repeat or read them. The constant reading of the new poems aloud was the surest way of helping him to find out any defects there might be. During his "sacred half-hours" and his other working hours and even on the Downs, he would murmur his new passages or new lines as they came to him, a habit which had always been his since boyhood, and which caused the Somersby cook to say "What is master Awlfred always a praying for?"

Aubrey de Vere writes of this year:

In 1854 I went from Swainston, the residence of Sir John Simeon, my friend, and the friend no less of Alfred Tennyson, in whose elegiac lines his memory is embalmed for ever, to Farringford, where the poet then made abode with his wife and two children. The eldest was about two years old; the other an infant in arms; and I was so much struck by his eyes, the most contemplative which I had ever seen, that I exclaimed, "When that child grows to be a man he must be a Carthusian monk!" "Nothing of the sort," was the answer I received; "but a happy husband, and a happy father, in a happy home." The home I stood in was a happy home; and the fortnight I spent in it was one I can never forget. The recollection of it is all the more delightful because it carries with it little sense of variety, "So like, so very like was day to day." The year had reached its zenith: the sky was almost always blue, and the lovely gleam of sea was a somewhat darker blue, while the healthful breezes of Freshwater prevented even the noontide from feeling sultry. The earlier part of the day I spent chiefly in reading and writing: in the afternoon we sometimes read aloud in the open air, or rather we listened to the Poet's reading, with such distractions alone as were caused by a bird-note louder than the rest or a distant sea-gleam more bright. On one occasion our book, which we agreed in greatly admiring, was Coventry Patmore's *Angel in the House*, then recent. Alfred and I had many a breezy walk along the Downs and as far as The Needles, sometimes with distant views of the coast flushed by sunset, sometimes with a nearer

one of the moonbeams "marbling" the wet sea-sands, as the
wave recoiled, which last always reminded me of Landor's
lines,

> "And the long moonbeam on the hard wet sands
> Lay like a jasper column half uprear'd."

Tennyson was engaged on his new poem "Maud." Its origin
and composition were, as he described them, singular. He had
accidentally lighted upon a poem of his own which begins, "O
that 'twere possible," and which had long before been published
in a selected volume got up by Lord Northampton for the aid of
a sick clergyman. It had struck him, in consequence, I think, of
a suggestion made by Sir John Simeon, that, to render the poem
fully intelligible, a preceding one was necessary. He wrote it;
the second poem too required a predecessor; and thus the
whole work was written, as it were, *backwards*. The readers of
"Maud" seldom observe that in the love-complexities of that
poem the birds take a vehement part. The "birds in the high
Hall-garden" are worldly birds, factious for the young Lord and
the millionaire Brother:

> Where is Maud, Maud, Maud,
> One is come to woo her?

The "birds in our wood" are as ardent partizans of the
lovers. I remarked to the Poet on this circumstance; but his
answer was as vague as the "mowt a beän" of the "Northern
Farmer."

This summer my father wrote of Freshwater to a
friend: "Ours is by far in my opinion the most note-
worthy part of the island, with an air on the Downs
'worth,' as somebody said, 'sixpence a pint.'"

Through the autumn and winter evenings he translated aloud to my mother the sixth *Æneid* of Virgil and
Homer's description of Hades, and they read Dante's
Inferno together. Whewell's *Plurality of Worlds* he
also carefully studied. "It is to me anything," he writes,
"but a satisfactory book. It is inconceivable that the
whole Universe was merely created for us who live in
this third-rate planet of a third-rate sun."

The excitement about the Crimean War was intense. On October 10th the papers were full of the particulars of the battle of the Alma[1]. The journal says: " Looking from the Beacon and seeing the white cliffs and the clear sea, their violet gray shading seemed to us tender and sad; perhaps the landscape seemed so sad because of the sorrowful news of the death-roll in the Crimea and of the death of our neighbour Colonel Hood in the trenches."

In November an unknown friend sent an account of the charge of the Heavy Brigade at Balaclava on October 25th, — how the Scots Greys and the Inniskilleners flung themselves against the solid Russian column. The writer says: "Our ears were frenzied by the monotonous incessant cannonade going on for days together."

On November 22nd Millais' long promised visit was paid. He was " beguiled into sweeping up leaves and burning them[2]. He made sketches of Hallam and his mother, Hallam appearing in the illustration to ' Dora.' " There were talks with Millais " as to the limits of realism in painting." My father hated the modern realism in painting and literature, notably as shown by the French schools. With regard to certain English pictures he said to Millais that from his point of view, " if you

[1] My father wrote the first stanza of a song entitled " The Alma River," which my mother finished and set to music:

> Frenchman, a hand in thine!
>   Our flags have waved together!
> Let us drink to the health of thine and mine
>   At the battle of Alma River.
>
> Our flags together furl'd,
>   Henceforward no other strife —
> Than which of us most shall help the world,
>   Which lead the noblest life.
>
> Then pledge we our glorious dead,
>   Swear to be one for ever,
> And God's best blessing on each dear head
>   That rests by the Alma River.

[2] Perhaps this suggested his fine early picture upon the subject.

have human beings before a wall, the wall ought to be picturesquely painted, and in harmony with the idea pervading the picture, but must not be made obtrusive by the bricks being *too* minutely drawn, since it is the human beings that ought to have the real interest for us in a dramatic picture."

When Millais left, my parents read together Souvestre's account of the Bretons. The fact that their most popular songs are religious and that, when the cholera was among them, they would not listen to the doctors until they put their advice in song, set to national airs, struck my father. On Dec. 2nd he wrote " The Charge of the Light Brigade[1]" in a few minutes, after reading the description in the *Times* in which occurred the phrase " some one had blundered," and this was the origin of the metre of his poem. Christmas Eve is kept by his " blowing bubbles for the children, and making fun for them by humping up his shoulders high, and pretending to be a giant."

At the end of the year he received Professor Ferrier's *History of Philosophy*, with the following letter:

ST ANDREWS, *Dec.* 17*th*, 1854.

DEAR SIR,

You were among the very first to whom my book was to be sent and I supposed that you had received it some six weeks ago. Possibly Blackwood did not know your address and therefore sent it to your publisher.

If anything strikes you as inconsecutive in the reasoning you will do me a favour by pointing it out.

One eminent authority has given it as his opinion that there is a non sequitur in the passage from Prop. I. to Prop. II. To me this seems odd. I esteem it a high honour to have now made your acquaintance and a great privilege to be allowed to subscribe myself

Very truly yours, F. FERRIER.

[1] Published in the *Examiner*, Dec. 9th.

Frederick Tennyson wrote from Florence:

Dec. 30th, 1854.

MY DEAR E. AND A.,

Browning comes in occasionally, but poor Mrs B. never stirs out during the winter. Under the rose, they are both preparing new poems, Browning a batch of Lyrics which are to be the real thing, Mrs B. a kind of Metrical Romance. Though I have the highest esteem for Browning, and believe him to be a man of infinite learning, jest and bonhommie, and moreover a sterling heart that reverbs no hollowness, I verily believe his school of poetry to be the most grotesque conceivable. With the exception of the "Blot on the 'Scutcheon," through which you may possibly grope your way without the aid of an Ariadne, the rest appear to me to be Chinese puzzles, trackless labyrinths, unapproachable nebulosities. Yet he has a very Catholic taste in poetry, doing justice to everything good in all poets past or present, and he is one who has a profound admiration of Alfred. I hear from Palgrave that A. has a new poem on the stocks; a few of the best stanzas in your next letter I should prize highly, and the Brownings would be delighted to see a specimen of it. I suppose the poem on the "Charge of the Six Hundred" in the *Examiner*, signed A. T., is really by Alfred. Browning sent me the paper but I could give him no information on the subject.

Your affectionate brother, F. TENNYSON.

On Jan. 10th, 1855, my father had "finished, and read out, several lyrics of 'Maud.'" The weather in January and February was arctic and the waves froze on the beach.

The news of the loss of Sir John Franklin, my mother's uncle, in the Arctic Regions was at this time "a great shock [1]." It is interesting to note that Dr Kane, who was on the second Grinnell Expedition in search of Sir John, honoured my father by naming a natural rock

---

[1] My mother thought that her uncle's last words to her were: "If I am lost, remember, Emily, my firm belief that there is open sea at the North Pole."

column 480 feet high, on a pedestal 280 feet high, to the
north of latitude 79 degrees, " Tennyson's Monument."

Dr Kane wrote :

I remember well the emotions of my party as it first broke
upon our view.   Cold and sick as I was, I brought back a sketch
of it, which may have interest for the reader, though it scarcely
suggests the imposing dignity of this magnificent landmark.
Those who are happily familiar with the writings of Tennyson
and have communed with his spirit in the wilderness, will apprehend the impulse that inscribed the scene with his name.

In February my father " translated aloud three Idylls
of Theocritus, *Hylas, The Island of Cos,* and *The Syracusan Women.*"   In March " Woolner made a medallion
of him (the best likeness that had yet been made)."

On March 22nd my father received this letter from
Ruskin :

DENMARK HILL, CAMBERWELL,
21st March, 1855.

DEAR MR TENNYSON,

I venture to write to you, because as I was talking
about you with Mr Woolner yesterday, he gave me more pleasure than I can express by telling me that you wished to see my
" Turners."

By several untoward chances I have been too long hindered
from telling you face to face how much I owe you.   So you see
at last I seize the wheel of fortune by its nearest spoke, begging
you with the heartiest entreaty I can, to tell me when you are
likely to be in London and to fix a day if possible that I may
keep it wholly for you, and prepare my " Turners " to look
their rosiest and best.   Capricious they are as enchanted opals,
but they must surely shine for you.

Any day will do for me if you give me notice two or three
days before, but please come soon, for I have much to say to
you and am eager to say it, above all to tell you how for a
thousand things I am gratefully and respectfully yours,

J. RUSKIN.

In April my father walked to Bonchurch, and wrote
to my mother : " If I stop another day here, I may have

a chance of seeing double stars thro' a telescope of Dr Mann's, a very clever interesting doctor with whom I spent two hours this morning. He showed me things thro' his microscope."

He was home again on April 25th, and "copied out 'Maud' for the press, and read 'The Lady of the Lake,' having just finished Goethe's 'Helena.'"

On June 6th he writes: "I have strangely enough accepted the Oxford Doctorship. Friends told me I ought to accept it, so I did." Temple[1] had suggested my father for that degree. My parents stayed at Balliol; and my father said, as he sat in the Balliol gardens, "The shouts of the Undergraduates from the theatre are like the shouts of the Roman crowd, 'Christiani ad Leones!'" He was very nervous before going, but entered the theatre quite calmly with Sir John Burgoyne, the stately-looking Montalembert, and Sir de Lacy Evans. He sat on the steps nearly under Lord Derby, then there was one great shout for "In Memoriam," one for "Alma" and one for "Inkermann." The sea of upturned faces was very striking, and my father had a "tremendous ovation" when he received his degree. The new doctor ordinarily borrows a doctor's robes from a tailor and just wears them in the Sheldonian Theatre for the ceremony. But my father after luncheon asked the Master of Balliol whether it would be against rule and propriety if he might have a smoke, as it was his fancy to do so, among the green trees when clad in his red doctorial robes. The Master said that he might do so, and he smoked in the then walled-in Master's garden, now open to the college. "In the evening at Magdalen he had long talks with Mr Gladstone and Montalembert." Next day Arthur Butler and Max Müller took my father and mother about Oxford, and to the Bodleian, to see the

---

[1] Now Archbishop of Canterbury.

Illuminated Missals, and Dr Wellesley showed them the Raffaelle sketches. At night they had tea with Professor Johnson and Professor Adams, and looked at the Nebulæ in Cassiopeia through the big telescope, the Ring Nebula in Lyra and also some double stars.

On July 7th they reached home, and the last touch was put to " Maud," before giving it to the publisher. Up to the time of my father's death, when his friends asked him to read aloud from his own poetry, he generally chose " Maud," the " Ode on the Duke of Wellington," or " Guinevere."

Translations into French of " Ring out, wild bells," and " Mariana in the Moated Grange," were sent him from France.

He pointed out " what a poor language French is for translating English poetry, although it is the best language for delicate *nuances* of meaning. How absurd ' Ring out, wild bells ' sounds in the translation ' Sonnez, Cloches, Sonnez,' and what a ridiculous rendering of ' He cometh not, she said ' is ' Tom ne vient pas '! [1] "

August 6th. " The Balaclava Charge " with the following short preface was forwarded to John Forster to be printed on a fly-leaf for the Crimean Soldiers.

---

[1] About this time he wrote a letter to the Breton poet Hippolyte Lucas :

Une Lettre inédite d'Alfred Tennyson à Hippolyte Lucas.

CHER MONSIEUR,
　　　Ce m'est véritablement une douce chose que d'avoir trouvé une âme poétique qui puisse fraterniser avec la mienne de l'autre côté de la grande mer. Les poètes, comme vous le dites fort bien, sont ou plutôt devraient être reliés ensemble par une chaîne électrique, car ils ne doivent pas parler seulement pour leurs compatriotes. J'ai lu vos vers plusieurs fois, et ils m'ont causé plus de plaisir à chaque nouvelle lecture. Je suis particulièrement flatté de leur ressemblance avec mon propre poème.

Si jamais je fais un voyage en Bretagne, j'aurai l'honneur et le plaisir de vous faire une visite. Votre province est riche en légendes poétiques de toute espèce, et par cela même particulièrement chère aux Anglais. J'espère la voir un jour, et vous en même temps.

En attendant, croyez-moi, cher monsieur, votre tout dévoué
　　　　　　　　　　　　　　　　　ALFRED TENNYSON.

August 8th, 1855.

Having heard that the brave soldiers before Sebastopol, whom I am proud to call my countrymen, have a
liking for my ballad on the charge of the Light Brigade
at Balaclava, I have ordered a thousand copies of it to
be printed for them.   No writing of mine can add to the
glory they have acquired in the Crimea; but if what I
have heard be true they will not be displeased to receive
these copies from me, and to know that those who sit
at home love and honour them.

ALFRED TENNYSON.

To John Forster.

[*Undated.*]

MY DEAR FORSTER,

In the first place thanks for your critique
which seems to me good and judicious.   Many thanks,
my wife will write to you about it; but what I am writing
to you now about is a matter which interests me very
much.   My friend Chapman of 3, Stone Buildings,
Lincoln's Inn, writes to me thus: — "An acquaintance
of mine in the department of the S.P.G. as he calls it
(Society for the Propagation of the Gospel) was saying
how a chaplain in the Crimea sent by the Society
writes to the Society — (neither he nor the Society being
suspected of any Tennysonian prejudices) — 'The *greatest
service you can do*[1] just now is to send out on printed
slips Mr A. T.'s 'Charge at Balaclava.'   It is the greatest
favourite of the soldiers — half are singing it, and all
want to have it in black and white, so as to read what
has so taken them.'"

Now, my dear Forster, you see I cannot possibly be
deaf to such an appeal.   I wish to send out about 1000
slips, and I don't at all want the S.P.G. or any one to

[1] Thus underscored in the original.

send out the *version last printed*: it would, I believe,
quite disappoint the soldiers.   Don't you live quite close
to the S.P.G.?   Could you not send Henry over to say
that *I* am sending over the soldiers' version of my ballad,
and beg them not to stir in the matter?   The soldiers
are the best critics in what pleases them.   I send you
a copy which retains the " Light Brigade," and the
" blunder'd "; and I declare it is the best of the two,
and that the criticism of two or three London friends (not
yours) induced me to spoil it.   For Heaven's sake get
this copy fairly printed at once, and sent out.   I have sent
it by this post likewise to Moxon, but you are closer to
your printer.   Concoct with him how it is all to be
managed : I am so sorry that I am not in town to have
done it at once.   I have written a little note to the
soldiers which need not be sent — just as you like.   It
might be merely printed " From A. Tennyson."   Please
see to all this : and see that there are *no mistakes ;* and
I will be bound to you for evermore, and more than ever
yours in great haste,

A. Tennyson.

P.S.   I am convinced now after writing it out that
this *is* the best version.

The following tribute was received from Scutari :

We had in hospital a man of the Light Brigade, one of the
few who survived that fatal mistake, the Balaclava charge ; but
which, deplorable as it was, at least tended to show the high
state of discipline attained in the British army.   I spoke to
several of those engaged in that deadly conflict, and they could
describe accurately the position of the Russian cannon ; were
perfectly aware when obeying that word of command, that they
rode to almost certain death.   This patient had received a kick
in the chest from a horse long after the battle of Balaclava, while
in barracks at Scutari.   He was depressed in spirits, which
prevented him from throwing off the disease engendered by the
blow.   The doctor remarked that he wished the soldier could be

roused.   Amongst other remedies leeches were prescribed. While watching them I tried to enter into a conversation with him, spoke of the charge, but could elicit only monosyllabic replies.   A copy of Tennyson's poems having been lent me that morning, I took it out and read it.   The man, with kindling eye, at once entered upon a spirited description of the fatal gallop between the guns' mouths to and from that cannon-crowded height.   He asked to hear it again, but, as by this time a number of convalescents were gathered around, I slipped out of the ward.   The chaplain who had lent me the poem, under-standing the enthusiasm with which it had been received, afterwards procured from England a number of copies for distribution.   In a few days the invalid requested the doctor to discharge him for duty, being now in health ; but whether the cure was effected by the leeches or the poem it is impossible to say.   On giving the card the medical man murmured, "Well done, Tennyson ! "

On one of the anniversaries of the Balaclava charge a banquet was given in London, and my father was pressed to attend.   Being unable to do so, he sent the following letter to the chairman of the committee:

FARRINGFORD, FRESHWATER.
DEAR SIR,

I cannot attend your banquet, but I enclose £5 to defray some of its expenses, or to be distributed as you may think fit among the most indigent of the survivors of that glorious charge.   A blunder it may have been, but one for which England should be grateful, having thereby learnt that her soldiers are the most honest and most obedient under the sun.   I will drink a cup of wine on the 25th to the health and long life of all your fine fellows ; and, thanking yourself and your comrades heartily for the cordial invitation sent me, I pray you all to believe me, now and ever, your admiring fellow-countryman,

A. TENNYSON.

He had intended to write a poem on the soldiers' battle of Inkermann, but only got as far as the first line: "Strong eight thousand of Inkermann."

At this time my father's friend Harry Lushington, who with his brother Franklin had published some stirring poems on the Crimean war, died in Paris.

My father's letter-diary of days in the New Forest.

August 31*st.* Haven't had the heart to get further than Winchester and Salisbury. I am going to-day to take a gig across country to Lyndhurst.

Lyndhurst, Sept. 1*st.* Tho' I had said that the New Forest, for didn't I expect that it was disforested, would not do again; tho', when I started this morning, I got on the wrong track for four miles or so out of the way of the great timber; the vast solemn beeches delighted me, but my soul was not satisfied, for I did not meet with any so very large beech as I had met with before. Yet I rejoiced in the beeches and have resolved to stay till Monday and see them twice again. I have lost the tobacco case which Simeon gave me; I am grieved, but it was so like the colour of last year's beech leaves that I did not see it when I turned to leave the spot where I had smoked.

Crown Hotel, Lyndhurst. Sept. 2*nd.* I lost my way in the Forest to-day, and have walked I don't know how many miles. I found a way back to Lyndhurst by resolutely following a track which brought me at last to a turnpike. On this I went a mile in the wrong direction, that is towards Christchurch, then met a surly fellow who grudgingly told me I was four miles from Lyndhurst, whereby I turned and walked to Lyndhurst. My admiration of the Forest is great: it is true old wild English Nature, and then the fresh heath-sweetened air is so delicious. The Forest is grand.

London, Sept. 28*th.* I dined yesterday with the Brownings and had a very pleasant evening. Both of them are great admirers of poor little " Maud." The two Rossettis came in during the evening[1].

October 1*st.* I dined at Twickenham, my mother looking very well and intending to keep the house on another year. I also dined with the Camerons last night, she is more wonderful than ever I think in her mild-beaming benevolence. I read " Maud " to five or six people at the Brownings (on Sept. 28th).

Mrs Browning writes thereupon to my mother:

13 DORSET STREET, *October*, 1855.

MY DEAR MRS TENNYSON,

If I had not received your kindest of letters I had yet made up my mind not to leave England without writing to you to thank you (surely it would have been your due) for the deep pleasure we had in Mr Tennyson's visit to us. He didn't come back as he said he would to teach me the " Brook " (which I persist nevertheless in fancying I understand a little), but he did so much and left such a voice (both him " and a voice! ") crying out "Maud " to us, and helping the effect of the poem by the personality, that it's an increase of joy and life to us ever. Then may we not venture to think now of Alfred Tennyson *our friend* ? and was it not worth while coming from Italy to England for so much ? Let me say too another thing, that though I was hindered (through having women friends with me, whom I loved and yet could not help wishing a little further just then) from sitting in the smoke and hearing the talk of the next room, yet I heard some sentences which, in this materialistic low-talking world, it was comfort and triumph to hear from the lips of such a man. So I thank you both, and my husband's thanks go with mine.

As to a visit to you, how pleasant that you should ask us!

---

[1] Gabriel Rossetti wrote to William Allingham about this evening in an unpublished letter: " He is quite as glorious in his way as Browning in his, and perhaps of the two even more impressive on the whole personally."

This year we could not have gone, next year perhaps we shall not be able any more * * * but every year of our lives it will be pleasant to think that you have wished it.   Dear Mrs Tennyson, you do not mind the foolish remarks on " Maud " * * * do you? These things are but signs of an advance made, of the tide rising. People on the shore are troubled in their picking up of shells a little.

Kiss your children for me: I hope my child may play with them before long.   My husband's " Men and Women " shall go to Mr Tennyson on the publication, not to trouble him (understand) with exaction of a letter or opinion, but simply as a sign of personal regard and respect.

Dear Mrs Tennyson and dear Mr Tennyson, believe us *both* very affectionately yours, though I have but the name of

ELIZABETH BARRETT BROWNING.

P.S. (We leave England to-morrow.)   God bless you, dear and admirable friends.   My wife feels what she says, and I feel with her.

Affectionately yours,

ROBERT BROWNING.

On his return the evening books were Milton, Shakespeare's *Sonnets*, Thackeray's *Humourists*, some of Hallam's *History* and of Carlyle's *Cromwell*.

This Christmas " Mr. Lear paid us a visit and sang his settings of ' Mariana,' ' Lotos-Eaters,' ' Let not the solid earth,' and ' Oh that 'twere possible.' "

One day my father received " an interesting letter telling him of a man who had been roused from a state of suicidal despondency by ' The Two Voices.' "

At the end of the year an unknown Nottingham artizan came to call.   My father asked him to dinner and at his request read " Maud."   It appears that the poor man had sent his poems beforehand.   They had been acknowledged, but had not been returned, and had been forgotten.   He was informed that the poems, thus sent, were always looked at, although my father and mother had not time to pass judgment on them. A most pathetic incident of this kind, my father told me, happened to him at Twickenham, when a Waterloo soldier brought twelve large cantos on the battle of Waterloo. The veteran had actually taught himself in his old age to read and write that he might thus commemorate Wellington's great victory. The epic lay for some time under the sofa in my father's study, and was a source of much anxiety to him. How could he go through such a vast poem? One day he mustered up courage and took a portion out. It opened on the heading of a canto: "The Angels encamped above the field of Waterloo." On that day, at least, he "read no more." He gave the author, when he called for his manuscript, this criticism: "Though great images loom here and there, your poem could not be published as a whole." The old man answered nothing, wrapt up each of the twelve cantos carefully, placed them in a strong oak case and carried them off. He was asked to come again but he never came.

Let not the solid ground
   Fail beneath my feet
Before my life has found
   What some have found so sweet.
Then let come what come may,
What matter if I go mad,
I shall have had my day.

Let the sweet Heavens endure
   Not close & darken above me,
Before I am quite quite sure
   That there is one to love me
Then let come what come may
To a life that has been so sad
I shall have lived my day.

From the Original MS.

CHAPTER XIX.

"MAUD[1]."

After reading "Maud":

Leave him to us, ye good and sage,
Who stiffen in your middle age.
Ye loved him once, but now forbear;
Yield him to those who hope and dare,
And have not yet to forms consign'd
A rigid ossifying mind.

Ionica.

Pure lyrical poetry of every form had been essayed by my father before 1855, but a monodramatic lyric, like "Maud," was a novelty. In consequence its meaning and drift were widely misunderstood even by educated readers, which partly accounts for the outburst of hostile criticism that greeted its appearance. It is a "Drama of the Soul," set in a landscape glorified by Love, and according to Lowell, "The antiphonal voice to 'In Memoriam[2].'" Nothing perhaps more justified what has been said of my father, that had he not been a poet, he might have been remarkable as an actor, than his reading of "Maud," with all its complex contrasts of motive and

---

[1] The volume contained "Maud" (*written at Farringford*), "The Brook," "The Letters," "Ode on the death of the Duke of Wellington," "The Daisy," "To the Rev. F. D. Maurice," "Will," "The Charge of the Light Brigade."

[2] My father sometimes called "In Memoriam," "The Way of the Soul."

393

action. He generally prefaced his reading with an explanation, the substance of which has been given by Dr Mann in his *Maud Vindicated*.

[1] "At the opening of the drama, the chief person or hero of the action is introduced with scenery and incidents artistically disposed around his figure, so as to make the reader at once acquainted with certain facts in his history, which it is essential should be known. Although still a young man, he has lost his father some years before by a sudden and violent death, following immediately upon unforeseen ruin brought about by an unfortunate speculation in which the deceased had engaged. Whether the death was the result of accident, or self-inflicted in a moment of despair, no one knows, but the son's mind has been painfully possessed by a suspicion of villainy and foul play somewhere, because an old friend of his family became suddenly and unaccountably rich by the same transaction that had brought ruin to the dead. Shortly after the decease of his father, the bereaved young man, by the death of his mother, is left quite alone in the world. He continues thenceforth to reside in the retired village in which his early days have been spent, but the sad experiences of his youth have confirmed the bent of a mind constitutionally prone to depression and melancholy. Brooding in loneliness upon miserable memories and bitter fancies, his temperament as a matter of course becomes more and more morbid and irritable. He can see nothing in human affairs that does not awaken in him disgust and contempt. Evil glares out from all social arrangements, and unqualified meanness and selfishness appear in every human form, so he keeps to himself and chews the cud of cynicism and discontent apart from his kind. Such in rough outline is the figure the poet has sketched as the foundation and centre of his

[1] My father desired that the passage by Dr Mann, here quoted, should be inserted among his notes 1891-92.

plan * * *. Since the days of his early youth up to
the period when the immediate action of the poem is
supposed to commence, the dreamy recluse has seen
nothing of the family of the man to whom circumstances
have inclined him to attribute his misfortunes. This
individual, although since his accession to prosperity
the possessor of the neighbouring hall and of the
manorial lands of the village, has been residing abroad.
Just at this time however there are workmen up at the
dark old place, and a rumour spreads that the absentees
are about to return. This rumour, as a matter of course,
stirs up afresh rankling memories in the breast of the
recluse, and awakens there old griefs. But with the
group of associated recollections that come crowding
forth, there is one of the child Maud, who was in
happier days his merry playfellow. She will now
however be a child no longer. She will return as the
lady mistress of the mansion (being the only daughter
of the Squire, who is a widower). What will she be
like? He, who wonders, has heard somewhere that
she is singularly beautiful. But what is this to him?
Even while he thinks of her, he feels a chill presentiment,
suggested no doubt by her close relationship to one who
he considered had already worked him so much harm,
that she will bring with her a curse for him."

I shall never forget his last reading[1] of " Maud," on
August 24th, 1892. He was sitting in his high-backed
chair, fronting a southern window which looks over the
groves and yellow cornfields of Sussex toward the long
line of South Downs that stretches from Arundel to
Hastings (his high-domed Rembrandt-like head outlined
against the sunset-clouds seen through the western
window). His voice, low and calm in everyday life,
capable of delicate and manifold inflection, but with

---

[1] He owned that " Some of the passages are hard to read because they
have to be taken in one breath and require good lungs."

"organ-tones" of great power and range, thoroughly brought out the drama of the poem. You were at once put in sympathy with the hero. As he said himself, "This poem is a little *Hamlet*," the history of a morbid poetic soul, under the blighting influence of a recklessly speculative age. He is the heir of madness, an egotist with the makings of a cynic, raised to sanity by a pure and holy love which elevates his whole nature, passing from the height of triumph to the lowest depth of misery, driven into madness by the loss of her whom he has loved, and, when he has at length passed through the fiery furnace, and has recovered his reason, giving himself up to work for the good of mankind through the unselfishness born of his great passion. My father pointed out that even Nature at first presented herself to the man in sad visions.

And the flying gold of the ruin'd woodlands drove thro' the air.

The "blood-red heath" too is an exaggeration of colour; and his suspicion that all the world is against him is as true to his nature as the mood when he is "fantastically merry." "The peculiarity of this poem," my father added, "is that different phases of passion in one person take the place of different characters."

The passion in the first Canto was given by my father in a sort of rushing recitative through the long sweeping lines of satire and invective against the greed for money, and of horror at the consequences of the war of the hearth.

Then comes the first sight of Maud, and "visions of the night," and in Canto IV. a longing for calm, the reaction after a mood of bitterness, and yearning for

A philosopher's life in the quiet woodland ways.

But the clarion call of the "voice by the cedar tree" singing

> A passionate ballad gallant and gay,

awakens a love in the heart which revolutionizes and inspires the whole life. In Canto XI. my father expressed the longing for love in

> O let the solid ground
> Not fail beneath my feet:

in Canto XVII. the exultation of love, knowing that it is returned:

> Go not, happy day,
> From the shining fields.

But this blessedness is so intense that it borders on sadness, and my father's voice would break down when he came to

> I have led her home, my love, my only friend.
> There is none like her, none.

Joy culminates in "Come into the garden, Maud," and my father's eyes, which were through the other love-passages veiled by his drooping lids, would suddenly flash as he looked up and spoke these words, the passion in his voice deepening in the last words of the stanza.

> She is coming, my own, my sweet;
>   Were it ever so airy a tread,
> My heart would hear her and beat,
>   Were it earth in an earthy bed;
> My dust would hear her and beat,
>   Had I lain for a century dead;
> Would start and tremble under her feet,
>   And blossom in purple and red.

Then we heard after the duel the terrible wail of
agony and despair in

The fault was mine,

and the depth of forlorn misery in

Courage, poor heart of stone!

when the man feels that he is going mad, both read with
slow solemnity: then the delirious madness of

O me, why have they not buried me deep enough?

The lyrics in "Maud" which my father himself
liked best were

I have led her home,

and   O that 'twere possible,

and   Courage, poor heart of stone!

About the mad-scene one of the best-known doctors
for the insane wrote that it was "the most faithful
representation of madness since Shakespeare."

It is notable that two such appreciative critics as
Mr Gladstone and Dr Van Dyke wholly misapprehended
the meaning of "Maud" until they heard my father read
it, and that they both then publicly recanted their first
criticisms. "No one but a noble-minded man would
have done that" my father would say of Mr Gladstone.
Dr Van Dyke's recantation he did not live to read[1].

Mr Gladstone's recantation runs thus:

I can now see, and I at once confess, that a feeling, which had
reference to the growth of the war-spirit in the outer world at
the date of this article (*Quarterly Review*, 1855), dislocated my

[1] When Fanny Kemble heard that my father read his "Maud" finely,
she wrote: "I do not think any reading of Tennyson's can ever be as striking
and impressive as that 'Curse of Boadicea' that he intoned to us, while the
oak trees were writhing in the storm that lashed the windows and swept
over Blackdown the day we were there." (Unpublished MS.)

frame of mind, and disabled me from dealing even tolerably with the work as a work of imagination. Whether it is to be desired that a poem should require from common men a good deal of effort in order to comprehend it; whether all that is put into the mouth of the Soliloquist in "Maud" is within the lines of poetical verisimilitude, whether this poem has the full moral equilibrium which is so marked a characteristic of the sister-works; are questions open, perhaps, to discussion. But I have neither done justice in the text to its rich and copious beauties of detail, nor to its great lyrical and metrical power. And what is worse, I have failed to comprehend rightly the relation between particular passages in the poem and its general scope. This is, I conceive, not to set forth any coherent strain, but to use for poetical ends all the moods and phases allowable under the laws of the art, in a special form of character, which is impassioned, fluctuating and ill-grounded. The design, which seems to resemble that of the Ecclesiastes in another sphere, is arduous; but Mr Tennyson's power of execution is probably nowhere greater. Even as regards the passages devoted to war-frenzy, equity should have reminded me of the fine lines in the *latter* portion of x. 3 (Part i), and of the emphatic words v. 10 (Part ii):

> I swear to you, lawful and lawless war
> Are scarcely even akin.
>
> W. E. G. 1878[1].

Among the few who recognized merit in "Maud" were Henry Taylor, Jowett and the Brownings.

From Henry Taylor.

COLONIAL OFFICE, LONDON,
31*st July*, 1855.

MY DEAR TENNYSON,

I thank you much for sending me "Maud." I have only read it twice, but I have already a strong feeling of what it is. I say a feeling and not an opinion, for I am always disposed to have as little as possible to say to opinions in matters poetical.

---

[1] Gladstone's *Gleanings*, Vol. ii.

I felt the passion of it and the poetic spirit that is in it, and the poetic spirit that it seemed in some measure to bring back unto me. I am glad that there is some one living who can do me that service and glad that you are he.

Ever yours sincerely, H. TAYLOR.

In December Jowett writes:

I want to tell you how greatly I admire "Maud." No poem since Shakespeare seems to show equal power of the same kind, or equal knowledge of human nature. No modern poem contains more lines that ring in the ears of men. I do not know any verse out of Shakespeare in which the ecstasy of love soars to such a height.

He adds that the critics have "confused the hero with the author[1]."

Some of the reviews accused him of loving war,

[1] I take from Dr Mann, with some condensation, the following remarks about "Maud," because in the light of present criticism they are curious. "One member of the fraternity of critics immediately pronounced the poem to be a 'spasm,' another acutely discovered that it was a 'careless, visionary, and unreal allegory of the Russian War.' A third could not quite make up his mind whether the adjective 'mud' or 'mad' would best apply to the work, but thought, as there was only one small vowel redundant in the title in either case, both might do. A fourth found that the 'mud' concealed 'irony'; and the fifth, leaning rather to the mad hypothesis, nevertheless held that the madness was only assumed as an excuse for pitching the tone of the poetry in 'a key of extravagant sensibility.' Others of the multifold judgments were of opinion that it was 'a political fever,' an 'epidemic caught from the prevalent care-lessness of thought and rambling contemplativeness of the time'; 'obscurity mistaken for profundity,' 'the dead level of prose run mad'; 'absurdity such as even partial friendship must blush to tolerate,' 'rampant and rabid bloodthirstiness of soul.' These are but a few of the pleasant suggestions which critical acumen brought forward as its explanations of the inspiration of numbers that must nevertheless be musical."

Maud Vindicated.

One of the anonymous letters my father received he enjoyed repeating with a humorous intonation:

SIR, I used to worship you, but now I hate you. I loathe and detest you. You beast! So you've taken to imitating Longfellow.

Yours in aversion * * *.

and urging the country to war, charges which he
sufficiently answered in the "Epilogue to the Heavy
Brigade," ending with these lines:

> And here the singer for his Art
> Not all in vain may plead,
> The song that nerves a nation's heart
> Is in itself a deed.

The truth is that though he advocated the war of defence
and of liberty, and often said, "Peace at all price implies
war at all cost," no one loathed war more than he did, or
looked forward more passionately to the

Parliament of man, the Federation of the world,

when the earth at last should be one.

> A warless world, a single race, a single tongue,
> I have seen her far away, for is not Earth as yet so
> young?
> Every tiger madness muzzled, every serpent passion
> kill'd,
> Every grim ravine a garden, every blazing desert till'd,
> Robed in universal harvest up to either pole she
> smiles,
> *Universal ocean softly washing all her warless isles*[1].

What even his hero in "Maud" says is only that the
sins of the nation, "civil war" as he calls them, are
deadlier in their effect than what is commonly called war,
and that they may be in a measure subdued by the war
between nations which is an evil more easily recognized.

At first my father was nettled by these captious remarks of the "indolent reviewers," but afterwards would
take no notice of them, except to speak of them in a
half-pitiful, half-humorous, half-mournful manner. About

---

[1] This line he held to be one of the best of the kind he had ever written.

"Maud" and other monodramatic poems (the stories of which were his own creation) he said to me: "In a certain way, no doubt, poets and novelists, however dramatic they are, give themselves in their works. The mistake that people make is that they think the poet's poems are a kind of 'catalogue raisonné' of his very own self, and of all the facts of his life, not seeing that they often only express a poetic instinct, or judgment on character real or imagined, and on the facts of lives real or imagined. Of course some poems, like my 'Ode to Memory,' are evidently based on the poet's own nature, and on hints from his own life."

The poem was first entitled "Maud or the Madness." My father thought that part of the misunderstanding of "Maud" had arisen from a misconception of the story, so left me the following MS headings and notes.

PART I.

Sections

I.   Before the arrival of Maud.

II. First sight of Maud.

III. Visions of the night. The broad-flung ship-wrecking roar. In the Isle of Wight the roar can be heard nine miles away from the beach. (Many of the descriptions of Nature are taken from observations of natural phenomena at Farringford, although the localities in the poem are all imaginary.)

IV. Mood of bitterness after fancied disdain.

V.   He fights against his growing passion.

VI. First interview with Maud.

VII. He remembers his own and her father talking just before the birth of Maud.

VIII. That she did not return his love.

IX. First sight of the young lord.

X. The *Westminster Review* said this was an attack on John Bright. I did not know at the time that he was a Quaker. (It was not against Quakers but against peace-at-all-price men that the hero fulminates.)

XI. This was originally verse III. but I omitted it.

Will she smile if he presses her hand,
This lord-captain up at the Hall?
Captain! he to hold a command!
He can hold a cue, he can pocket a ball;
And sure not a bantam cockerel lives
With a weaker crow upon English land,
Whether he boast of a horse that gains,
Or cackle his own applause....

What use for a single mouth to rage
At the rotten creak of the State-machine;
Tho' it makes friends weep and enemies smile,
That here in the face of a watchful age,
The sons of a gray-beard-ridden isle
Should dance in a round of an old routine.

XII. Interview with Maud.

"Maud, Maud, Maud" is like the rook's caw.
"Maud is here, here, here" is like the call of the little birds.

XIII. Mainly prophetic. He sees Maud's brother who will not recognize him.

XVI. He will declare his love.

XVII.　Accepted.

XVIII.　Happy.　The sigh in the cedar branches seems
to chime in with his own yearning.

"*Sad astrology*" is modern astronomy, for of
old astrology was thought to sympathize with
and rule man's fate.

Not die but live a life of truest breath.　This is
the central idea, the holy power of Love.

XXI.　Before the Ball.

XXII.　In the Hall-Garden.

Part II.

Sections

I.　The Phantom (after the duel with Maud's
brother).

II.　In Brittany.　The shell undestroyed amid the
storm perhaps symbolizes to him his own
first and highest nature preserved amid the
storms of passion.

III.　He felt himself going mad.

IV.　Haunted after Maud's death.

" O that 'twere possible " appeared first in the
Keepsake.　Sir John Simeon years after
begged me to weave a story round this
poem and so " Maud " came into being.

V.　In the mad-house.

The second corpse is Maud's brother, the
lover's father being the first corpse, whom
the lover thinks that Maud's father has
murdered.

PART III.

VI. Sane but shattered. Written when the cannon
was heard booming from the battle-ships in
the Solent before the Crimean War.

Letters to and from friends, 1854–55.

To Gerald Massey.

FRESHWATER, I. OF WIGHT,
April 1st, 1854.

MY DEAR SIR,

In consequence of my change of residence I
did not receive your captivating volume till yesterday.
I am no reader of papers and Reviews and I had not
seen, nor even heard of any of your poems: my joy was
all the fresher and the greater in thus suddenly coming
on a poet of such fine lyrical impulse, and of so rich
half-oriental an imagination. It must be granted that
you make our good old English tongue crack and sweat
for it occasionally, but time will chasten all that. Go on
and prosper, and believe me grateful for your gift, and

Yours most truly, A. TENNYSON.

Letters to Dr Mann, author of "Maud Vindicated."

1855.

Thanks for your *Vindication.* No one with this
essay before him can in future pretend to misunderstand
my dramatic poem, " Maud ": your commentary is as
true as it is full, and I am really obliged to you for
defending me against the egregiously nonsensical imputation of having attacked the Quakers or Mr Bright:
you are not aware, perhaps, that another wiseacre accused me of calling Mr Layard an "Assyrian Bull!"

Yours very truly, A. TENNYSON.

Without the prestige of Shakespeare, *Hamlet* (if it came out now) would be treated in just the same way, so that one ought not to care for their cackling, not that I am comparing poor little "Maud" to the Prince, except as, what's the old quotation out of Virgil, *sic parvis componere, etc.* Would it not be better that all literary criticisms should be signed with the name or at least the initials of the writer? To sign political articles would be perhaps unadvisable and inconvenient, but my opinion is that we shall never have a good school of criticism in England while the writer is anonymous and irresponsible.

Believe me yours ever, A. T.

I am delighted with Miss Sewell's gift[1], tho' yet unseen. I should like as I have told her to learn something of the history of the naming of it: can you tell me anything? Please get it framed, we shall be half a year getting it done here. I think it should not have a great white margin except the artist herself desires it. Perhaps the lake was not called after your humble servant but another. I enclose you the note to Miss Sewell which please deliver and read if you choose.

A. T.

I wished for you much yesterday. Merwood[2] brought me a lump of snake's eggs, and I picked carefully out two little embryo snakes with bolting eyes and beating hearts. I laid them on a piece of white paper. Their hearts or blood-vessels beat for at *least* two hours after extraction. Does not that in some way explain why it is so very difficult to kill a snake? I was so sorry not to have you and your microscope here.

A. T.

[1] Miss Sewell had painted a picture of Lake Tennyson in New Zealand, so named by Sir Frederick Weld.

[2] Tenant at Farringford farm.

From Mrs Vyner, a stranger[1].

RIVER, NEW SOUTH WALES, 1855.

DEAR FRIEND,

I know that the poet's life must have its common-place daily sorrows and toils and that there must be moments when he even doubts his own gift, but I fancy a poet's heart must be so large and loving that he can feel for and forgive even folly. Folly it may be, and yet I *must* write and thank you with a true and grateful heart for the happy moments your thoughts and your pen have given me. I am in the wildest bush of Australia, far away from all that makes life beautiful and endurable excepting the strong and stern sense of duty, the consciousness that where God has placed us is our lot to be, and that our most becoming posture is to accept our destiny with grateful humility. You must let me tell you how in a lonely home among the mountains, with my young children asleep, my husband absent, no sound to be heard but the cry of the wild dog or the wail of the curlew, no lock or bolt to guard our solitary hut, strong in our utter helplessness I have turned (next to God's book) to you as a friend, and read far into the night till my lot seemed light and a joy seemed cast around my very menial toils: then I have said, "God bless the poet and put still some beautiful words and thoughts into his heart," and the burthen of life became pleasant to me or at least easy. If you are the man I feel you must be you will forgive this address: there are certain impulses which seem irresistible, and I believe these are the genuine, truthful moments of our life, and such an impulse has urged me to write to you, and I know that the blessing of a faithful heart cannot be bootless: and may He who seeth not as man seeth spare you to plead the cause of truth and to spurn foolish saws and sickly conventionalities. Farewell.

God bless you: always your friend,

MARGARET ANNA VYNER.

My father's aunt Mrs Russell was vexed at what she thought an attack on coal-mine owners in " Maud,"

---

[1] My father was deeply touched by this letter: and kept it among the things he most prized.

and so he writes: "I really could find it in my heart to be offended with such an imputation, for what must you think of me if you think me capable of such gratuitous and unmeaning personality and hostility? I am as sensitive a person as exists, and sooner than wound anyone in such a spiteful fashion, would consent never to write a line again; yea, to have my hand cut off at the wrist. Why, if you had the least suspicion that I had acted in this way, did you not inquire of me before? Now see, you the kindliest and tenderest of human beings, how you have wronged me, and cherished in your heart this accusation as baseless, no, more baseless, than a dream, for dreams have some better foundation in past things: but pray put it all out of your head."

To George Brimley.

FRESHWATER, I. W.
Nov. 28th, 1855.

SIR,

I wish to assure you that I quite close with your commentary on "Maud." I may have agreed with portions of other critiques on the same poem, which have been sent to me; but when I saw your notice I laid my finger upon it and said, "There, that is my meaning." Poor little "Maud," after having run the gauntlet of so much brainless abuse and anonymous spite, has found a critic. Therefore believe her father (not the gray old wolf) to be

Yours not unthankfully, A. TENNYSON.

P.S. But there are two or three points in your comment to which I should take exception, e.g. "The writer of the fragments, etc.," surely the speaker or the thinker rather than the writer; again, as to the character of the love, do any of the expressions "rapturous," "painful," "childish," however they may apply to some of the poems, fully characterize the 18th? is it not something deeper? but perhaps some day I may discuss these things with you, and therefore I will say no more here, except that I shall be very glad to see you if ever you come to the Isle of Wight.

To F. G. Tuckerman.

1855.

DEAR MR TUCKERMAN,

I have just returned home (i.e. to Farringford) from a visit to London, during which I called on Moxon, and found your kind present of books waiting for me. I fear that you must have thought me neglectful in not immediately acknowledging them: and so I should have done had I not been waiting to send along with my thanks a small volume of my own, containing some of the things I repeated to you in my little smoking-attic here. These poems, when printed, I found needed considerable elision and so the book has hung on hand.

When I arrived here I found that my small smoking-room did not smell of smoke at all, nay was even fragrant. I could not at first make it out. At last I perceived it was owing to the Russian leather on your Webster which you made mine. Even so (as some one says),

> " The actions of the just
> Smell sweet and blossom in the dust "—

and there was dust enough on the table almost to justify the application.

You will find in my little volume " The Charge of the Light Brigade." * * * * It is not a poem on which

I pique myself, but I cannot help fancying that, such as it is, I have improved it.

Farewell and forgive my silence hitherto. I shall always remember with pleasure your coming to see me in the frost and our pleasant talk together. Did you see in your paper that the Oxford University would make me a Doctor the other day, and how the young men shouted?

I am, dear Mr Tuckerman,

Ever yours, A. TENNYSON.

To the Rev. G. G. Bradley[1].

FARRINGFORD,
August 25th, 1855.

DEAR MR BRADLEY,

Many thanks for the Arnold: nobody can deny that he is a poet. "The Merman" was an old favourite of mine, and I like him as well as ever. "The Scholar Gipsy" is quite new to me, and I have already an affection for him, which I think will increase. There are several others which seem very good, so that altogether I may say that you have conferred a great boon upon me. I have received a Scotch paper, in which it is stated that poor "Maud" is to be slashed all to pieces by that mighty man, that pompholygous, broad-blown Apollodorus, the gifted X. Her best friends do not expect her to survive it!

I am yours very truly,

A. TENNYSON.

[1] Dean of Westminster.

From J. Ruskin.

DENMARK HILL, 12*th November*, 1855.

MY DEAR SIR,

I hear of so many stupid and feelingless misunderstandings of "Maud" that I think it may perhaps give you some little pleasure to know my sincere admiration of it throughout.

I do not like its versification so well as much of your other work, not because I do not think it good of its kind, but because I do not think that wild kind quite so good, and I am sorry to have another cloud put into the sky of one's thoughts by the sad story, but as to the general bearing and delicate finish of the thing in its way, I think no admiration can be extravagant.

It is a compliment to myself, not to you, if I say that I think with you in *all* things about the war.

I am very sorry you put the "Some one had blundered" out of the "Light Brigade [1]."

It was precisely the most tragical line in the poem. It is as true to its history as essential to its tragedy.

Believe me sincerely yours, J. RUSKIN.

From Herbert Spencer (about "The Two Voices").

7 MARLBOROUGH GARDENS,
ST JOHN'S WOOD, LONDON, 1855.

SIR,

I happened recently to be re-reading your Poem "The Two Voices," and coming to the verse

Or if thro' lower lives I came —
Tho' all experience past became
Consolidate in mind and frame —

it occurred to me that you might like to glance through a book which applies to the elucidation of mental science, the hypothesis to which you refer. I therefore beg your acceptance of *Psychology* which I send by this post.

With much sympathy yours,

HERBERT SPENCER.

[1] Some friends of excellent critical judgment prevailed upon him to omit this phrase which was however soon re-inserted: for it was originally the keynote of the poem.

With the proceeds of the sale of "Maud" Farringford was bought, and my mother's journal says:

April 24th, 1856.   This morning a letter came from Mr G. S. Venables saying that Mr Chapman pronounced the title of Farringford good.   We have agreed to buy, so I suppose this ivied home among the pine-trees is ours.   Went to our withy holt: such beautiful blue hyacinths, orchises, primroses, daisies, marsh-marigolds and cuckoo-flowers.   Wild cherry trees too with single snowy blossom, and the hawthorns white with their "pearls of May."   The park has for many days been rich with cowslips and furze in bloom.   The elms are a golden wreath at the foot of the down; to the north of the house the mespilus and horse-chestnut are in flower and the apple-trees are covered with rosy buds.   A. dug the bed ready for the rhododendrons.   A thrush was singing among the nightingales and other birds, as he said "mad with joy."   At sunset, the golden green of the trees, the burning splendour of Blackgang Chine and St Catharine's, and the red bank of the primeval river, contrasted with the turkis-blue of the sea (that is our view from the drawing-room), make altogether a miracle of beauty.   We are glad that Farringford is ours.

FARRINGFORD

From a Water-colour Drawing by Mrs Allingham

CHAPTER XX.

HOME LIFE AND "IDYLLS OF THE KING."

1856–1859.

A thousand thanks for your charming letter from the Isle of Wight with suggestive date of Bonchurch (the only church you went to that day), and the spirited outline sketch of the Idyllic Poet serenely ploughing his windy acres. How must you have enjoyed!... The "Idylls (of the King)" are a brilliant success. Rich tapestries, wrought as only Tennyson could have done them, and worthy to hang by the *Faerie Queen*. I believe there is no discordant voice on this side of the water.

(From H. W. Longfellow to James T. Fields, 1854.)

1856.

My father went to the Grange (Lord Ashburton's) in January, and met the Carlyles, Venables, Brookfields, Tom Taylors, Goldwin Smith and Spedding. Brookfield wrote: "Alfred has been most cheerful and the life of the party." The note by my father is: "It seems a house not uneasy to live in, only I regret my little fumitory at Farringford. Here they smoke among the oranges, lemons, and camellias....I cannot see in Lady Ashburton a touch of the haughtiness which fame attributes to her. She is most perfectly natural, tho' like enough she sometimes snubs her own grade now and then, when she sees presumption and folly. But as Brookfield said this morning, 'She is very loyal to her *printers*.'"

During the winter evenings of 1855 my father would translate the *Odyssey* aloud into Biblical prose to my mother, who writes, "Thus I get as much as it is possible to have of the true spirit of the original."

He had been evolving the main scheme of the "Idylls of the King" at different periods during the last twenty years and more: the Morte d'Arthur episode had appeared in the volume of 1842. He resumed the plan with "Merlin and Nimue" (called "Vivien") in February; and in the "Forest of Broceliande" are many reminiscences of what was now the near scenery of the New Forest[1]. This Idyll was finished by March 31st, and "Geraint and Enid" begun on April 16th.

Meantime for daily exercise he planted trees and shrubs; rolled the lawn and dug in the kitchen garden, taking all the while a loving note of Nature. Thus as he was digging one day a well-known line formed itself:

> As careful robins eye the delver's toil.

Farringford being now his property, the Twickenham furniture was brought over to the new home. As it was unpacked, my father's eye was struck by a certain crimson-covered sofa and some oak chairs grouped together in the farmyard in front of the old thatched farmstead and the ivy-covered wall through which the kitchen garden is entered. "What a picture it would make!" he said; repeating his new song in "Enid," that then for the first time came to him:

> Turn fortune, turn thy wheel and lower the proud.

Presently, within doors, while the books were being sorted and rearranged, all imaginable things strewed over the drawing-room floor, and the chairs and tables in wild disarray, Prince Albert called. He had driven over suddenly from Osborne. The parlour-maid went to the front door, heard the Prince's name announced, and, being bewildered and not knowing into what room to show him, stood stock still; so the Equerry, I have been told, took

---

[1] On one occasion he stayed in the New Forest with his friend, the well-known ornithologist, Lord Lilford, in order to observe the bird-life there.

her by the shoulders and turned her round, bidding her
lead them in.   The Prince expressed great admiration of
the view from the drawing-room window, and one of the
party gathered a bunch of cowslips which H. R. H. said
he must take to the Queen.

From the first the Prince was very cordial, and
impressed my father as being a man of strong and
self-sacrificing nature.

In June news came that R.'s bank would probably
break and that all my father's little savings might be lost.
On July 2nd my mother wrote: " A. showed a noble
disregard of money, much as the loss would affect us."
That evening, so as to give her courage, he asked her
to play and sing the grand Welsh national air, " Come
to battle": and afterwards, to divert themselves from
dwelling on the possible loss, they hung their Michael
Angelo engravings round the drawing-room.

In July and August my father and mother took us
children to Wales, and here " Enid " was all but finished.
We stayed at Llangollen, then at Dolgelly, and at Barmouth.   My father spoke of " the high rejoicing lines of
Cader Idris."   My mother wrote: "*Sept. 8th.* A. climbed
Cader Idris.   Pouring rain came on.   I and the children
waited a long time for him.   I heard the roar of waters,
streams and cataracts, and I never saw anything more
awful than that great veil of rain drawn straight over
Cader Idris, pale light at the lower edge.   It looked as
if death were behind it, and made me shudder when I
thought he was there.   A message came from him by the
guide that he had gone to Dolgelly."

It was near Festiniog that he heard the roar of a
cataract above the roar of the torrent, and wrote that
Virgilian simile :

For as one,
That listens near a torrent mountain-brook,
All thro' the crash of the near cataract hears

> The drumming thunder of the huger fall
> At distance, were the soldiers wont to hear
> His voice in battle.

He particularly admired the still pools of the torrent in the " Torrent Walk " at Dolgelly, and the mysterious giant steps of Cwn Bychan. Harlech, Festiniog, Llanid-loes, Builth, Caerleon were the next halting-places; and on September 16th he wrote: " The Usk murmurs by the windows, and I sit like King Arthur in Caerleon. This is a most quiet, half-ruined village of about 1500 inhabitants with a little museum of Roman tombstones and other things." From Caerleon he made expeditions to Caerphilly, Merthyr Tydvil, Raglan; and then we all returned by Brecon, Gloucester and Salisbury home. With the help of local schoolmasters in Wales my parents had learned some Welsh, and now read together the *Hanes Cymru* (Welsh History), the *Mabinogion* and *Llywarch Hen.*

On Dec. 31st a characteristic letter was sent to a stranger who had forwarded a volume of verse:

I have as you desired considered your poem, and though I make it a rule to decline passing any judgment on poems, I cannot in this instance refrain from giving you a word of advice.

Follow your calling diligently, for be assured, work, far from being a hardship, is a blessing, and if you are a poet indeed, you will find in it a help not a hindrance. You might, if you chose, offer these lines to some maga-zine, but you must not be surprised if they are refused, for the poetic gift is so common in these days that hundreds must have to endure this disappointment, and I should not be an honest friend if I did not prepare you for that.

I should by no means recommend you to risk the publication of a volume on your own account. The publication of verse is almost always attended with loss. As an amusement to yourself and your friends, the writing is all very well. Accept my good wishes and believe me,

Your obedient servant,

A. TENNYSON.

1857.

An invitation was sent in January to Mr and Mrs Carlyle. The latter answered:

5 CHEYNE ROAD, CHELSEA,
21st January, 1857.

MY DEAR MRS TENNYSON,

You *are* a darling woman to have gone and written to me on the "voluntary principle" such a kind little note! *You* to have been at the trouble to know that *I* was ill! *You* to express regret at *my* illness. I feel both surprised and gratified, as if I were an *obsolete* word that some great Poet (Alfred Tennyson for example) had taken a notion to look up in the Dictionary.

In *London*, when one is sick, especially when one continues sick for three months, one falls so out of thought! it is much if even your female friend, in the next street, do not weary of you and then forget you! I say female advisedly for, to give the Devil his due, I find that men hold out longer than women against the loss of one's "powers of pleasing."

Now however I begin to be about: and have no longer the pretext of illness for straining what Mr Carlyle calls " the inestimable privilege of being as ugly and stupid and disagreeable as ever one likes!" and my friends drop in more frequently and sit much longer!

The heartiest thanks for your invitation to Freshwater.

Wouldn't I like to go and visit you if that man would leave his eternal *Frederick* and come along! nay wouldn't I like to go on my own small basis, if only I had the *nerve* for it, which I have not yet! *He* goes nowhere, sees nobody, only for two hours a day he rides, like the wild German Hunter, on a horse he has bought, and which seems to like the sort of thing! Such a horse! he (not the horse) never wearies, in the intervals of *Frederick*, of celebrating the creature's "good sense, courage and sensibility!" "Not once," he says, "has the creature shown the slightest disagreement from *him* in *any question of Intellect*" (more than can be said of most living Bipeds)! I wrote to a relation in Scotland, "If this horse of Mr C.'s dies, he will certainly write its biography," and that very day he said to me, "My dear, I wish I could find out about the genealogy of that horse of mine! and some particulars of its life! I am beginning to feel sure it is a Cockney."

Poor Lady Ashburton has made nothing by leaving the Grange deserted this winter, she has been quite ill ever since she went to Nice.

May I offer my affectionate regards to your husband? And may I give yourself a kiss?

Yours very truly,

JANE WELSH CARLYLE.

In April a report reached us that Tom Moore was dying. A friend writes: "This darling old poet is only just alive, mind and body. X goes over frequently to see him and read him your poems, which he cries over and delights in."

"Enid" and "Nimue, or The True and the False" were put into print this summer.

In June the American translator of *Faust*, Bayard Taylor, stayed at Farringford and was full of talk. Among other things he told my father that the most beautiful sight in the world was a Norwegian forest in winter, sheathed in ice, the sun rising over it and making the whole landscape one rainbow of flashing diamonds.

Taylor published the following account of his visit to us:

As we drew near Freshwater, my coachman pointed out Farringford, a cheerful gray country mansion with a small thick-grassed park before it, a grove behind, and beyond all, a deep shoulder of the chalk downs, a gap in which, at Freshwater, showed the dark blue horizon of the Channel. Leaving my luggage at one of the two little inns, I walked to the house, with lines from "Maud" chiming in my mind. "The dry-tongued laurel" shone glossily in the sun, the cedar "sighed for Lebanon" on the lawn, and "the liquid azure bloom of a crescent of sea" glimmered afar. I had not been two minutes in the drawing-room before Tennyson walked in. So unlike are the published portraits of him, that I was almost in doubt as to his identity. The engraved heads suggest a moderate stature, but he is tall and broad-shouldered as a son of Anak, with hair, beard and eyes of southern darkness. Something in the lofty brow and aquiline nose suggests Dante, but such a deep mellow chest-voice never could have come from Italian lungs. He proposed a walk, as the day was wonderfully clear and beautiful. We climbed the steep comb of the chalk cliff, and slowly wandered westward till we reached the Needles, at the extremity of the Island and some three or four miles from his residence. During the conversation with which we beguiled the way, I was struck with the variety of his knowledge. Not a little flower on the downs, which the sheep had spared, escaped his notice, and the geology of the coast, both terrestrial and submarine, was perfectly familiar to him. I thought of a remark I once heard from the lips of a distinguished English author (Thackeray), that "Tennyson was the wisest man he knew," and could well believe that he was sincere in making it.

July 9th. My mother writes in her journal: "A. has brought me as a birthday present the first two lines that he has made of 'Guinevere' which might be the nucleus of a great poem. Arthur is parting from Guinevere and says:

'But hither shall I never come again,
Never lie by thy side; see thee no more:
Farewell!'"

July 25th. The following letter was received from Mr Ruskin about the edition of the *Poems* illustrated by Dante Gabriel Rossetti, Millais, Holman Hunt and others, in which my father had taken great interest, having called on most of the artists so as to give them his views of what the illustrations ought to be.

EDINBURGH,
July 24th, 1857.

MY DEAR SIR,

It is a long time since I have heard from you and I do not like the mildew to grow over what little memory you may have of me.

It is however no excuse for writing to say that I wanted to congratulate you on the last edition of your poems. Indeed it might be and I hope will be some day better managed, still many of the plates are very noble things, though not, it seems to me, illustrations of your poems.

I believe in fact that good pictures never can be; they are always another poem, subordinate but wholly different from the poet's conception, and serve chiefly to show the reader how variously the same verses may affect various minds. But these woodcuts will be of much use in making people think and puzzle a little; art was getting quite a matter of form in book-illustrations, and it does not so much matter whether any given vignette is right or not, as whether it contains thought or not, still more whether it contains any kind of plain facts. If people have no sympathy with St Agnes, or if people as soon as they get a distinct idea of a living girl who probably got scolded for dropping her candle-wax about the convent-stairs, and caught cold by looking too long out of the window in her bedgown, feel no true sympathy with her, they can have no sympathy in them.

But we P. R. B.'s [1] must do better for you than this some day: meantime I do congratulate you on "The wind is blowing in turret and tree," and Rossetti's Sir Galahad and Lady of Shalott, and one or two more.

[1] Pre-Raphaelite Brotherhood.

Please send me a single line to Denmark Hill, Camberwell, and believe me

Faithfully yours,

J. RUSKIN.

This summer the tour was to Manchester, Coniston, Inverary Castle, and Carstairs (the home of my father's college friend Monteith). On this journey he read aloud *Tom Brown's School-Days* to my mother, enjoying it thoroughly.

When at Manchester my parents heard Dickens recite his *Christmas Carol.*

A visit was made to the Exhibition held there, and much time spent in studying Holman Hunt's pictures, the Turner sketches, Mulready's drawings, and various fine Gainsboroughs and Reynolds.

Hawthorne was in the same room, and my father afterwards expressed great regret that he had not been introduced to the author of *The Scarlet Letter.* Hawthorne wrote: "Gazing at him with all my eyes I liked him well, and rejoiced more in him than in all the wonders of the Exhibition."

After the tour Mrs Browning wrote to enquire after his health:

ALLA VILLA TOSCANA,
BAGNI DI LUCCA.
September 6th, 1857.

MY DEAR MRS TENNYSON,

We see in the *Galignani* that Mr Tennyson is not well, by the side of threats of fall of our Indian empire and other disasters; and it disquiets us to the point that I must write to ask you whether it is true or not and how far? The trade of newspapers is to blow bubbles, and a little breath more or less determines the size of the bubble.

May this be a mere bubble! write one word to say so. Oh may you be able to smile at my question from over the sea!

But remember we have lost our friend, your brother Frederick, from whom we could always hear about you! He has devastated our Florence for us by going to live at Pisa; and now he is farther off still, at Genoa, while we are mountain-locked here with no news from anybody.

The spring and summer have been heavy to me from a family grief[1], but we three are well, thank God, living quietly in the shade till the sun shall have done his worst and best alas! in this beautiful Italy. Little Penini[2] is very happy, gossiping with the Contadini, among whom he passes for un Vero Fiorentino, though he talks English inside the house as fast as Italian out of it. I hope that one day he may know your boys. How sorry I was to leave England last year without seeing them or you, or "King Arthur"!

My husband made me envious by the advantage he had over me in having listened to a certain exquisite music of which I could only dream.

Just before we left Florence to come hither, we saw your brother Frederick who went there for a day or two. We thought we never saw him looking so well. It was provoking to hear, very provoking; but he maintained that he *slept* at Pisa as he never could at Florence. I was very cross, and inclined to retort that at Pisa one slept by day as well as by night, the place was so dull.

Think of our loss having to lose him!

Dear Mrs Tennyson, will you send me just a few words? Really we are anxious. Being in all affection to both of you, his and yours,

ELIZABETH BARRETT BROWNING
& R. B.

A letter came about this time from Colonel Phipps, saying that the Queen desired that a stanza should be added to *God save the Queen* for a concert to be given at Buckingham Palace on the evening of the Princess Royal's wedding-day. These two stanzas were sent in answer, and published in the *Times*, January 26th, 1858:

---

[1] Death of her father.
[2] Familiar name of their son.

God bless our Prince and Bride!
God keep their lands allied,
　　God save the Queen!
Clothe them with righteousness,
Crown them with happiness,
Them with all blessings bless,
　　God save the Queen.

Fair fall this hallow'd hour,
Farewell our England's flower,
　　God save the Queen!
Farewell, fair rose of May!
Let both the peoples say,
God bless thy marriage-day,
　　God bless the Queen.

For the last few months the Indian Mutiny had excited the profoundest interest throughout the country, and on Christmas Day the account of the relief of Lucknow arrived. Havelock's death, which had occurred on Nov. 25th, was not then known. When this sad news came, my father wrote the following lines:

Havelock. Nov. 25th, 1857. (Unpublished.)

Bold Havelock march'd,
Many a mile went he,
Every mile a battle,
Every battle a victory.

Bold Havelock march'd,
Charged with his gallant few,
Ten men fought a thousand,
Slew them and overthrew.

Bold Havelock march'd,
Wrought with his hand and his head,
March'd and thought and fought,
March'd and fought himself dead.

Bold Havelock died,
Tender and great and good,
And every man in Britain
Says " I am of Havelock's blood ! "

1858.

In January "The Parting of Arthur and Guinevere"
was finished and my mother records her first impression
— " It is awe-inspiring."   On March 8th the entry in
her journal is: " To-day he has written his song of
' Too Late,' and has said it to me "; and on March
15th, " ' Guinevere ' is finally completed."

My father then occasionally wrote in his new summer-
house looking towards the down and the sea; and on
the windows of which he was painting marvellous
dragons and sea-serpents.   " One day " (she says),
" while writing his ' Guinevere,' A. spoke of ' the want
of reverence now-a-days for great men, whose brightness,
like that of the luminous bodies in the Heaven, makes
the dark spaces look the darker.' "

At this time he sent a letter to Dr Mann in Natal:

Our winter has been the mildest I have ever known.
I read of ripe pomegranates hanging on a houseside at
Bath, and I myself counted scores of our wild summer
roses on a hedge near, flourishing in December and lasting
on into January, tho' now gone, for the temperature has
changed.   They were perfectly fragrant, and I brought
home a bouquet of them and put them in water.   You
ask after the farm?   I cannot say that * * is going on
satisfactorily, very niggard of manure in the fields and
ever doing his best to 'reave me of my rent by working
at little odd jobs as a set off, so that at the end of the
year, all things deducted, I get almost nothing.   I am
now building a little summer-house to catch the southern

sun in Maiden's Croft, if you remember what field that is. I shall sit there and bask in the sunbeams and think of you far south. How I should love to rove about that parklike scenery of which you give such a fascinating account!

Yours ever, A. TENNYSON.

P.S. I may tell you however that young Swinburne called here the other day with a college friend of his, and we asked him to dinner, and I thought him a very modest and intelligent young fellow. Moreover I read him what you vindicated[1], but what I particularly admired in him was that he did not press upon me any verses of his own. Good-bye. How desolate No. 7 B. T. must feel itself!

Several friends urged the immediate publication of the newly-written Idylls, among them Jowett, who says:

I have great pleasure in sending some books which I hope you will accept, the best books in the world (except the Bible), Homer and Plato.

I take the opportunity also of enclosing Lemprière's *Dictionary*. The price is 1s. 6d. The bookseller valued it so little that he offered to give me the book. I have added two or three other books which I thought you might like to see, the translation of the Vedas as a specimen of the oldest thing in the world, Hegel's *Philosophy of History*, which is just "the increasing purpose that through the ages runs" buried under a heap of categories. If you care to look at it will you turn to the pages I have marked at the beginning? It is a favourite book of mine. I do not feel certain of the impression it will make on anyone else.

I also send you the latest and best work on Mythology, and Bunsen's new *Bibelbuch*, which, from the little I have read, seems to be an interesting and valuable introduction to Scripture. What

---

[1] Later Swinburne writes: "'Maud' is the poem of the deepest charm and fullest delight, pathos and melody ever written, even by Mr Tennyson."

a cartload of heavy literature! Do not trouble yourself to read or to send it back to me : I will carry it away some day myself.

I fear I have no news to tell you, and "the art of letter-writing" Dr Johnson says "consists solely in telling news."

May I say a word about "mosquitoes[1]"? Anyone who cares about you is deeply annoyed that you are deterred by them from writing or publishing. The feeling grows and brings in after years the still more painful and deeper feeling that they have prevented you from putting out half your powers. Nothing is so likely to lead to misrepresentation. Persons don't understand that sensitiveness is often combined with real manliness as well as great intellectual gifts, and they regard it as a sign of fear and weakness.

A certain man on a particular day has his stomach out of order and the stomach "getteth him up into the brain," and he calls another man "morbid." He is morbid himself and wants soothing words, and the whole world is morbid with dissecting and analysing itself and wants to be comforted and put together again. Might not this be the poet's office, to utter the "better voice" while Thackeray is uttering the worse one? I don't mean to blame Thackeray, for I desire to take the world as it is in this present age, crammed with self-consciousness, and no doubt Thackeray's views are of some value in the direction of anti-humbug.

But there is another note needed afterwards to show the good side of human nature and to condone its frailties which Thackeray will never strike. That note would be most thankfully received by the better part of the world.

Give my love to Hallam and Lionel. Tell Hallam I have put his letter "where I can always see it," and that I read every day about "Louise."

No more about "mosquitoes," I have bored you enough. With most kind regards to Mrs Tennyson,

Ever yours truly,

B. JOWETT.

At this time Lord Dufferin wrote from Highgate, with a copy of his *Letters from High Latitudes*.

---

[1] Spiteful critics.

My dear Mr Tennyson,

I am going to do a very bold thing, but in asking you to accept the accompanying book I hope you will consider I am only obeying an impulse I have felt for many many years, but to which until now I have never had any excuse for giving way.

For the first 20 years of my life I not only did not care for poetry, but to the despair of my friends absolutely disliked it, at least so much of it as until that time had fallen in my way. In vain my mother read to me Dryden, Pope, Byron, Young, Cowper and all the standard classics of the day, each seemed to me as distasteful as I had from early infancy found Virgil: and I shall never forget her dismay when at a literary dinner I was cross-examined as to my tastes, and blushingly confessed before an Olympus of poets that I rather disliked poetry than otherwise.

Soon afterwards however I fell in with a volume of yours, and suddenly felt such a sensation of delight as I never experienced before. A new world seemed open to me, and from that day, by a constant study of your works, I gradually worked my way to a thorough appreciation of what is good in all kinds of authors.

Naturally enough I could not help feeling very grateful to the Orpheus whose music had made the gate of poet-land fly open, and for years I longed to make your acquaintance. Now that I have done so I cannot help wishing to make you a little thank-offering as a token of my sense of what I owe to you, and however insignificant, I trust you will accept it as being the best and only thing I have to give.

Ever yours sincerely, DUFFERIN.

April 5th. Professor Tyndall, Mr Newman and Mr Dicey called: my father said of Tyndall: "He is such a good fellow, so unscornful and genial, so full of imagination and of enthusiasm for his work!"

In July we stayed at Little Holland House, Kensington, with the Prinseps: and here my father began

"The Fair Maid of Astolat," and read aloud "The Grandmother."

Watts was at work on what his friends called "the great moonlight portrait" of the Bard.

It was then that my father met Ruskin again. A voice from the corner of the room exclaimed: "Jones, you are gigantic." This was Ruskin apostrophizing Burne Jones as an artist.

From Little Holland House my father started on a trip to Norway, and he wrote in his Letter-Diary:

Started from Hull on July 23rd. Saw E. on board the little New Holland Steamer, and waved my handkerchief as both our boats were moving off: watched the two lights of Spurn Point till they became one star and then faded away. Next day very fine but in the night towards morning storm arose and our topmast was broken off. I stood next morning a long time by the cabin door and watched the green sea looking like a mountainous country, far off waves with foam at the top looking like snowy mountains bounding the scene ; one great wave, green-shining, past with all its crests smoking high up beside the vessel[1]. As I stood there came a sudden hurricane and roared drearily in the funnel for twenty seconds and past away.

Christiansand. Went up into the town and saw the wooden houses.

---

[1] They couch'd their spears and prick'd their steeds, and thus,
   Their plumes driv'n backward by the wind they made
   In moving, all together down upon him
   Bare, as a wild wave in the wide North-sea,
   Green-glimmering toward the summit, bears, with all
   Its stormy crests that smoke against the skies,
   Down on a bark, and overbears the bark,
   And him that helms it, so they overbore
   Sir Lancelot and his charger.
                              "Lancelot and Elaine."

Alfred Tennyson.
from the portrait in the possession of Lady Henry Somerset
painted by G. F. Watts, R.A. in 1859.

August 1st. Christiania. Magnificent seas on the way here. At Christiansand called on a Mr Murch, and the Frau Murch gave me a splendid bouquet of flowers : arrived here at 6 this afternoon. I write this at the house of Mr Crowe, consul, looking over the Sound — very pretty in the evening light. Am not quite certain whether I shall join Barrett and the other.

August 2nd. Christiania. I let Barrett and Tweedie go by themselves to Bergen. I am starting to-day to see the Riukan Foss with Mr Woodfall, a very quiet sensible man, and we shall take our time. I have had great kindness from the Crowes. Yesterday a Norwegian introduced himself at the hotel, and began to spout my own verses to me ; and I likewise rather to my annoyance found myself set down in the Christiania papers as " Den berömte engelske Digter."

I have seen the Riukan Foss. Magnificent power of water ; weird blue light behind the fall.

On his return the Frederick Maurices visited us at Farringford. Mr Maurice read family prayers in the morning, and my mother notes : "A. rejoiced as much as I did in his reading — ' the most earnest and holiest reading,' A. said, ' he had ever heard.' "

In the evenings my father recited his new poems " The Grandmother " and "Sea Dreams [1]," saying that the rascal in " Sea Dreams " was drawn from a man who had grossly cheated him in early life. Mr Maurice was charmed with the place :

> Groves of pine on either hand,
> To break the blast of winter, stand ;
> And further on, the hoary Channel
> Tumbles a billow on chalk and sand.

[1] First published in *Macmillan's Magazine*, Jan. 1860.

If his doctrine had been somewhat more within ordinary comprehension, my father was of opinion that he would have taken his place as foremost thinker among the Churchmen of our time. Consequently the following dedication of Maurice's *Theological Essays* gave him great pleasure.

> MY DEAR SIR,
>
> I have maintained in these *Essays* that a Theology which does not correspond to the deepest thoughts and feelings of human beings cannot be a true Theology. Your writings have taught me to enter into many of these thoughts and feelings. Will you forgive me the presumption of offering you a book which at least acknowledges them and does them homage?
>
> As the hopes which I have expressed in this volume are more likely to be fulfilled to our children than to ourselves, I might perhaps ask you to accept it as a present to one of your name, in whom you have given me a very sacred interest[1]. Many years, I trust, will elapse, before he knows that there are any controversies in the world into which he has entered. Would to God that in a few more he may find that they have ceased! At all events, if he should look into these *Essays*, they may tell him what meaning some of the former generation attached to words, which will be familiar and dear to his generation, and to those that follow his, how there were some who longed that the bells of our churches might indeed
>
> > Ring out the darkness of the land,
> > Ring in the Christ that is to be.
>
> Believe me, my dear Sir,
>
> > Yours very truly and gratefully,
> >
> > > F. D. MAURICE.

Two ideas which Maurice expressed my father would quote with approbation, that the "real Hell was the

---

[1] See p. 358.

absence of God from the human soul, and that all
religions seemed to him to be imperfect manifestations
of the true Christianity."

I remember too his reading with admiration this
passage from Maurice's *Friendship of Books.* " If I do
not give you extracts from any of Milton's specially
controversial writings, it is not that I wish to pass them
over because the conclusions in them are often directly
opposed to mine, for I think that I have learnt most
from those that are so."

Oct. 4th. " To-day," my mother says, " A. took a
volume of the *Morte d'Arthur* and read a noble passage
about the battle with the Romans.   He went to meet Mr
and Mrs Roebuck at dinner at Swainston : and the comet
was grand, with Arcturus shining brightly over the nucleus.   At dinner he said he must leave the table to look
at it and they all followed.   They saw Arcturus seemingly dance as if mad [1] when it passed out of the comet's
tail.   He said of the comet's tail, ' It is like a besom of
destruction sweeping the sky.' "   When he returned next
night he " observed the comet from his platform [2], and,
when he came down to tea, read some *Paradise Lost.*"

Oct. 17th.   He read aloud " The Rape of the
Lock," and noted the marvellous skill of many of
the couplets.

November.   My father writes : " I have just seen
Ruskin : he says that the Signor's (G. F. Watts') portrait
of me is the grandest thing he has seen in that line,
but so he said of (Woolner's) bust [3]."

During these last months of the year he was full of
the Queen's wise proclamation to India after the trans-
ference of the government from the Company to the

---

[1] Alluded to in "Harold."

[2] The platform on the top of the house was a favourite place with him at
night, and there he continually observed the stars.

[3] Now in the Library of Trinity College, Cambridge.

Crown.   The Indian Mutiny had stirred him to the depths.

Letters from the Rev. B. Jowett.

Dec. 1858.

DEAR MRS TENNYSON,

We shall long remember your kind hospitality, which made the Easter Vacation a very happy time to us.

You asked me whether I could suggest any subjects for poetry.   I have been so presumptuous as to think of some.   I don't believe that poetical feelings and imagery on subjects can ever be exhausted.   That is only a fancy which comes over us when our minds are dry or in moments of depression.   This generation is certainly more poetical and imaginative than the last, and perhaps in spite of the critics the next may be more poetical than our own.

And as to the critics their power is not really great.   Waggon-loads of them are lighting fires every week or on their way to the grocers.

I often fancy that the critical form of modern literature is like the rhetorical one which overlaid ancient literature and will be regarded as that is, at its true worth in after times.   One drop of natural feeling in poetry or the true statement of a single new fact is already felt to be of more value than all the critics put together.

I suggested "old age" to Mr Tennyson, a sort of "In Memoriam" over a lost child, wandering in soothing strains over all the thoughts and feelings of the aged.   It always seems to me that "old age" has been badly treated by poets notwithstanding Burns' beautiful ballad.   Its beauty, its sadness, its peace, its faded experience of life are good elements of poetry. An old lady once said to me quite simply, "The spirits of my children always seem to hover about me[1]."   Might not something of the kind be expressed in verse?   If it could, like "The May Queen," it would touch the chords of many hearts.

The 2 Sam. xix. 34, 35 is to me a very affecting passage.

---

[1] My father had heard this saying before, and it was the germ of "The Grandmother."

I wish Mr Tennyson could be persuaded to put the "Dogma of Immortality" to verse, not the fanciful hope of Immortality from "recollections of childhood," nor the conceptions of a future life derived from the imagery of Scripture such as are common in devotional poetry, but an heroic measure suited to manly minds embodying the deep ethical feeling which convinces us that the end of the Maker though dark is not here. I believe such a poem might be a possession for the world and better (what a bathos!) than ten thousand sermons.

Subjects like blackberries seem to me capable of being gathered off every hedge. (That shows the folly of suggesting what anybody can find for themselves anywhere.) I do not see why the Greek Mythology might not be the subject of a poem; not Wordsworth's "Lively Grecian," but such as it is in the philosophical idea of it as the twilight of the human mind, which lingers still among forms of sense and is unable to pierce them.

Have not many sciences such as Astronomy or Geology a side of feeling which is poetry? No sight touches ordinary persons so much as a starlight night.

I think you once said to me that "Whole philosophies might be contained in a line of verse." Is it not true also that whole periods of history, seen by the light of modern ideas, admit of being described in short passages of poetry? Representative men such as Charlemagne or Hildebrand seem to me safer than the shadowy personages of the legends of romance. The Coronation of Charlemagne, and the scene of Hildebrand and the Emperor might help to form the situation. New friends or foes with old faces might occasionally peep out.

A representative from one of the Monastic orders similar in idea to St Simeon Stylites and to be called St Francis of Assisi, more Christian and less barbarous, would perhaps be possible.

Painters like to teach new lessons in nature. The successive phases of the human mind in different ages are subjects for poetry even more than for philosophy. Might not the poet teach many lessons of that sort, not in the æsthetical, artistic manner of Goethe but with simpler English poetic feeling?

Now I have said enough foolish things and will conclude. You will do me a great favour if you will let me know of any books that I can send Mr Tennyson which you think may be useful or suggestive. Almost anything can be got here, or if you will tell me the subjects, I can find the books.

I hold most strongly that it is the duty of everyone who has the good fortune to know a man of genius, to do any trifling service they can to lighten his work.

I will write to Mr Tennyson in a few days. Remember me to him and

Believe me most truly yours,

B. JOWETT.

BALL. COLL.
Dec. 12th, 1858.

DEAR MRS TENNYSON,

I cannot but feel greatly ashamed of my ingratitude and disrespect in not having answered your last kind letter which gave me great pleasure at the time I received it. I believe that ingratitude is not the real cause (for that I could not possibly feel) but inveterate indolence about certain things, among which I fear come some of the duties of friendship.

You return me good for evil by sending me the two sweet letters of the children; which I recognize as most genuine productions. Give my love to the two "little birds." Lionel's epistle especially is just a picture of a child's mind.

I hope Mr Tennyson is well and has good success in his great work[1]. Authors great and small have some trials in common and some joys when a "book is born into the world."

I think I have read somewhere a description of Burns' wife and child coming to meet him when he was in a sort of ecstasy, "with the tears rolling down his cheeks," writing "Tam o' Shanter" at the side of a stream. That must be a great alleviation. I am sure it is only success (in the higher sense) and not resignation or philosophy that can make an author happy.

I do not doubt that the world will be charmed with the "Arthur Idylls." No malice will be able to prevent people from seeing that they are most beautiful poems. I have more

---

[1] The "Idylls of the King."

hesitation (shall I go on?) about the other poem respecting the clerk and wife [1], and could wish that the fortunes of it were tried alone so as not to interfere with the good-will towards "Arthur."

The scene and the satirical passage appear to me the doubtful points.   It seems to me quite as fine as the "Idylls," but I speak with reference to its effect on the public.

You told me that I might suggest to you any subjects that I dreamed of.   Did I mention "Jupiter Olympius," the statue of Phidias?   The subject could partly be the Olympic games and the interest the Classical Greek feeling of the poem.   But now I want to suggest something that would "express the thoughts of many hearts," which I must always think to be the highest excellence of poetry, and afford a solace where it is much needed.   The subject I mean is "In Memoriam" for the dead in India.   It might be done so as to include some scenes of Cawnpore and Lucknow; or quite simply and slightly, "Relatives in India," the schemings and hopings and imaginings about them, and the fatal missive suddenly announcing their death. They leave us in the fairness and innocence of youth, with nothing but the vision of their childhood and boyhood to look back upon, and return no more.

Perhaps you know what sets my thoughts upon this, the death of my dear brother, the second who has died in India.   It matters nothing to the world, for they had never the opportunity of distinguishing themselves, but it matters a great deal to me. They were dear good disinterested fellows, most unselfish in their ways, and as grateful to me for what I did for them when they were boys, as if it had been yesterday.   I like to think of them in the days of their youth busying themselves with engineering which was their great amusement.   They were wonderfully attached to each other.   The younger one especially, who died first about five years ago, was one of the sweetest dispositions I ever knew.

If I did not venture to look upon you and Mr Tennyson as something like friends, I should not venture to trouble you with this sorrow about persons whom you have never seen or heard of.

I hope to have the pleasure of coming to see you about the

[1] " Sea Dreams."

6th or 7th of January for a few days. But I could come at any
other time if more convenient.

Ever truly yours, B. JOWETT.

1859.

The sudden death of Henry Hallam was a great
grief to my father, for the historian had been a good
friend through thirty years. On hearing of Mr Hallam's
last days he read some "In Memoriam" aloud and
dwelt on those passages which most moved him. Generally when he was asked to read the poem he would
refuse, saying: "It breaks me down, I cannot." In the
spring of the year the four "Idylls of the King,"
"Enid," "Vivien," "Elaine," "Guinevere," were prepared for publication.

"Boadicea" was also written, the metre being "an
echo of the metre in the 'Atys' of Catullus[1]": he wished
that it were musically annotated so that it might be read
with proper quantity and force.

"Riflemen, Form!" appeared in May in the *Times*
after the outbreak of war between France, Piedmont,
and Austria; when more than one power seemed to be
prepared to take the offensive against England; and it
rang like a trumpet-call through the length and breadth
of the Empire. It so happened that three days later an
order from the War Office came out, approving of the
formation of Volunteer rifle corps. To Colonel Richards,
who was one of the prominent promoters of the movement, my father wrote: "I must heartily congratulate
you on your having been able to do so much for your
country; and I hope that you will not cease from your
labours until it is the law of the land that every male
child in it shall be trained to the use of arms." On the
same day that "Riflemen, Form!" was forwarded for

[1] A. T. MS.

publication, the proofs of the last " Idyll " (" Elaine ")
were finally corrected for press [1].

He made too a song for sailors:

Jack Tar. (*Unpublished.*)

They say some foreign powers have laid their heads
  together
  To break the pride of Britain, and bring her on
    her knees,
There's a treaty, so they tell us, of some dishonest
  fellows
  To break the noble pride of the Mistress of the
    Seas.
      Up, Jack Tars, and save us!
      The whole world shall not brave us!
      Up and save the pride of the Mistress of the
        Seas!

We quarrel here at home, and they plot against us
  yonder,
  They will not let an honest Briton sit at home
    at ease:
Up, Jack Tars, my hearties! and the d—l take the
  parties!
Up and save the pride of the Mistress of the Seas!
      Up, Jack Tars, and save us!
      The whole world shall not brave us!
      Up and save the pride of the Mistress of the
        Seas!

[1] Mr Coventry Patmore wrote to my father in May 1859: " It will please
you to hear that 'Riflemen, Form!' is being responded to. I hear that
four hundred clerks of the War Office alone have at once answered to the
Government invitation, and on my proposing that our department should send
a contingent, almost every man in the place put his name down, although a
large cost will be incurred, and we are nearly all poor. If things go through
the country at that rate, there never will be an invasion."

The lasses and the little ones, Jack Tars, they look to
    you!
The despots over yonder, let 'em do whate'er they
    please!
God bless the little isle where a man may still be
    true!
God bless the noble isle that is Mistress of the
    Seas!
    Up, Jack Tars, and save us!
    The whole world shall not brave us!
    If *you* will save the pride of the Mistress of
    the Seas.

In *Once a Week*, July 16th, was published "The
Grandmother's Apology" with a beautiful illustration by
Millais.

With a view to some new "Idylls of the King" my
father was studying "Pelleas and Ettarre" and "La
belle Isoude"; and, after working at those already in
print, went for a holiday in August with Mr Palgrave to
Portugal.

*My father's letter-diary. Journey to Portugal
    with F. T. Palgrave and F. C. Grove*[1].

August 16*th*. Radley's Hotel, Southampton. Have
been over the Vectis, the name of the vessel, not Tagus,
Tagus being repaired, or running alternately with the
Vectis. She is very prettily got up and painted, and
apparently scrupulously clean. Brookfield[2] keeps up my
spirits by wonderful tales, puns, etc. I find that neither
Palgrave nor Grove wants to move except as I will and
they are quite content to remain at Cintra.

August 17*th*. Have passed a night somewhat broken
by railway whistles.

---

[1] Eldest son of Judge Sir W. Grove.
[2] Brookfield had come to see his friends off from Southampton.

[This — writes Palgrave — was Tennyson's second voyage (so far as I know) of more than Channel length. It was strange, that sensation of the little moving island, the vessel which was bridging for us the ocean between England and Iberia: "like a world hung in space," as Tennyson called it. Tennyson's flow and fertility in anecdote, such as I have elsewhere tried to sketch it, was wonderful.

No need to dwell on the few incidents which broke the pleasant monotony of the voyage : porpoises plunging and re-appearing round the ship, like black wheels ploughing the gray-blue waters : small whales spouting their fountains on the near horizon : the meridian observations ; the rocks of Ushant : the beacon light on Finisterre : I name them only because of the vivid interest with which they were studied by Tennyson. But we desired nothing better than the *far niente* of those cloudless days. Presently, however, that craving for "the palms and temples of the South" which he was never to gratify, fell upon Tennyson ; and he began to long in vain to push onward to Teneriffe.]

August 21st. Braganza Hotel, Lisbon. Just arrived at Lisbon and settled at the Braganza Hotel after a very prosperous voyage tho' with a good deal of rolling. We merely touched at Vigo which looked fruitful, rolled up in a hot mist, and saw Oporto from the sea, looking very white in a fat port-wine country. It is here just as hot as one would wish it to be but not at all too hot. There was a vast deal of mist and fog all along the coast as we came. Lisbon I have not yet seen except from the sea, and it does not equal expectation as far as seen [1]. Palgrave and Grove have been helpful and pleasant companions, and so far all has gone well. We shall go to Cintra either to-morrow or next day. It is said to be Lisbon's Richmond and rather cockney tho' high and cool. The man who is landlord here is English and an Englishman keeps the hotel at Cintra. I hope with good hope that I shall not be pestered with the plagues of Egypt. I cannot say whether we shall stick at Cintra or go further on. Brookfield gave a good account of the cleanliness of Seville.

[1] Except the convent chapel at Belem.

August 23*rd*. Cintra. We drove over Lisbon
yesterday in a blazing heat and saw the Church of
St Vincent, and the Botanical Gardens where palms and
prickly pears and huge cactuses were growing, and
enormous oleanders covered all over with the richest red
blossom, and I thought of our poor one at Farringford
that won't blossom. There were two strange barbaric
statues at the gate of the garden, which were dug up on
the top of a hill in Portugal: some call them Phœnician
but no one knows much about them. I tried to see the
grave of Fielding the novelist, who is buried in the
Protestant cemetery, but could find no one to let me in;
he lies among the cypresses. In the evening we came
on here: the drive was a cold one, and the country dry,
tawny, and wholly uninteresting. Cintra disappointed
me at first sight, and perhaps will continue to disappoint,
tho' to southern eyes from its ever green groves, in
contrast to the parched barren look of the landscape, it
must look very lovely. I climbed with Grove to the
Peña, a Moorish-looking castle on the top of the hill,
which is being repaired, and which has gateways fronted
with tiles in pattern; these gates look like those in the
illustrated *Arabian Nights* of Lane [1].

August 26*th*. It is, I think, now decided that we are
to go on to Cadiz and Seville on the 2nd, and then to
Gibraltar and possibly to Tangiers, possibly to Malaga
and Granada. The King's Chamberlain has found me
out by my name: his name is the Marquis of Figueros
or some such sound; and yesterday even the Duke of
Saldanha came into the *salle à manger*, described himself
as "having fought under the great Duke, and having
been in two and forty combats and successful in all, as
having married two English wives, both perfect women,"
etc., and ended with seizing my hand and crying out

[1] Then they strolled to the Bay of Apples.

" Who does not know England's Poet Laureate? I am
the Duke of Saldanha." I continue pretty well except
for toothache ; I like the place much better as I know it
better. A visit to Santarem (the city of convents) was
greatly enjoyed.

[The town itself proved a labyrinth of narrow and filthy streets,
though here also were many large ecclesiastical buildings, ending in a
vast ruined castle, which from an immense height commanded the river
valley. Here we two (for our pleasant comrade had now left us) sat
long, and beneath us saw miles on miles of level land, forest and
vineyard, dotted with unknown villages, and lighted up by the long
curves of the Tagus. This undoubtedly is one of the great panoramic
landscapes of Europe, and I suppose the least visited. Nearer the city,
thorny lines of glaucous aloe, here and there throwing out lofty flower-
stems, ran up the hill-sides planted thick with olive-trees, beneath
which the sun now cast down long separate shadows, and illuminated
the Tagus flowing right below our eyes between wide tawny sandbanks
to the deepest fold of its green and sinuous channel[1].]

Sept. 2nd. Lisbon. The heat and the flies and the
fleas and one thing or another have decided us to return
by the boat to Southampton which starts from this place
on the 7th. We propose on arriving at Southampton to
pass on to Lyndhurst to spend two or three days in the
Forest.

[Our visit, we gradually found, was not at the most favourable
season : the fields browned and burnt by heat, the mosquitoes afflicting.
Against the latter, Tennyson had provided himself with an elaborate
tent (first contrived, I believe, by Sir C. Fellowes for use in Asia
Minor, during the night-time) : a sheet formed into a large bag, but
ending in a muslin canopy, which was distended by a cane circle, and
hung upwards, to accommodate head and shoulders, from a nail which
I took the freedom to run into his bedroom wall. Into this shelter the
occupant crept by a narrow sheet-funnel, which he closed by twisting ;
and once in, he was unable to light a match outside for fear lest the
action should set the muslin on fire. Hence one night Tennyson, able
to command the bell, summoned the waiter. I brought him in through
my (contiguous) room with a light ; and the man's terror at the spectacle of the great ghost, looking spectral within its white canopy, was

[1] Palgrave MS.

delightful. He almost ran off. But I think that after this experience Tennyson abandoned the tent and took his chances : only pretending to wish that he had a little baby in bed with him, as a whiter and more tempting morsel to the insect world.

More serious than the mosquito was the sun. This so wrought upon and disturbed Tennyson, in a manner with which many English travellers to Italy during the heat will be unpleasantly familiar, that he now began gravely to talk about leaving his bones by the side of the great novelist Fielding, who died and was buried at Lisbon in 1754 [1].]

Sept. 13*th.* Southampton. Arrived, and going on to-morrow to Lyndhurst, where I shall stop two or three days, then I am going on to Cambridge with Palgrave from a longing desire that I have to be there once more.

Crown Hotel, Lyndhurst. Palgrave has been as kind to me as a brother, and far more useful than a valet or courier, doing everything. His father is away at Spa, he (Palgrave) is horrified at being alone. I gave him hopes of his being with me till his father returned and I do not therefore like to leave him.

Sept. 20*th.* Cambridge. I have been spending the evening with my old tobacconist in whose house I used to lodge, and to-morrow I am to dine with Macmillan. I admire Jesus Chapel which is more like a Church than a Chapel.

[Palgrave writes : Cambridge was in Long Vacation, but Munro, the great Latin scholar, and W. G. Clark, then charming and gay, and unforeseeing the shadow destined to eclipse his later days, feasted us ; welcoming Tennyson once again back to Trinity. He showed me, with pathos in his voice of memories distant and dear, Arthur Hallam's rooms ; the "Backs," to which Oxford (he would have it) "has no rival," and the curious Jacobean brickwork of Queens' College, where in his time the "Combination room" had yet a sanded floor, and the table was set handsomely forth with long "church-wardens."]

In the autumn my father returned to Farringford and entertained the American statesman, Charles Sumner.

[1] Palgrave MS.

In November he was reading with intense interest an early copy of Darwin's *Origin of Species*, sent him by his own desire; and was finishing his "Tithonus," which he forwarded to Thackeray for the *Cornhill Magazine*[1]. A letter came from Charles Kingsley:

EVERSLEY, 1859.

MY DEAR TENNYSON,

        I wrote for *Fraser*, September 1850, a review of you, and especially of "In Memoriam." I am now going to publish a set of Miscellanies and thought of including that review. But when I read it through I thought I ought to ask your leave. I felt it almost too personal toward you in its expression of admiration and gratitude for your influence, and in its expression about "In Memoriam." It was necessary to be so then; for, while penny-a-liners were talking vulgar and unkind personalities, I felt bound to tell all whom I could make listen, what a gentleman and a Christian ought to think of you and your work; but I am not sure that you would like all I said there republished now that the bubble is over. Will you say "Yes" or "No"? and if you will say "Yes," you will deeply gratify me; for I wish to leave behind me some record of what I owe you. Pray remember me to Mrs Tennyson and to your children, whom I do not know alas! I seem destined never to see you. Here I live, as busy as a bee in my parish, and never leave home but for urgent business.

                Believe me your devoted C. KINGSLEY.

Soon after this the Kingsleys paid us a visit. "Charles Kingsley," so my father told me, "talked as usual on all sorts of topics and walked hard up and down the study for hours smoking furiously, and affirming that tobacco was the only thing that kept his nerves quiet." Among the topics discussed were the "Idylls" which Kingsley admired only less than "In Memoriam." Ten thousand copies had been sold in the first week of publication, and hundreds more were selling monthly. The reviews that were best in my father's estimation appeared

[1] February, 1860.

in the *Spectator*, the *Edinburgh* and the *Quarterly*, the last by Mr Gladstone [1].

Letters to and from friends about the "Idylls."

From Henry W. Longfellow.

MY DEAR MR TENNYSON,

I have requested my publishers in London, Messrs Routledge, to send you a copy of a translation of the *Divina Commedia*, which I have had the temerity to make, and which they are now publishing. In the notes I have taken the liberty to quote your beautiful song of Fortune (from " Enid "), and also part of " Ulysses," at which, I hope, you will not be displeased, as you are in very good company. Many thanks for your kind letter acknowledging the (Red Indian) red stone pipe of peace. To a civilized human being I fancy it can never be of any practical use. But it is pretty, and has a certain value as coming from those far-away Western mountains.

Always with great regard yours truly,

HENRY W. LONGFELLOW.

From W. M. Thackeray.

FOLKESTONE, *September*.
36 ONSLOW SQUARE, *October*.

MY DEAR OLD ALFRED,

I owe you a letter of happiness and thanks. Sir, about three weeks ago, when I was ill in bed, I read the " Idylls of the King," and I thought, " Oh I must write to him now, for this pleasure, this delight, this splendour of happiness which I have been enjoying." But I should have blotted the sheets, 'tis ill writing on one's back. The letter full of gratitude never went as far as the post-office and how comes it now ?

D'abord, a bottle of claret. (The landlord of the hotel asked me down to the cellar and treated me.) Then afterwards sitting here, an old magazine, *Fraser's Magazine*, 1850, and I come on a poem out of " The Princess " which says " I hear the horns of

[1] For chapter on the " Idylls," see Vol. II., p. 121.

Elfland blowing blowing," no, it's "the horns of Elfland faintly blowing" (I have been into my bedroom to fetch my pen and it has made that blot), and, reading the lines, which only one man in the world could write, I thought about the other horns of Elfland blowing in full strength, and Arthur in gold armour, and Guinevere in gold hair, and all those knights and heroes and beauties and purple landscapes and misty gray lakes in which you have made me live.   They seem like facts to me, since about three weeks ago (three weeks or a month was it?) when I read the book.   It is on the table yonder, and I don't like, somehow, to disturb it, but the delight and gratitude!   You have made me as happy as I was as a child with the *Arabian Nights*, every step I have walked in Elfland has been a sort of Paradise to me. (The landlord gave *two* bottles of his claret and I think I drank the most) and here I have been lying back in the chair and thinking of those delightful "Idylls," my thoughts being turned to you : what could I do but be grateful to that surprising genius which has made me so happy?   Do you understand that what I mean is all true and that I should break out were you sitting opposite with a pipe in your mouth?   Gold and purple and diamonds, I say, gentlemen and glory and love and honour, and if you haven't given me all these why should I be in such an ardour of gratitude?   But I have had out of that dear book the greatest delight that has ever come to me since I was a young man ; to write and think about it makes me almost young, and this I suppose is what I'm doing, like an after-dinner speech.

P.S.   I thought the "Grandmother" quite as fine.   How can you at 50 be doing things as well as at 35 ?

October 16*th*. (I should think six weeks after the writing of the above.)

The rhapsody of gratitude was never sent, and for a peculiar reason ; just about the time of writing I came to an arrangement with Smith and Elder to edit their new magazine, and to have a contribution from T. was the publishers' and editor's highest ambition.   But to ask a man for a favour, and to praise and bow down before him in the same page seemed to be so like hypocrisy, that I held my hand, and left this note in my desk, where it has been lying during a little French-Italian-Swiss tour which my girls and their papa have been making.

Meanwhile S. E. and Co. have been making their own

proposals to you, and you have replied not favourably I am sorry to hear: but now there is no reason why you should not have my homages, and I am just as thankful for the "Idylls," and love and admire them just as much, as I did two months ago when I began to write in that ardour of claret and gratitude. If you can't write for us you can't. If you can by chance some day, and help an old friend, how pleased and happy I shall be! This however must be left to fate and your convenience: I don't intend to give up hope, but accept the good fortune if it comes. I see one, two, three quarterlies advertized to-day, as all bringing laurels to laureatus. He will not refuse the private tribute of an old friend, will he? You don't know how pleased the girls were at Kensington t'other day to hear you quote their father's little verses, and he too I daresay was not disgusted. He sends you and yours his very best regards in this most heartfelt and artless

(note of admiration)!

Always yours, my dear Alfred,

W. M. THACKERAY.

To W. M. Thackeray.

FARRINGFORD.

MY DEAR THACKERAY,

Should I not have answered you ere this 6th of November? surely: what excuse? none that I know of: except indeed, that perhaps your very generosity and boundlessness of approval made me in a measure shame-faced. I could scarcely accept it, being, I fancy, a modest man, and always more or less doubtful of my own efforts in any line. But I may tell you that your little note gave me more pleasure than all the journals and monthlies and quarterlies which have come across me: not so much from your being the Great Novelist I hope as from your being my good old friend, or perhaps from your being both of these in one. Well, let it be. I have been ransacking all sorts of old albums and scrap books but cannot find anything worthy sending you.

Unfortunately before your letter arrived I had agreed to give Macmillan the only available poem I had by me ("Sea Dreams")[1]. I don't think he would have got it (for I dislike publishing in magazines) except that he had come to visit me in my Island, and was sitting and blowing his weed vis-à-vis. I am sorry that you have engaged for any quantity of money to let your brains be sucked periodically by Smith, Elder & Co.: not that I don't like Smith who seems from the very little I have seen of him liberal and kindly, but that so great an artist as you are should go to work after this fashion. Whenever you feel your brains as the "remainder biscuit," or indeed whenever you will, come over to me and take a blow on these downs where the air as Keats said is "worth sixpence a pint," and bring your girls too.

Yours always, A. TENNYSON.

From the Duke of Argyll.

LONDON, July 14th, 1859.

MY DEAR MR TENNYSON,

I think my prediction is coming true, that your "Idylls of the King" will be understood and admired by many who are incapable of understanding and appreciating many of your other works.

Macaulay is certainly not a man incapable of *understanding* anything but I knew that his tastes in poetry were so formed in another line that I considered him a good test, and three days ago I gave him "Guinevere."

The result has been as I expected, that he has been *delighted with it*. He told me that he had been greatly moved by it, and admired it exceedingly. Altho' by practice and disposition he is eminently a critic, he did not find one single fault. Yesterday I gave him the "Maid of Astolat" with which he was delighted also.

I hear the article in the *Edin. Review* is not to contain

---

[1] "Tithonus" was sent to Thackeray for the *Cornhill*, February, 1860.

much criticism, it consists to a great extent of long extracts. But I have not seen it myself, nor am I sure who wrote it.

How are you standing this tropical heat, and Mrs Tennyson? Let us have a good account of yourselves.

This Peace is abominable, and you should be perpetually, telescope in hand, watching for the "Liberator of Italy," who has proclaimed to his soldiers that he stops because the contest is no longer in the *interests of France!*

Yours most sincerely, ARGYLL.

To the Duke of Argyll.

FARRINGFORD,
Monday, July 18*th*, 1859.

MY DEAR DUKE,

Doubtless Macaulay's good opinion is worth having and I am grateful to you for letting me know it, but this time I intend to be thick-skinned; nay, I scarcely believe that I should ever feel very deeply the pen-punctures of those parasitic animalcules of the press, if they kept themselves to what I write, and did not glance spitefully and personally at myself. I hate spite.

*   *   *   *   *   *

Yours ever, A. TENNYSON.

Best remembrances to the Duchess.

From the Rev. B. Jowett.

19 GLOUCESTER TERRACE,
July 17*th*, 1859.

MY DEAR TENNYSON,

Thank you many times for your last: I have read it through with the greatest delight, the "Maid of Astolat" twice over, and it rings in my ears. "The Lily Maid" seems to me the fairest, purest, sweetest love-poem in the English language. I have not seen any criticisms nor do I care about them. It moves me like the love of Juliet in Shakespeare (though that is not altogether parallel), and I do not doubt whatever opinions are expressed about it that it will in a few years be above criticism.

There are hundreds and hundreds of all ages (and men as well as women) who, though they have not died for love (have no intention of doing so), will find there a sort of ideal consolation of their own troubles and remembrances.

Of the other poems I admire "Vivien" the most (the naughty one), which seems to me a work of wonderful power and skill.

It is most elegant and fanciful. I am not surprised at your Delilah reducing the wise man, she is quite equal to it.

The allegory in the distance *greatly strengthens, also elevates, the meaning of the poem.*

I shall not bore you with criticisms. It struck me what a great number of lines —

> He makes no friends, who never made a foe — [1]
> Then trust me not at all, or all in all —

will pass current on the lips of men, which I always regard as a great test of excellence, for it is saying the thing that everybody feels.

I am sure that the "Grandmother" is a most exquisite thing.

I hope you will find rest after toil and listen to the voice that says "Rejoice, Rejoice."

Next week I shall probably be in London. I am afraid that I shall not be able to manage going abroad. But I should like to come and look in upon you if you are at any house where it would be convenient to you to see me.

With most kind regards to Mrs Tennyson and love to the children,

Believe me ever most truly yours,

B. JOWETT.

---

[1] This line my father generally wrote in autograph albums.

From Arthur H. Clough.

COUNCIL OFFICE,
18*th July*, 1859.

DEAR MRS TENNYSON,

The Welsh books appeared suddenly one morning, by what agency I do not know, and I have already appeased my uncle's bibliomaniac fears by communicating the fact of their arrival.

The reception of the "Idylls of the King" will I hope satisfy all Farringford.

I have heard no words of dispraise: and in my own opinion they are just what we had a right to hope for, better, because more fully given, without any disparagement to what went before.

Faithfully yours, A. H. CLOUGH.

From the Duke of Argyll.

July 20th, 1859.

MY DEAR MR TENNYSON,

I hope you will give me note of your arrival in town.

The applause of the "Idylls" goes on crescendo, and so far as I can hear without exception. Detractors are silenced.

Macaulay has repeated to me several times an expression of his great admiration. Another well-known Author, himself a Poet, whom I shall not name, who heretofore could go no further than a half unwilling approval of the "Lotos-Eaters," has succumbed to the "Idylls," has laid down his arms, without reserve. I consider him a test and index of a large class of minds. I have heard of several other obdurate sinners who have been converted from the error of their ways.

Gladstone, who is not one of the class, has spoken to me, and has written to the Duchess of Sutherland that the impression of the power and beauty of these Poems increases daily in reading them.

I am delighted, specially from my love of natural history, with some of your imagery from natural things.

The passage comparing the voice of Enid to the first heard song of the nightingale is singularly beautiful in expression. So is that passage comparing the dispersion of Geraint's foes to the shoals of fish among the "crystal dykes of Camelot."

By the bye I have always omitted to ask you what you mean in one of your old poems by "The Red-Cap[1] whistled." I know of no such bird: don't you mean the *Black*-Cap, which does whistle beautifully? The Golden-crested Wren is never called "Red-Cap," nor can it be said to whistle, tho' it has a loud song.

L. Nap.'s explanation of the Peace is, I have no doubt, a tolerably correct account. But it will seem a bitter mockery to those whose "illusions" he encouraged, and now contemns.

Can you send me a copy of your song "The Great Name of England round and round"? Do.

Yours ever, ARGYLL.

To the Duke of Argyll.

E. L. Lushington's,
PARK HOUSE, MAIDSTONE,
July 29th, 1859.

MY DEAR DUKE,

Your last note was very welcome to me and if I did not answer it earlier, why, I was all the more to blame; answered partly it was by my wife's copy of the song[2] requested, which I hope arrived safely. She has set it to music far more to the purpose than most of Master Balfe's.

"Red-cap" is, or was when I was a lad, provincial for "Gold-finch"; had I known it was purely provincial I should probably not have used it. Now the passage has stood so long that I am loth to alter it.

Ever yours, A. TENNYSON.

[1] Provincial name for the goldfinch.
[2] "Riflemen, Form!"

From my father's mother.

ROSE MANOR, WELL WALK.
Monday, Jan. 10th, 1860.

DEAREST ALLY,

I received a nice kind note from Alan Ker a short time since, which I now enclose, thinking it will give thee pleasure to know what he says about thy last beautiful and interesting poems. It does indeed (as he supposes it would) give me the purest satisfaction to notice that a spirit of Christianity is perceptible through the whole volume. It gladdens my heart also to perceive that Alan seems to estimate it greatly on that account. O dearest Ally, how fervently have I prayed for years that our merciful Redeemer would intercede with our Heavenly Father, to grant thee His Holy Spirit to urge thee to employ the talents He has given thee, by taking every opportunity of endeavouring to impress the precepts of His Holy Word on the minds of others. My beloved son, words are too feeble to express the joy of my heart in perceiving that thou art earnestly endeavouring to do so. Dearest Ally, there is nothing for a moment to be compared to the favour of God: I need not ask thee if thou art of the same opinion. Thy writings are a convincive proof that thou art. My beloved child, when our Heavenly Father summons us hence, may we meet, and all that are dear to us, in that blessed state where sorrow is unknown, never more to be separated. I hope Emmy and thyself continue well, also the dear little boys. All here join me in kindest love to both.

Ever, dearest Ally,

Thy attached and loving mother,

E. TENNYSON.

From J. Ruskin.

STRASBURG.

DEAR MR TENNYSON,

I have had the "Idylls" in my travelling desk ever since I could get them across the water, and have only not written about them because I could not quite make up my mind about that increased quietness of style. I thought you would like a little to know what I felt about it, but did not quite know myself what I did feel.

To a certain extent you yourself of course know better what the work is than anyone else, as all great artists do.

If you are satisfied with it, I believe it to be right. Satisfied with bits of it you must be, and so must all of us, however much we expect from you.

The four songs seem to me the jewels of the crown, and bits come every here and there, the fright of the maid for instance, and the " In the darkness o'er her fallen head," which seem to me finer than almost all you have done yet. Nevertheless I am not sure but I feel the art and finish in these poems a little more than I like to feel it[1]. Yet I am not a fair judge quite, for I am so much of a realist as not by any possibility to interest myself much in an unreal subject to feel it as I should, and the very sweetness and stateliness of the words strike me all the more as *pure* workmanship.

As a description of various nobleness and tenderness the book is without price : but I shall always wish it had been nobleness independent of a romantic condition of externals in general.

" In Memoriam," " Maud," " The Miller's Daughter," and such like will always be my own pet rhymes, yet I am quite prepared to admit this to be as good as any, for its own peculiar audience. Treasures of wisdom there are in it, and word-painting such as never was yet for concentration, nevertheless it seems to me that so great power ought not to be spent on visions of things past but on the living present. For one hearer capable of feeling the depth of this poem I believe ten would feel a depth quite as great if the stream flowed through things nearer the hearer. And merely in the facts of modern life, not

---

[1] So far as the word *art*, as used here by Mr Ruskin, suggests that these Idylls were carefully elaborated, the suggestion is hardly in accordance with the fact. The more imaginative the poem, the less time it generally took him to compose. " Guinevere " and " Elaine " were certainly not elaborated, seeing that they were written, each of them, in a few weeks, and hardly corrected at all. My father said that he often did not know why some passages were thought specially beautiful, until he had examined them. He added : " Perfection in art is perhaps more sudden sometimes than we think ; but then the long preparation for it, that unseen germination, *that* is what we ignore and forget."

drawing-room formal life, but the far away and quite unknown growth of souls in and through any form of misery or servitude, there is an infinity of what men should be told, and what none but a poet can tell. I cannot but think that the intense masterful and unerring transcript of an actuality, and the relation of a story of any real human life as a poet would watch and analyze it, would make all men feel more or less what poetry was, as they felt what Life and Fate were in their instant workings.

This seems to me the true task of the modern poet. And I think I have seen faces, and heard voices by road and street side, which claimed or conferred as much as ever the loveliest or saddest of Camelot. As I watch them, the feeling continually weighs upon me, day by day, more and more, that not the grief of the world but the loss of it is the wonder of it. I see creatures so full of all power and beauty, with none to understand or teach or save them. The making in them of miracles and all cast away, for ever lost as far as we can trace. And no " in memoriam."

I do not ask when you are likely to be in London for I know you do not like writing letters, and I know you will let Mrs Prinsep or Watts send me word about you, so that I may come and see you again, when you do come; and then on some bright winter's day, I shall put in my plea for Denmark Hill.

Meanwhile believe me always

Faithfully and gratefully yours, J. RUSKIN.

Part of a letter from Aubrey de Vere.

1860.

Love to Alfred, from whom I hope to have more of those glorious chivalrous legends. * * *

Alfred seems to be founding a school just as Raffaelle and Titian founded their respective Roman and Venetian schools. There cannot be a truer tribute to genius than this. It proves that it has struck roots in the national mind.

From H.R.H. Prince Albert.

BUCKINGHAM PALACE,
17th May, 1860.

MY DEAR MR TENNYSON,

Will you forgive me if I intrude upon your leisure
with a request which I have thought some little time of making,
viz. that you would be good enough to write your name in the
accompanying volume of your "Idylls of the King"? You
would thus add a peculiar interest to the book, containing those
beautiful songs, from the perusal of which I derived the greatest
enjoyment. They quite rekindle the feeling with which the
legends of King Arthur must have inspired the chivalry of old,
whilst the graceful form in which they are presented blends
those feelings with the softer tone of our present age.

Believe me always yours truly, ALBERT.

From the Rev. Charles Kingsley.

EVERSLEY RECTORY, WINCHFIELD,
Nov. 10th, 1859.

MY DEAR TENNYSON,

I was amused to-night at a burst of enthusiasm in
your behalf from a most unenthusiastic man (though a man of
taste and scholarship), Walter the proprietor of the *Times*. He
confest to having been a disbeliever in you, save in "Locksley
Hall," which he said was the finest modern lyric; but he
considered you had taken liberties, and so forth. But the
"Idylls," he confest, had beaten him. He thought them the
finest modern poem. There was nothing he did not or would
not say in praise of them. He now classed the four great
English poets as Shakespeare, Spenser, Byron, Tennyson, and
so on, and so on, very pleasant to me though little worth to you.
But I like to tell you of a "jamjam efficaci do manus scientiæ"
from anyone who has not as yet appreciated you, to his own
harm. He did not write the disagreeable review of you in the
Times some years back. It was, I believe, a poor envious,
dyspeptic, poetaster parson, ——. I tell you this for fear you
should think Walter, who is really a fine fellow, had anything to
do with it.

God bless you, C. KINGSLEY.

To the Duke of Argyll.

FARRINGFORD,
Oct. 3rd, 1859.

MY DEAR DUKE,

We are delighted to hear that your Duchess
has added another scion to your race, and that mother
and child are both prospering. I had fancied that the
event would have come off while I was in Portugal (for
in Portugal I have been), and made enquiries thereanent
of Mr Henry Howard[1] but he could tell me nothing.

If I came back with "bullion" in the "Tagus," it was
nowhere in my packages. I went to see that Cintra
which Byron and Beckford have made so famous : but
the orange-trees were all dead of disease, and the crystal
streams (with the exception of a few sprinkling springlets
by the wayside) either dried up, or diverted thro' unseen
tunnels into the great aqueduct of Lisbon. Moreover
the place is cockney, and, when I was there, was crammed
with Lisbon fashionables and Portuguese nobility; yet
Cintra is not without its beauties, being a mountain of
green pines rising out of an everywhere arid and tawny
country, with a fantastic Moorish-looking castle on the
peak, which commands a great sweep of the Atlantic and
the mouth of the Tagus : here on the topmost tower sat
the king (they say) day by day in the old times of Vasco
da Gama watching for his return, till he saw him enter
the river : there, perhaps, was a moment worth having
been waited for. I made some pleasant acquaintances,
but I could not escape autograph hunters; a certain Don
Pedro Something even telegraphed for one after I had
returned to Lisbon.

As to Macaulay's suggestion of the Sangreal, I doubt
whether such a subject could be handled in these days,
without incurring a charge of irreverence. It would be

---

[1] English Minister at Lisbon in 1859.

too much like playing with sacred things. The old writers *believed* in the Sangreal. Many years ago I did write " Lancelot's Quest of the Grail " in as good verses as I ever wrote, no, I did not write, I made it in my head, and it has now altogether slipt out of memory.

My wife, I am sorry to say, has been very unwell.

Yours ever, A. TENNYSON.

UNPUBLISHED POEM OF THIS PERIOD.

The Philosopher.

He was too good and kind and sweet,
    Ev'n when I knew him in his hour
    Of darkest doubt, and in his power,
To fling his doubts into the street.

Truth-seeking he and not afraid,
    But questions that perplex us now —
    What time (he thought) have loom or plough
To weigh them as they should be weighed?

We help the blatant voice abroad
    To preach the freedom of despair,
    And from the heart of all things fair
To pluck the sanction of a God.

CHAPTER XXI.

TOUR IN CORNWALL AND THE SCILLY ISLES.

1860.

So great had been the success of the first four "Idylls of the King" that my father's friends begged him to "continue the epic." He received a letter from the Duke of Argyll again urging him to take up as his next subject the Holy Grail, but he said he shunned handling the subject, for fear that it might seem to some almost profane. He answered:

1860.

My dear Duke,

I sympathised with you when I read of Macaulay's death in the *Times*. He was, was he not, your next-door neighbour? I can easily conceive what a loss you must have had in the want of his brilliant conversation. I hardly knew him: met him once, I remember, when Hallam and Guizot were in his company: Hallam was showing Guizot the Houses of Parliament then building, and Macaulay went on like a cataract for an hour or so to those two great men, and, when they had gone, turned to me and said, "Good morning, I am happy to have had the pleasure of making your acquaintance," and strode away. Had I been a piquable man I should have been piqued, but I don't think I was, for the movement after all was amicable.

Alfred Tennyson.

Engraved by G. J. Stodart

from a photograph by O. G. Rejlander. 1859.

Of the two books I should, I think, have chosen the
Crabbe, though Macaulay's criticisms on poetry would
be less valuable probably than his historical ones. Peace
be with him !

  As to the *Sangreal*, as I gave up the subject so
many long years ago I do not think that I shall resume
it. You will see a little poem of mine in the *Cornhill
Magazine*. My friend Thackeray and his publishers
had been so urgent with me to send them something,
that I ferreted among my old books and found this
" Tithonus," written upwards of a quarter of a century
ago, and now queerly enough at the tail of a flashy
modern novel. It was originally a pendent to the
" Ulysses " in my former volumes, and I wanted Smith
to insert a letter, not of mine, to the editor stating this,
and how long ago it had been written, but he thought
it would lower the value of the contribution in the
public eye. Read in Browning's *Men and Women*
" Evelyn Hope" for its beauty, and "Bishop Blougram's
Apology " for its exceeding cleverness, and I think that
you will not deny him his own. The *Cornhill Magazine* gives a very pleasant account of Macaulay.

Yours ever, A. TENNYSON.

  The Duke and the Duchess spent some days at
Farringford, and were most emphatic that the " Grail "
ought to be written forthwith. My father said that he
was not "at present in the mood for it," and read aloud
his " Boadicea," which he had now quite finished. He
gloried in his new English metre, but he "feared
that no one could read it except himself, and wanted
someone to annotate it musically so that people could
understand the rhythm." " If they would only read
it straight like prose," he said, " just as it is written,
it would come all right." Among other guests was

Lord Dufferin, full of Cyril Graham's discoveries of the white marble cities in the black basaltic land of the Hauran with their inscriptions in an unknown tongue. Then the missionary Dr Wolff stayed with us, recounting his hairbreadth escapes in Central Asia, and giving an awe-inspiring description of an earthquake in Bokhara.

It was not until August that my father was able to go on his summer tour to Cornwall and the Scilly Isles, in company with Woolner, Palgrave, Holman Hunt and Val Prinsep.

My father's letter-diary. Tour in Cornwall and the Scilly Isles.

August 18*th*. All Souls' Reading Room, Oxford. Before my departure Palgrave called with his Syrian brother, a very interesting man in an Eastern dress with a kind of turban, having just escaped from his convent in the Syrian Deserts where several of his fellow monks were massacred. Palgrave is obliged to stop for a week at Hampstead till the brother goes to Paris, where he will have an interview with the Emperor on the affairs of the East. I started off alone, and I believe that in a week's time Holman Hunt, Val Prinsep and Frank Palgrave will join me at Penzance. Woolner, like a good fellow, followed me here yesterday that I might not feel lonely, and this morning we breakfasted with Max Müller, and are going to dine with him at 7.

August 21*st*. Bideford. We came here last night at 7 o'clock. I and Woolner are going down the coast to Tintagel, where we shall stop till the others join us.

August 23*rd*. Bude. Fine sea here, smart rain alternating with weak sunshine. Woolner is very kindly. We go off to-day to Boscastle which is three miles from Tintagel.

August 23*rd*. Arrived at Tintagel, grand coast, furious rain. Mr Poelaur would be a good name to direct to me by.

August 25*th*. Tintagel. Black cliffs and caves and storm and wind, but I weather it out and take my ten miles a day walks in my weather-proofs. Palgrave arrived to-day.

To Hallam.

TINTAGEL,
Aug. 25*th,* 1860.

MY DEAR HALLAM,

I was very glad to receive your little letter. Mind that you and Lionel do not quarrel and vex poor mamma who has lots of work to do; and learn your lessons regularly; for gentlemen and ladies will not take you for a gentleman when you grow up if you are ignorant. Here are great black cliffs of slate-rock, and deep, black caves, and the ruined castle of King Arthur, and I wish that you and Lionel and mamma were here to see them. Give my love to grandpapa and to Lionel, and work well at your lessons. I shall be glad to find you know more and more every day.

Your loving papa, A. TENNYSON.

August 28*th*. Tintagel. We believe that we are going to-morrow to Penzance or in that direction. We have had two fine days and some exceedingly grand coast views. Here is an artist, a friend of Woolner's (Inchbold), sketching now in this room. I am very tired of walking against wind and rain.

[Mr Palgrave writes: Following the publication of the first four "Idylls of the King" in 1859, when he was intending to write further Idylls, this was, perhaps, specially entitled to be named Tennyson's Arthurian journey.

At a sea inlet of wonderful picturesqueness, so grandly

modelled are the rocks which wall it, so translucently purple the waves that are its pavement, — waves whence the "naked babe" Arthur came ashore in flame, — stand the time-eaten ruins of unknown date which bear the name Tintagel. To these of course we climbed, — descending from "the castle gateway by the chasm," and at a turn in the rocks meeting that ever graceful, ill-appreciated landscapist, Inchbold: whose cry of delighted wonder at sight of Tennyson still sounds in the sole survivor's ear. Thence, after some delightful wandering walks, by a dreary road (for such is often the character of central Cornwall), we moved to Camelford on the greatly-winding stream which the name indicates. Near the little town, on the edge of the river, is shown a large block of stone upon which legend places Arthur, hiding or meditating, after his last fatal battle. It lay below the bank; and in his eagerness to reach it and sit down (as he sat in 1851 on that other, the *Sasso di Dante* by Sta. Maria del Fiore), Arthur's poet slipped right into the stream, and returned laughing to Camelford.

The next halting-place I remember was Penzance; whence, by Marazion, we crossed to and saw our English smaller but yet impressive and beautiful St Michael's Mount[1].]

August 31*st.* Union Hotel, Penzance. I am so very much grieved for poor Simeon's loss of his wife; it casts a gloom on my little tour: what will he do without her and with all those children? I have now walked 10 miles a day for 10 days, equal 100, and I want to continue doing that for some time longer. I am going to-morrow to Land's End and then I must return here, and then I go to the Scilly Isles and then again return here.

Sept. 5*th.* Land's End Inn. I will write to Simeon to-day, tho' I rather shun writing to him on such a subject, for what can one say, what comfort can one give? We are here at this racketty, rather dirty inn, but we have had four glorious days and *magnificently coloured seas.* To-day the Scilly Isles look so dark and clear on the horizon that one expects rain.

[1] Palgrave MS.

[I was struck — Mr Palgrave notes again — on the plateau of Sennen by the likeness between the masses of rock, piled up by Nature only, and those cromlechs which also occur in Cornwall; "Do you not remember that Wordsworth has a sonnet on this point?" Tennyson said, alluding to that beginning

"Mark the concentred hazels..."

adding, "He seems to have been always before one in observation of Nature [1]."]

Sept. 6th. Penzance. I start in an hour by the boat for the Scilly Islands. The weather is splendid, and the sea as calm as any lake shut in on all sides by hills. Woolner goes back to London and Palgrave continues with me.

Sept. 9th. St Mary's, Scilly Isles. Captain Tregarthen, who has the packet and the hotel here, has brought me my letters: the packet only goes three times a week. I shall stop here till Wednesday; there are West Indian aloes here 30 feet high, in blossom, and out all the winter, yet the peaches won't ripen; vast hedges of splendid geraniums, a delight to the eye, yet the mulberry won't ripen. These Islands are very peculiar and in some respects very fine. I never saw anything quite like them.

Sept. 11th. Three Tuns, Lizard. At the Lizard; and intend coming on to Falmouth. Hope to be at Brockenhurst next Saturday, but if not there, I shall have turned aside to see Avebury and Silbury Hill.

Sept. 20th. Falmouth. Have not found it easy to write every day in the bustle and bother of travellers' inns. I am now writing on my knees in my bedroom at a fishmonger's, there being no room at the hotel, and the whole town mad with a bazaar for riflemen, who get drunk every night and squabble and fight and

---

[1] Palgrave MS.

disgrace themselves and their corps. We left Hunt and Val Prinsep hard at work at the Lizard, sketching on a promontory.

[Mr Palgrave concludes his notes on this tour thus: From Falmouth [1] a little river-steamer was to carry us to Truro. We sat on deck enjoying the fresh air and sight of the fine estuary. But upon *l'incognito* Tennyson had reckoned too soon. Our captain presently came forward with a tray and a squat bottle, and said with unimpeachable good manners that " he was aware how distinguished a passenger, etc., and that some young men sitting opposite, and he, would be much honoured if Mr Tennyson would take a tumbler of stout with them." With as much courteous ease as if he had been a royal prince he stepped forward, said a few words of graceful thanks, pleased, and looking so; bowed to the hospitable party; and drank off his glass to their good health.

Presently the Captain reappeared, and this time it was the ladies in the cabin who begged that the Laureate would only step down among them. But the height of that small place of refuge, Tennyson declared, would render the proposed exhibition impossible; might he not be kindly excused? The good women however were not to be baulked; and one after another presented her half-length above the little hatchway before us, gazed, smiled and retreated. " It was like the crowned figures who appear and vanish in *Macbeth*," he said; and so, talking with our fellow-passengers and the captain, in due time we disembarked at Truro.

Next day a long and pleasant walk took us to Perranporth, a little village on the coast, which here was a stretch of level golden sands, barred at each end by fine rocks. Some way hence, we were directed through a little labyrinth of dunes

[1] Caroline Fox described my father on this tour in *Memories of Old Friends:* " Tennyson is a grand specimen of a man, with a magnificent head set on his shoulders like the capital of a mighty pillar. His hair is long and wavy, and covers a massive head. He wears a beard and moustache, which one begrudges, as hiding so much of that firm, forceful, but finely chiselled mouth. His eyes are large, gray (?), and open wide when a subject interests him; they are well shaded by the noble brow, with its strong lines of thought and suffering. I can quite understand Sam. Laurence calling it the best balance of head he had ever seen."

to the famous buried church of Perranzabuloe. Only a few sand-heaped lines of wall remain. But St Piran is assigned to the fifth century, and the church might be of Arthur's age, if we place him about that period[1].]

A vivid picture of my father, from a letter addressed to my mother (23rd Sept. 1860) by Woolner, may be added:

"I expect idling about so long will make his brain so fertile that when he gets back to Farringford he will do an immense deal of work. He was physically better, there can be no question, for he actually ate breakfasts! and partook of tarts not once but *twice* at dinner! which he had not done before for many years: and his face had grown a reddish bronze, a very healthy colour; and he was perpetually making jokes at expense of Palgrave, or at mine, and taking long walks, and swimming, and not smoking much, and drinking scarcely any wine. So you may consider all this as flourishing."

In my father's note-book are written as below the following Verse-Memoranda of tours in Cornwall, Isle of Wight and Ireland[2].

(*Babbicombe.*)　Like serpent-coils upon the deep.

(*Torquay.*)　　　　　　As the little thrift
Trembles in perilous places o'er the deep.

(*From the Old Red Sandstone.*)
　　　　　　　　　　As a stony spring
Blocks its own issue (tho' it makes a fresh one of course).

(*Fowey.*)　A cow drinking from a trough on the hill-side. The netted beams of light played on the wrinkles of her throat.

---

[1] Palgrave MS.

[2] When I was walking with my father almost for the last time, he said to me: "I generally take my nature-similes direct from my own observation of nature, and sometimes jot them down, and if by chance I find that one of my similes is like that in any author, my impulse is not to use that simile." If he was in the vein during a walk, he would make dozens of similes that were never chronicled.

(*Cornwall.*) The wildflower, called lady's finger, of a golden yellow when open'd, is, unopen'd, of a rich orange red, frequently at least in Cornwall when I observed it.

The open sea.)   Two great ships
        That draw together in a calm.

(*Bonchurch.*)   A little salt pool fluttering round a stone upon the shore.

(*I. of Wight.*)

    As those that lie on happy shores and see
    Thro' the near blossom slip the distant sail.

(*Park House.*)   Before the leaf,
    When all the trees stand in a mist of green.

After his tour in Ireland he had written on the same page:

(*Valencia.*)   Claps of thunder on the cliffs
        Amid the solid roar.

(*Bray Head.*)

    O friend, the great deeps of Eternity
    Roar only round the wasting cliffs of Time.

(*The river Shannon, on the rapids.*)
        Ledges of battling water.

CHAPTER XXII.

FARRINGFORD FRIENDS.

THE PYRENEES. DEATH OF THE PRINCE CONSORT.

1860–1862.

Some of the journals of this period have been mislaid, and Mrs Bradley has allowed me to make use of the Reminiscences written by her during the visits which she and the present Dean of Westminster paid to us at Farringford. They begin with the first impression of my father:

Here is Farringford, Tennyson's home, with its "careless ordered garden close to the ridge of a noble down" buried in trees. He invited Granville to dine with him to meet "Lear the artist, not the king," at Farringford two or three times, and Granville has had walks and talks with him and brings away memories full of pleasure and interest. To have come near the *man* and found in him all one could have desired in a great poet! I must write down my first sight of him. I was on the top of the stack in the yard having a birthday feast, very gay under a blue tent with decorations of flowers, etc. A carriage drove up to the little gate of the yard, I could not see who it was but guessed it was he. He came to the stack and looked up. I saw a tall large figure, cloak and large black wide-awake. He had no beard or moustache, I recollect being impressed with the beauty and power of his mouth and chin.

His face is full of power and thought, a deep furrow runs from nose to chin on either side, and gives a peculiar expression to the face, a lofty forehead adds to this. I remember the splendour of his eyes. He asked me who I was and told me to "throw the little maid into his arms" promising to catch her. He asked Edith how old she was, she said "thwee to-day." He said, "Then you and I have the same birthday, August 6th." He did not say much, but walked into the little parlour. Granville came in and they talked a little. Mr Tennyson took up the books on the table and remarked to himself about them.

He and Granville have been on an expedition to Brooke Bay, geologising, botanising, poetising, talking of everything great and small, of life inward and outward, at home and abroad, of religious and social difficulties; they talked from 12 noon to 10 p.m. almost incessantly this day, Mr Tennyson walking back with him to the Warren Farm still talking; Granville says that beneath all the slight allusions to various subjects in his poems lies a mine of knowledge. "He speaks of poetry as a great master only can do."

1860. Mr Tennyson has read "Maud" to us. He is a little vexed at the reception of "Maud." He said: "You must always stand up for 'Maud' when you hear my pet bantling abused. Perhaps that is why I am sensitive about her. You know mothers always make the most of a child that is abused." He commented on the poem as he read, pointed out certain beauties of metre and meaning which he admired himself. He excuses all that people pronounce sardonic in his poems, by saying, he does not cry out against the age as hopelessly bad, but tries to point out where it is bad in order that each individual may do his best to redeem it; as the evils he denounces are individual, only to be cured by each man looking to his own heart. He denounced evil in all its shapes, especially those considered venial by the world and society.

Speaking of Alexander Smith: "He has plenty of promise, but he must learn a different creed to that he preaches in those lines beginning 'Fame, fame, thou art next to God.' Next to God — next to the Devil say I. Fame might be worth having if it helped us to do good to a single mortal, but what is it? only the pleasure of hearing oneself talked of up and down the street."

[*Death's Jest-Book* by Thomas Lovell Beddoes he also praised.] He tells stories very well, ghost and other stories, and has plenty of humour. Amongst others he told us several stories of queer letters he has had from all sorts of people, companies, associations, etc. One young lady wrote imploring him to write some poetry for her to produce at a picnic when everyone was to recite an original poem! He said the deceit of passing off his poem as her own disgusted him, on the other hand he thought it plucky to tell him what she meant to do, and he would have written it for her, but unfortunately she signed her note "Kate" and sent no address.

Those evenings when the poet, sitting in his old oak arm-chair after dinner in the drawing-room, talked of what was in his heart, or read some poem aloud, with the landscape lying before us like a beautiful picture framed in the dark-arched bow-window, are never to be forgotten. His moods are so variable, his conversation so earnest, his knowledge of all things he writes about is so wide and minute. It is a rare treat to be in his domestic circle, where he talks freely and brightly without shyness or a certain morbidity which oppresses him occasionally in society. Crabbe, Gray and Keats were the chief poets he read to us.

There is a look in his face like a bright burning light behind it, like an inward fire that might consume his very life.

The reference in the following letter from my father is to an article on "English Metrical Critics" contributed by Mr Patmore to the *North British Review* for 1857 (Vol. XXVII. pp. 127–161).

This is the passage referred to:

The six-syllable "iambic" is the most solemn of all our English measures. It is scarcely fit for anything but a dirge; the reason being, that the final pause in this measure is greater, when compared with the length of the line, than in any other verse. Here is an example, which we select on account of the peculiar illustration of its nature as a "dimeter brachy-catalectic," which is supplied by the *filling up* of the measure in the seventh line:

> How strange it is to wake
> And watch, while others sleep,
> Till sight and hearing ache
> For objects that may keep
> The awful inner sense
> Unroused, lest it should mark
> The life that haunts the emptiness
> And horror of the dark.

We have only to *fill up* the measure in every line as well as the seventh, in order to change this verse from the slowest and most mournful, to the most rapid and high-spirited of all English metres, the common eight-syllable quatrain; a measure particularly recommended by the early critics, and continually chosen by poets of all times for erotic poetry, on account of its joyous air.

It will be seen that my father's second specimen is constructed by "filling up" Mr Patmore's lines in the manner that he suggests.

MY DEAR C. P.

Specimen of the "most solemn" English metre.

How glad am I to walk
  With Susan on the shore!
How glad am I to talk!
  I kiss her o'er and o'er.
I clasp her slender waist,
  We kiss, we are so fond,
When she and I are thus embraced,
  There's not a joy beyond.

Is this C. P.'s most solemn?

Specimen of the "most high-spirited" metre.

How strange it is, O God, to wake,
  To watch and wake while others sleep,
Till heart and sight and hearing ache
  For common objects that would keep
Our awful inner ghostly sense
  Unroused, lest it by chance should mark
The life that haunts the emptiness
  And horrors of the formless dark.

Is this C. P.'s rapid and high-spirited? A. T.

1861.

January. The Bensons[1] and Bradleys here. My father spoke of seeing Freshwater cliffs and the Needles from Bournemouth, and said, " The Isle of Wight looked like a water-lily on a blue lake." Talking of some poems published by an advanced young lady, which were instantly suppressed and the edition bought up by her friends, he quoted two or three passages to show how she had poetic perception rendered worthless by bad taste. One line ran: " whose looks were well-manured with love[2]."

January 22nd. My father said on the evening when the Bradleys were leaving: " You are going away —it is taking away a bit of my sunshine: I've been cutting down trees to let in some, and now you are taking away a bit of it." He continued: " All that sounds like flattery: there is no need for us to make fine speeches. By this time you know I never do, and it is just a plain truth that your going takes away some of my sunshine."

On Feb. 17th my father told my mother about his plan for a new poem, " The Northern Farmer."

By the evening of Feb. 18th he had already written down a great part of " The Northern Farmer " in one of the MS books bound in blue and red paper (which my mother always made for him herself). They also read of Sir Gareth in the *Morte d'Arthur.* About this time we went with my father to the National Gallery to see what he called " some of the great pictures of the world," the

---

[1] The late Archbishop of Canterbury and his wife.

[2] I may observe that my father was by no means a severe critic of the poems sent him. I remember his saying to Millais (about 1879) : — " The average poems which I get are not at all bad, but there is just the something, I suppose, wanted, that I cannot explain." Millais assured him that he found the same difficulty in criticizing pictures by young painters, that there was a good level of performance throughout their work, yet somehow failing short of excellence.

"Titians," the new "Veronese[1]," and the portrait of Ariosto.

In March my mother received a letter from Mr Jowett, a passage in which refers to some advice my father had given him with regard to the manner of expressing his theological opinions.

BALLIOL.

I had not the courage to follow Mr Tennyson's advice about the Essay[2]. It was, however, of great use to me, for I have modified the objectionable passages. I will send you a copy in a few days.

Believe me ever most truly yours,

B. JOWETT.

In May it was decided that my father should receive a degree at Cambridge, but we were unable to go further than Oatlands Park Hotel, for he had such a bad attack of palpitation of the heart that Cambridge had to be given up. After a few days spent in walking to Hampton Court and about the country round, we returned to Farringford, my father stopping at Winchester and Lyndhurst on the way.

Auvergne and the Pyrenees (July and August).

In the summer of 1861 we travelled in Auvergne and the Pyrenees. Some things we could not but be glad to have seen, but the difficulty of getting rooms, carriages, or even donkeys to ride in those days, and the impossibility of finding food not soaked in garlic, took away much of our pleasure.

The Cathedral at Bourges, its great pillars and its gorgeous windows, was what struck my father most on the journey out. On our arrival at Clermont, the comet

[1] The great picture, "Darius and his family before Alexander," brought from the Pisani Palace, Venice, in 1857.

[2] The famous essay in *Essays and Reviews*.

was flaring over the market-place. Here we should have been content to stay, had it not been for the bad drainage.

My father and Mr Dakyns [1] climbed the Puy de Dôme and several of the extinct volcanoes in the neighbourhood. Afterwards we drove to Mont Dore and La Bourboule; the plain of Clermont, where Peter the Hermit preached the First Crusade, and over which we looked during the drive, is very fine. At Mont Dore, while my father was reading some of the *Iliad* out aloud to us, little boys came and stood outside the window in open-mouthed astonishment. He took long walks there by the Dordogne, and one day when he came in from his walk we heard him call " Clough, come upstairs," and in walked Mr Clough. My father, Mr Clough and Mr Dakyns made many expeditions to waterfalls and up mountains, Mr Clough riding. We were delighted with the gorgeous meadows of forget-me-nots, and yellow anemones. We left Mr Clough at Mont Dore and drove to Tulle and Perigueux, a quaint place with its old Roman Tower and Cathedral with grass-grown tower, church of St Etienne, and city walls. Thence to Bordeaux, Tarbes, Bagnères de Bigorre where there was a magnificent thunderstorm at night, forked lightning of different colours striking the mountains on either hand. From this place my father and Mr Dakyns made an expedition up the Pic du Midi. When the climbers reached the summit, three great eagles, they said, kept swooping round without any perceptible movement of wing. On our drive from Bigorre to Bagnères de Luchon, a brigand cut one of our trunks from behind the carriage and was making off with it, when our driver looked round and caught sight of him, whereat the rascal ran off into the mountains, our driver cracking his whip at him and shouting out volleys of break-jaw oaths. At Bagnères

---

[1] Mr Dakyns had recently come to be our tutor; previously my mother had taught my brother and myself.

de Luchon we lodged in a house among the maize fields, and one night there was in the town a grand puppet show, a sham fight between the French and the Chinese, illustrating some of the incidents in the Chinese war of 1860. The English were conspicuous by their absence. My father walked with Mr Dakyns to the Port de Venasque and into Spain, and to see the Cascade d'Enfer and other cascades, and the Lac D'Oo, and the Lac Vert, and up several mountains: or sometimes he would ride on a white pony about the mountain valleys, one of these being the Vallée de Lys, which he much admired. Mr Clough joined us again at Luchon. He and my father went together to the Cascade des Demoiselles. He was with us too at Luz. My father was enchanted with the torrent of the Gave de Pau, he "sat by it and watched it, and seemed to be possessed by the spirit of delight." Mr Dakyns and he climbed toward the Brèche de Roland, Mr Clough meeting them on their return in the Cirque de Gavarnie, where my father said that the phrase "slow dropping veils of thinnest lawn" was taken from the central cataract which pours over the cliff. He observed that Gavarnie did not impress him quite so much this time as when he was here before. It seemed to him "different, but still the finest thing in the Pyrenees." Mr Clough noticed how silent my father was, and how absorbed by the beauty of the mountains. On August 6th, my father's birthday, we arrived at Cauteretz, — his favourite valley in the Pyrenees. Before our windows we had the torrent rushing over its rocky bed from far away among the mountains and falling in cataracts. Patches of snow lay on the peaks above, and nearer were great wooded heights glorious with autumnal colours, bare rocks here and there, and greenest mountain meadows below. He wrote his lyric "All along the Valley[1]" "after hear-

---

[1] Extract from Clough's *Journal*: "Sept. 1st. The Tennysons arrived here at 6.30 yesterday. Tennyson was here with Arthur Hallam thirty-one

ing the voice of the torrent seemingly sound deeper as
the night grew" (in memory of his visit here with
Arthur Hallam).

And all along the valley, by rock and cave and tree,
The voice of the dead was a living voice to me.

My father, Mr Clough and Mr Dakyns climbed to
the Lac de Gaube, a blue, still lake among fir woods,
where my father quoted to Mr Clough the simile of the
"stately pine" in " The Princess," which he made from
a pine here on an island in mid-stream between two
cataracts. More pines he found had grown by the side
of this solitary pine that he remembered years ago.

> And standing like a stately Pine
> Set in a cataract on an island-crag,
> When storm is on the heights, and right and left
> Suck'd from the dark heart of the long hills roll
> The torrents, dash'd to the vale: and yet her will
> Bred will in me to overcome it or fall.

My father clambered on to the Lac Bleu; he said
that the water was marvellously blue except where the
shadow of the mountains made parts of the lake purple.
My mother writes in her journal:

" We had a sad parting from Mr Clough at Pau.
There could not have been a gentler, kinder, more
unselfish or more thoughtful companion than he has
been. Among other kind things he corrected the boys'
little journals for them ; we called him the ' child-angel.'

---

years ago; and really finds great pleasure in the place: they stayed here
and at Cauteretz. He is very fond of this place evidently."

" Clough," said my father, " had great poetic feeling: he read me then his
' In Mari Magno' and cried like a child over it."

My father was vexed that he had written "two and thirty years ago " in
his " All along the Valley " instead of " one and thirty years ago," and as late
as 1892 wished to alter it since he hated inaccuracy. I persuaded him to
let his first reading stand, for the public had learnt to love the poem in its
present form: and besides "two and thirty " was more melodious.

After stopping at Pau for a few days we journeyed home by Dax, St Emilion, Libourne, Tours and Amiens: and on our return A. said to me: 'I have seen many things in this tour I shall like to remember.'"

My father wrote to the Duke of Argyll on his return:

THE TEMPLE, LONDON, 1861.

MY DEAR DUKE,

I had intended to write yesterday so that my answer might have reached Cliveden on the 10th, and I scarce know why I did not: perhaps because in these chambers I had lighted on an old and not unclever novel *Zohrab the Hostage;* partly perhaps because I had fallen into a muse about human vanities and "the glories of our blood and state" (do you know those grand old lines of Shirley's?). This must have been suggested by the progress of His Majesty the Mayor down the Strand, where I was entangled for half an hour in a roaring crowd and hardly escaped unbruised;—however, what with the novel and what with the musing fit, I let the post slip; but this morning let me say that I am grateful for the enquiring after myself and mine: of myself indeed I have no good account to render, being very far from well, living at a friend's rooms here in the Temple, and dancing attendance on a doctor. France, I believe overset me, and more especially the foul ways and unhappy diet of that charming Auvergne: no amount of granite craters or chestnut-woods, or lava-streams, not the Puy de Dôme which I climbed, nor the Glen of Royat, where I lived, nor the plain of Clermont seen from the bridge there, nor the still more magnificent view of the dead volcanoes from the ascent to Mont Dore could make amends for those drawbacks: so we all fell sick by turns: my wife is better since our return, and the boys are well enough, tho' they suffered too at the time; but I remain with a torpid liver, not having much pleasure in anything: yet I can still grieve with my friends' griefs, and therefore I am sorry for the occasion which exiles your good and kind Duchess, tho' it be but for this December.   I am sure the Duchess will sympathise with my disgust at having my Freshwater (where I had pitched my tent, taken with its solitariness) so polluted and defiled with brick and mortar, as is threatened; they talk of laying out streets and crescents, and I oscillate between my desire of purchasing land at a ruinous price in order to keep my views open, and my wish to fly the place altogether.   Is there no millionaire who will take pity on the wholesome hillside and buy it all up?

"Boadicea," no, I cannot publish her yet, perhaps never, for who can read her except myself?   I have half consented to write a little ode on the opening of the International Exhibition.   The commissioners prest me: I should never have volunteered; for I hate a subject given me, and still more if that subject be a public one. Present my best remembrances to your Duchess and to [her mother] the Duchess of Sutherland.   I am half afraid to inquire after her Grace's eyesight lest I should hear ill news.

Yours, my dear Duke, always,

A. TENNYSON.

In September Lord Dufferin wrote:

CLANDEBOY, BELFAST, Sept. 24th, 1861.

MY DEAR MR TENNYSON,

I wonder if you will think me very presumptuous for doing what at last, after many months' hesitation, I have determined to do.

You must know that here in my park in Ireland there rises a high hill, from the top of which I look down not only on an extensive tract of Irish land, but also on St George's Channel, a long blue line of Scotch coast, and the mountains of the Isle of Man.

On the summit of this hill I have built an old-world tower which I have called after my mother "Helen's Tower."

In it I have placed on a golden tablet the birthday verses which my mother wrote to me on the day I came of age, and I have spared no pains in beautifying it with all imaginable devices. In fact my tower is a little "Palace of Art." Beneath is a rough outline of its form and situation.

Now there is only one thing wanting to make it a perfect little gem of architecture and decoration and that is "*a voice.*" It is now ten years since it was built and all that time it has stood silent. Yet if he chose there is one person in the world able to endow it with this priceless gift, and by sending me some little short distich for it to crown it for ever with a glory it cannot otherwise obtain, and render it a memorial of the personal friendship which its builder felt for the great poet of our age.

Yours ever, DUFFERIN.

In answer my father sent the following lines, and annotated, as below, the words "recurring Paradise":

Helen's Tower.

Helen's Tower, here I stand,
Dominant over sea and land.
Son's love built me and I hold
Mother's love engrav'n in gold.
Love is in and out of time,
I am mortal stone and lime.
Would my granite girth were strong
As either love to last as long!
I should wear my crown entire
To and thro' the Doomsday fire,
And be found of angel eyes
In earth's recurring Paradise [1].

[1] The fancy of some poets and theologians that Paradise is to be the renovated earth, as, I dare say, you know.

The death of the Prince Consort in December my

father felt was a great loss to Britain and the Empire. He sent the first copies of his *Dedication* of the "Idylls" to the Princess Alice with the following letter:

MADAM,

Having heard some time ago from Sir C. B. Phipps that your Royal Highness had expressed a strong desire that I should in some way "idealize" our lamented Prince, and being at that time very unwell, I was unwilling to attempt the subject, because I feared that I might scarce be able to do it justice; nor did I well see how I should idealize a life which was in itself an ideal.

At last it seemed to me that I could do no better than dedicate to his memory a book which he himself had told me was valued by him. I am the more emboldened to send these lines to your Royal Highness, because having asked the opinion of a lady who knew and truly loved and honoured him, she gave me to understand by her reply that they were true and worthy of him: whether they be so or not, I hardly know, but if they do not appear so to your Royal Highness, forgive me as your Father would have forgiven me.

Though these lines conclude with an address to our beloved Queen I feel that I cannot do better than leave the occasion of presenting them to the discretion of your Royal Highness.

Believe me, as altogether sympathizing with your sorrow,

Your Royal Highness'

faithful and obedient servant,

A. TENNYSON.

1862.

Jan. 9th. My father recited in a rolling voice his new Ode for the opening of the Exhibition in the summer [1]. He explained that the rhythm and composition were hampered by the necessity of arranging it for a choir of 4000 voices: " I think for that kind of Ode the wild irregular bursts are an addition to its effectiveness." The lines on the death of the Prince Consort had to be put in after the first draft was written. My father was deeply grieved, not only by the death of the Prince, but also by the deaths of his two friends Clough and Godley. He wrote: " We have lost Clough: he died at Florence of a relapse of malaria-fever: it gave me a great shock. I see that Godley too has gone: so we fall, one by one."

Jan. 19th. Princess Alice wrote to my father about the *Dedication* of the " Idylls " to the Prince Consort:

If words could express *thanks* and *real* appreciation of lines so beautiful, so truly worthy of the great pure spirit which inspired the author, Princess Alice would attempt to do it; — but these failing, she begs Mr Tennyson to believe how much she admires them, and that this just tribute to the memory of her beloved Father touched her deeply. Mr Tennyson could not have chosen a more beautiful or true testimonial to the memory of him who was so really good and noble, than the dedication of the 'Idylls of the King' which he so valued and admired. Princess Alice transmitted the lines to the Queen, who desired her to tell Mr Tennyson, with her sincerest thanks, how much moved she was on reading them, and that they had soothed her aching, bleeding heart. She knows also how *he* would have admired them.

---

[1] Sung May 1, 1862; set by Sterndale Bennett. One newspaper reported that the poet-laureate was present, " clothed in his green *baize* " (probably a misprint for " bays ").

The Crown Princess of Prussia also wrote:

February 23rd, 1862.

The first time I ever heard the "Idylls of the King" was last year, when I found both the Queen and Prince quite in raptures about them. The first bit I ever heard was the end of "Guinevere," the last two or three pages: the Prince read them to me, and I shall never forget the impression it made upon me hearing those grand and simple words in his voice! He did so admire them, and I cannot separate the idea of King Arthur from the image of him whom I most revered on earth!

I almost know the "Idylls of the King" by heart now: they are really sublime!

Surely it must give the Author satisfaction to think that his words have been drops of balm on the broken and loving hearts of the widowed Queen and her orphan children.

Victoria,

Crown Princess of Prussia, Princess Royal.

Even the "calm Spedding" wrote enthusiastically about the "Dedication":

The thing I had to say was merely that the Dedication was, and continues to be, the most beautiful and touching thing of the kind that I ever read, to which I have nothing to add except that I find *that* to be the general opinion of men and women within my small circle of acquaintance. Not that I have heard it much talked of. But I think that is because people are afraid of not meeting with the sympathy they require in such a case. With some of my most intimate friends, whom I was frequently meeting, not a word passed about it for weeks, till at last some accident brought it shyly out, and we found we had been all the time thinking exactly alike.

Hitherto I have enjoyed the quiet dignity belonging to the editor of a book of good repute which everybody is willing to be thought familiar with, but nobody reads, so the critics have taken their information from the preface, and passed me to the respectable shelf with compliments. But now I come on ground [the *Life of Francis Bacon*] where they have opinions of their own, and must be prepared for the rougher side of the critic tongue.

Of all creatures that feed upon the earth, the professional critic is the one whose judgment I least value for any purpose except advertisement, but of all writers, the one whom he sits in judgment on is also the one whom he is least qualified to assume a superiority over. For is it likely that a man, who has written a serious book about anything in the world, should not know more about that thing than one who merely reads his book for the purpose of reviewing it? But so it must be: and a discreet man must just let it be. What I want to know is whether men and women and children who care nothing about me, but take an intelligent interest in the subject, find the book readable. What its other merits are nobody knows so well as [I].

Letters to the Duke of Argyll.

FARRINGFORD, *Feb.* 1862.

MY DEAR DUKE,

Many thanks for your very interesting letter. Very touching is what you tell me about the Queen. I am of course exceedingly gratified that anything which I have written should have the power to console one whom we all love; strange that a book[1] which, when it first appeared, was pronounced by more than one clergyman as Pantheistic, if not, as (I think) one wiseacre commented on it, Atheistic, should have such a power, but after all it is very little that words can do. Time, time!

I have written out for the Princess Royal a morsel from "Guinevere." I do so hate rewriting my own things that my pen refuses to trace the "Dedication."

Her critique on the "Idylls" is enthusiastic, and mingled up with the affection of her father, as I would wish it to be. As to joining these with the "Morte d'Arthur," there are two objections, — one that I could scarcely light upon a finer close than that ghostlike passing away of the king, and the other that the "Morte"

---

[1] " In Memoriam."

is older in style[1].   I have thought about it and arranged
all the intervening Idylls, but I dare not set to work
for fear of a failure, and time lost.   I am now about my
" Fisherman," which is heroic too in its way.

Yours ever, A. TENNYSON.

If you call me Mr Tennyson any longer, I think that
I must Your-grace you till the end of the chapter.

MONDAY, March 3rd, 1862.

MY DEAR DUKE,

    I have been out on a visit (a very unusual
proceeding on my part), and on returning found your
letter, which a little dismayed me, for, as you in the prior
one had bound me by no promise of secrecy, I, in talking
of Her Majesty and her sorrow, did say to two friends,
whom I bound by such a promise, that she had found
comfort in reading " In Memoriam," and had made the
private markings therein.

I don't suppose much harm would result even if these
broke their promise, for that is all that could be reported ;
still I am vexed, because if the Queen heard of the
report she might fancy that her private comments were
public prey.   As to those very interesting ones communicated in your last, whether you had bound me to secrecy
or not, I should not have dreamt of repeating them : they
are far too sacred ; and possibly your caution of silence
only refers to these.

I hope so.   I think it <i>must</i> be so.   I wrote off the
very day I returned to both my friends, urging them to
abide by their promise, for in these days of half-
unconscious social treachery and multitudinous babble
I felt that I ought to make assurance doubly sure.   You
can scarce tell how annoyed I have been.   I hope the

---

[1] " ' The Coming and the Passing of Arthur ' are simpler and more severe
in style, as dealing with the awfulness of Birth and Death."   A. T.

Princess Royal got my note and inclosure, but she has not acknowledged it. My letters, I believe, have ere this been opened and stopt at our little Yarmouth P. O. but not in the present Postmaster's time.

My best remembrances to the Duchess.

Yours ever, A. TENNYSON.

March 26th, 1862.

MY DEAR DUKE,

I am a shy beast and like to keep in my burrow. Two questions, what sort of salutation to make on entering Her[1] private room? and whether to retreat backward? or sidle out as I may?

I am sorry to hear that you were the worse for your journey. I myself am raven-hoarse with cold.

Yours ever, A. TENNYSON.

April, 1862.

MY DEAR DUKE,

As you were kind enough to say that you would mention Woolner's name to the Queen, I send a photograph of a work of his, which Gladstone, who saw it the other day, pronounced the first thing he had seen after the antique. The children are Thomas Fairbairn's, deaf and dumb, not pretty certainly, but infinitely pathetic.

I do not say, show this to her Majesty, you know best, but admit that myself and Gladstone are justified in our admiration.

Yours ever, A. TENNYSON.

[1] The Queen's.

My father's first visit to the Queen, April, 1862 [1],
after the death of the Prince Consort.

A. was much affected by his interview with the
Queen. He said that she stood pale and statue-like
before him, speaking in a quiet, unutterably sad voice.
" There was a kind of stately innocence about her." She
said many kind things to him, such as " Next to the
Bible ' In Memoriam' is my comfort." She talked of
the Prince, and of Hallam, and of Macaulay, and of
Goethe, and of Schiller in connection with him, and said
that the Prince was so like the picture of Arthur Hallam
in " In Memoriam," even to his blue eyes. When A.
said that he thought that the Prince would have made a
great king, she answered, " He always said that it did
not signify whether *he* did the right thing or did not, so
long as the right thing was done."

A. said, " We all grieve with your Majesty," and the
Queen replied, " The country has been kind to me, and
I am thankful."

When the Queen had withdrawn, Princess Alice
came in with Princess Beatrice.

After the interview my father wrote to Lady Augusta
Bruce [2]:

FARRINGFORD, *April* 17*th,* 1862.

MY DEAR LADY AUGUSTA,

Accept my very best thanks for your kind
letter. I perceive that it was written on the evening of
that day when I called at Osborne, but I received it
only yesterday; then I thought that I would wait till

[1] This account was written down by my mother immediately after my
father's return from Osborne.

[2] Afterwards the wife of Dean Stanley, then Lady-in-Waiting to the
Queen.

the prints [1] arrived, but as they have not, I will not delay my answer.

I was conscious of having spoken with considerable emotion to the Queen, but I have a very imperfect recollection of what I did say. Nor indeed — which perhaps you may think less excusable — do I very well recollect what Her Majesty said to me: but I loved the voice that spoke, for being very blind I am much led by the voice, and blind as I am and as I told Her I was, I yet could dimly perceive so great an expression of sweetness in Her countenance as made me wroth with those imperfect cartes de visite of H.M. which Mayall once sent me. Will you say, as you best know how to say it, how deeply grateful I am to Her Majesty for the prints of Herself and of Him which She proposes to send me, and how very much I shall value Her Gift? I was charmed with Princess Alice. She seemed to me what Goethe calls *eine Natur*. Did he not say that was the highest compliment that could be paid to a woman? and the little Beatrice with her long tresses was very captivating. Thank you also for what you tell me of your own family. True, as you write, I often receive similar communications, but the value of these depends on the value of those from whom they come. I often scarce believe that I have done anything, especially when I meet with too flowery compliments: but when I know that I am spoken to sincerely, as by your Ladyship, I lift my head a little, and rejoice that I am not altogether useless.

Believe me, yours very truly,

A. Tennyson.

[1] Portraits of the Queen and Prince Consort.

CHAPTER XXIII.

DERBYSHIRE AND YORKSHIRE.

LETTERS.

1862–1864[1].

During this summer, after finishing his "Enoch Arden[2]," or "The Fisherman" as he called it then, my father went with Palgrave for a tour to Derbyshire and Yorkshire. On his return I remember hearing him express delight at the beauties of Haddon Hall, and at the glories of the Peak cavern. The guide had asked the travellers, before entering the cavern, at what scale they would wish to see the Great Hall illuminated, for when the Emperor of Russia had been there, he had chosen the most magnificent of the illuminations offered. My father answered : "Let us be as grand as Emperors for once": and Palgrave and he were amply rewarded by the wonderful colour-effects produced, and especially by the display of the crimson fire. From Castleton they went to Ripon, Leyburn, Middleham, Wensleydale, Bolton, and Skipton. My father told me that it was at Middleham Castle he had made the lines in "Geraint and Enid":

And here had fall'n a great part of a tower,
Whole, like a crag that tumbles from the cliff,
And like a crag was gay with wilding flowers.

[1] See Appendix, p. 511, for Reminiscences by Thomas Wilson and William Allingham, 1863–64.

[2] See Fitzgerald's "Hints for 'Enoch Arden'" in Appendix, p. 515.

At Christmas a greeting from Edward Fitzgerald came:

MARKET RISE, WOODBRIDGE,
1862.

Let me hear how you both are and your boys, and where you have been this summer.

I have as usual, nothing to tell of myself: boating all the summer and reading *Clarissa Harlowe* since; you and I used to talk of the book more than 20 years ago. I believe I am better read in it than almost any one in existence now. No wonder, for it is almost intolerably tedious and absurd. But I can't read the *Adam Bedes*, *Daisy Chains*, etc. at all: I look at my row of Sir Walter Scott, and think with comfort that I can always go to him of a winter evening, when no other book comes to hand.

I think you must come over here one summer-day, not till summer, but before more summers are gone. Else, who knows? Do you smoke? I sometimes talk with seafaring men who come from Boston in billyboys, and from Goole, and other places in the Humber, and then I don't forget the coast of Locksley Hall.

1863.

In January my father wrote to Frederick Locker, sending at the same time a volume of his poems for his daughter Eleanor:

FARRINGFORD,
Jan. 31*st,* 1863.

DEAR MR LOCKER,

I am glad that your young lady approves of my little book. Why wouldn't you let me give it to her? As to this canard of a Baronetcy, I remember the same foolish rumour arising some years ago, and with some little trouble I put it down, or it died down of itself. In this instance the notice had been out in the *Athenæum* several days before I heard of it, but I

answered the first letter which alluded to it, by declaring
that the rumour was *wholly* unfounded; so that, as no
Baronetcy has been offered, there is less reason for considering your friendly pros and cons as to acceptance or
refusal; if it had, I trust that I should have had grace
and loyalty enough to think more of the Queen's feelings
than my own in this matter. I mean whichever way I
answered. Both myself and my wife have been somewhat vexed, and annoyed, by all this chatter.

Kind regards to Lady Charlotte. I shall be glad to
see you here, whenever you like to come our way.
Froude promised me he would come in January, but
January is breathing his last to-day.

Yours very truly,

ALFRED TENNYSON.

On March 6th my father sent off his "Welcome to
Alexandra." He would like to have seen the pageant
at the Prince of Wales' wedding, but his ticket for the
Chapel only arrived on the 10th, having been mis-sent.

After the arrival of the Princess of Wales in England,
Lady Augusta Bruce wrote:

WINDSOR CASTLE,
March 8th, 1863.

DEAR MR TENNYSON,

Last night, a few minutes after the advent of the
lovely Bride, while I felt my heart still glowing from seeing the
look of inexpressible brightness, confidence, and happiness, with
which she alighted on the threshold of Windsor Castle and threw
herself into the arms of her new family, your letter, and
the beautiful lines of welcome it enclosed, were put into my
hands.

I cannot convey to you the impression they made on me, or
how I longed to put them into the hands of our beloved Queen,
how I longed that the heart of the nation should be moved and
touched by them, as mine had been, that the noble, soul-inspiring

feeling of which we have witnessed the outburst, should find itself so expressed. The Queen's response to your words was all that I had expected. Her Majesty desires me to thank you very warmly, and to tell you with how much pleasure she has read the lines [1], and how much she rejoices that the sweet and charming Princess should be thus greeted.

One looks at her with trembling hope, but every expression, every act, word, and gesture more than justifies one's most sanguine expectations and desires. God grant it for the sake of the Prince, the Country, and I am tempted to feel above all, for the sake of that sorrowing heart, which is ever more and more being lifted up to the divine height of which you speak. Truly the royal mourner is bearing this joy as she has borne the sorrow, and it is a spectacle that would move a heart of stone. I should have liked you and dear Mrs Tennyson to see the light on Her Majesty's countenance, as she read your lines and as she speaks of the young joyous bride, so joyous but so tender and gentle to the widowed mother; also when Her Majesty speaks of the feeling manifested by her people, realizing as she does all that is contained in it.

I remain yours truly,

AUGUSTA BRUCE.

At this time my father's indignation against Russia for her treatment of Poland was boundless. He was filled with horror too at the gigantic civil war in America, although he had always looked forward anxiously to the total abolition of slavery [2]: but he had hoped that it might have been accomplished gradually and peacefully.

In May the Queen asked my father what she could do for him, and he said: "Nothing, Madam, but shake my two boys by the hand. It may keep them loyal in the troublous times to come." So on the 9th Her Majesty sent for us all to Osborne. We lunched with

---

[1] "A Welcome," published by Moxon (March, 1863).

[2] He would sing with enthusiasm the great chorus of the "Battle-hymn of the Republic":

> "Singing 'Glory, Glory, Hallelujah!'
> His soul goes marching on..."

Lady Augusta Bruce, and drove with her in the grounds.

After returning to the Palace we waited in the drawing-room, and the Queen came to us. All the Princesses came in by turns, Prince Leopold also.

My mother wrote:

The Queen is not like her portraits, her face is full of intelligence and is very mobile and full of sympathy. A. was delighted with 'the breadth and freedom of her mind.' We talked of everything in heaven and earth. Shades of pain and sadness often passed over the Queen's face.

On the 11th a Queen's messenger rode over, bringing from Her Majesty Guizot's edition of Prince Albert's *Speeches*, *In der Stille* by Karl Sudhoff, *Lieder des Leides* by Albert Zeller, and an Album of the Queen's, in which A. was to write something." He wrote out "All along the Valley," and the next day sent the following letter to Lady Augusta Bruce:

May 12th, 1863.

Dear Lady Augusta,

I had no time yesterday to overlook the volume which Her Majesty sent me. I did but see the inscription in the beginning by the Duchess of Kent and Goethe's "Edel sei der Mensch" in the Prince's hand-writing — a poem which has always appeared to me one of the grandest things which Goethe or any other man has written. Perhaps some time or other the Queen will allow me to look at the book again.

The little song which I inserted in it was repeated to H.M. last year by the Duke of Argyll who told me that she approved of it, and I thought it more graceful to give an unpublished than an already printed one.

Cauteretz, which I had visited with my friend before

I was twenty, had always lived in my recollection as a sort of Paradise; when I saw it once more, it had become a rather odious watering-place, but the hills wore their old green, and the roaring stream had the same echoes as of old. Altogether I like the little piece as well as anything I have written: I hope I wrote it out correctly — for I was very much hurried — and I feel sure that in my note to yourself I somewhere or other made pure nonsense of a sentence by putting an ' of ' for an ' a ' or ' and.'

I have read Guizot's Preface, which is just what it ought to be — compact, careful, reverential: I have also dipt slightly into the *Meditations* and what I have read of them I can quite approve of: their one defect to me being that I discern the German through the translation. Passages here and there which would look quite natural in the original read a little too quaintly in our English: yet I find my appreciation of these essays scarce lessened by feeling that they are a translation. They are true-hearted, tender, and solacing, and contrasting advantageously with our disquisitions on these subjects. Does H.M. know the sermons of Robertson of Brighton? he died young, not very long ago. These have always appeared to me the most spiritual utterances of any minister of the church in our times.

I am glad that the Queen remembers my visit with pleasure, and refers to the conversation she held with us, not without interest.

It was very good of you to think of bringing the book: we were sorry, it could not be.

> Believe me, dear Lady Augusta,
>
> > Yours very truly,
> >
> > > A. TENNYSON.

My father wrote to the Duke of Argyll:

FARRINGFORD,
May 28th, 1863.

MY DEAR DUKE,

I have delayed so long granting the "absolution[1]," that like enough by this time you may have forgotten that you desired it.

However it is granted.

Only do not, after absolution, begin sinning the sin again with a greater gusto.

Of course I am glad to have given a moment's satisfaction to our poor Queen, glad too that you give a somewhat better account of her.

I had a very pleasant two days' visit to Cliveden. I sat in your favourite seat which looks over the reach of the river, and regretted that you were not at my side. Gladstone was at C. with me. I had met him before, but had never seen him so nearly. Very pleasant, and very interesting he was, even when he discoursed on Homer, where most people think him a little hobbyhorsical: let him be. His hobby-horse is of the intellect and with a grace.

Yours ever, A. TENNYSON.

In the summer we went on a tour to York, Harrogate, Ripon and Fountains Abbey: my father was busy with his translation of Homer, and with his Alcaics to Milton.

> O mighty-mouth'd inventor of harmonies,
> O skill'd to sing of Time and Eternity,
>   God-gifted organ-voice of England,
>   Milton, a name to resound for ages.

---

[1] Because the Duke had repeated to the Queen "All along the Valley."

After the different experiments in Classical metre had been published in the *Cornhill* for December, my uncle Frederick wrote as follows:

I got a letter from Fitzgerald yesterday, in reply to a note from me communicating to him poor Thackeray's sudden death, which I thought it very possible he might never have learnt in his solitude and indifference to newspapers. He tells me he has been ill with his old complaint, blood to the head, and expects to be taken off by it in the end; he hopes it may be suddenly, that he may not linger after an attack in a paralysed state. But there is " a Providence that shapes our *ends*," and whatever those ends may be, whether apoplexy, paralysis, or the painless separation of the *man* from his integuments, or natural death, not a very different thing from putting off your clothes to go to bed, no doubt (tho' poor Fitz cannot see a hand's breadth before him in these matters) all is for the best. I read Alfred's experiments in Classical metres in the *Cornhill*, and think them clever, though I prefer the translation from Homer. I send him an Italian sonnet which I am rather proud of, though Petrarch would stand aghast at it, and Dante would tell me to mind my own business.

At Christmas, Mr Jowett, Mr W. G. Clark (Public Orator at Cambridge), Dr and Mrs Butler, and the Bradleys visited us. The flow of my father's jests and stories, when he had sympathetic listeners, was inexhaustible: and this party was particularly sympathetic.

One evening they were talking of repartee, and my father said, laughing: "I would give all my poems to have made the two following retorts courteous. (1) A certain French king, seeing at Court a man said to be very like him, blurted out, 'You are very like our family: is it possible that your mother was much at Court?' 'No! sire,' said the man, 'but my father was.' (2) The Prince Regent, being in Portsmouth one day and seeing Jack Towers across the street, shouted out in his royal way, ' Hulloa, Towers, I hear you are the greatest blackguard in Portsmouth!' Towers replied with a low bow, 'I hope your Royal Highness has not come here to take away my character!'"

He also thought that two of the neatest repartees were (1) the reply of Margaret More to a Lady Manners, both having had honours conferred on their families. To the satirical remark of Lady Manners "Honores mutant Mores," Margaret More replied: "That goes better in English, Madam, — 'Honours change Manners.'" (2) The reply of the Italian lady to Napoleon who said to her, "Tutti Italiani sono perfidi." "Non tutti, ma Buona parte."

At the end of December my father was finishing "Aylmer's Field." He said "The story is incalculably difficult to tell, the dry facts are so prosaic in themselves." He often pointed out how hard he had found such and such a passage, how much work and thought it had cost him; for instance, the lawyer at work in chambers; the pompous old Aylmer in his wrath; the suicide. He liked his own descriptions of English landscape, and of cottages covered with creepers; and especially the passage about the Traveller's Joy.

The following letter was written by my father to a stranger who questioned him as to his belief in a hereafter.

SIR,

I have been considering your questions, but I am not a God or a disembodied spirit that I should answer them. I can only say that I sympathize with your grief, and if faith mean anything at all it is trusting to those instincts, or feelings, or whatever they may be called, which assure us of some life after this.

A. TENNYSON.

He also wrote to Mr Swinburne about "Atalanta in Calydon":

My DEAR SIR,

Accept my congratulations on the success of your Greek play. I had some strong objections to parts of it, but these I think have been modified by a re-perusal, and at any rate I daresay you would not care to hear them; here however is one. Is it *fair* for a Greek chorus to abuse the Deity something in the *style* of the Hebrew prophets?

Altogether it is many a long day since I have read anything so fine; for it is not only carefully written, but it has both strength and splendour, and shows moreover that you have a fine metrical invention which I envy you.

Yours very truly, A. TENNYSON.

APPENDIX.

(P. 7.) Professor Hales' account of Louth School.

They (the masters) were not cruel-hearted men; to make ears tingle, bones ache, life generally a burden and a misery, was no extreme pleasure to them. Small specimens of humanity leaping and dancing, and wringing their hands, and shrieking as if engaged in the worship of some Baal who perchance slept, and must needs be awakened, could scarcely have been agreeable objects of contemplation; but they knew not of any other method in which instruction might possibly be imparted.... To shew how completely we lay at the mercy of the headmaster, I perhaps ought to state that we generally sat when "up" to him upon one long form, opposite to which stood a chair, on which was seated the particular boy who was "going on." Our master adopted for himself the peripatetic, or, more strictly perhaps, the ana- or katapatetic method; his beat was immediately in front of the form on which we sat, so that he could get at the centre class as he paced up and down. He very frequently availed himself of his opportunities; and with the masterly dexterity and quickness which distinguished him, often succeeded in "touching up" each one of us in the course of a single promenade. But most pitiable was the position of the poor boy on the chair on the other side of the master's line of walk. That chair was a sort of altar on which boy-sacrifices were offered. There the youth sat, exposed on every side to the blast of blows and boxes that might descend on him at any moment, which were sure to descend upon him sooner or later in a hideous hurricane.

(P. 43.) Ghosts. (Prologue of my father's paper written for the "Apostles.")

He who has the power of speaking of the spiritual world, speaks in a simple manner of a high matter. He speaks of life and death, and the things after death. He lifts the veil, but the form behind it is shrouded in deeper obscurity. He raises the cloud, but he darkens the prospect. He unlocks with a golden key the iron-grated gates of the charnel house, he throws them wide open. And forth issue from the inmost gloom the colossal Presences of the Past, majores humano; some as they lived, seemingly pale, and faintly smiling; some as they died, still suddenly frozen by the chill of death; and some as they were buried, with dropped eyelids, in their cerements and their winding sheets.

The listeners creep closer to each other, they are afraid of the drawing of their own breaths, the beating of their own hearts. The voice of *him* who speaks alone like a mountain stream on a still night fills up and occupies the silence. He stands as it were on a vantage ground. He becomes the minister and expounder of human sympathies. His words *find* the heart like the arrows of truth. Those who laughed long before, have long ago become solemn, and those who were solemn before, feel the awful sense of unutterable mystery. The speaker pauses:

"Wherefore," says one, "granting the intensity of the feeling, wherefore this fever and fret about a baseless vision?" "Do not assume," says another, "that any vision *is* baseless."

(P. 108.) Letters about Arthur Hallam (after his death).

From R. J. Tennant to my father.

Nov. 26th, 1833.

My dear Alfred,

I wish I were gifted with a far sight to reach over hills and towns even as far as Somersby and thro' the windows of the house, that I might see you, how you look when you come down to breakfast, and after breakfast whether you sit reading, writing or musing, whether you are gloomy or cheerful; I hope the latter; and that you can look back upon the mournful past without that bitterness of spirit which you felt when I saw you. I would rather not allude to this; but I wish to talk to you of what has been much in my thoughts since you were in town, and on which I have spoken to many of our friends. It appears to be a universal wish among them, that whatever writings Arthur has left should be collected and published; that there may be some memorial of him among us, which, tho' it will fall very far short of what was hoped and expected of him, will yet be highly gratifying to his friends, and as we think will not be without interest and value to many others. A great number of his poems are such as everyone will delight in, and there are several essays that will do honour to his powers of original thought and expression. It seemed the most proper way to cause this to be done if you were to intimate it to Mr Hallam as the general wish of his friends. His desire that you would suggest to him whatever you think that Arthur would have wished to be done, gives you ample opportunity to do this without being in the least obtrusive. I asked Spedding's opinion and he entirely agreed with me ; and he is one whose opinion on such a matter is of great weight. It is possible that Mr Hallam may himself intend to do this ; but even if it be so, it will probably be a great satisfaction to him to learn that this feeling and wish prevails so generally among us, and that such a wide circle of men are unanimous in seeking to pay honour to one who by his nearer friends was so deeply loved. You are not perhaps aware how widely his loss is felt ; one circumstance will show it ; *many* of his *less intimate* acquaintance have been exerting themselves to cause a tablet to be placed in Trinity Chapel to his memory : the intention failed only because he was in fact not on the foundation. I hope you will not think it ill-timed in me to recall your memory to what I fear you already dwell too much upon. To me the remembrance of Arthur is full of delight, looking back upon the days when he gave light and life to my spirit ; it is only when I need his counsels and know that I cannot any more receive them, or when I think upon you and your sorrow, that regret is mixed with bitterness. God bless you all. You are all in my thoughts night and day.

Ever your affectionate

R. J. Tennant.

From Robert Monteith to my father.

1833.

My dear Alfred,

I assure you I have never been quite easy without having had some communication between us since the news of the loss sustained by you. I say *you* because, though it was and still is to myself one of those dreadful things which at moments one cannot bring oneself to believe, yet the sorrow of all others combined cannot be supposed equal to that of you and your family. I assure you all with whom I have spoken about it have been full of sympathy with you, and all wish, as I do, for still stricter friendship with you, if it might be (which is all but impossible) that together we might help to fill up the gap. One feeling that remains with me is a longing to preserve all those friends whom I know Hallam loved and whom I learnt to love through him. He was so much a centre round which we moved that now there seems a possibility of many connections being all but dissolved. Since Hallam's death I almost feel like an old man looking back on many friendships as something bygone. I beseech you, do not let us permit this, you may even dislike the interference of common friendship for a time, but you will be glad at length to gather together all the different means by which you may feel not entirely in a different world from that in which you knew and loved Hallam. I will write you a long letter some day which I daresay will trouble you : if it does I shall be sorry, but it will rather prove the propriety of our not leaving you alone. I wish you were abroad with us and am revolving some schemes for seeing the south together. All Mr Garden's family desire to be most kindly remembered to you.

Believe me your very sincere friend,

R. MONTEITH.

(P. 117.) MARIANA IN THE SOUTH.

Arthur H. Hallam to W. B. Donne[1].

TRINITY,
Sunday. [1831.]

MY DEAR DONNE,

I rejoice exceedingly at the admiration you express for Alfred Tennyson in general, and the Indian ditty[2] in particular.

I expect you to be properly grateful to me for sending you by these presents another poem, of which to say that I love it would be only saying that it is his. It is intended, you will perceive, as a kind of pendant to his former poem of "Mariana," the idea of both being the expression of desolate loneliness, but with this distinctive variety in the second, that it paints the forlorn feeling as it would exist under the influence of different impressions of sense. When we were journeying together this summer through the South of France we came upon a range of country just corresponding to his preconceived thought of a barrenness, so as in the South, and the portraiture of the scenery in this poem is most faithful. You will, I think, agree with me that the

---

[1] Afterwards "Examiner of plays." This hitherto unpublished letter has been kindly given to me by his son Mr Mowbray Donne.

[2] "Anacaona," p. 56.

essential and distinguishing character of the conception requires in the "Southern Mariana" a greater lingering on the outward circumstances, and a less palpable transition of the poet into Mariana's feelings, than was the case in the former poem. Were this not implied in the subject it would be a fault : "an artist," as Alfred is wont to say, "ought to be lord of the five senses," but if he lacks the inward sense which reveals to him what is inward in the heart, he has left out the part of Hamlet in the play. In this meaning I think the objection sometimes made to a poem, that it is too picturesque, is a just objection ; but according to a more strict use of words, poetry cannot be too pictorial, for it cannot represent too truly, and when the object of the poetic power happens to be an object of sensuous perception it is the business of the poetic language to paint.

It is observable in the mighty models of art, left for the worship of ages by the Greeks and those too rare specimens of Roman production which breathe a Greek spirit, that their way of imaging a mood of the human heart in a group of circumstances, each of which reciprocally affects and is affected by the unity of that mood, resembles much Alfred's manner of delineation, and should therefore give additional sanction to the confidence of our praise.

I believe you will find instances in all the Greek poems of the highest order, — at present I can only call into distinct recollection the divine passage about the sacrifice of Iphigenia in Lucretius and the desolation of Ariadne in Catullus, and the fragments of Sappho, in which I see much congeniality to Alfred's peculiar power. I beg pardon for this prose, here comes something better.

(Here the "Southern Mariana" is copied at length.)

Your very sincere friend,

A. H. HALLAM.

(P. 207.) THE RECEPTION OF THE EARLY POEMS, BY AUBREY DE VERE.

1832–1845.

There are moments when the day on which I first made acquaintance with Alfred Tennyson's poetry seems to me less remote than those days upon which events comparatively recent took place. It is more clearly marked in my memory than the day on which I first met the poet himself. My acquaintance with him as a poet had been so long and familiar, that to have made acquaintance with him as a man would have been to me something remarkable only if the man and the poet had been in striking contrast. On the contrary they were very like each other.

The mode in which I first made acquaintance with Alfred Tennyson's poetry is recorded in a letter which was written by me after the death of the late Lord Houghton and published in his recent biography by Mr Wemyss Reid. Lord Houghton, then Richard Monckton Milnes, a Cambridge friend of my eldest brother's, drove up to the door of our house at Curragh Chase one night in 1832, and in a few days had quite won our hearts by his pleasant ways, his wit, and his astonishing acquaintance with all the modern European Literatures. He had brought with him the first number of a new magazine entitled *The Englishman* containing Arthur Hallam's essay on Tennyson's *Poems, chiefly Lyrical.* The day on which I first took the slender volume into my hands was with me a memorable one. Arthur Hallam's essay had contrasted two different schools of modern poetry, calling one of these classes Poets of Reflection, and the other class Poets of Sensation, the latter represented by Shelley and Keats. Of Keats I knew nothing, and of Shelley very little ; but the new poet seemed to me, while he had about him a touch of both the classes thus characterized, to have yet little in common with either. He was eminently original, and about that originality there was for me a wild, inexplicable magic and a deep pathos, though hardly as simple as Wordsworth's pathos, and with nothing of its homeliness ; and the character of its language was nearly the opposite of that which Wordsworth had, at least in his youth, asserted to be the true poetic diction, viz. the language of common life among the educated. The diction of the new poet was elaborate in accordance with a certain artificiality belonging to the time, that is, whenever strange combinations of words were needed in order to produce a corresponding exactitude of significance. The youthful poet very soon afterwards discarded that elaborateness, perceiving that the loss of simplicity caused by it could not be compensated for by any degree of expressiveness, and adopted a style especially marked by its purity. But the subtle exquisiteness of his imagination remained unchanged and had never required any such artificial aid. It had ever "fed among the lilies" of a "Fairy Land," which to it had ever been a native land. With the bleating of the lamb or the lowing of the herd there mingled from afar "the horns of Elfland faintly blowing." I remember my dear friend, Sara Coleridge, daughter of the poet, once remarking to me that, however inferior the bulk of a young man's poetry may be to that of the poet when mature, it generally possesses some passages with a special freshness of their own, and an inexplicable charm to be found in them alone. Such was the charm with which many of those early poems

captivated me, a charm which they have never lost. Still, as in that
old time, the old oak-tree, "thick-leaved, ambrosial," sighs over the
grave of "Claribel." The new interpretation of Nature given to me
then remains, and the beauty mingled with the pathos, when the scene
described is one of Nature's forlornest, as in "The Dying Swan," or
in the weird lines

> Low-flowing breezes are roaming
> The broad valley dimm'd in the gloaming—

never cease to possess me as they did the day that I read them first.
The sea beside which the minstrel lover chanted the ballad of "Oriana"
seemed to me to uplift a clamour of woe such as no sea had ever
uttered before, and reminded me of the "sad prophet's" cry, "Magnum
sicut mare lamentatio mea." Another image of grief, if in a form less
terrible, yet more drearily desolate, was presented to me by "Mariana
in the Moated Grange," with the blackened pool close by, and the
poplar that "shook alway" above it. The "Recollections of the
Arabian Nights" seemed all the more wonderful because the picture
presented with such truthfulness was one taken less from Nature's page
than that of art, because its very excess of magnificence precluded
that effect of tawdriness which commonly characterizes descriptions of
Oriental splendours; and also because the harmony of the poem's
metre so fully sustained the brilliancy of its imagery. It was

> "A world of bright vision set floating in sound[1]."

Many of the other poems impressed me not less vividly, and I remember most of them by heart still. Day after day my sister and
I used to read them as we drove up and down the "close green ways"
of our woods. Our pony soon detected our abstracted mood. Several
times he nearly upset us down a bank; and often choosing his path
according to his private judgment, stood still with his head hanging
over a gate. We sometimes sketched an imaginary likeness of the unknown poet. We determined that he must be singularly unlike Shelley;
that his step must not be rapid but vague, that there would be on his
face less of light, but more of dream; that his eye would be that of
one who saw little where the many see much, and saw much where
the many see little. Wholly unlike the young poet we thought must
be the countenance of him who had long been the chief object of our
poetic veneration, the great contemplative Bard who had forsaken "the
fortunate Isles of the Muses" for his "Tower of Speculation on the
mountain top," Coleridge.

[1] Leigh Hunt.

In two years more Alfred Tennyson met us again in the gift of a new volume : it had been eagerly waited for and it was eagerly read. The second volume was in several particulars a decided advance upon the earlier; yet we enjoyed it less at first. Though its subjects were more important and were also treated with more skill, a something seemed to be wanting. That something was probably the spontaneity and unconsciousness which belongs to very youthful poetry in its most felicitous specimens; for its failures are more numerous than its successes. A third and maturer period comes, in which the best qualities that mark the first and the second period are found united. A few poems in the later volume touched us nearly in the same way as those in the earlier. One of these was "The Lady of Shalott," destined to reappear at the interval of many years in a nobler, ampler and richer form, but not one which challenged more vividly the youthful imagination. Another was "Margaret," to which might be added "The Death of the Old Year," and "The Miller's Daughter"; but most of them were remoter themes, characteristic of memorable epochs, or involving some metaphysical problems. Those poems were written with very great power and skill: they were unlike each other; they showed that the author's genius possessed an extraordinary versatility, and that besides what was most characteristic in that genius he possessed an exquisite taste and a high art. "Mariana in the South" breathes the air of Southern France; and its sadness is touched by an amenity which never mitigates the wintry dreariness of "Mariana in the Moated Grange." "Œnone" is thoroughly Greek in spirit, though far richer in detail than the Greek art, a severe thing, as this commonly is. "The May Queen" is an enchanting Idyl of English Rural Life, not rendered dull by its moral but ennobled by it. The "Dream of Fair Women" does not illustrate any particular country or period; but it is a marvellous specimen of one especial class of poetry, that of Vision, which reached its perfection in Dante, whose verse the young aspirant may have been reading with a grateful desire to note by this poem the spot on which his feet had rested for a time. There is however nothing of plagiarism in it. "The Lotos-Eaters" is not more admirable for its beauty than for its unity; everywhere the luxuriously lovely scenery corresponds with the voluptuous sentiment; though voluptuous only in the way of enervate thought, not of passion. I remember the poet's pointing out to me the improvement effected later by the introduction of the last paragraph setting forth the Lucretian Philosophy respecting the Gods, their aloofness from all human interests and elevated action, an Epicurean and therefore hard-hearted repose, sweetened not troubled by the endless wail from the earth. The sudden change of metre in the last paragraph has a highly artistic effect, that of throwing the bulk of the poem as it were into a remote distance. This poem should be contrasted with another and later one, "Ulysses," which illustrates the same lesson in a converse form. It shows us what Heroism may be even in old age, though sustained by little except the love of knowledge, and the scorn of sloth. Carlyle said that it was "Ulysses" which first convinced him that "Tennyson was a true poet." I remember hearing that Bishop Thirlwall made the same statement respecting "St Simeon Stylites."

Another poem in the second volume, which, if it has not the spontaneousness of many in the first, at least illustrates a great theme with a great and manifold mastery, is "The Palace of Art." In its extreme subjectivity it reminds us of German genius; but though its scope is a philosophical and spiritual one, its handling is as strikingly objective; and it consists almost wholly of images which though subordinated to moral, not material ends, yet possess a vividness and a concentrated power rarely found elsewhere, and reminds us of Matthew Arnold's assertion that German Literature, however profound it may be in thought, is cumbrous and clumsy in style compared with English. Its theme is the danger resulting from that "Art Heresy" of modern times, which substitutes the worship of Art for its own sake in place of that reverence which man should feel for it, only when it knows its place, and is content to minister at the altars of Powers greater than itself, viz. Nature and Religion. In this poem nearly every stanza is a picture condensed within four lines. It describes a Palace not a Temple, one created by the imagination exclusively for its own delight, an imagination so great that it refuses all human sympathy, "O God-like isolation which art mine," and yet so small that it can dream of nothing greater than itself.

> I sit as God, holding no form of Creed,
> But contemplating all.

The root of the evil, as the poet clearly intimates, is to be found not in the Sense, but in Pride, a greater crime, the sole expiation of which is Humility.

> "Make me a cottage in the vale," she said,
> "Where I may mourn and pray."

This poem is far greater in thought and in power than any of those in the earlier volume, though less attractive to some, perhaps on account of an apparently didactic purpose. I remember a legend about it, whether authentic or not. Alfred Tennyson and Richard Chenevix Trench had been friends at Cambridge, and had a common love of poetry. Soon after his ordination the future Archbishop paid a visit to the future Laureate. He spoke about the new heresy which substituted Art for Faith and Beauty for Sanctity. His brother-poet, it is said, contested nothing, but simply listened, occasionally replenishing his pipe. When Trench had taken his departure the auditor took up his pen, and the single thought became a poem. Later the same thought was illustrated by Trench in two poems, viz. "The Prize of Song," one of the stateliest lyrics of modern times, and a noble representative of Hellenic Song: and, secondly, in a sonnet, beginning, "What good soever in thy heart or mind."

Two short poems of an extraordinary strength and majesty were written at this time: one would have thought that they had been written at a maturer period; but, if I remember right, they were suggested by some popular demonstrations connected with the Reform Bill of 1832, and its rejection by the House of Lords. Their political teaching shows that when but twenty-three years of age Tennyson's love of Liberty, which at all periods so strongly characterized his poetry, was accompanied by an equally strong conviction that Liberty must ever be a Moral Power beginning upon the spiritual "heights" of wisdom, mutual respect and self-control; and that no despotism could be more fatal than that *tyranny of a majority* in which alone a material omnipotence is united with a legal one. These two poems begin respectively with the lines, "You ask me, why, tho' ill at ease," and "Of old sat Freedom on the heights." Their massive grandeur results mainly from their brevity, and the austere simplicity of their diction, which belongs to what has sometimes been called the "lapidary" style. Each might indeed have been carved upon the entablature of a temple; and I remember hearing an aged statesman exclaim that they reminded him of what he felt when, driving across the lonely plain of Paestum, he found himself confronted by its two temples. Their power consists largely in that perfection of poetic form with which each of them is invested. In this respect they may be profitably contrasted with a third poem which begins "Love thou thy land, with love far-brought." In thought and imagination that poem is equal to the former two; yet it bears no comparison with them as regards weight and effectiveness, because the same perfection of form was forbidden to it by the extent and complexity of its theme. It could not have been caused by want of pains on the part of the poet. An anecdote will illustrate his solicitude on the subject of poetic form, the importance of which was perhaps not as much appreciated by any other writer since the days of Greek poetry. One night, after he had been reading aloud several of his poems, all of them short, he passed one of them to me and said, "What is the matter with that poem?" I read it and answered, "I see nothing to complain of." He laid his fingers on two stanzas of it, the third and fifth, and said, "Read it again." After doing so I said, "It has now more completeness and totality about it; but the two stanzas you cover are among its best." "No matter," he rejoined, "they make the poem too longbacked; and they must go, at any sacrifice." "Every short poem," he remarked, "should have a definite shape, like the curve, sometimes a single, sometimes a double one, assumed by a severed tress or the rind of an apple when flung on the floor."

In 1842, twelve years after the publication of Alfred Tennyson's first volume, a new edition of his poems appeared in two volumes, the earlier of which included his poems previously published, with a few exceptions, while the second was wholly new. It was this edition which carried his poetry beyond a narrower circle and fixed it in the heart of the nation : but in winning the many the poet did not cease to delight the "fit and few." They gladly recognised the progress which his art had made, a progress the result of well-directed pains, as well as of the poet's moral characteristics and peculiarities.

Genius is often frittered away by the social popularity which greets its earlier achievements, one among the worst forms of adulation. Henry Taylor amusingly describes his own immunity from such perils. He was, he tells us,

> "From social snares with ease
> Saved by that gracious gift, inaptitude to please."

The younger poet was as little open to such snares. He was proof against them through the absence of vanity, even more than through shyness, indolence, or any other peculiarity. He was born a poet; and had no ambition except the single one of first meriting and then receiving the poet's crown, an ambition the unselfish character of which is so asserted by Shelley in the expression "Fame is Love disguised." No matter how much courted he might be, no attraction, whether of wit, beauty or fashion, could prevail on him to frequent any society except that of those whom he cordially liked; and in none did he ever talk for effect. Neither did he allow himself, as so many of our best modern poets have done, to be diverted from poetry by inferior forms of labour; though the loss very frequently sustained by poetry is doubtless much compensated by the signal aptitude which the poetic faculty sometimes shows for tasks not properly its own, whether literary or practical. He delighted in all forms of knowledge, but he was faithful to his own gift, and drew all things beside into the service of poetry, as their Suzerain. For this task the largeness of his sympathies specially qualified him, though it might have produced the opposite effect if he had not possessed a great unity of purpose as well as a great imaginative versatility.

Another gift contributed to make these twelve years fruitful to him, that of a singular common sense. This gift, often regarded as but an humble one, is in reality nothing less than a form of inspiration, for, like the loftier inspiration, it works it knows not how, and spontaneously. It is often, as obviously in the case of Shakespeare, united with the highest genius; and it is as often signally defective in men of high abilities, but men who in genius have no part. The gift of common sense united with that of imagination attracted Alfred Tennyson to the humorous side of things as well as to the pathetic, and thus made him learned in Life, the Life of the Humanities. All those things in them which others see but in their accidents, the mind thus dowered with a twofold inspiration sees in their essence.

Those English Idyls[1] were a gift such as no other writer of Idyls had ever given to his countrymen. No Englishman can read them in far lands without the memory coming back to him of the days when he sat on an English stile, and watched English lambs at play, or walked beneath hedgerow trees in " a land of ancient peace " listening to the last note of the last bird-song as the twilight deepened into night. He will see an English Ruth adorning with flowers the hat of the child that is not hers, in the hope of winning his grandfather's heart, or sitting on the poppied ground amid the wheat, while

> The reapers reap'd
> And the sun fell and all the land was dark.

He will see " The Gardener's Daughter," and her garden described, to quote Henry Taylor's words, " as only Tennyson could describe it," that Garden bordered by

> A league of grass, wash'd by a slow broad stream
> That stirr'd with languid pulses of the oar,
> Waves all its lazy lilies, and creeps on,
> Barge-laden, to three arches of a bridge
> Crown'd with the minster towers.

It would be hard to find two Idyls more perfect than " Dora " and " The Gardener's Daughter," or more unlike each other — the former so Hebraic in its stern and unadorned simplicity; the latter so pure in its richness, sweetness and pathos, a pathos not of sorrow, but of joy, one that delights, not wounds. I remember an incident connected with " The Gardener's Daughter." The poet had corrected

---

[1] My father used to spell Idyls then with one " *l*" for these shorter Idyls, and Idylls with two " *l*'s " for the epic " Idylls of the King."

it as carefully as he had originally composed it in his head, where he was in the habit of keeping more than one poem at a time before he wrote down any of them. I found him one day in James Spedding's rooms. He shewed me the MS and said, "The corrections jostled each other, and the poem seemed out of gear. Spedding has just now remarked that it wants nothing but that this passage, forty lines, should be omitted. He is right." It was omitted.

Few of these Idyls are more perfect than "Audley Court," short as it is. What can be more vigorous than these lines illustrative of simple aversion, as distinguished from hatred or resentment?

> Oh! who would love? I woo'd a woman once,
> But she was sharper than an eastern wind,
> And all my heart turned from her, *as a thorn*
> *Turns from the sea;* but let me live my life.

Those descriptions of nature owe half their charm to the circumstance that the illustrations of men and manners are in entire harmony with them. In them material nature and human life are mirrors that mutually reflect each other. There exist pictures in which the landscape is by one artist and the figures by another. Compared with these poems they are failures.

Among the Idyls none are more delightful than those which illustrate the life of young Englishmen and Englishwomen. Such are "Edwin Morris," "Locksley Hall," "The Day-Dream," and "Will Waterproof's Lyrical Monologue." To me the most delightful of these is "The Talking Oak." It is more difficult to make the Manor House poetical than the Cottage; but here as in "The Princess" and elsewhere that arduous problem is solved. In it the poet's gift of expressive, harmonious and richly coloured language reaches its highest:

> O rock upon thy towery top
> All throats that gurgle sweet!
> All starry culmination drop
> Balm-dews to bathe thy feet!

> All grass of silky feather grow —
> And while he sinks or swells
> The full south-breeze around thee blow
> The sound of minster bells.

Very remarkable is the skill with which "The Talking Oak," while depicting the country life of England, connects with it a series of sketches illustrating, each in but a few happy touches, many of her past historical periods. Its author told me that this poem was an experiment meant to test the degree in which it is within the power of poetry to *humanize* external nature. The *subtlety* of his own sympathies with Nature probably rendered it easier for him than for any other poet to invest tree or stream with human affections and sympathies. He mentioned that he had written, as a companion to this poem, another one, dealing in similar fashion with a rivulet, but that it was lost: and he repeated a line the syllables of which imitated the sound of a stream running over a stony bed, "I babble with my pebbles." The lost poem seems to survive in "The Brook," the most artistic, I think, of that kind of Idyl. To this Idyl series many were added in later volumes, such as "The First Quarrel," "The Sisters," "The Village Wife," "The Spinster's Sweet-'arts," "The Children's Hospital," and "Rizpah," among the strongest of the series.

In this series Idylic Poetry was raised to a height after which it had never before aspired. In most of the old Idyls, and the modern imitations of them, a couple of shepherds piped their loves in rivalry. One of them gained his prize, and thanked Faunus; another lost it, as he had already lost the treacherous object of his affections, and went home seriously distressed but not without hope of "better luck the next time." There was in them no attempt at descriptive poetry: the trees and the pastures were generally as like each other as sheep is like sheep. It was otherwise with these new Idyls. In them there was room for the whole range of human affections, passions and interests; and their descriptive passages delineated nature in all her moods and aspects, the humblest as well as the greatest. Had those poems included nothing but their descriptive portions they would hence still have possessed a great charm: but they were yet more remarkable for the dramatic skill with which the characters were discriminated, whether they belonged to the cultured or the humbler classes of society. How unlike are the self-satisfied and harmless babbler of "Philip's Farm," and the sturdy yeoman who starves his son because he will not marry Dora, and who later weeps over that son's orphan child! How different from both is that Northern farmer of "the old style," with a heart hard as a stone, and a mind that seems but animated matter, and yet with a single spot of tenderness in him, one for the soil itself, from which he seems to have risen full-grown, on which he has laboured so long, and over which he cannot bear that the new-fangled steam-plough and the hiss of the "kettle" should ever pass! Many a year before Tennyson wrote drama, his Idyls had proved that in his poetic gift there lived a latent but admirable dramatic insight.

The volume of 1842 was welcomed not only with gratitude for all that it bestowed, but as an augury of gifts greater yet sure to follow whenever a genius so potent and so various measured itself with a theme worthy of it, and capable of testing all its powers. That augury was fulfilled by the publication of "In Memoriam" and the "Idylls of the King." "In Memoriam" showed how great a thing man's love is, by revealing the greatness of that love, that grief and that deliverance from grief, of which it is capable. The "Idylls of the King," more of a complete great Epic than any of the great Epics, showed how high is that aim which every commonwealth of men is bound to propose to itself; and it showed not less that that high aim, political at once and spiritual, when frustrated, owes its doom not to mischance, or external violence chiefly, but to moral evil that saps the State's foundations.

(P. 487.) REMINISCENCES BY THOMAS WILSON AND WILLIAM ALLINGHAM.

1863–64.

Mr Wilson writes:

We used frequently to walk together with the boys, sometimes drawing Mrs Tennyson in her little four-wheeled carriage along the Downs, towards the Needles, through Maiden's Croft over the little rustic bridge across the lane, where sometimes inquisitive strangers used to lie in wait to catch a sight of the Poet.

Maiden's Croft reminds me of Mr Tennyson's resentment of Mr Ruskin's criticising his line in "Maud" as a "pathetic fallacy":

And left the daisies rosy.

"Why," he said, "the very day I wrote it, I saw the daisies rosy in Maiden's Croft, and thought of enclosing one to Ruskin labelled 'A pathetic fallacy.'" I remember asking him if unselfishness was the essence of virtue? his reply was "Certainly."

Not unfrequently I used to have evening talks with him on the way up to bed, looking at the many pictures that adorned the staircase: these he said he looked at far more frequently than pictures in the room. On one of these occasions, as he was holding a candle to examine some book or picture (for he was very near-sighted), his wavy dark hair took fire; I was for putting it out: "Oh, never mind," he said, "it depends upon chance burnings."

He spoke of "the wind torturing the roof," and used often to mount outside the roof from his attic-chamber, to admire the moonlight, and the sound of the breakers in the Bay. He was so short-sighted that the moon, without a glass, seemed to him like a shield across the sky[1].

He came into my room one day looking for any new book to feed upon: he took down one by Stevenson called *Praying and Working*, an account of German Ragged Schools; he told me afterwards he had read it with great pleasure; he was keen to get De Morgan's *From Matter to Spirit*.

On Lionel's birthday we acted a little Play or Charade: the first scene, to represent the word 'lion,' was the interlude of Pyramus and Thisbe from *Midsummer Night's Dream;* the servants were admitted to the performance, and laughed heartily at Wall, the Moon, and other grotesque characters. Tennyson remarked that this confirmed his opinion of the enduring popularity of broad Comedy in England.

Tennyson always said that his childhood had been at times very unhappy; and his desire was to make Hallam and Lionel's childhood as happy as possible: he encouraged Lionel, who had some talent for drawing, to copy natural objects.

He used sometimes to read aloud in the evening, in a deep sustained sonorous voice. I remember little Hallam warning me not to trouble him when he was smoking his first morning pipe, when he used to think that his best inspirations came.

At the time of these Recollections I was not in good health, sometimes suffering from fits of melancholy; on one such occasion he said, "If you wish to kill yourself don't do it here: go to Yarmouth and do it decently"; on another occasion he said, "Just go grimly on." I once spoke of Christ as an example of failure. "Do you," said he, "call that failure which has altered the belief and the social relations of the whole world?"

Mr Allingham writes:

Oct. 3rd, 1863. Saturday. We drove to Farringford (Mrs A., Clough and W. A.), picking up on the way Pollock and his son. Drawing-room tea, Mrs Tennyson in white, I can sometimes scarcely hear her low tones. Mrs Cameron, dark, short, sharp-eyed, one hears very distinctly. I wandered to the book-table where Tennyson joined me. He praised Worsley's *Odyssey*. In a book of Latin versions from his own poetry he found some slips in Lord Lyttelton's Latin *Cytherea Venus*, etc. "Did I find Lymington very dull?" I told him that

---

[1] He said that he never saw the two end stars in the tail of "Ursa Major" separate. To his eyes they intersected one another.

since coming there I had heard Cardinal Wiseman lecture (on Self-culture), Spurgeon preach, and seen Tom Sayers spar. "More than I have," he remarked. In taking leave he said, "Come to-morrow."

Oct. 4th. I walked over alone to Farringford, found first Mrs Tennyson, the two boys and their tutor. Tennyson at luncheon. "What do we know of the feelings of insects? Nothing." Tennyson takes me upstairs to his "den" on the top storey, and higher, up a ladder, to the leads. He often comes up here at night to look at the heavens....Then we went down and walked about the grounds, looking at a cedar, a huge fern, an Irish yew. The dark cedar in "Maud," "sighing for Lebanon," he got at Swainston, Sir John Simeon's....We went down the garden, past a large fig-tree growing in the open, "like a breaking wave." Contradictions *from him* are no way disagreeable: and so to the farmyard. "Have you a particular feeling about a farm-yard?" he asked, "a special delight in it? I have. The first time I read Shakespeare was on a hay-stack, *Othello.* I said, 'This man's overrated.' Boys can't understand Shakespeare." We spoke a little of the Shakespeare "Tercentenary," next year. "Most people pronounce 'Arbutus' wrong, with the second syllable long. 'Clematis' too, which should be 'Clē-mătis.'" In the passage, or somewhere near it, I noticed a dusty phial hanging up with some dried brown stuff in it (left by the last owners of Farringford). "It is a Lar," he said, with a twinkle in his eyes. "And what else is it?" I asked. "An old bottle of Ipecacuanha." We looked at the great magnolia stretching up to the roof; then into the hall and saw some fossils. "Man is so small!" he said, "but a fly on the wheel." Mrs Clough was in the house, and she and I now departed, Tennyson coming with us as far as the little south postern opening on the lane....In parting he said to me, "We shall see you sometimes?" which gladdened me.

Later. We (W. A. and Rev. W. Barnes, the Dorsetshire poet) drove in a fly to Farringford, where Tennyson, Mrs Tennyson, Miss Tennyson, met us in the hall. Tennyson and Barnes at once on easy terms, having simple poetic minds and mutual good-will. Talk of "Ancient Britons, barrows, roads," etc. I to upper room to dress, Tennyson comes in to me, and we go down together. Dinner: stories of Ghosts and Dreams. To drawing-room as usual, where Tennyson had his port. Barnes no wine. Tennyson said, "Modern fame is nothing: I'd rather have an acre of land. I shall go down, down! I'm up now. Action and reaction." Tennyson went upstairs by him-self. Tea. Enter Mrs Cameron (in a funny red open-work shawl) with two of her boys. Tennyson reappeared, and Mrs Cameron showed a small firework toy called "Pharaoh's Serpents," a kind of pastille which when lighted twists about in a wormlike shape. Mrs Cameron said they were poisonous, and forbade us all to touch. Tennyson in defiance put out his hand. "Don't touch 'em," shrieked Mrs Cameron. "You shan't, Alfred!" But Alfred did. "Wash your hands then!" But Alfred wouldn't, and rubbed his moustache instead, enjoying Mrs Cameron's agonies. Then she said to him, "Will you come to-morrow to be photographed?" He, very emphatically, "No!" Then she turned to me, "You left a Great Poet out of *Nightingale Valley*, and have been repenting ever since in sackcloth and ashes, eh?" She meant Henry Taylor. I tried to say that the volume was not a collection of specimens of poets, but she did not listen. Then she said graciously, "Come to-morrow and you shall be taken, and (whispers) you shall see Madonna, eh?" Madonna, otherwise called Island Mary, being one of her pretty servants whom she photographs as the Virgin, etc. This eh! and hm! makes a droll little finish to many of Mrs Cameron's sentences. She is extremely clever, and good-natured. Tennyson and I went out to the porch with Mrs Cameron, where her donkey-chair was waiting in the moonlight. We looked at some of her own photographs on the walls, and at one of Henry Taylor. Tennyson said to one of the Cameron boys, "All your mother's geese are swans and all her Taylors are gods!" "What's that?" says Mrs Cameron, who only heard part; upon which Tennyson repeated the words, introducing them with "Your son says," at which we all laughed, whether the lady enjoyed it or not. But she was candid enough on her part. Tennyson asked her would she photograph Mr Barnes? But she said "No." She objected to the top of his head.

Tennyson now took Barnes and me to his top room. "Darwinism, Man from Ape, would that really make any difference?" "Time is nothing (said T.): are we not all part of Deity?" "Pantheism," hinted Barnes, who was not at ease in this sort of speculation. "Well," says Tennyson, "I think I believe in Pantheism, of a sort." Barnes to bed, Tennyson and I up ladder to the roof and looked at Orion; then to my room, where more talk. He liked Barnes, he said, "but he is not accustomed to strong views theologic." We talked of Browning, for whom Tennyson had a very strong personal regard. "I can't understand how he should care for my poetry. His new poem has 15,000 lines: there's copiousness! Good night." Bed about 1.

(P. 487.) *Hints for "Enoch Arden" from Edward Fitzgerald*
(1862), *in a letter to my mother.*

How is it that your note has been. unanswered this month or more?
Why, a fortnight of the month I didn't see it at all : being away with a
sister in Norfolk ; and the remaining fortnight? Why I kept thinking
I might tell you something about the *fishing* questions you ask me : I
mean, about telling you "*anything*" about fishermen, etc. Well, somehow, what little I know on such matters won't turn up on demand :
perhaps it would undemanded if you and A. T. were in my boat one
summer day on this poor river, or plunging over its bar into the German
Seas. Ah ! Alfred should never have left his old county with its
Mablethorpe sea. As to the definite questions you ask on the subject,
I can only answer for the customs in such matters *hereabout.*

1. There is no *apprenticeship* to fishing : anyone takes anyone who
comes handy, etc., even in the *Deep-Sea* fishing, i.e. not along the
coast, but out to the Dogger bank, Scotland, Ireland, etc. (for cod-fish) ;
anyone *may* go who *can* get a berth. Only a little while ago, a lad was
telling me at Aldbro' how *he* first went, as a boy of 13 : he *hid* himself
in the *stern* of the boat that was pushing off to the *smack :* and when
they were well off shore, he pushed up his head from under ropes, etc.,
and the " Master " only said, " What ! is thee that devil of a boy ? You'll
be glad enough to be at home again before along ! " and so took him
out to sea ; and now the lad has his 14*s.* a week (grown to 19 years old)
like the rest.

2. " May *fishermen* act as pilots, or must they be of a *Guild* of
pilots ? " *Yes*, properly : no one is *authorized* to become a pilot, unless
he has served his time as *mate* in a *square-rigged vessel* (i.e. nothing
under *a brig :* even a *schooner* won't do). When he has so served a
certain time, he has to pass examinations before (I *think*) the *Trinity
Board* and so is admitted or not to be of the Guild. But, when all the
authorized pilots in a place are exhausted (as will happen when many
foreign ships pass, etc.), then a *fisherman* or other *un*authorized sailor
will go : being called a "*Brummagem Pilot.*"

Oh dear ! this is very learned, very useless, I dare say. But you ask
me and I tell my best. I have been almost tempted to write you out
some morsels of Dampier's *Voyages* which I copied out for myself : so
fine as they are in their way I think, but they would be no use unless
A. T. fell upon them by chance : for, of all horses, Pegasus least likes
to be dragged to drink. I love Captain Cook too : what fine English
his, in the Johnsonian days ! I remember, 10 years ago, telling Alfred
at Brighton of some poor little verses found in the Prayer-Book of a

seafaring son of our old coachman, who died at sea : and Alfred took
the pipe out of his blessed old lips to remurmur one, which *Thackeray*
pooh-poohed.   Along the coast here are many peculiar and fine Scandi-
navian words, which are not registered even by our provincial glossarists
(who have dealt chiefly with the inland husbandman people).

Well, I shan't go on more about this unless you desire some more.
About the photographs of A. T., thank you for them : as *you* think one
of them very good, I have no doubt it is so : but what becomes of the
eyes?   I had seen some bigger ones, which made a sort of Rembrandt
Burgomaster of him : but in reality I don't much love photographs :
though I asked you for one, because I knew they were always going on :
and I sincerely thank you for sending me (I dare say) the best.

This is vile weak scribbling, after two glasses of b-r-n-d-y and water
too (Sunday evening).

I saw (in Norfolk) that Yarrell does give that human note to the
plover : so I dare say he is right, and my friends on the river here
wrong.   I see too that Yarrell writes the word " Curlew " as French
"*Couvre lieu*" (*I think*), supposed to be from its *cry*.   (Query.   Will
A. T. say anything better than an Aldbro' fisherman said of *a* boat —
(Humph) " Ah ! — She go like *a Wiolin*, she do ! ")

Some Summer — some Summer day send the old wretch here, where
nobody scarce knows his name (don't be angry, Mrs A. T.), though a
duller place is not ! but an ugly river

                    (and a dirty sea)
                    (and E. F. G.)

which is my poem Q. E. D.

(P.S.   Leave the scrap of *Cook* on the floor, in Alfred's way : don't
give it him.)